# 英语国家概况
## 第二版

张富生　张红梅　祝乃荣 ◎编著

# A Survey of Major English-Speaking Countries

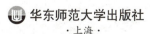

华东师范大学出版社
·上海·

图书在版编目(CIP)数据

英语国家概况/张富生,张红梅,祝乃荣编著.—2版.—上海:华东师范大学出版社,2023
ISBN 978-7-5760-3588-9

Ⅰ.①英… Ⅱ.①张…②张…③祝… Ⅲ.①英语—阅读教学—高等学校—教材②世界—概况 Ⅳ.①H319.37

中国国家版本馆 CIP 数据核字(2023)第 056844 号

### 英语国家概况(第二版)

| 编　　著 | 张富生　张红梅　祝乃荣 |
| --- | --- |
| 责任编辑 | 李恒平 |
| 责任校对 | 林小慧　时东明 |
| 装帧设计 | 俞　越 |

| 出版发行 | 华东师范大学出版社 |
| --- | --- |
| 社　　址 | 上海市中山北路 3663 号　邮编 200062 |
| 网　　址 | www.ecnupress.com.cn |
| 电　　话 | 021-60821666　行政传真 021-62572105 |
| 客服电话 | 021-62865537　门市(邮购)电话 021-62869887 |
| 地　　址 | 上海市中山北路 3663 号华东师范大学校内先锋路口 |
| 网　　店 | http://hdsdcbs.tmall.com |

| 印 刷 者 | 常熟市文化印刷有限公司 |
| --- | --- |
| 开　　本 | 787 毫米×1092 毫米　1/16 |
| 印　　张 | 14.75 |
| 字　　数 | 434 千字 |
| 版　　次 | 2023 年 6 月第 2 版 |
| 印　　次 | 2023 年 6 月第 1 次 |
| 书　　号 | ISBN 978-7-5760-3588-9 |
| 定　　价 | 52.00 元 |

出版人　王　焰

(如发现本版图书有印订质量问题,请寄回本社客服中心调换或电话 021-62865537 联系)

# 前言（第二版）

自《英语国家概况》2012年8月由华东师范大学出版社出版至今，已逾十年。其间，我先后收到很多读者发来的电子邮件，他们对本书提出了许多问题和建议，我虽无法一一回复，但在修订时都纳入考虑，在此一并表示感谢。

这次再版修订与时俱进，体现了时代性。一是当前加强国际传播能力建设，全面提升国际传播效能，需要我们更好地了解世界并做好国别和区域研究。而且十来年间风云变化，世界发生了许多大事，世界又一次站在历史的十字路口。根据教学过程中得到的反馈，此次修订在保持原书框架和特点的基础上，增加了英美等国家发生的重大历史事件，如英国脱欧、中美贸易摩擦，更新了内容和相关数据，替换了部分图片等。

二是因为技术发展日新月异，教学理念和教学手段也发生了重大转变。此次再版特地融入了新的思路和技术，尤其是注重课程思政元素的融入，这也得益于以本书为基础的团队成功创建成为省级"课程思政示范课程"。根据学生的反馈意见，此次再版兼顾了英语专业学生研究生入学考试、英语本科生专业八级考试和英语成人自学考试等需求，注重任务性教学和拓展性训练。另外，教材增设了拓展阅读、课程导学视频和练习答案二维码等。编者团队还以"英语国家概况"课程为依托，建设了网络学习资源，不断补充更新试题库和教辅资料。线上课程先后被评为校级"网络精品开放课程"、省级线上线下混合式一流本科课程等。线上课程（单月点击量超过2万次，单学期点击量高达16万次）得到了全国80多所大学（包括北京外国语大学、上海外国语大学、广东外语外贸大学、北京大学、中国人民大学、国防科技大学、中国科学院大学、河南大学等）学生的选读和好评。

在本书编写和修订过程中，我得到了华东师范大学出版社李恒平老师的大力支持；美国Timothy Ralph Osgood博士对修订书稿再次进行了语言润色，并提出了宝贵建议；《英语国家概况》教学团队中的刘星光、常霜林、李燕、王浩、田歌以及赵娟老师在视频的录制及PPT的制作过程中做了大量的工作；周淑蕊、李景燕在数据更新、修订编排方面也投入了大量精力，再次一并表示感谢。

本书初版以来，先后收到很多读者的宝贵意见和建议，我在此表示衷心的感谢！由于所涉知识体系庞大，加上个人水平所限，《英语国家概况（第二版）》仍难免会有错漏，欢迎大家继续指正。

张富生
2023年1月

# 前言（第一版）

　　随着国际交往的深入和全球一体化的发展，英语文化已成为一门独立的学科，得到了学界普遍的关注。在教学领域，英语文化受到的关注尤为广泛，英语专业研究生考试、英语专业本科专业八级考试、英语专业成人自学考试中无不如此。二十多年来，有关英语文化方面的著作出版不少，专家学者见仁见智，从不同的角度为介绍英语文化作出了卓越贡献。然而，由于英语国家的政治、经济、文化等方面的情况变化很快，不少著作中的数据及资料已显得陈旧，某些提法也存在一定局限。鉴于此，我们编写了这本《英语国家概况》。

　　本书主要介绍了英国、美国、澳大利亚、加拿大、新西兰和爱尔兰六个国家。它主要有以下特点：

1. 力争内容新颖，注重数据更新：收入了最新的重大事件，如 2010 年 5 月英国大选、美国金融危机、2010 年 8 月美韩黄海军事演习及 2010 年温哥华冬季奥运会；数据援引自国际权威机构发布的报告，大多为 2011 年最新数据。
2. 章节布局新颖：根据英语教学规律进行编排，既保持了章节的相对独立，有利于教师备课，又保持了全书的完整性。
3. 图文并茂：在一些专有名词、术语和习惯用法旁边，增加了相关的图片，便于理解。
4. 厚今薄古：除了介绍客观事实和历史外，侧重于对六国当前政治、经济和文化情况的介绍，添加了与中国相关的内容。
5. 兼顾其他：在系统介绍六国文化的前提下，兼顾了英语研究生入学考试、英语本科生专业八级考试和英语成人自学考试的需求，并增加了相应的练习题。
6. 注重任务型教学和拓展性训练：在每个章节增加了标题导读、相关思考题及 mini-task，丰富了内容，增强了互动，增加了趣味性。

　　在本书编写过程中，我们得到了华东师范大学出版社李恒平老师的大力协助。美国 Timothy Ralph Osgood 博士对书稿的语言文字进行了修改润色，并对有关章节提出了宝贵的意见。另外，我们还引用了有关部门提供的大量数据，在此我们一并表示真诚谢意！

　　限于作者水平，《英语国家概况》中仍难免会有疏漏和不妥之处，欢迎读者批评指正。

编　者

2011 年 8 月

# VOLUME ONE — THE UNITED KINGDOM OF GREAT BRITAIN AND NORTHERN IRELAND

## Chapter One  Geography and Population ........ 3
- Part One  **Names and Position** ........ 3
  - Official and Geographical Names ........ 3
  - Position ........ 3
- Part Two  **Geographical Features** ........ 3
  - The Highland Zone ........ 4
  - The Lowland Zone ........ 4
- Part Three  **Climate** ........ 4
  - Features of Climate ........ 4
  - Factors Influencing Climate ........ 4
- Part Four  **Natural Resources** ........ 5
  - Minerals ........ 5
  - Fisheries ........ 5
  - Forests and Farmlands ........ 5
  - Waters ........ 5
- Part Five  **The People** ........ 6
  - Origins of the British Nationalities ........ 6
  - Characteristics of the British People ........ 6
- Part Six  **Languages and Religions** ........ 7
  - Languages ........ 7
  - Religions ........ 7
- Exercises ........ 8

## Chapter Two  Government and Politics ........ 10
- Part One  **Political System** ........ 10
- Part Two  **The Constitution** ........ 10
- Part Three  **The Monarch** ........ 10
  - Functions of the Monarch ........ 10
  - *Act of Settlement* ........ 11
  - Elizabeth II & Charles III ........ 11
- Part Four  **Parliament** ........ 12
  - The House of Commons ........ 12
  - The House of Lords ........ 12
- Part Five  **The Cabinet** ........ 13
  - Functions of the Cabinet ........ 13
  - Two-Party System ........ 13
- Part Six  **The Judiciary** ........ 13
  - The Lord Chancellor ........ 13
  - Law and Courts ........ 14
- Exercises ........ 14

## Chapter Three  Education and Social Life ........ 16
- Part One  **Education** ........ 16
  - Types of Schools ........ 16
  - Levels of Education ........ 16
- Part Two  **Social Welfare** ........ 17
- Part Three  **Class Structure and Social Problems** ........ 18
- Exercises ........ 18

## Chapter Four  Economy and Major Cities ........ 20
- Part One  **Economic Profile** ........ 20
- Part Two  **Structure of Economy** ........ 20

## Contents

|  |  |  |  |
|---|---|---|---|
|  |  | The Primary Industries | 20 |
|  |  | The Secondary Industries | 21 |
|  |  | The Tertiary Industries | 21 |
|  | Part Three | **Major Cities** | 21 |
|  |  | London | 21 |
|  |  | Cardiff | 22 |
|  |  | Edinburgh | 22 |
|  |  | Belfast | 23 |
|  | Exercises |  | 23 |

### Chapter Five  History ............ 25

| | | |
|---|---|---|
| Part One | **The Early and Medieval History** | 25 |
|  | The Native Celts and the Roman Conquest | 25 |
|  | The Anglo-Saxon Conquest | 25 |
|  | The Viking Invasions | 26 |
|  | The Norman Conquest | 26 |
| Exercises |  | 26 |
| Part Two | **The Decline of Feudalism and the Rise of the English Bourgeoisie** | 27 |
|  | Henry II and His Reforms | 27 |
|  | King John and the Great Charter | 28 |
|  | Beginning of Parliament | 29 |
|  | The Hundred Years' War | 29 |
|  | The Black Death | 30 |
|  | The Peasants' Revolt | 30 |
|  | The Wars of the Roses | 31 |
|  | The New Monarchy | 31 |
| Exercises |  | 33 |
| Part Three | **English Bourgeoisie Revolution in the 17th Century** | 34 |
|  | James I and the Parliament | 34 |
|  | Charles I | 35 |
|  | The Short Parliament and the Long Parliament | 35 |
|  | The Civil War | 36 |
|  | Restoration | 36 |
|  | The Glorious Revolution | 37 |
| Exercises |  | 37 |
| Part Four | **The Rise of the British Empire** | 38 |
|  | The Industrial Revolution | 38 |
|  | The Chartist Movement | 39 |
|  | Queen Victoria and Her Time | 40 |
|  | Foreign Expansion | 40 |
| Exercises |  | 41 |
| Part Five | **The Fall of the British Empire** | 42 |
|  | Britain and World War I | 42 |
|  | Britain and World War II | 43 |
|  | Major Events After World War II | 44 |
|  | Conservative in Power | 45 |
|  | Labour in Power | 48 |
|  | Relations with China | 48 |
| Exercises |  | 51 |

## VOLUME TWO  THE UNITED STATES OF AMERICA

### Chapter One  Geography and Population ............ 55

| | | |
|---|---|---|
| Part One | **Names and Position** | 55 |

| | Part Two | **Geographical Features** | 55 |
|---|---|---|---|
| | | The Eastern Part | 55 |
| | | The Central Part | 56 |
| | | The Western Part | 56 |
| | Part Three | **Climate** | 57 |
| | | Features of Climate | 57 |
| | | Factors Influencing Climate | 57 |
| | Part Four | **Natural Resources** | 58 |
| | | Waters | 58 |
| | | Forests | 59 |
| | | Minerals | 59 |
| | Part Five | **The People** | 60 |
| | | Immigration to America | 60 |
| | | Composition of Population | 61 |
| | Exercises | | 63 |
| **Chapter Two** | **Government and Politics** | | 65 |
| | Part One | **Government Principles** | 65 |
| | Part Two | **The Federal Government** | 65 |
| | | The President | 65 |
| | | The Congress | 66 |
| | | The Supreme Court | 67 |
| | | Notable Government Agencies | 67 |
| | Part Three | **State and Local Governments** | 69 |
| | Exercises | | 69 |
| **Chapter Three** | **Economy and Major Cities** | | 71 |
| | Part One | **Economic Profile** | 71 |
| | Part Two | **Economic System** | 71 |
| | | The Giant Corporations | 71 |
| | | The Small Businesses | 72 |
| | | Role of Government in Economy | 72 |
| | Part Three | **Structure of Economy** | 72 |
| | | The Primary Industries | 73 |
| | | The Secondary Industries | 73 |
| | | The Tertiary Industries | 74 |
| | Part Four | **Imports and Exports** | 74 |
| | Part Five | **Energy** | 75 |
| | Part Six | **Current Problems** | 75 |
| | Part Seven | **Major Cities** | 75 |
| | | Washington, D. C. | 75 |
| | | New York City | 76 |
| | | Boston | 76 |
| | | Los Angeles | 76 |
| | | San Francisco | 77 |
| | Exercises | | 77 |
| **Chapter Four** | **Education and Social Life** | | 79 |
| | Part One | **American Education** | 79 |
| | | Elementary and Secondary Education | 79 |
| | | Higher Education | 79 |
| | Part Two | **Employment and Social Welfare** | 80 |
| | | Employment in America Today | 80 |
| | | Types of Social Welfare | 81 |
| | Exercises | | 82 |
| **Chapter Five** | **History** | | 84 |
| | Part One | **The Thirteen Colonies and the War of Independence** | 84 |

|  |  |  |
|---|---|---|
|  | Columbus Discovering the New World | 84 |
|  | The Founding of the Colonies | 84 |
|  | The Early Immigrants | 86 |
|  | Relations Between England and the Colonies | 87 |
|  | Conflicts Leading to Armed Revolution | 87 |
|  | The First Continental Congress | 88 |
|  | The First Armed Clash | 88 |
|  | The Declaration of Independence | 88 |
|  | The War of Independence | 89 |
| Exercises |  | 90 |
| Part Two | **Appearance of the American Constitution and Territorial Expansion** | 91 |
|  | The Confederation and the Constitution | 91 |
|  | Washington as the First President | 92 |
|  | John Adams | 93 |
|  | The Administration of Thomas Jefferson | 94 |
|  | The War with Britain Between 1812 and 1814 | 94 |
|  | The Monroe Doctrine | 95 |
|  | Jackson and Spoils System | 95 |
|  | The Mexican War | 96 |
|  | The Westward Movement | 96 |
| Exercises |  | 97 |
| Part Three | **The United States During and After the Civil War** | 98 |
|  | The American Civil War | 98 |
|  | After the Civil War | 99 |
|  | Economic Development | 100 |
|  | Social Reforms During Industrialization | 101 |
|  | The Growth of U. S. Imperialism | 102 |
| Exercises |  | 102 |
| Part Four | **The United States During and After World War I** | 103 |
|  | World War I | 103 |
|  | American Red Scare | 104 |
|  | Changes of America After World War I | 104 |
|  | The Great Depression | 105 |
|  | President Roosevelt's "New Deal" | 106 |
| Exercises |  | 107 |
| Part Five | **The United States During and After World War II** | 108 |
|  | World War II | 108 |
|  | Cold War and America's Containment | 109 |
|  | The Korean War | 110 |
|  | McCarthy Era | 110 |
|  | Cuban Missile Crisis | 111 |
|  | John Kennedy and New Frontier | 111 |
|  | Demands for Reform | 112 |
|  | The Beat Generation | 113 |
|  | The Vietnam War | 113 |
|  | The Watergate Affair | 113 |
|  | Present America | 114 |
|  | The Retreat of American Troops from Afghanistan in 2021 | 122 |
|  | Relations with China | 122 |
| Exercises |  | 125 |

# VOLUME THREE  THE COMMONWEALTH OF AUSTRALIA

**Chapter One**  **Geography and Population** — 129
- Part One  **Position** — 129
- Part Two  **Geographical Features** — 129
  - The Eastern Highlands — 129
  - The Central Eastern Lowlands — 129
  - The Great Western Plateau — 129
- Part Three  **Climate** — 130
  - Features of Climate — 130
  - Factors Influencing Climate — 130
- Part Four  **The People** — 130
- Exercises — 131

**Chapter Two**  **Government and Politics** — 133
- Part One  **Constitution** — 133
- Part Two  **Parliament** — 133
- Part Three  **The Judiciary** — 134
- Part Four  **Parties** — 134
  - The Australian Labor Party — 134
  - The Liberal Party of Australia — 134
  - The National Party of Australia — 135
- Exercises — 135

**Chapter Three**  **Education** — 137
- Part One  **Primary Education** — 137
- Part Two  **Secondary Education** — 137
- Part Three  **Tertiary Education** — 138
- Exercises — 138

**Chapter Four**  **Economy and Major Cities** — 140
- Part One  **Structure of Economy** — 140
  - Agriculture — 140
  - Mining Industry — 140
  - Service Industries — 141
- Part Two  **Current Problems** — 141
- Part Three  **Major Cities** — 142
  - Canberra — 142
  - Sydney — 142
  - Melbourne — 143
- Exercises — 144

**Chapter Five**  **History** — 146
- Part One  **Australia to Federation** — 146
  - The Natives in Australia Before 1788 — 146
  - Australia as a Colony from 1788 to 1900 — 146
- Exercises — 148
- Part Two  **Australia Since Federation** — 149
  - Founding of Australia-Federation — 149
  - Australia and World War I — 149
  - Australia and World War II — 150
  - Australia After World War II — 150
  - Present Australia — 151
  - Scott Morrison — 151
  - Anthony Albanese — 152
  - Relations with China — 152

Exercises ... 153

## VOLUME FOUR — CANADA

**Chapter One  Geography and Population** ... 157
- Part One **Geographical Features** ... 157
  - Position ... 157
  - Landform ... 157
  - Climate ... 159
- Part Two **Natural Resources** ... 159
  - Minerals ... 159
  - Waters ... 159
  - Forests ... 160
- Part Three **The People** ... 160
  - Distribution of Population ... 160
  - Multinationality ... 160
- Part Four **Culture** ... 160
  - Multiculturalism ... 160
  - Bilingualism ... 161
  - Sports ... 161
  - Religion ... 161
- Part Five **Education** ... 161
- Exercises ... 162

**Chapter Two  Government and Politics** ... 164
- Part One **Political System** ... 164
- Part Two **Parties** ... 165
- Part Three **Quebec's Problem** ... 165
- Exercises ... 166

**Chapter Three  Economy and Major Cities** ... 168
- Part One **Structure of Economy** ... 168
  - Changes and Adjustments ... 168
  - Agriculture ... 169
  - Manufacturing ... 169
- Part Two **Current Problems** ... 169
- Part Three **Major Cities** ... 170
  - Ottawa ... 170
  - Montreal ... 170
  - Toronto ... 170
  - Vancouver ... 171
  - Calgary ... 171
  - Quebec City ... 171
  - Winnipeg ... 172
- Exercises ... 172

**Chapter Four  History** ... 174
- Part One **Discovery by the European** ... 174
- Part Two **Colony of Britain** ... 174
- Part Three **Autonomous Government and the Commonwealth of Nations** ... 175
- Part Four **Independence** ... 175
- Part Five **Present Canada** ... 176
- Part Six **Foreign Relations** ... 177
- Exercises ... 178

## VOLUME FIVE — NEW ZEALAND

**Chapter One  Geography and Population** — 183
- Part One  **Geographical Features** — 183
- Part Two  **Climate** — 184
- Part Three  **Biodiversity** — 184
- Part Four  **The People** — 185
- Part Five  **Culture** — 185
- Part Six  **Education** — 186
  - Primary and Secondary Education — 186
  - Higher Education — 186
- Exercises — 187

**Chapter Two  Government and Politics** — 188
- Part One  **Political System** — 188
- Part Two  **Government** — 188
- Part Three  **Parliament** — 188
- Part Four  **Election System** — 189
- Part Five  **The Judiciary** — 189
- Exercises — 190

**Chapter Three  Economy** — 191
- Part One  **Structure of Economy** — 191
- Part Two  **Export and Import Products** — 192
  - Agriculture — 192
  - Industry — 193
  - Energy — 193
- Exercises — 193

**Chapter Four  History** — 195
- Part One  **The *Treaty of Waitangi* in 1840** — 195
- Part Two  **The Independence of New Zealand** — 195
- Part Three  **Post-war New Zealand** — 196
  - Jacinda Ardern — 196
- Part Four  **Foreign Relations** — 197
- Exercises — 198

## VOLUME SIX — THE REPUBLIC OF IRELAND

**Chapter One  Geography and Population** — 201
- Part One  **Geographical Features** — 201
- Part Two  **Climate** — 201
- Part Three  **Population and Language** — 202
- Part Four  **Culture** — 202
  - Religion — 202
- Part Five  **Education** — 203
- Exercises — 203

**Chapter Two  Government and Politics** — 205
- Part One  **Constitution** — 205
- Part Two  **Political System** — 205
  - The Executive — 205
  - The Legislative — 205

|  |  | The Judiciary | 206 |
|---|---|---|---|
|  | Part Three | **Parties** | 206 |
|  |  | Exercises | 206 |

# Chapter Three  Economy — 208
                      Exercises — 209

# Chapter Four  History — 210
                      Exercises — 212

# Appendix: Supplementary Materials for Reference — 213
1. 英国历代国王、女王世系表 — 213
2. 英国历届首相一览表 — 215
3. 美国主要地名表 — 217
4. 美国历届总统一览表 — 219

# VOLUME ONE

# THE UNITED KINGDOM
# OF
# GREAT BRITAIN AND NORTHERN IRELAND

# Chapter One  Geography and Population

*Before going into this chapter, try to get some information about the following items through movies, books, the Internet and other resources available:*
1. *Characteristics of geography and climate in Great Britain.*
2. *Detailed information about one of the rivers or lakes in Great Britain, such as the Thames River.*

## Part One  Names and Position

### Official and Geographical Names

The United Kingdom of Great Britain and Northern Ireland refers to the state consisting of the British Isles and the northeast of the island of Ireland. It is often shortened to the United Kingdom, the UK, Great Britain, or Britain for the sake of convenience. Since the 5th century, the southern part of the island of Great Britain has been named England, and the English language in this area has become the official language of the state. As England has been playing an important role in British politics and economy, many foreign people tend to call the whole country England rather than Britain.

### Position

As an island state, the UK lies to the west of the **North Sea**, facing **Belgium**, the **Netherlands**, **Germany**, **Denmark** and **Norway**; to the west of the UK is the **Republic of Ireland**, with the **Irish Sea** separating the island of Great Britain from the island of Ireland; the UK is opposite **the United States** and **Canada** across the **Atlantic Ocean** and neighbours **Iceland** to the north and **France** to the south, covering an area of 244,100 square kilometres with a population of 67.53 million (2019). The island of Great Britain, surrounded by over 1,000 smaller islands and isles, is the largest one of the British Isles as well as the largest island in Europe and the eighth largest one in the world, running nearly 1,000 kilometres from the south to the north and extending about 500 kilometres from the east to the west. With rich coastline resources, the UK abounds in vast excellent deepwater ports offering inexpensive transportation. It consists of **four chief districts** as follows: **England** is in the south as the largest political division, **Scotland** in the north as the second largest one, **Wales** in the southwest, and **Northern Ireland** in the northwest. The first three districts are on the British Isles, and the fourth one is on the island of Ireland, the second largest island to the west of Great Britain. Northern Ireland has become an inseparable part of the United Kingdom since the 17th century when the English Protestant settlers immigrated and occupied the northeast corner of the island of Ireland.

## Part Two  Geographical Features

As one of the island countries with a long coastline, Britain is separated from the European Continent by the English Channel to the south and the North Sea to the east. The **Channel Tunnel**, also known as the Chunnel, is a 51-kilometre undersea rail tunnel linking Folkestone, Kent in the UK with Coquelles, near Calais in northern France beneath the English Channel at the Strait of Dover.

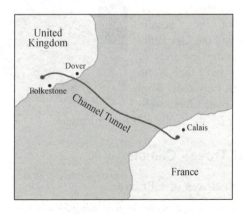

In general, Britain can be divided into two parts on geographical basis: the highland zone in the north and the west, and the lowland zone in the east and the southeast.

### The Highland Zone

The highland zone mainly covers Scotland, North England, Wales and Northern Ireland. Its geographical features are as follows: the **Scottish Highlands** consist of many great mountains with rounded outlines, which form a barren plateau with a sparse population devoted to sheep and cattle farming; to the south of the Scottish Highlands is the **Middle Valley**, which was ever suitable for the growth of swamp forests and now becomes one of the British Central Coalfields, famous for its industry and cultivated farmland; the southern highlands border on the Middle Valley and are characterised by pasture and woods; the **Pennines**, known as the **"Backbone of England"**, runs from the highest west to the lowest east and borders on the North Sea, and is featured by moorland; to the west of the Pennines is the **Lake District**, notable for its lakes and mountains as well as its inspiration for the 19th-century Lake Poets represented by William Wordsworth, Samuel Coleridge and Robert Southey; the **Welsh Massif** rises steeply with smooth hilltops, most of which is pasture suitable for feeding sheep and cattle, and southern Wales abounds in coal deposits; Northern Ireland, half surrounded by the barren rocky coastline, has several gulfs penetrating into the inland, and the landform of the **Antrim Plateau** in Northern Ireland is high around the circuit with mountains and low in the centre with a lake and flatlands.

### The Lowland Zone

The lowland zone is distributed mainly over England, consisting of the Cheshire Plain and the Lancashire Plain, the lowlands of York and the North Eastern Lowlands. These three plains are well-known for the fertile soil for agriculture.

## Part Three  Climate

### Features of Climate

The climate of the United Kingdom is classified as **mid-latitude oceanic** with summers not so hot, winters not so cold and plentiful precipitation throughout the year. The average temperature in January ranges approximately from 4°C to 7°C, and in July from 13°C to 17°C. The annual rainfall in the mountainous area of the west and the north is over 2,000 mm, while that in the east and the south varies from 600 mm to 700 mm.

On the whole, the most distinct feature of the British climate lies in **mildness**. Another feature is **abundant precipitation**, steady and reliable throughout the whole year. But the precipitation distribution in Britain is a little uneven — there is a water surplus in the north and the west, and a water deficit in the south and the east. On the other hand, the west part in winter and the east part in summer have the greater proportion of the annual precipitation. In addition, the British weather is characterised by **variability**. As the convergence between the warm tropical air and the cold polar air lies over Britain, the large temperature variation creates instability and works as a major factor that influences the notoriously **changeable** and often **unsettled** weather in this country, where many types of weather can be experienced in a single day. Therefore the British people often say, "There is no climate but weather in Britain." Such variable weather makes people more cautious when they go outside. Foreigners may be taken aback at the sight of those carrying raincoats and umbrellas in a sunny and bright weather, but they will understand the need after an unexpected downpour. It is so changeable that even the experienced weather experts find it difficult to produce a reliable weather forecast. Maybe that's the reason why weather has become the main topic for the British people to socialise with each other.

### Factors Influencing Climate

In general, there are four factors that contribute to the mild climate and variable weather. First of all, the **North Atlantic Current** flows through and warms up the west coastline of the British Isles. Climate in Britain is primarily influenced by the Atlantic Ocean and its latitude. Northern Ireland, Wales and the western parts of England and Scotland, being closest

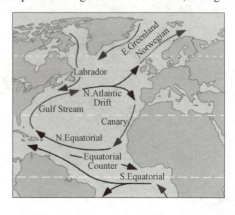

to the Atlantic, are generally the mildest, wettest and windiest regions of Britain, and the temperature ranges here are seldom extreme. By contrast, the eastern areas are drier, cooler, and less windy, going through the greatest daily and seasonal temperature variations. The northern areas are generally cooler,

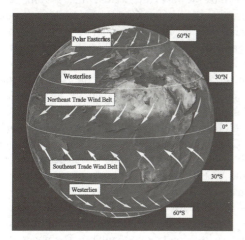

wetter and have a smaller temperature range than the southern areas. Secondly, the **westerly wind**, warm and wet, stays for the whole year and brings warm and wet air to the island. Britain is mostly under the influence of the maritime tropical air mass from the southwest, but different regions are susceptible to different air masses: Northern Ireland and the west of Scotland are mostly exposed to the maritime polar air mass which brings cool moist air; the east of Scotland and the northeast of England are more affected by the continental polar air mass which brings cold dry air; the south and the southeast of England are under the control of the continental tropical air mass which brings warm dry air; Wales and the southwest of England are chiefly influenced by the maritime tropical air mass which brings warm moist air. Thirdly, the surrounding sea waters balance the differences of the seasons, keeping it cool in summer and warm in winter because of the relatively slow warming and cooling of sea water. Last but not least, the numerous inlets of the rivers sweep the barriers to the incoming westerly wind and moisture.

> **? Questions for discussion:**
>
> It is well-known that the British people prefer to talk about weather when they meet, no matter whether they are strangers or good friends. Weather seems to be an eternal topic to start a conversation for them. Why?

## Part Four  Natural Resources

### Minerals

Great Britain is abundant in mineral resources which played an essential part in the industrialisation of Great Britain. The major minerals were coal, iron, tin, copper, lead and silver, but recently, the discovery of petroleum and natural gas on the UK Continental Shelf has changed the situation. With the increase of petroleum production, Britain has been self-reliant in oil since 1980.

### Fisheries

Abundant fisheries are another feature of Great Britain. As an island country, Britain has developed a fishing industry with rich sea waters and has become an important fishing source in Europe.

### Forests and Farmlands

By contrast, Britain is short of forest and farmland resources. Forests, only covering 13.1% of the country, are insufficient to meet the need for wood in Britain, 90% of which depends on import. On the other hand, the lack of farmlands also means that Britain can not provide enough food for the residents by itself.

### Waters

Britain has sufficient water resources. Rivers and lakes are not very large but in great number. Many of the rivers flow throughout the whole year under the influence of the mild climate, and the lakes can provide rich surface water as large reservoirs do, mostly distributed in the north of Scotland, the northwest of England and the north of Ireland. In addition, the abundant rainfall benefits the development of farmlands, and the surrounding sea waters bring convenience to transportation and fishing industries. In a sense, the sufficient water supply confronts Britain with the problem of drainage rather than irrigation.

The **Severn River** is the longest river in Britain, the length of which is 354 kilometres. It originates from the Welsh Massif and runs into the Bristol Strait.

The **Thames River** is the second longest river with a length of 346 kilometres. It derives from the southwest of England, runs through six counties in the south of England and empties up into the North Sea. The Thames River is of great importance in its heavy transportation, serving as the most important commercial channel in the world.

**Lough Neagh** in the centre of Northern Ireland is the largest freshwater lake in Britain. It is 29 kilometres long, 24 kilometres wide and 12 metres deep in average, covering an area of 396 square kilometres. It is also a place where the most ancient human handicrafts in Britain are found.

**Loch Lomond** is the largest lake in Scotland, situated in the south of the Scottish uplands. It is triangle in shape and reaches 190 metres at the deepest. The tree-covered islands in the south of the lake make it a well-known scenic spot.

**The Lake District** is another famous scenic spot, situated in the northwest of England. It contains 16 lakes, several waterfalls and some peaks of Cambrian Mountains, covering an area of 2,362 square kilometres.

## Part Five　The People

### Origins of the British Nationalities

The UK has a population of over 66 million (2019) that can be divided into four nationalities: the English, the Scottish, the Welsh and the Irish. The present British people derive from many different groups and tribes that invaded Britain at various times from the European mainland.

Between 1000 B.C. and 100 B.C., Britain suffered three invasions by the Celts who lived in the west of the European continent with three branches: the Gaels, the Britons and the Belgae. The first invaders were the **Gaels** who had already learned to use bronze wares; afterwards, the **Britons** as the iron-users drove the Gaels into Wales, Scotland, Ireland and the Pennines; and then, the aggressive **Belgae** took up residence in the south of Britain. The Belgae turned the southeastern Britain into the political and economic centre of the island, taking the advantage of their knowledge in agriculture and techniques, arm forces, money casting and trade with the European continent. And later on, the Gaels of the Celts became the ancestors of the Scottish and the Irish, while the Britons of the Celts became the origin of the Welsh. And from then on the whole island got its name as Britain.

In the first century A.D., the Celts in England were conquered by the **Romans** who infiltrated into Britain with economy and culture. The upper class in Britain began to follow the Roman tradition and customs, turning the Celts into their slaves. But with the decline of the Roman Empire and the intense resistance of the Celts, the Romans withdrew from Britain in the 5th century A.D.

After the invasion by the Romans, Britain was invaded by some Germanic tribes known as the **Angles, Saxons** and **Jutes**. The Anglo-Saxon Conquest laid a foundation for the English nation. They brought in Old English, traditions and cultures, keeping the ruling position as the master of England for several hundred years. Many of the Celts fled into the mountainous areas in Scotland and Wales after being defeated. That's why the present-day Scottish and Welsh are the descendants of the Celts, while the English are the descendants of the Anglo-Saxons.

Subsequently, Britain experienced two invasions by the Danes and the last invasion by the Normans from the northern Europe, which had a great influence on the political system, tradition, culture and language in Britain.

### Characteristics of the British People

The British people have a strong sense of national division and preference for their own languages except the English. As the English make up the majority of the nation, it is conventional for foreigners to call a British man "an Englishman". If a Welshman is called English, he will correct it by saying "I am Welsh". The British people prefer to distinguish their own nationalities by Englishmen, Scotsmen, Welshmen and Irishmen, because each of them possesses a language, culture and religion of their own.

**Conservatism** is a common characteristic of the British people. They have a tendency to accept something familiar and to suspect anything different. Many examples illustrate the influence of it. The existence of the Monarchy and the House of Lords, the national song "God Save the Queen" and the long wigs of the judges in law courts are the remainder of the past. On the other hand, many of the British people suspect new plans of the government and the European integration plans, holding numerous protests in the country.

**Reservedness** is well-known as a characteristic of the British personality. Most of the British people do not like to express their ideas openly or to take the initiative in talking, especially about their private business. Weather is a common topic in conversation, while many other topics, such as marriage, income and employment, are taboos in casual talks. Therefore, reading books and newspapers serves as a way to avoid conversing with each other.

**Courtesy** is what the British people attach importance to. Appropriate dressing for dinners and interviews indicates a person's fine breeding, and well-educated persons are supposed to observe the table manners such as keeping silent, taking good care of the table wares, never laughing and talking loudly.

**Localism** and **individualism** are the conspicuous features of the British people. With a sense of nostalgia about the past, they have their own traditions, customs and even the way of thinking that are different from the rest of the world, while many of the individuals enjoy different clothes styles, clubs, speaking different dialects with various accents.

**Deference** was another feature of the British people, who used to be rigidly status-conscious and obedient to those with more wealth and higher status. But now since the new demand for equality is on the rise, more and more British people have become advocates of equality, freedom and open-mindedness.

> **? Question for discussion:**
> Britain has experienced numerous invasions by foreign settlers. Can you list the current constitution of the British people according to their origins?

## Part Six  Languages and Religions

### Languages

The English language is the official language of the UK. It originates from the dialect spoken by some Germanic tribes known as the Anglo-Saxons. In addition, there are many other languages in different areas of Britain such as Welsh, Scots and Irish.

The development of the English language can be divided into three major periods: Old English, Middle English and Modern English.

### Religions

Britain is a country that advocates freedom of religious belief. Almost half of the British people are Christians who believe in God and the Bible. Churches can be found all over the country. Christianity embraces three main groups: **the Roman Catholic Church**, **the Eastern Orthodox Church** and **the Protestant Church**. The Eastern Orthodox Church was separated from the Roman Catholic Church in 1054, and the Protestant Church was separated from the Roman Catholic Church at the Protestant Reformation in the 16th century and began to spread over Britain.

There are two famous state churches established by law: the Church of England and the Church of Scotland. The former was a product of the religious reformation in the 16th century; the latter instituted the Presbyterian system of government. A top-down religious reform proceeded due to the divorce case of Henry VIII, and the Church of England was gradually established and separated from the Roman Catholic Church in the early 16th century. As the most important denomination in Britain, the Church of England (also named the Anglican Church or Anglicanism) re-claimed its independence from the Roman Catholic Church by the *Act of Supremacy of 1559*, with Parliament conferring on Elizabeth I the title Supreme Governor of the Church of England. Basing its teachings on the Bible, the ancient Catholic teachings and some of the doctrinal principles of the Protestant Reformation, the Church of England can be described as reformed Catholic. In practice, the Church of England has mixed views within itself. There are three parties in the Church of England,

which are sometimes called High Church (or Anglo-Catholic) favouring Roman Catholicism, Low Church (or Evangelical) with Protestant practices and Broad Church (or Liberal) in which a variety of beliefs and practices coexist.

### ❓ Question for discussion:

Nearly every nation has its own belief, and generally speaking, people's behaviours conform to their beliefs or religions. Can you do a little research after class, and list some rules that Christians should obey?

## Exercises

### Ⅰ. Fill in the blanks.

1. Since the 5th century, the name England has been applied to the southern part of Great Britain, and the _____ has become the official language of the nation.
2. _____ is the largest one of all the British Isles; _____ is the second largest island to the west of Great Britain.
3. Britain is an island country with the longest coastline. It is situated in the _____ Ocean and separated from the European continent by _____ to the south and _____ to the east.
4. In general, British climate is featured by _____ and _____. The British weather is characterised by _____.
5. The discovery of _____ and _____ on the UK Continental Shelf has made Britain self-sufficient in energy since 1980.
6. Great Britain is abundant in _____, _____ and _____, but short of _____ and _____.
7. _____ is the second longest river in Britain, with a length of 346 kilometres. It is of importance in its _____, as the most important commercial channel in the world.
8. Lough Neagh in the centre of Northern Ireland is the largest _____ lake in Britain. It is also the place where the most ancient human _____ in Britain were produced.
9. The population of the UK can be divided into four nationalities: _____, _____, _____ and _____.
10. Most of the British people dislike expressing their ideas openly and taking the initiative in talking, especially about their _____, which reflects a well-known personality — _____.

### Ⅱ. Define the following terms.

1. Backbone of England
2. the Church of England
3. the Scottish Highlands
4. the Middle Valley
5. the Lake District

### Ⅲ. Multiple choice.

1. As the official language of the UK, the English language originates from the dialect spoken by some Germanic tribes known as _____.
   A. the Anglo-Saxons
   B. the English
   C. the Welsh
   D. the Irish
2. Britain is a country that advocates freedom of religious belief. Almost half of the British people believe in _____.
   A. Islam              B. Buddhism
   C. Christianity       D. Catholicism
3. Christianity embraces three main groups: the Roman Catholic Church, the Eastern Orthodox Church and the _____.
   A. Presbyterian Church
   B. Protestant Church
   C. Methodist Church
   D. Pentecostal Church
4. The _____ Church was separated from the Roman Catholic Church in the early 16th century.
   A. Quakers
   B. Eastern Orthodox
   C. Baptist
   D. Anglican
5. There are two famous state churches established by law: _____ and the Church of Scotland.
   A. the Church of England
   B. the Church of Ireland
   C. the Church of Welsh
   D. the Church of Protestants
6. Modern English started from the end of the _____, when London English had been accepted as a standard literary language in most parts of the country.
   A. 14th century
   B. 17th century
   C. 16th century
   D. 15th century
7. Middle English began with the Norman Conquest in the _____ century.
   A. 9th                B. 10th
   C. 11th               D. 12th
8. Old English began in the 5th century when Britain was invaded by the _____.
   A. Anglos             B. Anglo-Saxons
   C. Saxons             D. Germans

9. The last invasion of Britain by the _____ from the northern Europe had a great influence on the political system, tradition, culture and language in Britain.
   A. Normans  B. Danes
   C. Romans   D. Germans

Ⅳ. **Translate the following terms into English.**
   1. 塞文河
   2. 泰晤士河
   3. 诺曼征服
   4. 英国国教
   5. 罗马天主教

Ⅴ. **Answer the following questions in a few sentences.**
   1. What contributes to Britain's mild climate and variable weather?

   2. What's the consensus of the Protestants and other denominations in their beliefs?

Mini-tasks:

1. The English Channel separates Great Britain from France, and has proven to be very hazardous for marine travel. That is why efforts to build a physical link between Great Britain and France have been made throughout centuries. In 1994, the Channel Tunnel was opened. But how much benefit has it brought to Britain and France? Please search for information about the impact of the completion of the Channel Tunnel.

2. The English Lake District is not only famous for the natural scenery, but for the settings of the Lake Poets in British literature, main figures being William Wordsworth, Samuel Taylor Coleridge and Robert Southey. Try to search for more information about the Lake Poets as well as their masterpieces.

3. Religion has been playing a great part in Britain. Various churches are commonly seen in Great Britain. The Church of England, also known as the Anglican Church, does not belong to Protestantism, nor is it beholden to the Roman Pope. Through several centuries' evolution, the appointment of the head of the Church has been transferred from the British King or Queen to the Archbishop. Search for information about the doctrine and the system of the Anglican Church.

# Chapter Two  Government and Politics

> *As a capitalist country based on the system of triumvirate, Britain has some differences from America in the political system. Try to find some examples to illustrate the differences between them by researching other materials available.*

## Part One  Political System

Britain adopts **constitutional monarchy** as its form of government. This system started at the end of the 17th century. The British Constitution prescribes that the head of state must be the Monarch (the King or Queen), in the name of whom the British government administers the country. The King or Queen undertakes the function of the propriety, performing the formal rights in the light of the decisions made by the government. The Prime Minister and the Cabinet (established by the Party with the majority of Parliamentary seats; consisting of all the most senior government department heads) are collectively accountable for their policies and actions to the Sovereign, to Parliament, to their political party and ultimately to the electorate.

The British government is the first one to be established on the basis of the **separation of powers**, that is, the three branches of the national power: the legislature, the executive and the judiciary. In principle, the legislative power is in the charge of Parliament; the executive power is in the hand of the government and the judicial the Court. But in practice, the legislature and the executive in Britain are integrated into a unity, because the Prime Minister and the Cabinet members of the executive come from the legislature: Parliament. Therefore, the constitution of Britain is often described as having "a weak separation of powers".

Britain is also the first country to form the two-party system. The chief political parties include the **Conservative**, the **Labour**, and the **Liberal Democrats**.

## Part Two  The Constitution

Britain is the first country to carry out the constitutional system, but has no written constitution. In other words, the British Constitution is composed of many separate legal documents, the common laws and usual practices produced in different historical periods. The most important separate legal documents are as follows:

*The Great Charter* was promulgated by the Monarch after the conflict between the king and the feudalist nobles. It limited the monarchical power and made way for the democratic constitutional system. What's more, it laid the foundation for the later establishment of Parliament.

The *Petition of Right*, another important political document, was produced in the British bourgeois revolution, further limiting the monarchical power.

The *Bill of Rights*, as the most important constitutional document in the British history, was issued in 1689 when the bourgeoisie and the new nobles staged a *coup d'état* and overthrew the feudal dynasty. In substance, it made Parliament superior to the monarch. Parliament became the supreme power organisation, which laid a foundation for the constitutional monarchy.

The **common law** mainly refers to some court cases involved in the civil right of freedom and so on. The so-called usual practices have no written documents, but contain some old practices related to the national system of Britain.

## Part Three  The Monarch

### Functions of the Monarch

The hereditary monarchy results from the compromise between the bourgeoisie and the feudalists. Besides, Britain still keeps such organisations founded in the period of feudalism as the **House of Lords** and the **Privy Council**. According to the British Constitution, the Monarch is the head of the jurisdiction, the commander-in-chief of the national armed forces, the temporal head of the established Church of England as well as the head of state. The King or Queen is regarded as the origin of all the powers and the personification of the state, so

the government is called His or Her Majesty's government, the armed forces are crowned with "the royal", and even the opposition party is viewed as the party loyal to the British Majesty.

But the King or Queen is just the symbol of the whole nation with no practical power. Everything that the Monarch does has been decided in advance by **Parliament** and the **Cabinet**, such as the appointment of the ministers in the government, the opening speech of Parliament, the outline of the government's programme and the declaration of wars, etc. The King or Queen carries them out without any alternative. The reasons for the existence of the Monarchy lie in the following two aspects: On the one hand, as the Monarch is highly respected by the whole nation, the bourgeoisie make use of such a supreme figure to rule the country; on the other hand, the King or Queen, as the head of Britain as well as that of the British Commonwealth, is the symbol of the unity of the British Empire and the connection between all the members of the Commonwealth, which makes the British Empire an inseparable unity.

### *Act of Settlement*

The *Act of Settlement* was passed in 1701 in order to rule out the possibility of the restoration of a Catholic King. It prescribes the conditions and order for succeeding to the throne, based on the right of primogeniture, that is, the eldest son of the reigning Monarch ought to be the first one to succeed to the throne, then the younger sons in turn, and daughters take turns in the end. Several months after the wedding of Prince William and Kate in October, 2011, British royal succession law adopted absolute primogeniture, that is, the first child of the Duke and Duchess, whether male or female, would be next in line to the throne after their father. In reality, most of the qualified successors are Protestants, claiming in public to be members of the Anglican Church. In addition, it also prescribes that the succession of the throne is not decided by the Monarch, but by Parliament.

### Elizabeth II & Charles III

Queen Elizabeth II served as the head of state of the United Kingdom of Great Britain and Northern Ireland as well as that of the British Commonwealth from 1952 to 2022. She was born on 21 April, 1926, and received education in the royal palace, majoring in constitutional history and law. She could

fluently speak French, Spanish and German, with achievements in history, language and music. Elizabeth II got married to Prince Philip of Greece and Denmark in 1947. As the eldest daughter of British King **George VI**, she began to be present on various formal occasions in 1951. After George VI passed away in 1952, Princess Elizabeth immediately ascended to the throne and the coronation ceremony was held on 2 June, 1953. She has proven to be an experienced and skillful adviser of successive prime ministers, but careful to abide by main constitutional conventions and not to take a political stand in public. Under Elizabeth II, members of the royal family maintain their important charitable roles. In October, 1986, Queen Elizabeth II made a visit to China, which was the first time that the head of state visited China in British history.

The present Sovereign King Charles III, Queen Elizabeth's firstborn child, was born in 1948. He was crowned Prince of Wales in 1969. Charles attended both the Royal Air Force College and Royal Naval College, Dartmouth and served with the Royal Navy from 1971  to 1976. Charles is perhaps most well-known for his marriage to Princess Diana. They were wed in 1981 in a historic, televised marriage ceremony. Together, they had two sons: William, who will succeed his father, and Harry. Charles and Diana divorced in 1996. Diana died a year later in a car crash. In 2005, Charles married Camilla in a private civil ceremony. Charles is now the king of Britain at the age of 73 after his mother, Queen Elizabeth II, died at the age of 96 on 8 September, 2022.

The death of Elizabeth II marks the end of an era. It deprives Britain of a thread that wove the nation together and linked it to its past. Her death marks the severing of a bond which ties modern Britain to the wartime era which, through the language of debate, continues to cast a huge defining shadow across the modern British political landscape, sometimes to the bafflement of other countries. Her passing is also the end of an era for the world, as of all the world's major political leaders and heads of state, only US President Joe Biden, born in 1942, shares any connection to World War II. She is now the past, and her successor, King Charles III, is the future. As the head of the Commonwealth, the Queen has limited political power, but she has always been committed to acting as a good monarch, maintaining the image of the royal family, and playing a role in uniting the people and gathering strength. By keeping the Commonwealth together, it has also maintained

Britain's global influence. This is why many British people love the Queen and accept the existence of the monarchy. Polls show that although support for the monarchy is still high in Britain, the public is not optimistic about its long-term existence. Many people believe the monarchy will only maintain the status quo for a while after the Queen's death. How long the monarchy can survive depends on whether it can keep up with the times and speak out on issues of social concern, and, more importantly, on the attitudes of the British public. For a long time, the Queen has been the cornerstone of the stable existence of the British royal family and monarchy. When Charles III came to the throne, there was a lot of public anger against him because of his previous outspoken comments and controversy over Princess Diana. Where Britain goes from here, in what state of mind, and how it handles the challenge of striking a balance between dealing with its past, grappling with its present challenges, and embracing its future, remains to be seen.

## Part Four    Parliament

The British system of Parliament started in 1264, chiefly made up of two parts: the House of Lords (or the Upper House) and the House of Commons (or the Lower House). The early purpose of Parliament was to solve the financial problem. It originally stood for the benefits of feudal nobles, while now it functions as a product of the bourgeoisie. In the middle of the 17th century, the bourgeoisie began to limit the monarchical power through Parliament and established its dominant position in the fight against the monarchical power. The *Bill of Rights* in 1689 and the *Act of Settlement* in 1701 established Parliament as the supreme legislative body superior to the monarch. Parliament enjoys a number of major powers such as budget decision and succession of the throne.

According to the official introduction, Parliament consists of three elements: the King or Queen, the House of Lords and the House of Commons. But the King or Queen is just the official head of Parliament, performing the decisions made by the House of Commons that possesses the real political power, and the House of Lords has no real power but provides high-level debates about big problems and performs the passage of the legislation already approved by the House of Commons. Therefore, the House of Commons plays a key role in Parliament. The House of Commons is created by voters in election and is responsible to voters. It performs the legislative procedure along with the head of state and the House of Lords, and enjoys the right of questioning government actions, but possesses the policy decision on its own. On the other hand, the government is just responsible to the House of Commons.

### The House of Commons

Members of the House of Commons are elected by the over-18-year-old citizens of Britain except some professionals such as judges, bishops and soldiers, and they have to be reelected at the end of the five-year term. Parliament can be dissolved by the Prime Minister with the permission of the Queen. In 2019, they elected 650 members. Each constituency produces only one Parliament member through general elections. The Speaker of the Lower House, who can hold his office until his retirement, is elected by the Commons as the chairman to conduct spirited debates. In general, the Speaker has to give up his party politics in order to remain impartial in carrying out his duties. The duty of the Lower House is to present and debate about the bills. The accepted bills will go to a special group of people for technical consideration and improvement of wording. Then the approved bills by vote go to the Upper House for its deliberation. In the end, the passed bills are sent to the Monarch for the ceremonial formality of royal consent before becoming laws. As far as the British Parliament is concerned, the general assembly of the House of Commons alone serves as the core of Parliament.

### The House of Lords

The House of Lords served on behalf of the feudal nobles in the beginning, and members of the Upper House were mostly descendants of those feudal lords. They have no pay, no involvement in party politics as well as no right to vote in Parliament elections because of their noble titles, which means a lord

can never become the Prime Minister unless he gives up his noble title and becomes a common citizen. As the principles of election are denied in the creation of the House of Lords, and its members are produced via inheriting the rank of nobility or being granted the title of nobility by the King or Queen, the number of the members is unstable. The rank of nobility does not contain political privileges. In 2006, the membership of the Upper House reached 701. The Lord Chancellor presides over the debate as the chairman of the Upper House. Theoretically, the House of Lords has a veto power in introducing and approving bills before they become laws. But its power has been reduced greatly. According to an act passed in 1949, it can not veto the financial bills passed by the House of Commons because its members are not elected, but can prevent a common bill for no more than one year from being passed as a law. However, it has the absolute veto over the bill of extending the term of Parliament. As a result, many lords refuse to attend meetings, and only big problems can attract a large attendance. As many of the members are experts in various fields, the Prime Minister attaches importance to their valuable debates.

### ? Questions for discussion:
1. The British King or Queen has been out of the real power, but Britain still keeps the system of monarchy, why? Could you say something about the role of Queen Elizabeth II in the British social and political life?
2. As a product of the combination of reform and tradition, Parliament has been functioning well in British politics. How does Britain keep a balance between the House of Lords and the House of Commons?

## Part Five    The Cabinet

### Functions of the Cabinet

The Cabinet serves as the nucleus of the government. It is composed of the chiefs of the most important ministries and departments and headed by the Prime Minister, who decides the composition of the Cabinet. Most important bills debated in Parliament originate in the Cabinet and can often win the approval of Parliament. The organs of state power, such as the army, police and courts, are under the control of the Cabinet members, because the Cabinet is in the charge of the party that possesses the majority of seats in Parliament.

Historically, the British Cabinet evolved from the diplomatic committee of the Privy Council that was established in the reign of Henry VI in the 15th century as a consulting institute. By the time of Charles I, the diplomatic committee had become the most powerful in the Privy Council, and the biggest issues were discussed in the Cabinet of the royal palace. At the end of the 17th century, the Privy Council became less important and served as the symbol of power with the rise of the system of the Cabinet. The Cabinet meets in private once or twice a week in the Prime Minister's official residence, holding confidential discussions with no disclosure of any secret. The Cabinet members are bound by collective responsibility and act unanimously on all matters.

### Two-Party System

Standing for different political parties, the head of the Cabinet and members of Parliament are elected every five years through general elections. Britain carries out a system of party politics, that is, political parties control politics. The transfer of political power from one party to another is viewed as an effective way of making politicians more responsible for social problems in the western democracies. A number of political parties are granted equal treatment by the law in the UK. But in practice, politics in Britain is on the basis of a two-party system. British Parliament is now dominated by one of the two most important parties known as the major parties: the Conservative Party and the Labour Party. Since the 20th century, these two major parties have been competing for the position in power. The party who wins most of the seats in Parliament by election every five years has the right to organise the Cabinet, and becomes the party in power. The leader of the party in power takes up the post of the Prime Minister of the Cabinet, and virtually becomes the supreme political figure of the whole country with the power of appointment and the right to organise and speak for the government. The one who wins a minority of the seats serves as the Opposition, organising an unofficial Shadow Cabinet and supervising the work of each minister.

## Part Six    The Judiciary

### The Lord Chancellor

As there is no Minister of Justice in the British

government, the jurisdiction is in the charge of the Lord Chancellor who presides over the administration of Justice. As the supreme leader of the judiciary, the Lord Chancellor of the Court of Equity in Parliament also serves as the chief Judge of the Court of Equity, the Legal Adviser of the Cabinet as well as the Attorney General and Solicitor General. The Lord Chancellor is entitled to appoint the judge of the High Court and the judges of local courts.

### Law and Courts

British law consists of three elements: Statutes or Acts of Parliament, common laws and conventions in accordance with customs and previous court decisions. In general, the British judicial organ can be divided into two levels: the central courts and the local courts. The central courts include the High Court of Justice, the Court of Appeal, the House of Lords and the Privy Council, while the local courts consist of the Magistrate's Court, the County Court and others. According to the nature of law cases, the courts can be divided into two systems: the Civil Courts and the Criminal Courts. The civil cases are handled by the County Court, the High Court of Justice and the Court of Civil Appeal respectively in accordance with different levels, while the criminal cases are taken by the Magistrate's Court, the Criminal Court and the Court of Criminal Appeal in the light of the increasing level. The Magistrate's Court is the basic court, while the House of Lords is the final appealing organ to take civil and criminal cases.

> **? Questions for discussion:**
> 1. The Prime Minister serves as the head of the Cabinet, while the British Queen or King serves as the head of state. What's the relationship between them?
> 2. How does the two-party system reflect the principle of democracy in Britain? Which party is currently in power? What political actions have been taken to deal with the aftermath of the global financial crisis that broke out in 2008?

### Exercises

#### I. Fill in the blanks.

1. Britain adopts _____ as its political system, with the King or Queen as the head of state and a prime minister as the head of government.
2. The national organs consist of _____, _____ like Parliament, _____ like the Cabinet and _____ like the Court.
3. Britain is the first country to carry out the constitutional system, but has no _____ constitution.
4. As there is no Minister of Justice in the British government, the jurisprudence is in the charge of _____ who presides over the administration of Justice.
5. The King or Queen is just the _____ of the whole nation without any practical power. Everything that the monarch does has been decided in advance by _____ and the _____.
6. The British system of Parliament started in _____, which is chiefly made up of two parts: _____ and _____.
7. Parliament consists of three elements: _____, _____ and _____.
8. Parliament can be dissolved by _____ with the permission of the Queen.
9. In general, the Speaker has to give up his _____ in order to remain impartial in carrying out his duties.
10. The British Cabinet evolved from the diplomatic committee of _____ that was established in the reign of Henry VI in the 15th century as a consulting institute. By the time of _____, the diplomatic committee had become the most powerful in the Privy Council.

#### II. Explain the following terms.

1. the constitutional monarchy
2. the Cabinet
3. the two-party system
4. the House of Lords
5. the House of Commons

#### III. Multiple choice.

1. Members of the House of Commons are elected by the over-18-year-old citizens of Britain except some professionals such as judges, bishops and soldiers. They have to be reelected at the end of the _____ term.
   A. five-year   B. four-year
   C. three-year   D. two-year
2. Now in Britain, the two-party system mainly consists of _____ Party.
   A. the Liberty and the Labour
   B. the Conservative and the Democratic
   C. the National and the Liberty
   D. the Conservative and the Labour
3. In principle, the legislative power is under the control of _____, the executive power is in the hand of _____, and the judiciary is in the charge of _____.
   A. the Cabinet, Parliament, the Court

B. Parliament, the Government, the Court
　　C. the Government, Parliament, the Cabinet
　　D. the Court, the Government, Parliament
4. The Prime Minister and the Cabinet members of the executive must belong to the Parliament members of the legislature, which indicates that _____ in Britain are integrated into a unity.
　　A. the legislature and the judiciary
　　B. the legislature and the Party
　　C. the legislature and the executive
　　D. the judiciary and the executive
5. The system of the British government is the Constitutional Monarchy, which started at the end of _____.
　　A. the 14th century　　B. the 15th century
　　C. the 16th century　　D. the 17th century
6. _____ are collectively accountable for their policies and actions to the Sovereign, to Parliament, to their political party, and ultimately to the electorate.
　　A. The Prime Minister and the Cabinet
　　B. The Prime Minister
　　C. The Cabinet
　　D. The members of Parliament
7. The British Constitution is composed of many separate legal documents, _____ and usual practices produced in different historical periods.
　　A. the *Bill of Rights*
　　B. the common laws
　　C. the Petition of Right
　　D. the Great Charter
8. The present sovereign is _____.
　　A. Queen Victoria　　B. Queen Elizabeth
　　C. Queen Mary　　D. King Charles III
9. The King or Queen is just the official head of Parliament, performing the decisions made by _____ that possesses the real political power.
　　A. the House of Commons
　　B. the House of Lords
　　C. the Prime Minister
　　D. the Cabinet
10. _____ performs a vital role in the British government, because it is the origin of most important bills and in charge of the organs of state power.
　　A. The House of Commons
　　B. Parliament
　　C. The Cabinet
　　D. The Party in power

Ⅳ. **Translate the following terms into English.**
1. 王位继承法
2. 大法官
3. 权利法案
4. 地方法院
5. 枢密院

Ⅴ. **Answer the following questions in a few sentences.**
1. What's the reason for the existence of the monarchy?

2. How does a law come into being?

**Mini-task:**

　　In 1981, Princess Diana became well-known in the world for her fairy-tale marriage to Prince Charles. But in 1997, Princess Diana died in a car crash in Paris, which brought great sorrow to the whole British people. Why did Diana have such a great influence on the British people and even the world? Try to get information about the reasons.

# Chapter Three  Education and Social Life

> *Britain has been well-known for its education and social welfare programmes. It presents irresistable attractions to overseas students from all over the world. What are the advantages of Britain that attract so many overseas students? And what are the disadvantages of the British welfare system? Try to get information from other materials available.*

## Part One  Education

### Types of Schools

In general, there are two types of schools in British elementary and secondary education: the state schools which are in the majority and the public schools that are few in number but of great influence.

**State schools** are financed by the central government that has a loose state control over the schools. The Department of Education and Science establishes standards for schools and sends out inspectors to visit, giving advice and suggesting new ideas. The inspectors' function is advisory only, while the head teachers in the state schools have the autonomy in deciding teaching materials and methods.

**Public schools** (also known as independent schools) are supported entirely by fees and private funds for the improvement of teaching quality and facilities, but not for profit. As fees for boarders are rather expensive, only rich people can afford them. On the other hand, public schools are quite independent, because a board of governors controls the finances and appoints the headmaster, who in his turn appoints the other teachers, while the government has no right to operate schools and employ teachers. Public schools are generally controlled by governing bodies in certain aspects. Most public schools are named after the town or village where they are located. These schools aim at shaping character and individuality as well as study of classics and science. The school spirit is based on both team spirit and leadership that are developed through games.

In addition, there are many other kinds of schools established in various historical periods: grammar schools, comprehensive secondary schools and secondary modern schools. They all belong to the state system.

**Grammar schools** are for the children who get high marks in an entrance examination. These schools concentrate on academic subjects and expect their pupils to take higher level exams and go to university. Preparing pupils for the Scholarship Level Certificate and university entrance, they are called the sixth form college at the top of the secondary schools.

**Comprehensive secondary schools** provide a wide variety of subjects in the first two or three years, and then drop some of them and allow their pupils to choose their favourite subjects. Pupils at 15 or 16 can take the General Certificate of Secondary Education and enter a sixth form college to study for two or three years. At the age of 18, pupils can take another examination for the Advanced Level of the General Certificate of Education. The pupils who do well in it can enter a university.

**Secondary modern schools** provide general education for those up to the age of 15. They also offer some practical instructions and freedom to develop the pupils' talents.

### Levels of Education

The British educational system can be divided into three levels: elementary, secondary and higher education. All the children ranging from 5 to 16 in age must receive a full-time education as it is compulsory by law at this stage. Parents have no right to stop their children's education but possess an amount of choice as to which school to attend. If a child fails to attend school without good reasons, the parents may be prosecuted.

**Elementary education** includes two sections: One is for young children from the age of 5 to 7; the other is for children aged from 7 to 11. While public schools at elementary level may range from the age of 3 to 13, including preschool education, some children from the age of 3 to 5 have an opportunity to attend kindergartens (officially called nursery schools); others stay at home with their mothers. Most children attend the state schools where education and equipment are completely free. Hours for attendance are commonly from 9:00 to 12:00 in the morning and from 2:00 to 4:00 in the afternoon. Saturdays and Sundays are for rest. The academic year is divided into three terms with holidays at Christmas and Easter and in summer. The first term begins in September.

Most state schools are maintained by the local authorities such as churches and religious denominations, which provide not only general education but also religious instructions. The general curricula include Religion, English, Mathematics, History, Geography, Nature Studies, Hygiene, Art Handicraft, Music and Physical Education.

**Secondary education** comprises two systems: state schools and independent schools. The patterns of secondary schools are various. Some authorities introduce a two-tier pattern: the junior high school from 11 to 14 or 15, and the senior high school from 14 to 18; some concentrate on sixth form colleges where all pupils in the age of 16 to 19 do advanced work; others divide the primary and secondary education into three parts: primary school from 5 to 9, middle school from 9 to 13 and senior school from 13 to 18.

**Higher education** in Britain is not compulsory. All the university students have to pay their tuition, fees and living costs. But students in poor families are entitled to financial assistance from the local authority, which is enough to cover the full costs. Most students try to earn some money by taking jobs during summer holiday. There are over 40 universities in Britain for those who excel in the academic work, and many polytechnics and colleges of higher education for those who choose more practical courses or fail to enter university. There are three academic degrees in Britain: the Bachelor's, Master's and Doctor's degrees. The Bachelor's degree is given to the students who pass examinations at the end of three or four years of study. The Master's degree is granted to the postgraduates who present a thesis based on at least one year's full-time work, and the Doctor's degree is awarded to those who conduct exhaustive research and present a thesis with an original contribution to knowledge in their area of study. The well-known British universities with a long history include Oxford and Cambridge in England.

**Open University** is an innovation of higher education founded in 1969. Open to everyone, it does not demand the same formal qualifications as other universities. The university, with tutors and counselors all over Britain, offers courses through TV channel and by radio, provides residential courses for two or three weeks in summer, and sometimes holds some classes in the evening. Successful students are granted a university degree at the end of the courses. Up to now, Open University is the cheapest and most far-reaching method in spreading higher education.

### ❓ Questions for discussion:

1. Public schools have been established in both Britain and America, but hold different educational systems. What's the difference between them?
2. Compare British universities with Chinese universities in educational concept and system. Please do a little research after class and make a presentation.

### Part Two   Social Welfare

Britain is a well-known **welfare state** in which everybody should have the means for the minimum necessities of life, no matter whether they are in unemployment, old age, sickness or overly-large families. The operation of this state depends on the following strategies: the system of national insurance based on the contributions of the employed to help the unemployed, **the National Health Service (NHS)** that provides free or nearly free medical and dental care for everyone, supplementary benefits provided for those with lower income, and services such as compulsory education and family allowances for the benefit of children. But many people prefer the private service to the free medical service, probably because they do not like to join the commons, or want to establish a personal relationship with the doctor, or choose a specialist. The introduction of the Health Service was to improve the conditions of people's health, and is now achieving its main objectives with outstanding success. Moreover, the cost of the state welfare is not very high, especially in comparison with other European countries. The funds and expenditure for all the services depend on the public money contributed by the taxpayers and general taxation of the state.

The national insurance fund is based on the weekly obligatory contributions by everyone who is working and the supplementary contributions from general taxation, and used to help those unemployed, old or sick people. For example, any men from the age of 65 or women from the age of 60 can receive a state sponsored retirement pension. In addition to the state pension, many people adopt non-state methods to obtain additional retirement pensions. They can continue to work and pay higher contributions after the retirement age besides taking a life-insurance policy with an insurance company.

## Part Three  Class Structure and Social Problems

During the early period of feudalism, British people had their own distinctive class status. In general, people whose incomes depended on rents and payments belonged to the upper or noble class; those well-educated or in a profession were considered in the middle class; and the manual-laboured people made up the lower or working class. After the Norman Conquest in 1066, the noble class was subdivided into two parts: those with most of the land and privileges became the nobility or aristocracy, playing a key role in the House of Lords and local governments, while others with less land and privileges were called knights, squires, gentry or country gentlemen, playing a greater part in the House of Commons and the bourgeois revolutions in the 17th century. The British noble class had their own influence on society all the time because they kept their estate, status and the primogeniture inheritance system in the 17th century revolution. The middle class has grown significantly after the Industrial Revolution and played a major role in the British economy. They made a living by their knowledge and skills, and became wealthier by becoming involved in businesses and professions. Besides, they attached great importance to freedom and education of their children, which contributed to the development of democracy and equality in Britain. The working class predominantly referred to agricultural labourers before the Industrial Revolution, but now it is composed of mining and factory workers as fewer people are engaged in farming. At present, some class distinctions have been obscured as many new jobs require higher education and special skills and there is no definite distinction between the middle class jobs and the working class jobs. In addition, high income may turn the working class people into the middle class, or even the upper class status.

More and more people live a prosperous life in Britain, but there are still some people living under the poverty line in poor surroundings, who can barely support their children to finish school. Without enough knowledge for a decent job in modern society, their children have little hope to break away from poverty and then turn into the real lower class. As they usually live in the neglected neighbourhoods, vandalism and rowdiness by youths of the lower class become a problem in some big cities. But on the whole, Britain maintains a lower rate of unemployment and crime, especially crime involved in violence, which may be the result of the social welfare policy and the British characteristics such as self-control and mildness.

### ? Questions for discussion:
1. Compare the differences between Britain and China in social welfare.
2. According to the British government's Social Trends Report 2007, single parent families, bus fare hikes and civil partnerships are among the markers of Britain's changing society. Do a research after class and try to find out the causes of these social phenomena.

## Exercises

### I. Fill in the blanks.

1. There are two types of school in the British elementary and secondary education: the _____ schools which are in the majority and the _____ schools that are few in number but of great influence.
2. The inspectors' function is nothing but _____, while the head teachers in the state schools have the _____ in deciding the teaching materials and methods.
3. As fees for boarders are rather expensive, only rich people can afford the fees and send their children to the _____ schools.
4. All the children ranging from _____ to _____ in age must receive a full-time education as it is _____ by law at this stage.
5. Most state schools are maintained by the local authorities such as churches and religious denominations, which provide not only _____ but also _____.
6. _____ schools are for the children who get high marks in the examination.
7. _____ schools provide a wide variety of subjects in the first two or three years, and then drop some of them and allow their pupils to choose their favourite subjects.
8. _____ schools provide general education for those up to the age of 15.
9. _____ in Britain is not compulsory. All the

university students have to pay their tuition, fees and living costs. But students in poor families are entitled to _____ from the local authority.
10. There are over 40 universities in Britain for those who excel in the _____, and many _____ and _____ of higher education for those who choose more practical courses or fail to enter university.

## Ⅱ. Explain the following terms.
1. public schools
2. state schools
3. the Open University
4. the National Health Service
5. comprehensive secondary schools

## Ⅲ. Multiple choice.
1. Oxford University, started in _____, has 39 ordinary colleges for men and 5 for women, and is a sort of federation of colleges.
   A. the 11th century
   B. the 12th century
   C. the 13th century
   D. the 14th century
2. After the Norman Conquest in 1066, the noble class was subdivided into two parts: the _____ playing a key role in the House of Lords and local governments, and the _____ playing a great part in the House of Commons and the bourgeois revolutions in the 17th century.
   A. nobility, country gentlemen
   B. nobility, aristocracy
   C. gentry, knights
   D. squires, gentry
3. The _____ class has grown significantly after the Industrial Revolution and plays a major role in the British economy.
   A. middle         B. upper
   C. lower          D. aristocracy
4. _____ and rowdiness by youths of the lower class become a problem in some big cities.
   A. Vandalism      B. Unemployment
   C. Health care    D. Crimes
5. The public schools are supported entirely by _____.
   A. fees
   B. state funds
   C. fees and private funds
   D. private funds
6. The academic year in British schools is divided into _____ terms.
   A. five    B. four    C. two    D. three
7. The school hours in British elementary school are commonly from 9:00 to 12:00 in the morning and from 2:00 to _____ in the afternoon.
   A. 5:00    B. 4:00    C. 4:30    D. 5:30
8. The public schools at elementary level may range from the age of _____, including preschool education.
   A. 5 to 13         B. 3 to 11
   C. 3 to 13         D. 5 to 11
9. The school holidays are at Christmas, _____, and in summer.
   A. Easter          B. Halloween
   C. Thanksgiving Day    D. Spring festival
10. Preparing pupils for the Scholarship Level Certificate and university entrance, _____ are called the sixth form college as the top of the secondary schools.
    A. comprehensive secondary schools
    B. grammar schools
    C. secondary modern schools
    D. public schools

## Ⅳ. Translate the following terms into English.
1. 牛津大学
2. 剑桥大学
3. 长子继承制度
4. 福利国家
5. 文法学校

## Ⅴ. Answer the following questions in a few sentences.
1. What are the features of Oxford University?

2. What's the difference between Oxford University and Cambridge University?

### Mini-task:

Britain's educational system is characterised by its preciseness, complexity and flexibility, which make it popular with overseas students from around the world. It possesses a good number of ancient universities as well as newly-built colleges with uniqueness and creativity. If you have the desire to study abroad, please search for the relevant information about the application for the British universities.

# Chapter Four  Economy and Major Cities

*Britain has undergone a series of transformations in its economy. After reading this chapter, list some big changes in its economic development. As one of the biggest economic powers, how did Britain penetrate economically into other countries?*

## Part One  Economic Profile

As a major producer of industrial goods and provider of services as well as a centre of world trade and finance, Britain has been a leading force in the world economy. First of all, it is the first country to carry out the **capitalist system** in economy, which improves the economic efficiency. Secondly, British overseas investment goes beyond its domestic industrial investment. After World War II, Britain's economy fell into a relative decline and improved less rapidly than that in other European countries, because Britain was badly damaged by German bombing, forced into debt in order to fund World War II, and had lost its colonies that provided raw materials and big markets for British products. But by the year of 2019, Britain had become the second largest international investor in the world.

Generally speaking, Britain went through three stages in its economic development during the post-war period. First, it experienced stable development between the 1950s and the 1960s, and its economy was growing slowly but continuously with a low rate of unemployment. Second, in the 1970s, British economy, namely, the British Disease stepped into a sluggish growth and money inflation. The economic crisis went along with increasing prices of commodities, which led to the slowdown of production and high rate of unemployment. Third, in the 1980s, Britain began to enter a stage of economic recovery. Prime Minister Mrs. Margaret Thatcher planned a middle-term strategy to adjust and restore the economy, which aimed at reducing the government interference by means of **monetarism**, reforming the workers' union, reducing taxes, and adjusting the industrial structure. The features of the British economy in this period found expression in free competition, privatisation of state-owned enterprises, financial reduction, monetarism, the workers' union, tax reforms, and industry adjustment as well as the application of new technology. However, all of these measures served as means to ease economic problems, but did not resolve the problems once and for all.

The British economy can be divided into two types: the public sector and the private sector. The former refers to state-owned enterprises related to basic industries such as coal mining, electricity, post and telecommunications, railways, bus companies, oil and gas. Many of these nationalised industries ran poorly due to mismanagement and low efficiency. So in 1979, Prime Minister Thatcher advocated a radical economic programme — **privatisation**, which resulted in many state-owned businesses joining the private sector and a high rate of unemployment. Privatisation means that businesses are owned and managed by people as private individuals or groups, covering agricultural, mining, manufacturing, construction, financial as well as service industries with a feature of higher efficiency and profits.

## Part Two  Structure of Economy

The economic structure of Britain has undergone a lot of changes overtime. It has three main areas: the primary industries including agriculture, fishing and mining; the secondary industries which manufacture goods from the primary products; and the tertiary or service industries such as banking, insurance, tourism, etc. Great changes have been found in the economic structure of the post-war Britain: The proportion of the primary and secondary industries has been in a rapid decline, while the tertiary industries are constantly expanding.

### The Primary Industries

The agricultural sector in Britain occupies a small part in the national wealth, but produces about 60% of the Britain's food needs with less than 2% of its workforce, mostly located in the southeast

England. The fishery meets two-thirds of the British demand for fish, mainly distributed in the Scottish ports. The decline in agriculture is an inevitable outcome of modernisation. With the development of mechanisation, intensification and automation, productivity has been increasing by a large margin, which resulted in a great number of productive forces turning to other industries or unemployment.

### The Secondary Industries

In the 19th century, Britain was well-known for its shipping and manufacturing industries, and products made in Britain could be found all over the world. Pharmaceuticals, chemicals, aerospace, food and drink were the strong fields of the manufacturing industry. The privatised British Steel became the world's fourth largest steel company. However, the secondary industries have been slowing down due to the unbalanced development of the internal departments. For instance, oil development, chemicals, aerospace as well as electronic industries are in a great increase, while the traditional industries like iron, textiles and shipbuilding are in a continuous decline. Energy production, based on the older coal mining industry and the newly developed nuclear energy, plays an important part in the British economy, especially when oil and gas were discovered under the North Sea in the 1970s. Now Britain has become an overall exporter of energy as well as a major oil and gas producer.

### The Tertiary Industries

Service industries have gradually taken the place of the traditional industries in the form of banking, financial and insurance industries, producing three fourths of the national wealth. As a major provider of services, about 80.8% of the British workforce is employed in the service sector (2019). The financial sector is a prominent part of the service industry because London has become the world's leading centre of insurance and the world's largest centre for foreign exchange, currency and business. Advertising is another major service business with great success. In addition, the commercial sector has been developing from independent retailing to large chain stores. The tertiary industries have developed rapidly in post-war Britain and have always been in great proportion of GDP. At present, the service industries are characterised by IT, computer and electronic business. Besides, tourism is also of great importance and plays a key role in the development of the British economy as well as its major cities, especially in creating foreign exchange earnings and jobs in the process of transforming and adjusting the structure of economy.

> **? Questions for discussion:**
>
> Britain's state-owned enterprises have gone through the economic programme — privatisation advocated by Prime Minister Thatcher. Likewise, since China adopted the opening-up policy — the economic reform in the 1980s, many of China's state-owned enterprises have been privatised. What do you think of such major initiatives? What are the advantages and disadvantages of such initiatives in the economic development of both Britain and China?

## Part Three  Major Cities

### London

London, the capital of Great Britain as well as the political centre of the Commonwealth, is listed as one of the major cities in the world. Located in the southeast of England, it crosses the Thames River and is 88 kilometres away from the entrance of the North Sea. Greater London is composed of the City of

London, the Inner London (consisting of 12 boroughs) and the Outer London (consisting of 20 boroughs). Greater London occupies an area of 1,579 square kilometres, while the area of the City of London is only 1.6 square kilometres. As the centre of Greater London on the left bank of the Thames River, the City of London serves as the financial centre of the whole country with many famous domestic and foreign banks, insurance companies and stock exchanges. The west of the city is a booming business district, known as the **West End**. In the south of the West End stands the political centre of London — the City of Westminster, which is famous for **Downing Street**, the **Buckingham Palace** and the **Parliament Mansions**. By contrast, as a place for ports and industries, the **East End** has become the residence for poor people since the 16th century. Besides, London is a centre of labour movements, where the first **Chartist Movement** of the proletariat started in the 1930s.

London is also the centre of culture with many theatres, cinemas, museums, galleries and concert halls, including the well-known **British Museum**, Victoria and Albert Museum, the National Gallery, Tate Gallery, Covent Garden Royal Opera House and the Royal Festival Hall. **The British Library** growing out of the British Museum is the biggest library in the world. London also provides hundreds of free public libraries. If the key word "London" is input in the British Library, about 1,750,000 books can be found related to it. In addition, there are over forty universities and colleges in London. Some are located in the centre such as University College London and Westminster University, while others in the suburbs such as Kingston University and Brunel University. And London University that was established in 1836 is the largest in Britain.

London earned its nickname "**foggy town**" after the Industrial Revolution because of the serious air pollution. But now it is getting better due to the government management. The parks in London contribute greatly to the improvement of the environment, and the largest and most famous one is the Hyde Park.

## Cardiff

Cardiff is the capital of Wales as well as an important port on the Bristol Channel. It was the largest coal-exporting port in the world in the early 20th century, but by the year of 1963, the coal resources were nearly running out. Now it is developing light industries, serving as an important centre of business and services. It has many famous buildings like the National Museum of Wales founded in 1907 and the University of Wales in 1893. These modern public buildings coexist with the castle and medieval churches, forming the uniqueness of Cardiff.

## Edinburgh

Edinburgh is the capital of Scotland, established in the 6th century. It is the economic centre of Scotland and just secondary to London in tourism. It maintains the following ancient buildings: the Edinburgh Castle, the Holyrood Palace, etc.

Edinburgh is a centre of socialisation and culture as well as one of the most attractive cities. As an ancient cultural city, it holds the three-week Edinburgh International Festival of Music and Drama every year, attracting art groups from all over the world. The historic sites remind people of the European cultural city — Athens. Therefore, Edinburgh is called "Athens of the North".

### Belfast

Belfast, the capital of Northern Ireland, is a major port, a hub of railway transportation as well as the centre of business, administration and culture in Northern Ireland. It began to develop into the largest centre of the flax industry in the 17th century, and then into a port with a growing shipbuilding industry.

Belfast Castle is well-known to the world, the view of which reminds people of the brilliant Victorian Age. The Waterfront Hall attracts artists from all over the world to perform each year. Moreover, its shipbuilding industry enjoys a considerable reputation. Harland & Wolfe Shipyard manufactured the fastest and most extravagant ship in the world, and the Titanic was its masterpiece.

> **? Questions for discussion:**
> 1. As the capital city, London serves as the centre of politics, finance and culture. But there is a widening wealth gap between the West End and the East End. Do a little research after class and find out the reason for that. Are there any similarities to the capital of America — Washington, D.C.?
> 2. Since the British people's awareness of environmental protection has been increasing, London has gotten rid of the nickname "foggy town". Do a little research after class and give some examples to show the increasing awareness of environmental protection in Britain.

## Exercises

### I. Fill in the blanks.
1. The British economy can be divided into two types: the _____ sector and the _____ sector.
2. Now Britain has become an overall exporter of _____ as well as a major oil and gas _____.
3. The selling sector in Britain has been developing from independent retailing to large _____.
4. _____ was one of the earliest cities where Chinese inhabited in Britain, possessing the first Chinatown in Britain.
5. In the early 20th century, Cardiff was the largest _____ port in the world, now it is developing the light industries, serving as a major centre of _____ industry.
6. Belfast, the capital of _____, is a major port, a hub of railway transportation as well as the centre of business, administration and culture in Northern Ireland.

### II. Define the following terms.
1. the capitalist system
2. privatisation
3. foggy town
4. Athens of the North
5. the West End

### III. Multiple choice.
1. By the year of 2019, Britain has become the _____ biggest international investor in the world.
   A. first   B. fourth   C. third   D. second
2. Agriculture, fishing, and mining belong to the _____ industries.
   A. primary        B. secondary
   C. tertiary       D. state
3. The agricultural sector in Britain occupies a small part in the national wealth, mostly located in the _____ of England.
   A. northeast      B. southwest
   C. southeast      D. south
4. The fishing industry provides two-thirds of the UK demand for fish, mainly distributed in the _____ ports.
   A. English        B. Welsh
   C. Irish          D. Scottish
5. Oil and gas were discovered under _____ in the 1970s.
   A. the North Sea
   B. the Irish Sea
   C. the North Atlantic Ocean
   D. the English Channel
6. The privatised British Steel turns into the world's _____ largest steel company.
   A. first   B. second   C. third   D. fourth
7. Nowadays service industries take the place of the traditional industries and make a reputation for the _____, financial and insurance industries.
   A. manufacturing   B. banking
   C. farming         D. transporting
8. The largest university in Britain is _____.
   A. London University

B. Oxford University
C. Cambridge University
D. Manchester University

9. London crosses the _____ River and keeps 88 kilometres away from the entrance of the North Sea.
   A. Severn   B. Cam   C. Thames   D. Mersey

10. _____ has the second largest Chinatown in Britain.
    A. London        B. Manchester
    C. Liverpool     D. Birmingham

## IV. Translate the following terms into English.
1. 货币主义
2. 议会大厦
3. 唐宁街
4. 白金汉宫
5. 宪章运动

## V. Answer the following questions in a few sentences.
1. Why did Britain fall in a decline in economy during the post-war period?

2. What's the policy of Mrs. Margaret Thatcher in the restoration of British economy?

In 2002, Britain became one of the largest overseas investment countries in the world. Besides, tourism has become an important part of Britain's economy. Please search for information about the tourism regions and the scenic spots in Britain.

# Chapter Five  History

## Part One  The Early and Medieval History

> As a multi-national country, Britain has gone through several conquests, which laid a foundation for the progress of the British people. What are the historical conquests and their significance in British history? Try to get the information from the materials available.

### The Native Celts and the Roman Conquest

As there is no actual written history about the origin of the earliest natives in Britain, the **Celts** were taken as the early natives in British history. Their languages were assimilated into the English language and served as the origin of the Scots and Welsh languages. The Celtic tribes migrated from northwestern Europe to the British Isles from about 750 B.C. in search for empty land, living in a primitive society. They became the ancestors of the Scots, the Irish, and the Welsh, and created their own civilisation known as the historical Stonehenge.

In 55 B.C., **Julius Caesar** commanded the Roman army to invade Britain. This invasion is the well-known Roman Conquest which lasted nearly a century and marked the beginning of the recorded history in Britain. The Romans didn't succeed in conquering what is now England by driving the native Celts into the mountainous Scotland and Wales until 43 A.D. But they never conquered the whole nation because of the natives' resistance in the mountainous areas. The Romans introduced their own civilisation into England by building baths and temples, draining marshes, cultivating land, and clearing away forests. They also introduced the system of governing, with an intention to transform England into a slavery society. What's more, the Roman traders and soldiers brought their own religion — Christianity — to Britain.

Although England became a part of the **Roman Empire**, and even some of the native people served as slaves of the Romans, the Roman influence upon Britain was too limited to change the language and customs of the ordinary native people. Only the English upper classes were organised to become Roman landlords and officials. With the decline of the Roman Empire, the Romans had to withdraw from England to fight against the Germanic invasion in 410 A.D., which ended the Roman occupation.

### The Anglo-Saxon Conquest

After the Romans left, three groups of Germanic tribes from the European continent came to England in succession: the Angles, the Saxons, and the Jutes. The Angles and Saxons began to invade the British Isles in 450 A.D., but encountered fierce resistance of the Celts. Half a century later, the Celts were slaughtered or made slaves or driven to the mountainous areas in northern and western Britain or assimilated by the invaders. As the Scots in the mountainous areas began to plunder the native Britons in England who were defenseless without the protection and control of the Romans, the Jutes were invited by the English King to help him drive out the Scots. But the Jutes refused to leave and stayed in England when the war was over. This well-known movement in history is called the **Anglo-Saxon Conquest**. Their language is what we call the Old English or the Anglo-Saxon language. They also introduced their own **Teutonic religion**, which practised multi-gods, to England. Moreover, the Anglo-Saxons carried out the village system in which the arable land was fairly distributed among the villagers. Such concept of equality started the process of feudalism in Britain. By the early 7th century, the Angles, Saxons and the Jutes from north Germany settled and established seven kingdoms in England for lack of unity and were trapped in wars with each other for about 200 years, and was plundered by the vikings later on.

### The Viking Invasions

The Vikings from Norway, Denmark, and Scandinavia began to attack the northeast coast of Britain for farming land and settlement in the late 8th century. But under the leadership of **King Alfred the Great**, the Danes were unable to conquer England. In 1013, the Danes defeated Ethelred, and Sweyn, the Danish leader, was made king of England. After the death of his sons, the throne was passed to **Edward the Confessor**, the last Anglo-Saxon king in English history.

### The Norman Conquest

In the 9th century, the Normans, belonging to the same ethnic group as the Danes, began to ravage the northern coast of France. Finally the French king had to make an agreement by giving them a piece of land in the northern part of France, but forced them to accept the Christian religion, just as the English King Alfred had done before. Their country was then named Normandy. When the English King Edward died in 1066, many claimants scrambled for the English throne. Finally **William**, the **Duke of Normandy**, succeeded in conquering England and was crowned in Westminster Abbey. So William, known as the **Conqueror**, became the first Anglo-Norman King of England. This is the well-known Norman Conquest in British history.

**The Norman Conquest** had a huge influence on Britain. It enhanced the process of the British feudalism. After the conquest of England, **William the Conqueror** distributed the lands to the Norman followers in order to secure his own authority. In the feudal society, the nobles received their land from the King, to whom they were bound to be loyal and to pay certain duties. Actually the King became the ultimate owner of the land. What's more important,

he centralised the power of the Monarch by granting the Norman nobles several pieces of land in different parts of the country instead of a large piece, but retained most of the Old English customs of governing. Introducing French culture to England, the Normans intermingled with the Anglo-Saxons. Therefore, the English language kept its own structure, while adopting French words and terms employed by the Normans. As the last invasion of England, the Norman Conquest in 1066 marked the beginning of the period of Middle English.

> **? Questions for discussion:**
> 1. What great changes took place in England after the Anglo-Saxon Conquest?
> 2. What's the relationship between England and France before the Norman Conquest?

## Exercises

### I. Fill in the blanks.

1. _____ were taken as the early natives in British history, and their language was assimilated into the English language.
2. The Celts' language serves as the origin of the _____ and _____ languages.
3. In 55 B.C., _____ commanded the Roman army to invade Britain, but failed because of the Celts' resistance and bad weather.
4. Three groups of the Germanic tribes from the European continent came to England in succession: _____, _____, and _____.
5. _____ made a notable contribution to literature because his writings and translations have been taken as the beginning of prose in Britain.
6. Until in _____ did the Roman succeeded in conquering what is now England.
7. The Romans introduced the system of governing, intending to transform England into a _____ society.
8. The Roman traders and soldiers brought their own religion — _____ to Britain.
9. The Roman influence upon Britain was too limited to change the _____ and _____ of the ordinary native people.
10. The Romans had to withdraw from England to fight against the Germanic invasion of the Roman

Empire in _____.

## II. Define the following terms.
1. the Roman Conquest
2. the Anglo-Saxon Conquest
3. the Viking invasions
4. the Norman Conquest

## III. Multiple choice.
1. The Celtic tribes migrated from eastern and central Europe to the British Isles from about _____.
   A. 500 B.C.  B. 750 B.C.
   C. 200 A.D.  D. 750 A.D.
2. The _____ invasion marked the beginning of the recorded history in Britain.
   A. Roman  B. Anglo-Saxon
   C. Danish  D. Norman
3. The _____ language is what we call the Old English.
   A. Scottish  B. Welsh
   C. Anglo-Saxon  D. Jutes'
4. The process of feudalism in Britain started from the _____ conquest.
   A. Norman  B. Roman
   C. Celts  D. Anglo-Saxon
5. Without the protection and control of the _____ in the 5th century, the English king invited the Jutes to help him drive out the Scots.
   A. Normans  B. Romans
   C. Anglos  D. Saxons
6. The Anglo-Saxons carried out the _____ system in which the arable land was fairly distributed among the villagers.
   A. village  B. governing
   C. draining  D. cultivating
7. King Alfred attached great importance to education and religion by establishing schools and repairing churches, especially to the _____ culture.
   A. French  B. English
   C. German  D. Latin
8. _____, the Duke of Normandy, was known as the Conqueror and became the first Anglo-Norman king of England.
   A. Alfred  B. William
   C. Edward  D. Richard
9. After the conquest of England, William distributed the lands to the _____ followers in order to secure his own authority.
   A. French  B. English
   C. Norman  D. Roman
10. The _____ became the upper class, while the _____ turned into the lower class.
    A. Normans, Anglo-Saxons
    B. Romans, Anglo-Saxons
    C. Normans, Scots
    D. Romans, Jutes

## IV. Translate the following terms into English.
1. 凯尔特人
2. 罗马帝国
3. 阿尔弗雷德大帝
4. 条顿人宗教
5. 诺曼底君主

## V. Answer the following questions in a few sentences.
1. What's the influence of the Norman Conquest on Britain?

2. What's the contribution of King Alfred to Britain?

## Part Two  The Decline of Feudalism and the Rise of the English Bourgeoisie

*After the Hundred Years' War and the War of the Roses, the British feudal reign was weakened and the bourgeoisie began to establish their position on the British political stage. In addition, the spread of Renaissance into Britain reflected the spirit of the rising bourgeoisie. Try to get information about the essence of the spirit advocated by the bourgeoisie from the materials at hand.*

### Henry II and His Reforms

After the death of William the Conqueror, England and Normandy were governed by William II, Henry I, and Henry II in succession. During the reign of Henry II, the power of the crown was further strengthened. Henry II took the first step to destroy all the fortresses illegally built by the nobles, then ordered them to disband their hired soldiers, and stripped those resistant nobles of their

titles. By doing so, the King limited the power of the nobles who relied on their own military force to challenge the King's authority in order to consolidate the royal power. He imposed a new tax on the basis of a landowner's annual rents and all movable property, established circuit courts to improve the efficiency of law, and planned to reform the church courts.

Henry II stayed longer in Normandy than in England, but the area under his sovereignty was larger in England than that in Normandy. In order to make the administrative organs work properly, he expanded the power of the Exchequer, which contained well-trained secretaries, skillful officials, and proficient judges. Therefore, the Exchequer served as a financial organ and a decision-making court.

The major achievement of Henry II lies in his reform in the judiciary system. He appointed the circuit judges to try cases from town to town, who investigated the nobles' property and behaviour of abusing power, or even punished offenders, which laid a foundation for the jury system. **The jury** was originally made up of 12 persons who could verify the reputation and behaviours of the criminals on the basis of facts. In other words, members of the jury were only entitled to verification rather than verdict. But later on, the jury was gradually empowered to announce their verdict.

Another aspect of Henry II's reforms consisted in the church courts. The churches always interfered in the common arguments, which would prevent the King's reform in the judiciary. Therefore, Henry II was eager to restore the King's control over the churches. This conflict between the King and churches was reflected in the struggle between Henry II and **Thomas Becket**, the archbishop. In the beginning, Henry II put Chancellor Thomas Becket, his close friend, in the leading position of the Church in order to carry out the plan to reform the church courts. However, Thomas Becket was intensely opposed to the King's reforms in the churches, which frustrated the King's plan. As a result, Thomas Becket was murdered in 1170. The murder of Thomas Becket shocked the world of Christianity. Under the pressure of the churches and commons, Henry II had to make a compromise in his reforms. But on the whole, Henry II consolidated the British feudalism and enabled the country to experience a period of security and prosperity. Thomas Becket was respected as a saint martyred in the name of the Church, and his grave at Canterbury became a place of pilgrimage and an origin of creating well-known literature. *The Canterbury Tales* by Geoffrey Chaucer in the 14th century and *Murder in the Cathedral* by T. S. Eliot in the 20th century both derived from the story of Thomas Becket.

### King John and the Great Charter

After the death of Henry II, John (1167—1216) was considered the worst of the English Kings and was notorious for his tyranny and misgovernment. **King John**, like William I, was one of the most controversial monarchs of Medieval England and was closely related to the **Magna Carta** or the **Great Charter** of 1215.

As the youngest son of Henry II, John tended to be overshadowed by his older brother Richard and developed a bad reputation for violent rages, more resembling his father in character. With no land left to him, John was given the nick-name "Lackland". In 1189, all of Henry's territory went to his oldest son, Richard I (known as **the Lionheart**).

In 1191, Richard left England to embark on the **Third Crusade**. He left John in charge of the country. John's reputation as a leader had been severely dented as far back as 1185 when he was sent to rule Ireland and returned home for his poor reign capacity within six months. In 1192, Richard was imprisoned by Duke Leopold of Austria when he returned from the **Crusade**. John tried to seize the crown from his brother but in vain. In 1194, Richard finally returned to England and forgave his brother

John for his betrayal.

John succeeded to the throne after Richard was killed in France in 1199. He started his reign in an unfortunate way. In 1202 John's nephew, Arthur of Brittany, was murdered. A great number of people in Brittany (the northwest part of France) believed that John was responsible for his death and they began to rebel against John. With failure to suppress the rebellion in 1204, John had no choice but to retreat from Brittany to England. Hence he got a new nickname "Softsword" with the decline of his military standing among the nobles. The defeat in north France was a costly and major blow to John. He had to increase taxes to pay for the defeat.

On the other hand, as John quarreled with the Pope in 1207 over who should be Archbishop of Canterbury, the Pope excommunicated John and put England under a Church law with the provision that no christening or marriage would be legal without the permission of the Pope. The Church law said that only christened people could get to Heaven, while children born out of marriage were doomed to Hell. This placed people in England under terrible strain and they blamed King John for this provision.

In 1213, John had to surrender to the Pope. However, the Pope never fully trusted John and proclaimed in 1214 that anybody who tried to overthrow John would be legally entitled to do so. In the same year, John lost another battle to the French at Bouvines. This defeat resulted in England losing all her possessions in France, which brought about the rebellion of the English powerful barons in 1214. John was forced to sign the Great Charter (or the Magna Carta) at Runnymede in 1215.

The Great Charter prescribed what the King must observe. For instance, the King must permit free elections of churches, guarantee the nobles' and knights' right in succeeding to their manors and protect the citizens' free trade; no free man should be imprisoned or penalized or banished in any way unless convicted by a jury of his fellow citizens; no extra tax should be imposed on nobles without the permission of **the Great Council**; in addition, the nobles should be entitled to declare war against the King on condition that the King seriously violates the provisions of the Great Charter. But John had no intention to observe the Great Charter and launched a civil war against the nobles which came to an end with his death in 1216.

The Great Charter was of great importance as the turning point of English history and laid a foundation for the latter constitutional monarchy. Firstly, it established a legal relation between the King and the nobles by defining their respective rights and obligations. Secondly, it granted some power to the Great Council, which made it possible for the new-born bourgeoisie to enter politics. In addition, the Charter protected the rights of the merchant class, which later extended to the common people and established the guideline for the protection of civil rights in the Western World.

### Beginning of Parliament

King John started a war against the nobles, but was defeated. After his death, Henry III succeeded to the throne in 1216, showing his inability to govern the country and much obedience to the Pope. Simon de Montfort was a defender of the Great Charter. He is praised as a fighter for liberty in British history. In 1264, under the leadership of Munford, the nobles defeated the royal army and captured Henry III and the royal family. From then on, Munford began to rule England in the name of King Henry.

The Great Council was an advisory assembly of the King's chief feudal vassals and clergymen. In 1265, Munford called the **Great Council**, which was attended by the knights and representatives as well as the nobles and clergymen from counties and towns. It was the first time for the common people without noble titles to take part in discussions, thus the Great Council got the new name "Parliament", which comes from a French word and means a place for discussing and debating about problems. In the 14th century, Parliament was divided into two chambers, one was known as the House of Commons, the other was called the House of Lords. These two houses functioned as the law maker in England.

### The Hundred Years' War

Feudalism was established in Britain during the Norman Conquest, and then revealed its decline in the 14th century. William the Conqueror was the first English King to control a domain in France — Normandy, and Henry II expanded the domain almost to two thirds of the land of France, which caused a long-term conflict  between England and France. Consequently, the English domain in France had been reduced continuously since King John. However, the appearance of Parliament strengthened the English King's power and England gradually developed into a strong nation. The new-born bourgeoisie desired to expand markets for greater wealth, and the English King was eager to regain the lost territory.

Meanwhile France also developed into a strong nation, with an intention to enlarge its influence. The French kings wanted to stop English trade, while the English kings and merchants attempted to expand trade with France. Such an economic conflict between England and France resulted in the **Hundred Years' War (1337—1453)**, which started in 1337 and ended in 1453. On the other hand, the English King's succession to the French throne became an incident that touched off the war. The French King left no legitimate successor after death, and then the English King **Edward III** claimed to be the rightful King of France, for his mother was a sister of the former King. As soon as his claim was denied by the French nobles, Edward III landed in Normandy with his English army in 1337 and launched the well-known Hundred Years' War.

In the beginning of the war, the English army achieved numerous victories in the Battle of Crecy, Poitier and Argebcourt. But a turning point from victory to defeat came to England in 1429, partly because of the French peasant girl **Joan of Arc**. Joan of Arc was selected by the French King to head an army, protecting Orleans from being besieged by the English army. She was betrayed by the French nobles and died as a martyr in 1431, but her enthusiastic patriotism aroused the fighting will of French people from a variety of social strata and imbued the anti-England war with a widespread national character. Moreover, the use of guns and gunpowder in France was superior in effectiveness to the English cavalry. As a result, the Hundred Years' War ended with the defeat of England in 1453.

The Hundred Years' War had a great impact on England. In the early period of the war, English nobles secured a great deal of profits, but the long-lasting war made the common people suffer from great taxes, military service, and higher inflation, which intensified the class conflict. On the other hand, the military reverse and loss of the continental territory greatly weakened British feudal reign.

### The Black Death

England was struck by another disaster — the **Black Death (1348—1349)** during the Hundred Years' War. The Black Death referred to a deadly bubonic plague between 1348 and 1349, which spread throughout the whole Europe. Those falling victim to such a disease would die within two or three days. In August, 1348, the Black Death broke out in England. It was so acute that Britain's population decreased sharply by half. The surviving labourers were not enough to engage in work for manors, so the lords of manors had to employ free labourers with higher wages. Those serfs and tenant-peasants began to escape from their masters to other manors for higher wages. In view of this situation, Edward III issued the Statute of Labourers, which prescribed peasants must be employed with low wages, and the serfs were prohibited from leaving their original manors, otherwise, they would be put into jail or branded with a flatiron. This cruelty of the tyrant, along with poll taxes for the Hundred Years' War, accelerated the anti-feudal movement and finally led to the peasants' uprising in 1381.

### The Peasants' Revolt

In order to fund the Hundred Years' War, the British Parliament decided to impose and increase the poll taxes. What's more, they attempted to transfer the taxes to the British peasants. As a result, the peasants' opposition to the poll taxes directly triggered off the uprising in 1381, which was led by **Walt Tyler** and **John Ball**. Besides, John Ball, a poor churchman, called on a reform of churches against social injustice. His advocacy of human equality awakened the peasants and had a great effect on the poor mass, which laid the groundwork for the peasant uprising.

The uprising broke out first in Essex and Kent in 1381, and then spread to half of England. Many manors were destroyed and nobles were killed, but some merchants supported the uprising for more free labourers. After occupying London, the peasants forced King Richard II to negotiate with them. The King received their petition and pretended to meet their demands. The uprising peasants failed to see through the King's trickery and left London for home. Soon after that, the peasants joining the uprising were brutally killed, including the uprising leaders. The vigorous uprising failed, but it strongly struck the feudal serf system in Britain. By the end of the 14th century, most of the serfs became owner-peasants.

## The Wars of the Roses

**The Wars of the Roses (1455－1485)** followed up with the Hundred Years' War two years later. It was a series of civil wars, started by Edward III's descendants: the **House of York** and the **House of Lancaster**. The badge of the former was a white rose, while that of the latter was a red one. So the intermittent 30-year (1455－1485) war was called the Wars of the Roses.

The basic reasons for the Wars of the Roses were as follows: Many warlike nobles in England during the last years of the Hundred Years' War joined the fight in France and started a new contest for wealth and power after returning to England in order to make up for their loss. Large bands of soldiers followed their masters back home, but could not find proper jobs as they were unfit for the civil employment. On the other hand, the descendants of the English kings were married to the heirs of some most powerful nobles in order to win over their support, which turned these nobles into relatives of the royal house and strengthened the monarchical power, but made them more powerful and ambitious for the throne.

The Wars of the Roses went through two stages. Henry VI was the third king in the Lancaster Monarchy. He was so weak that he took direction from his French wife — Margaret. The House of York became dissatisfied with him, and began to fight for the throne. In 1461, Edward, the oldest son of the Duke of York reached London and ascended to the throne as Edward IV, and Margaret escaped to Scotland. The first stage of the wars came to an end. After that, the House of York had an internal conflict. George, Edward's younger brother, dethroned Edward IV in 1470 and returned the throne to Henry VI. Edward IV escaped to Netherlands for help, and then returned to capture Margaret and kill Henry VI. But after his death, his brother Richard usurped the power from Edward V and became Richard III, which led to the isolation of the whole House of York. They placed their expectations on **Henry Tudor** in the House of Lancaster. In 1485, Henry Tudor killed Richard III and ended the Wars of the Roses. Henry Tudor became Henry VII, who married Elizabeth, the daughter of Edward IV, and solved the long-term dispute between the two houses.

The Wars of the Roses started in 1455 and ended in 1485, marking the end of the middle-aged England. During the wars, feudal nobles killed each other and were in decline, which paved the way for the development of the bourgeoisie.

## The New Monarchy

⊙ Henry VII

With the support of the new nobles and bourgeoisie, Henry Tudor came to the throne as Henry VII and started the **Tudor Monarchy**. This was a new monarchy which differed from the old one. With the decline of the feudal nobles and promotion of the new nobles from the middle class, the position of the new monarchy was consolidated. Meanwhile, the influence of the newly born bourgeoisie increased. The new monarchy adopted a series of domestic policies to cut down expenses, increase revenues and promote the development of trade and industry. On the other hand, in order to promote the interests of its supporters, the monarchy needed to accumulate large amounts of wealth and encourage the expansion of the export market, which paved the way for the establishment of the capitalist mode of production. Moreover, Henry VII formed an alliance with Spain through his son's marriage to the Spanish Princess Catherine in order to enhance the prestige of the Tudor Monarchy in Europe. Therefore, Henry VII succeeded in restoring peace and centralising the monarchy. Furthermore, the English bourgeoisie grew stronger in preparation for the political power and laid the foundation for the establishment of capitalism in England.

⊙ Henry VIII and Church Reformation

**Henry VIII** was an intelligent, but cruel and suspicious king. He married Catherine, his widowed sister-in-law, in order to keep alliance with Spain. He expected to scramble for supremacy from Spain and France by risking military force, but lacked in military and political capacities. As a result, Henry

VIII almost ran out of the wealth accumulated by Henry VII. On the other hand, in order to win popular support after assuming the throne, he put to death, in the name of a fabricated charge, Richard Epson and Edmund Dudley who were loyal to his father. Henry VIII was strict  in carrying out policies. Thomas More, a famous English humanist and the author of *Utopia*, was executed for his disagreement with Henry VIII in the King's divorce case and church policies, which reflected Henry VIII's cruelty and suspicious nature.

However, Henry VIII set up the Privy Council and began to carry out reforms of the church. The Privy Council was officially set up in 1540, composed of the chief officials. It was similar to the modern Cabinet, but different in that the Privy Council was responsible for the King rather than Parliament. The Privy Council comprised a series of committees for special purposes, in which a group of smaller landowners served as Justices of the Peace with full power over law and administration in the rural areas, except for payment.

The reform of the church in England was directly caused by the divorce case of Henry VIII. As Henry VIII was indulgent in seeking pleasure and fell in love with Anne Boleyn, a young maid of **Queen Catherine** (Spain), he applied to **Pope Clement VII** for a divorce from Catherine on the ground that his marriage to the sister-in-law violated God's decree. In fact, the divorce was based on a political purpose: The marriage to the Spanish Princess inhibited Henry VIII from being allied with France. In addition, Catherine failed to produce a male heir for him. But the Pope refused his application for fear of offending the Spanish King — Catherine's nephew, because Rome was occupied by Spain and the Pope was actually a captive of the Spanish King. In 1533, Henry VIII defied the Roman Church by marrying **Anne Boleyn** and requiring Parliament to legitimize his marriage. In addition, he isolated the **Church of England** from the Pope in Rome and prohibited appeals to the Pope. The *Act of Supremacy* passed by Parliament in 1534 established the English King as the head of the Church of England. In 1536, Henry VIII  deserted Anne Boleyn and had her beheaded for the alleged adultery and her inability to give birth to a male heir, and subsequently married Jane Seymour who died soon after giving birth to Edward VI in 1537.

After the death of Henry VIII, the Council of Regency was retained to administer state affairs in the name of Edward VI. As most members of the Council of Regency were enthusiastic about religious reforms, the drastic Protestant theology was rapidly in the ascendant.

> **? Questions for discussion:**
> 1. The periods of Henry II and Henry VII were considered the turning points in British history. What contribution did they make to the progress of British history?
> 2. The divorce case of Henry VIII had a great impact on the religious system in Britain and helped establish the position of the Church of England. What was the relationship between the Church of England and the Pope at that time?

### ⊙ Mary I and Elizabeth I

Mary I, the daughter of Henry VIII and Catherine, was a devout Catholic. As she supported the authority of the Pope and tried to restore Roman Catholicism in England, Mary I cruelly suppressed and persecuted the Protestants. Approximately 300 Protestants were burnt to death as heretics, including  women and children. Therefore, she was known as **Bloody Mary** in British history. In addition, she married the Spanish King, Philip II, in 1553 and made England join the war between Spain and France that led to the loss of England's last domain in France — Calais.

**Elizabeth I** was the daughter of Henry VIII and

Anne Boleyn. She succeeded to the throne after the death of her half-sister Mary I in 1558. However, Elizabeth was different from her sister. She was clear about the necessity of resolving the religious problems. Without religious settlement, England would fall into another disaster. Therefore, she spared no efforts to make the  Church of England dominant and accepted by the majority. The Church of England was in the charge of the King or Queen, breaking away from the Roman Pope. It was Catholic in form and creed, but reformed in some degree, that is, it maintained the traditions of churches, but got rid of corrupt customs and doctrines. In essence, the English reforms in the church reflected the fight between the new-born bourgeoisie and the ruling feudal class.

During the period of Elizabeth I, the Spanish Armada, known as the "invincible fleet", was defeated by Britain. Thus the long-term combat between England and Spain came to an end. The English victory strengthened the position of England in Europe as a major sea power and consolidated the religious reform in England.

A group of sea risk-takers returned to England with numerous war trophies, which paved the way for its foreign expansion.

It was also in this period that the English began their disgraceful slave trade. Those risk-takers turned into pirates as well as slave traders. Their plunder provided the original accumulation of wealth for the development of capitalism.

Besides, many chartered companies were set up as organisations for traders and risk-takers to engage in commercial activities in the Tudor Monarchy. In the period of Elizabeth I, the English East India Company was established in 1600 and became the biggest company doing business in the Far East. Privileges were granted to these companies by the King or Queen, that is, the chartered companies were entitled to monopoly privilege of exploring, risking or migrating, which needed great amounts of capital and cooperation between the joint stockholders.

Elizabeth I had never been married because an alliance with France or Spain by marriage would get England involved in wars. Her devotion to the sovereignty made England prosperous and pushed forward the English Renaissance.

## Questions for discussion:

1. Mary I was notorious for her bloody policy in religion, while Elizabeth I served as the peacemaker in all parts of the British society. Make a comparison between the two British Queens in their beliefs, policies or even characters.
2. The Renaissance in Britain was featured by humanism, materialism and individualism, etc. Could you explore and interpret the connotation of these ideas and list some works related to these ideas?

## Exercises

### I. Fill in the blanks.

1. Henry II expanded the function of _____, which served as a financial organ and a decision-making court.
2. The major achievement of Henry II lies in his reform in the _____ system.
3. Until in the _____ century, Parliament was divided into two chambers: _____ and _____.
4. The Hundred Years' War between Britain and France started in _____ and ended in _____.
5. In view of _____, Edward III issued the Statute of Labourers, which prescribed the employers' payment could not be increased, and the serfs were prohibited from leaving their original manors.
6. The cruelty of the tyrant Edward III sped up the anti-feudal movement and led to the _____ in 1381.
7. Henry VII's policy paved the way for the establishment of the _____ mode of production and centralised the monarchy.
8. Humanists in the period of Renaissance advocated obeying _____ and justifying everything, and emphasised the _____ of the human world rather than the _____ preaching in religion.
9. Francis Bacon attached importance to the study of nature, which indicated that the characteristic of Renaissance in England changed from _____ to _____.
10. As _____ became the slogan of the humanists who claimed the right to liberty and individuality, _____ turned out to be a feature of the Renaissance in England.

## II. Define the following terms.
1. The Great Charter
2. The Hundred Years' War
3. The Wars of the Roses
4. Bloody Mary
5. The Church of England

## III. Multiple choice.
1. _____ limited the power of the nobles who relied on their own military force to challenge the king authority, and consolidated the royal power.
   A. William the Conqueror
   B. William II
   C. Henry I
   D. Henry II
2. In _____, the Great Council got the new name Parliament, as it was the first time for common people to attend the council.
   A. 1265    B. 1264
   C. 1170    D. 1215
3. With the support of the new nobles and bourgeoisie, Henry Tudor came to the throne as _____ and started the Tudor Monarchy.
   A. Henry II    B. Henry VII
   C. Henry VIII   D. Henry V
4. _____ set up Privy Council, and began to carry out the reform in church.
   A. Henry VII    B. Henry I
   C. Henry VIII   D. Henry VI
5. The Church of England became dominant in England during the reign of _____, with the King or Queen as the head, and broke away from the Roman Church.
   A. Mary I     B. Victoria
   C. Catherine  D. Elizabeth I
6. In the period of Elizabeth I, the English East India Company was established in _____ and became the biggest company doing business in the Far East.
   A. 1600    B. 1610
   C. 1601    D. 1620
7. Thomas Moore's prose writing _____ was the typical work in the English Renaissance.
   A. *Faerie Queen*
   B. *Utopia*
   C. *Paradise Lost*
   D. *Romeo and Juliet*
8. Privy Council was officially set up in _____ and composed of the chief officials.
   A. 1536    B. 1533
   C. 1524    D. 1540
9. The deadly plague which broke out in Britain in _____ was called the Black Death.
   A. 1438   B. 1431   C. 1348   D. 1381
10. The characteristic of the Renaissance in England gradually changed from _____ to materialism.
    A. humanism    B. idealism
    C. romanticism  D. feudalism

## IV. Translate the following terms into English.
1. 教皇
2. 黑死病
3. 文艺复兴
4. 都铎王朝
5. 大议会

## V. Answer the following questions in a few sentences.
1. What are the reasons for the Wars of the Roses?
2. What's the contribution of Elizabeth I to the British Empire?

## Part Three    English Bourgeoisie Revolution in the 17th Century

*Due to the religious difference, Puritans in popularity were severely persecuted in the reign of James I, which resulted in the migration of Puritans and the Gunpowder Plot. In addition, the conflict between the King and Parliament led to the Civil War and the death of Charles I. After the Monarchy was restored, the Glorious Revolution took place, which laid the foundation for the Constitutional Monarchy. Why didn't the bourgeoisie revolt in the 17th century? Try to find out the original reason for it by researching the materials available.*

### James I and the Parliament

As Elizabeth I never got married and died in 1603 without leaving an heir to succeed her, the Scottish King, **James I**, was welcomed to the English throne as a descendant of Henry VII. Therefore, England and Scotland were brought together under the reign of James I, and the unification of the two kingdoms gave birth to the name "Great Britain".

The first problem James I had to confront was related to religion. With the popularity of Puritanism increasing, the **Puritans** put forward the **Millenary Petition** and sought to reform the Church of England. But James I refused their demands for reform, condemning and forcing them to follow the Church of England. In order to escape from the persecution, many Puritans were compelled to leave England and immigrate abroad. The number of immigrating Puritans between 1603 and 1640 reached about 60 thousand. The voyage of the Mayflower to North America in 1620 was one of the well-known migrations of Puritans.

The Catholics also became dissatisfied with James I because he refused to allow further tolerance in religion. In 1605, five radical Catholics decided to hatch a gunpowder plot, planning to destroy both the King and members of Parliament by blowing up the Parliament building. One of the conspirators, **Guy Fawkes**, placed barrels of gunpowder in a cellar of the Parliament building and prepared to detonate the explosive charge on 5 November when Parliament would be in session. But the plot was betrayed and Guy Fawkes along with his conspirators were arrested and executed. This was known as the **Gunpowder Plot** of 1605 in British history. From then on, a bonfire night festival on 5 November would be annually celebrated with fireworks and bonfires to remind the English people of the danger of Catholic restoration.

Another problem existed in the conflict between the King and Parliament. Those who represented the interests of the bourgeoisie and new nobles in Parliament gradually formed the opposition to the royal court, criticising the autocratic policies of the government, while James I's belief in the Divine Right of King worsened the relations between the King and Parliament. On the other hand, James I resented any efforts of Parliament to have a different voice and even dismissed Parliament for a time.

Compared with Elizabeth I, James I was less popular in the eyes of the English people, but was quite learned in many fields except in politics. He wrote many a book on various subjects. What's more, he ordered translation of the Bible into English, which greatly influenced the English language and cultures.

### Charles I

**Charles I** followed his father's practice in dealing with his relationship with Parliament, but was even worse than James I. Charles I needed a large sum of money to support the war against Spain and France, but encountered refusal from Parliament. Intent on getting money from Parliament, Charles I unwillingly approved the Petition of Right proposed by Parliament, then immediately discarded it and raised an army without the agreement of Parliament. In 1629, Charles I dismissed Parliament as people were called on to refuse paying taxes. Not until 1640 was Parliament restored. During the absence of Parliament, Charles I strengthened the persecution of those opposing him.

### The Short Parliament and the Long Parliament

Due to the English people's resentment against Charles I and his interference in the Scottish religion, an uprising broke out in England. In 1638, the Scots organised an army to fight for their independence in religion and politics and occupied the border of England in 1639. So Charles I had to call a meeting of Parliament on 13 April, 1640, with an attempt to raise money for suppressing the uprising. Consequently, Parliament not only refused his requirement, but also put forward the Petition of Right. Charles I was so irritated that he dissolved Parliament immediately on 5 May, 1640. This Parliament existed for less than a month and was called the **Short Parliament** in the English history.

Besides the Scottish uprising, English uprisings took place one after another among the craftsmen and peasants. Charles I had to call another meeting of Parliament with the same attempt in November, 1640. This Parliament was known as the **Long Parliament** in English history, lasting until in 1653. It forced the King to issue the *Triennial Act*, which prescribed that Parliament must be convened every three years. The King had no right to dissolve or suspend Parliament. Parliament passed *Grand Remonstrance* in 1641, which advocated the freedom of commerce and trade and required that the government should be responsible for Parliament, etc. On the whole, *Grand Remonstrance* played an active role in calling on people to oppose the sovereign.

### The Civil War

In order to suppress the revolution, Charles I commanded his force to capture the leaders of his opponents, but was frustrated by armed citizens in London, and then escaped for gathering his followers. In August, 1642, he declared a war against Parliament. This was the beginning of the first civil war in England.

The King was supported by the feudal nobles and the upper clergymen of the Church of England, while Parliament was financed by the bourgeoisie and the new nobles. From the objective perspective, Parliament was on the absolute advantage, because the prosperous industrialised middle and southeastern England were under the control of Parliament. But in the initial stage, the army of Parliament was defeated continuously due to the leaders' passive attitude. Not until 1643, when Parliament formed an alliance with the Scots, was the situation reversed. In 1646, the surrender of Charles I to the Scots put an end to the civil war. During the period of the civil war, the Long Parliament served as the supreme authority in Britain, issuing a series of laws and decrees for the benefit of capitalism instead of the labourers.

After the end of the first civil war, Parliament was confronted with the establishment of a new political system, but the Presbyters in charge of Parliament did not resolve this issue. Instead, they regarded the Levelers, the representatives of the young bourgeoisie supported by the army, as their opponents, which led to the fight between Parliament and the army.

In 1647, the house-arrested Charles I escaped to the Isle of Wight and designed a plot to restore his sovereignty with the support of the Scottish feudal nobles. In February, 1648, a rebellion burst out in South Wales, which started the second civil war. At the end of August, 1648, the revolutionaries surrendered to the army of Parliament, and thus the second civil war came to an end. The Presbyters intended to help Charles I restore his throne, but met the opposition of the citizens and soldiers, who presented their petition that required the trial of the King. As the Upper House of Parliament denied the proposal to try the King, the Lower House passed the decision that the Lower House was prescribed as the highest authority and their decision could take effect directly without the approval of the Upper House and the King. On 30 January, 1649, Charles I was put to death after trial. On 19 May, 1649, Parliament officially proclaimed England to be a Commonwealth without the monarch and the Upper House. The establishment of the Commonwealth marked the summit of the English Bourgeoisie Revolution.

### Restoration

As the head of the army, **Oliver Cromwell** became the real ruler of the nation after Charles I was beheaded. He suppressed the soldiers' uprising and eliminated the **Diggers Movement** initiated by the Levelers who advocated the public ownership of land. Soon after that, Cromwell commanded his army to occupy Ireland and put down the Irish uprising. In 1652, Ireland was conquered and reduced to a colony of England. On the other hand, the Presbyters in Scotland were dissatisfied with the beheading of Charles I, they supported Charles I's son and put him on the throne as Charles II in Scotland. Therefore, Cromwell marched north and subdued the rebellion of Scots. Thus, Scotland was proclaimed to be integrated into the Commonwealth. In order to establish a powerful regime, Cromwell was announced to be a life-long Protector. He was in charge of military leadership and possessed power superior to Parliament. In essence, the **Protector system** belonged to the military dictatorship and had little difference from the monarchy. It was nothing but an access to the monarchy.

After the death of Cromwell in 1658, his son Richard Cromwell succeeded the Protector. However, many generals resigned due to his incapability as the Protector, and then the political power fell into the hand of some generals. They called a meeting of Parliament, declaring that the political power should belong to the King, nobles and commons. As a result, **Charles II** was invited to return to London in 1660 and mounted the throne. The Commonwealth came to an end and the monarchy was restored. Charles II attempted to restore the dictatorship and remove the effect of the revolution on social economy but failed. However, the development of capitalism could not be prevented by the restoration, and the bourgeoisie grew dissatisfied with the behaviours of Charles II. So they proposed the *Habeas Corpus of Act of 1679* in Parliament. This act limited the power of the monarch, and thus was rejected by the Upper House of Parliament. But with the support of the Lower House, it was finally passed as a law.

## The Glorious Revolution

In 1685, Charles II died and his brother succeeded the throne as **James II**. He backed up Catholics in public, regardless of the people's opposition and the provisions of laws. From 1679 to 1681, the problem had been discussed in Parliament about whether James was entitled to the succession of the throne.

Some members argued that James had no right to succeed the throne as he was a Catholic, and they were called the "Whigs" by their opponents, a derogatory name for cattle drivers in Scots. On the other hand, those who supported James were called the "Tories", an Irish word meaning thugs. These two sects represented the interests of different classes: the Whigs advocated limiting the power of the monarch on behalf of the financial capitalists, traders and some land-owners, while the Tories attempted to strengthen the power of the monarch, standing for the big land-owners and the upper churchmen. Later on, the Whigs together with dissident Tories turned into the Liberal Party, while the Tories became the forerunners of the Conservative Party.

In 1688, the Whigs and Tories came together to negotiate with William of Holland, who was the head of the United Netherlands and the son-in-law of James II. They invited William to England and asked for help to overthrow James II. William accepted the invitation and landed in England with his army in November, 1688. James II escaped to France without resistance.

In February, 1689, Parliament proposed the *Declaration of Rights*. It prescribed that laws can not be abolished by the King or Queen without agreement of Parliament, the financial administration belonged to Parliament, Parliament members must be produced through free election and had the freedom of speech, and any Catholic or anyone

marrying Catholic had no right to succeed the throne. As soon as William and his wife Mary accepted it, Parliament proclaimed them to be joint sovereigns: **William III and Mary II**. In October, 1689, the *Declaration of Rights* was passed to be a law, that is, the *Bill of Rights*. Such a coup d'etat without bloody fight was known as the **Glorious Revolution** in history. It was a compromise between the bourgeoisie and the nobles, but it overthrew the feudalism and established the capitalism in England based on the constitutional monarchy. As an epoch-making event in history, the Glorious Revolution paved the way for the speedy economic development that promoted the later Industrial Revolution.

> **? Questions for Discussion:**
> 1. What's the significance of the British Puritans' migration in American history?
> 2. Why did Oliver Cromwell perform the restoration of the monarchy instead of claiming to be the King?

## Exercises

### I. Fill in the blanks.

1. With the Scottish King succeeding the English throne in 1603, the two kingdoms — England and Scotland — were brought together under the reign of one King, which also gave birth to the name _____.
2. The voyage of the Mayflower to North America in _____ was the well-known migration of _____.
3. In August, 1642, Charles I declared a war against _____, which was the beginning of the first civil war in England.
4. In February, 1648, a rebellion burst out in _____, which started the second civil war between Parliament and the army.
5. On 30 January, 1649, _____ was put to death after trial.
6. In 1649, Parliament officially proclaimed England to be a _____.
7. In 1652, Ireland was conquered and reduced to the _____ of England.
8. _____ was invited to return to London in 1660 and mounted the throne. Thus the Commonwealth came to an end and _____ was restored.
9. The Whigs later became the _____ Party, while the Tories were the forerunners of the _____ Party.
10. As an epoch-making event in history, the Glorious Revolution paved the way for the speedy economic development that promoted the later _____.

## II. Define the following terms.

1. the Short Parliament
2. the Long Parliament
3. the Protector system
4. the Glorious Revolution
5. Restoration

## III. Multiple choice.

1. In order to escape from the persecution, many Puritans were forced to leave England and immigrated abroad in the period of _____.
   A. James I
   B. Henry VII
   C. William I
   D. Henry VIII

2. In 1629, _____ dismissed Parliament as people were called on to refuse paying taxes.
   A. James I        B. Charles I
   C. Elizabeth I    D. Mary I

3. In _____, the surrender of Charles I to the Scots put an end to the civil war.
   A. 1643    B. 1640
   C. 1642    D. 1646

4. The coup d'etat without bloody fight in _____ was known in history as the Glorious Revolution.
   A. 1681    B. 1689
   C. 1688    D. 1685

5. In October, _____, the *Declaration of Rights* was passed to be a law: the *Bill of Rights*.
   A. 1688    B. 1689
   C. 1685    D. 1687

## IV. Translate the following terms into English.

1. 清教徒
2. 千人请愿书
3. 火药阴谋
4. 掘地派运动
5. 大抗议书

## V. Answer the following questions in a few sentences.

1. What's the significance of the Glorious Revolution?
2. How did the Lower House of Parliament obtain the real power of Britain?

## Part Four  The Rise of the British Empire

*The Industrial Revolution, going hand in hand with the Chartist Movement of the working class, contributed to Britain's monopoly in the world's industry. Up to the Victorian Age, Britain had grown into an empire due to its foreign expansion policy. Could you list some examples to indicate the effect of Britain's foreign expansion on both economy and culture? Try to get the relevant information from the materials available.*

### The Industrial Revolution

The Industrial Revolution refers to the economic transition from agriculture and handicraft industry to the mechanised industry in England from 1760 to 1840. There were two prerequisites for the Industrial Revolution: One was the labourers deprived of the means of production, and the other was large sums of monetary capital. Both of them depended on the fulfillment of the following means: the Enclosure Movement, the colonial exploitation, slave trafficking and the development of the basic sciences.

Firstly, the enclosure movement reduced peasants to employees, and the political power of the state sped up the separation between labourers and the means of production. Meanwhile, the capitalist agriculture was set up on the enclosed land, which provided enough food for cities as well as labourers and materials for industry.

Secondly, England defeated Spain, Holland and France in fighting for colonies from the 1650s to the 1760s and held the monopoly in slave trafficking in the 18th century. Therefore, England accumulated great amounts of primitive capital by means of plundering colonial wealth and trafficking in slaves.

In addition, the development of basic sciences, such as the great contribution to mechanics and mathematics made by Isaac Newton, offered the necessary theory to the invention of machines. On the other hand, handicraft workplaces created the division of labour and specialised tools, which provided indispensable technology and skilled workers. All of these factors provided the foundation

for the Industrial Revolution in the 1760s.

The revolution began with the cotton textile industry, because without traditional limitations of guild regulations as a new trade, it was easy to adopt new technology to compete with each other. Moreover, the increasing demand for cheap cotton cloth made it urgent to improve techniques and increase production. For example, the invention of the **flying shuttle** in 1733 sped up spinning. Subsequently, the **spinning Jenny** and the **water frame spinning machine** were invented in 1765 and 1769 respectively. Based on them, the **mule spinning machine** was invented in 1779, combining the advantages of the two spinning machines and producing refined and durable yarn. The application of machines in cotton textile promoted innovative techniques in related industries such as the coal mining and metallurgical industry. By the end of the 17th century, the **steam engine** was invented and continuously improved. In 1784, the all-powerful steam engine was invented and finally applied in various industries, which led to the innovation of tools in transportation and started the age of locomotive. By the 1840s, England had been transformed from an agricultural country into a manufacturing country.

The Industrial Revolution had a great effect on Britain. Britain became the biggest industrial country as the workshop of the world. Its monopoly in industry, supremacy on seas and subsequent plunder in colonies turned Britain into a great overlord and exploiter in the world.

## The Chartist Movement

The Industrial Revolution produced two confronting classes: the bourgeoisie and the proletariat. What's worse, the gap between these two classes went to the extreme. The capitalists occupied the means of production and exploited the labourers, and then they grew wealthier, while the workers became poorer. As a result, the workers began to strive for better conditions and political rights. They organised the workers' union in secret and staged strikes. In practice, the proletariat realised that they couldn't benefit from the political movement of the bourgeoisie and was aware of the limitation of the labour union movement. So they set about establishing their own party in the Chartist Movement.

**The Chartist Movement** started in 1836, marking the workers' awareness in politics. It went through the following three stages.

The first stage started from the establishment of the London Working Men's Association in 1836 for the purpose of advocating general elections. The Association proposed a programme which was promulgated in 1838 as an act and called the *People's Charter*. Hence, the consequent campaign for carrying out the charter was called the Chartist Movement. But soon the movement was split into two parts due to the representatives' disagreement: the moral force Chartists advocating legal strategies like propaganda, meeting as well as petition, and the violence Chartists advocating uprising and strikes. However, both parts agreed to submit a petition to Parliament. The petition was passed by the Chartist Convention but denied by Parliament, which aroused the indignation of the mass and led to strikes in various places. The strikes were suppressed bloodily and drove the movement to the bottom. The second stage occurred in 1842. The Association held a meeting in London and decided to present a petition to Parliament. As soon as the petition was denied, strikes and even uprisings were held all over Britain. So the movement met a second bloody suppression. However, the movement forced the ruling class to make a compromise and pass several acts in favour of workers such as the *Coal Mine Act*, the *Factory Act* and the *Ten Hour Day Act*. The third stage took place in 1848 when the British workers were confronted with a new economic crisis and the revolution movement in the European Continent. The Association planned a demonstration to present a petition to Parliament, but gave it up. From then on, the Chartist Movement came into a decline. But it provided the workers of the world with abundant experience in later political combat as the first universal political movement of the proletariat.

## Queen Victoria and Her Time

Victoria was another famous Queen in British history, mounting the throne in 1837. The reign of Queen Victoria was one of the longest in Britain, and has come to be known as the **Victorian Age**. Britain stepped into the stage of the worldwide British Empire in this period, involving the colonies in Canada, Australia, India, New Zealand, and large parts of Africa. Therefore, Queen Victoria served as the official head of the United Kingdom and the British Empire as well.

The Victorian Age witnessed tremendous changes in almost every respect. In general, Britain enjoyed a boom in economy in spite of the social problems caused by the Industrial Revolution. With the innovation of new techniques, the British transportation and agriculture were mechanised; trade and commerce developed rapidly with an increase in urban population.

The economic prosperity advanced the development of sciences, literature, politics and education. For instance, the *Origin of Species*, written by Darwin in 1859, put forward the basic idea about the survival of the fittest in the natural selection and provided evidence to justify the theory of free competition, which became an important element of British values.

The cultural boom found expression in a group of famous writers such as William Thackeray, the Bronte Sisters, Charles Dickens, and George Eliot who produced lots of works with the intention of promoting social reforms. Compulsory education was adopted and universities began to enroll women as well as non-Anglican church believers. Besides, secret voting was introduced in 1876.

What's more, foreign expansion was another characteristic of the British Empire during this period. It suppressed the revolt of the Canadians, fought against the Russians, and started the Opium War against China. On the other hand, Britain granted its colonies self-government. It tried to transform its position from the world's workshop into the world's banker. Under the reign of Queen Victoria, Britain stepped into the stage of imperialism.

> **? Question for discussion:**
> As a conservative state, Britain has gone through a series of significant reforms in social and political areas. The British people tend to keep their own style in carrying out the social and political reforms. Can you list some examples to indicate the conservativeness of the British people in carrying out the reforms?

## Foreign Expansion

⊙ Process of foreign expansion

Foreign expansion actually started from the period of Elizabeth I, which laid the foundation for the **British Empire**. Britain defeated the **Spanish fleet** and seized the world hegemony in 1588; it defeated Holland and established its superiority in the sea trade in the 17th century. By the 18th century, France had become the major opponent to Britain. But not until the Industrial Revolution in the 18th and 19th century did the British Empire come into being. The Empire acquired a lot of colonies and seized countless wealth through foreign expansion. Moreover, the Empire turned the colonies into sources of raw materials and important markets for its industrial products.

In America, Bahama Islands and Canada were occupied by Britain and turned into British colonies one after another. The American Independence War, breaking out in the thirteen British colonies in 1776, was a blow to the British colonial expansion. After that, the British government granted Canada the right of self-government in order to avoid troubles alike.

In 1770, Australia was discovered by an English captain, **James Cook**, who claimed the east coast region for Britain. In 1788, the British government began to transport convicts to Australia. In 1816, free colonists started to settle in Australia. Later on, the gold rushes brought large numbers of free immigrants to Australia and laid the foundation for six separate colonies. In 1901, the six separate and self-governing colonies were united into one dominion, that is, the independent Commonwealth of Australia.

In addition, New Zealand was claimed for Britain after James Cook's arrival in the 1770s. In 1840, the New Zealand Company started systematic colonization and turned New Zealand into a colony by signing a treaty with the Maoris. New Zealand obtained the right of self-government in 1852 and became a dominion of Britain. Not until 1931 did it achieve complete independence.

India was the most important colony of Britain, and various chartered companies were set up there. The **East India Company** was the first one to be established in 1600. It traded with India through a few trading posts and had the right to use the British Navy. Therefore, the British aggression always followed up with commerce. In the 17th century, other countries also established trading posts in India one after another. Britain managed to edge out the French and Portuguese colonists in contending for the domination of India. In 1877, Queen Victoria was proclaimed the Empress of India, and thus Britain's control over India was strengthened.

China was another target of British colonists. In order to turn China into its own colony, Britain launched repeated aggression against China in the same pattern. As China's economy was based on agriculture and self-sufficiency, Britain used to suffer a deficit in its trade with China. British merchants began to traffic in opium in China. The opium trade had been banned since 1799, but some British merchants continued to smuggle opium into China. In 1839, about 20,000 chests of opium were confiscated and burned by the Imperial Commissioner Lin Zexu. The British used this event as a pretext to launch the **Opium War** against China in 1840 and to occupy Hong Kong in 1841. With its advanced military equipment, Britain forced China to sign a series of unequal treaties, by which China ceded territory to Britain, opened ports to British trade and paid war indemnity. These treaties reduced China to a British semi-colony.

Moreover, a number of places in Latin America and Africa as well as many islands in the Pacific and Atlantic oceans were also under the control of Britain or claimed by the British government.

By the time of World War I, the British colonial area had reached 33,500,000 square kilometres, which was 130 times more than the British native land. The population of the British colonies was 8 times more than that of the British natives. So Britain at that time was known as an Empire without sunset, crossing five continents in the world.

⊙ Effect of foreign expansion

On the whole, the foreign expansion contributed to the economic prosperity of Britain. The British Empire was characterised by monopoly, organising numbers of companies to monopolise the raw materials of the British colonies. From the middle 19th century, Britain had become a centre of world trade and finance, and five banks in Britain controlled the whole banking industry. Also, Britain expanded its investment in the colonies and semi-colonies. The incomes from the investment exceeded those from trade and industry.

However, the economic prosperity worsened class distinctions to the extreme. With the increasing gap between the rich and the poor, the government started to conduct reform under the pressure of the public demand. In 1893, the Independent Labour Party was established, and then in 1900, the Labour Representation Committee was set up, which was later changed into the Labour Party. In 1909, a social politician proposed the people's budget to raise taxes on the wealthy and fund extensive social programmes for the poor. The 1905 general election empowered the Liberal Party, and minimum wages were fixed in some industries. Subsequently, the *Act of Old Age Pensions* was passed in 1909, and the *National Insurance Act* of 1911 provided insurance against sickness and unemployment. Women's position in society was also improved as maternity grants were established and poor children were provided with free schools as well as free school meals. Therefore, the British workers' life got noticeably better, which eased the relations between the capitalists and the workers.

### ❓ Questions for Discussion:

1. What are the features of the British expansion around the world? What effect did Britain have on its colonies?
2. Why did Britain establish the East Indian Company in 1600 and launch the Opium War against China in 1840? Do you think Britain is still in the process of expansion?

### Exercises

I. **Fill in the blanks.**
1. There are two prerequisites to the Industrial Revolution: One is the _____ deprived of the means of production, the other is large sums of _____.
2. The Industrial Revolution started from the _____ industry.
3. Plundering the colonial wealth and trafficking in slaves made England accumulate great amounts of _____ capital.
4. In 1784, the all-powerful steam engine was invented and finally applied in all kinds of industry, which led to the innovation of tools in _____ and started the age of _____.
5. *Origin of Species*, written by _____ in 1859, put forward the basic principle of _____ in which the fittest survive.

6. During British foreign expansion, Britain granted its colonies self-government, trying to transform the position from the world's _____ into the world's _____.
7. After launching the Opium War against China, Britain occupied Hong Kong in _____.
8. The American Independence War broke out in 1776 in the thirteen British colonies and gave a blow to the British policy of _____.
9. India was the most important colony of Britain, and various _____ companies were set up there.
10. In 1770, _____ was discovered and its east coast region was claimed for Britain by James Cook, an English captain.

## II. Define the following terms.
1. the Industrial Revolution
2. the Chartist Movement
3. the Victorian Age
4. the Opium War

## III. Multiple choice.
1. By the _____, England had been transformed from an agricultural nation into a manufacturing country.
   A. 1840s   B. 1750s   C. 1760s   D. 1820s
2. The Chartist Movement started in _____, marking the workers' awareness in politics.
   A. 1837   B. 1836   C. 1842   D. 1847
3. In 1876, secret voting was introduced to Britain. Compulsory education was adopted and universities began to enroll women as well as _____ church believers.
   A. Irish        B. Scottish
   C. Germanic     D. non-Anglican
4. In 1588, England defeated the _____ fleet to seize world hegemony.
   A. French       B. Spanish
   C. Irish        D. Italian
5. The *National Insurance Act* in 1911 provided insurance against _____.
   A. old age
   B. sickness and old age
   C. sickness and unemployment
   D. old age and unemployment
6. In 1840, the _____ Company started systematic colonization and turned New Zealand into a British colony.
   A. Canada       B. New Zealand
   C. India        D. Australia
7. After the American Independence War, the English government granted _____ the right of self-government in order to save trouble.
   A. Australia    B. Canada
   C. India        D. America
8. In 1877, Queen Victoria was proclaimed Empress of _____.
   A. India        B. Australia
   C. Canada       D. New Zealand
9. The British launched the Opium War against China in _____.
   A. 1841   B. 1842   C. 1840   D. 1839
10. In 1788, the British government began to transport _____ to Australia.
    A. puritans     B. protestants
    C. immigrants   D. convicts

## IV. Translate the following terms into English.
1. 西班牙舰队
2. 大英帝国
3. 特许公司
4. 东印度公司
5. 十小时工作日法

## V. Answer the following questions in a few sentences.
1. What factors contributed to the Industrial Revolution?
2. What's the effect of foreign expansion on Britain?

## Part Five  The Fall of the British Empire

*The two world wars reduced Britain from a superpower to an honoured Commonwealth, but Britain still occupies an important position in the world's politics and economy. Try to find out the information from the materials available about Britain's importance as well as its diminishing power in the world after World War II.*

### Britain and World War I

World War I between 1914 and 1918 was actually a combat between two imperialist groups for a new division of the world as a result of unbalanced development among the imperialist countries. In a sense, World War I weakened the British hegemony in the world.

At the beginning of the 20th century, France, Germany and America grew up into strong competitive opponents of Britain in the world. The

newly-united Germany especially became most aggressive. As early as in 1882, Germany, Austria-Hungary, and Italy concluded the **Triple Alliance**. During the following decades, the relations between the nations of the Triple Alliance and the other European powers grew strained. In 1907, Britain, France and Russia made a rival pact known as the **Triple Entente**. On 28 June, 1914, the Austrian Crown Prince Franz was assassinated by a Serbian nationalist at Sarajevo. In response, Austria began to suppress Slav nationalists with the support of Germany and declared war against Serbia. Consequently, Russia immediately mobilised military actions, and France refused Germany's requirement to remain neutral. As a result, Germany declared war against Russia and France in succession. For fear of Germany's control over Europe and the British Empire, Britain declared war against Germany in August 1914. Because of the tense relations with its allies, Italy did not join in the war on the side of Germany and Austria-Hungary, but declared war against its former allies in 1915. Therefore, the Triple Alliance turned into **Central Powers** after the departure of Italy. On the contrary, the Triple Entente consequently developed into **Allied Powers** with 28 countries as its supporters. World War I involved 32 countries and mobilised 65 million men, among which more than 10 million were killed and 20 million wounded. Four years later, both sides were exhausted and eager to end the conflict. In 1918, the war came to an end with the surrender of Austria-Hungary and Germany in succession. Twenty-seven countries, including Britain, France, America and Italy held the **Paris Peace Conference** in the name of establishing post-war peace in January 1919, but in essence, the conference served as a chance to carve up the world in a fresh order and a scheme against Russia. The *Treaty of Versailles* was concluded on 28 June, 1919. According to the treaty, the victorious nations such as Britain, America and Japan redivided up the German colonies, demanding huge indemnities from Germany and limiting its future armament. As it was based on the conflicts among capitalist countries, the exploitation of national interests and the sacrifice of the defeated countries, the *Treaty of Versailles* became a prelude to the future World War II.

World War I gave a great blow to Britain. The number of British people killed in the war was over 750 thousand; Britain was deprived of one-third of its national wealth, with seventy percent of its commercial ships sinking during the war. Moreover, the increasing postwar unemployment caused many strikes in Britain. Funding the war transformed Britain from a creditor nation to a debtor nation, and London was replaced by New York as the world's financial centre. Furthermore, America took the place of Germany as a major world competitor against Britain and kept pace with Britain in aircraft passenger carrier, while Japan tried to enter the sphere of British influence. Meanwhile, the national industry in the British dominions and colonies developed rapidly. All of these factors reduced Britain's foreign market to the extent that an international trade deficit occurred in Britain. Subsequently, Britain lost its hegemony in the world due to the loss of its sea supremacy.

## Britain and World War II

After Germany was defeated in World War I, Britain was threatened by the increasing power of France. In order to keep the balance of power in diplomacy, Britain followed a non-intervention policy, dreaming of inhibiting the development of France and confronting Russia by means of propping up Germany. First of all, **Dawes Plan** was proposed and carried out by Britain and America in 1924, providing Germany with loans and investments, which sped up the restoration of the German economy and laid the foundation for Germany to rebuild its military equipment. Secondly, the *Pact of Locarno* was concluded in 1925 under the control of Britain. It guaranteed non-intervention on the border between Germany and France as well as that between Germany and Belgium, but excluded the border between Germany and Czech and that between Germany and Poland. This was actually to facilitate Germany's expansion to the East and tie up Russia. Thirdly, when the extreme Nazi leader, **Adolf Hitler**, was in charge of German power, Germany broke the *Treaty of Versailles* and placed large orders for arms and ammunition from Britain. Hitler informed Britain, France, and Italy that Germany possessed air forces and issued the

conscription law in 1935 and commanded his army to march into the Rhineland in 1936. Finally, Germany turned into a fascist nation and became the initiator of World War II. Soon Italy and Japan followed up with Germany as fascist nations.

However, Britain and America still adopted the appeasement policy to benefit from propping up those fascist nations. In 1931, Japan started to invade China, advocating the establishment of Manchuria government with an attempt to control northeastern China. In 1935, the Italian fascists launched the war against Abyssinia and occupied it without any response from Britain. Germany invaded and occupied Austria in 1938, and deprived Czech of the whole territory in 1939. Eventually, Britain and France respectively declared war against Germany in September 1939 when Germany invaded Poland. Thus World War II burst out.

Germany carried out a blitz on Denmark, Norway and Holland one by one, and then marched through northeastern France in 1940. The British government under the leadership of **Winston Churchill** continued to fight against Germany after France was defeated. The British and the allied forces landed at Normandy in North France in June 1944 and liberated Paris in August, 1944. Berlin was surrounded by the Russian army in 1945 when Hitler was forced to commit suicide. The surrender of Germany ended World War II in Europe.

In 1941, America and Britain were forced to declare war against Japan, as Japan made a sneak attack on the Pearl Harbor. Due to the involvement of America and Russia in the war as well as the Asian people's persistent resistance against the aggression, Japan declared unconditional surrender to the Allies on 14 August, 1945, which marked the end of anti-facist World War II.

Britain suffered great loss because of World War II. Over 300,000 people were killed and 25,000 million pounds were expended for the war. The damage to shipping and merchandise due to German attack amounted to 4,000 million pounds. What's more, Britain's economy fell into a subordinate position to America, because the industrial output in America surpassed that in Britain, and American investment gradually penetrated into the British dominions such as Canada, Australia, and New Zealand as well as the Far East, Southeast Asia and Latin America. Therefore, World War II resulted in the disintegration of the colonial system of the British Empire and the establishment of the **British Commonwealth of Nations**. Up to now, the Commonwealth, with the British Monarch as its symbol and head of state, is composed of fifty-four independent member states. All but two of these countries were formerly part of the British Empire. It is not a political union, but an intergovernmental organisation whose member states with diverse social, political and economic backgrounds are regarded as equal in status. The major function of the Commonwealth lies in its contribution to the cooperation among member states that can resign from the Commonwealth in the light of their own will.

### ? Questions for discussion:
1. What consequences did World War I bring to Britain?
2. Why was Britain involved in World War II?

## Major Events After World War II

### ⊙ Invasion of Egypt

Britain and France invaded Egypt after the nationalisation of the Suez Canal in 1956, which was known as **the second Middle-East War**. The Suez Canal is a vital waterway connecting the Mediterranean Sea with the Red Sea. The Suez Crisis was sparked when Britain and France were allied with Israel to invade Egypt for its decision to nationalise the Suez Canal. Under American pressure, the canal was handed back to Egypt and the invasion force was withdrawn. The crisis revealed Britain's declining world status and its subordination to the U.S.

### ⊙ The London Declaration

The London Declaration was an official statement made by the 1949 Commonwealth Prime Ministers' Conference on whether India continued its membership of the Commonwealth of Nations after its transition to a republican constitution. It was published on 28 April, 1949, symbolizing the birth of the modern Commonwealth. Drafted by the Indian statesman V. K. Krishna Menon, the declaration had two main provisions: For one thing, it allowed the Commonwealth to admit and retain members that were not Dominions, which thus included both republics and indigenous monarchies; for another, it changed the name of the organisation from the British Commonwealth to the Commonwealth of Nations, which reflected the first change. The Declaration recognised King George VI as Head of the Commonwealth. After his death, the Commonwealth leaders confirmed Queen Elizabeth II in that capacity.

### ⊙ Britain joined in the European Community

The United Kingdom European Communities membership referendum took place under the provisions of the *Referendum Act 1975* on 5 June, 1975 in the United Kingdom to gauge support for the country's continued membership of the European Communities (EC) often known at the time as the European Community and the Common Market. Britain had entered two and a half years earlier on 1 January, 1973 under the Conservative government of **Edward Heath**. The Labour Party's manifesto for the October 1974 general election had promised that the people would decide through the ballot box whether to remain in the EC.

⊙ Elizabeth's accession to the throne

During 1951, George VI's health declined, and Elizabeth frequently stood in for him at public events. On 6 February, 1952, Elizabeth and Philip had just returned to their Kenyan home, Sagana Lodge, after a tour of Australia and New Zealand when the King died, and consequently Elizabeth immediately accessed to the throne as Queen Elizabeth II. She and the Duke of Edinburgh moved into Buckingham Palace.

### Conservative in Power

⊙ Mrs. Margaret Thatcher

**Mrs. Margaret Thatcher** was the first woman to serve as the British Prime Minister, holding the office from 1979 to 1990. As a well-known Conservative Party leader since 1975, Mrs. Margaret Thatcher became the British Prime Minister with a majority of 43 seats in 1979. The Conservatives won 43.9% of the votes and 339 seats,  Labour 36.9% and 269 seats, and Liberals 13.8% and 11 seats. She came to power on the promise that the Conservatives would cut income taxes, reduce public expenditures, make it easier for people to buy their own houses, and restrain the power of the unions.

Thatcher gained the nickname of the "Iron Lady", due to her tough-talking rhetoric as well as her resolution and determination in leadership. In order to reverse Britain's economic decline, Thatcher put an emphasis on the reduced state intervention, free markets and entrepreneurialism in her political philosophy and economic policies. She gained much support after the 1982 Falklands War and was reelected as Prime Minister in the following year. After the 1983 election, the government sold off most of the large utilities, starting with British Telecom, which had been a publicly owned monopoly since 1912. Many people took advantage of the share offers. But as many sold their shares immediately for a quick profit, the proportion of shares held by individuals rather than institutions did not increase. Therefore, the policy of privatisation has become synonymous with **Thatcherism**. However, Thatcher took a hard line against trade unions, survived an assassination attempt in Briton hotel bombing, and defiantly opposed the Soviet Union.

She was reelected for an unprecedented third term in 1987. But the following years proved difficult, as her Community Charge plan was unpopular with many people and her views regarding the European Community (European Union) were not shared by others in her Cabinet. Facing large-scale opposition within her own parliamentary party, she resigned as Prime Minister in November 1990. Margaret Thatcher was widely seen as remote and autocratic, for the crisis of confidence in her leadership had been sparked by her attitude to Europe, and her support for the so-called "poll tax" had undermined her standing with the electorate.

⊙ John Major

The Conservative plans for a "poll tax" was introduced in England and Wales on 1 April, 1990, which provoked vocal opposition across Britain in the form of anti-poll tax rallies and acts of civil disobedience. A largely peaceful march in London, attended by 70,000 people, degenerated into serious  rioting on Trafalgar Square. The unpopularity of the tax contributed to the downfall of Margaret Thatcher. And then John Major succeeded her as the party leader and was elected the Prime Minister on 28 November, 1990, replacing the poll tax with the council tax. As the inner-party divergent opinion caused the crisis of confidence in the Conservative government, Major was compelled to resign in May, 1997.

⊙ David Cameron

The 2010 general election in the UK on 6 May, 2010 was to elect members to the House of Commons, involving 650 constituencies across the United Kingdom. The Conservative Party led by David Cameron won 306 seats but was still 20 seats short of a majority. As none of the parties achieved the 326 seats needed for an overall majority, Britain had a hung Parliament for the first time since World War II. As a consequence, no party was able to command a majority in the House of Commons, and the attempt to put together a Labour-Liberal Democrat coalition failed. Gordon Brown announced his resignation on 11 May, 2010, marking the end of 13 years of the Labour government. Queen Elizabeth II accepted Brown's resignation and invited David Cameron to form a coalition government of Conservatives and Liberal Democrats. Consequently, a coalition government of the Conservatives and the Liberal Democrats was formed.

**David Cameron** was the 53rd Prime Minister of the UK as the leader of the Conservative Party. He studied philosophy, politics and economics at Oxford, gaining a first class honours degree, and then joined the Conservative Research Department. He was elected as the Member of Parliament for the Oxfordshire constituency of Witney in 2001 and promoted to the Opposition front bench two years later. He rose rapidly to become the head of policy co-ordination during the 2005 general election campaign and won the 2005 Conservative leadership election with a public image of a young, moderate candidate appealing to young voters. In the 2010 general election, the Conservatives gained a plurality of seats in a hung Parliament and Cameron was appointed Prime Minister on 11 May, 2010 as the head of a coalition joining the Conservatives and the Liberal Democrats. At the age of 43, Cameron became the youngest British Prime Minister since the Earl of Liverpool 198 years earlier. And the Cameron Ministry was the first coalition government in the UK since World War II.

⊙ Brexit Referendum

When Cameron took over as prime minister, the British Conservative party had been severely divided into Europhiles and Eurosceptics because of the coalition government's controversial policies, such as raising university tuition fees, and the fact that Eurosceptics had been opposed to Cameron's leadership and coalition with the Liberal Democrats. But these oppositions did not hurt Cameron's leadership, and the coalition government under his leadership took a more moderate line than previous Conservative governments.

On 24 October, 2011, some Conservative backbenchers ignored Cameron's opposition and called a referendum as more than 100,000 Britons had signed up to demand a British exit from the EU. With Liberal Democrat and Labour MPs voting, the referendum was voted down by 111 in favour to 483 against, but the fact of the Tories getting 81 votes in favour of Brexit represented a clear defection from the party and from Prime Minister Cameron's position on Europe, which was a serious blow to Cameron's authority to govern. Downing Street said after the vote that it respected the views of the MPs who had supported Brexit, but the government must lead the country and remaining in the EU was in Britain's best interest.

⊙ Scottish Independence Referendum

Cameron's government oversaw the referendum on Scottish independence. In 2014, the British government led by Cameron reached an agreement with the Scottish National Party, which advocates Scottish independence, to hold the 2014 Scottish independence referendum on 18 September. It was a referendum held by the Scottish Government to allow Scottish voters to decide on whether Scotland should be independent from the United Kingdom. All Scots over the age of 16 can vote, and the number of participants amounted to more than four million. The referendum turned out that the "Remain" camp won 55% of the votes, and thus Scotland remained part of the United Kingdom.

⊙ Cameron's resignation

When the Conservatives secured an unexpected majority in the 2015 general election, Cameron remained Prime Minister, this time leading a Conservative-only government. As promised in the election manifesto, Cameron set a date for a referendum on Britain's exit from the European Union, and unexpectedly became one of the leaders who actually led the "Remain" campaign for Britain's membership in the EU, while the "Leave" campaign was effectively led by his political rival, Greater London Mayor Boris Johnson. Hence a criticism pointed that the "Brexit" referendum was in effect an internal political struggle within the Conservative Party. The referendum was held on 23 June, 2016, and the vote was 51.9% in favour of leaving the EU. Cameron announced that he would resign the office of Prime Minister by the start of the Conservative Party Conference in October, 2016, taking responsibility for the failure of the referendum to keep Britain in the EU, and making way for the new Prime Minister, Theresa May.

⊙ Theresa May

**Theresa May** was the second female Prime Minister in Britain after Margaret Thatcher. She grew up in Oxfordshire and attended St Hugh's College, Oxford. After graduating in 1977, she worked at the Bank of England and the Association for Payment Clearing Services. She succeeded in being elected to the House of Commons in 1997 and joined the front bench the following year as the opposition speaker on education and employment. She was invited to join the Shadow Cabinet in 1998, holding several roles in it from then on. Following the formation of the coalition government after the 2010 general election, she was appointed Home Secretary and Minister for Women and Equalities, but gave up the latter role in 2012. Reappointed after the Conservative success in the 2015 general election, she became the longest-serving Home Secretary in over 60 years. During her tenure she pursued reform of the Police Federation, implemented a harder line on drugs policy including the banning of khat and brought in additional restrictions on immigration.

⊙ General election & coalition

In June, 2016, Cameron decided to resign as both Prime Minister and party leader because of the Brexit referendum. Theresa May, who was also part of the Remain campaign, did not take a high profile position during the referendum, which allowed her to contest for the party leadership on behalf of her party's Remain wing. In July, 2016, Theresa May was elected Conservative Party leader and became the UK's second female Prime Minister after Margaret Thatcher.

The ruling Tories remained the largest party in the general election on 8 June, 2017, but failed to secure a majority in the House of Commons, resulting in a hung parliament. The loss of an overall majority prompted May to enter a confidence and supply agreement with the Democratic Unionist Party (DUP). This means that the DUP would give the Tories a vote of confidence at the start of the new session of the House of Commons and offer them financial support to pass the budget.

⊙ Brexit Referendum

In June, 2016, Britain passed a referendum on leaving the European Union. On 2 October, 2016, Prime Minister Theresa May announced that the process of leaving the EU would start by the end of March, 2017. It was expected that the negotiations on Brexit would take two years, and Britain would formally leave the EU in 2019. British Foreign Secretary Boris Johnson said the UK would continually focus on European affairs after leaving the EU and become more active and dynamic on the international stage. On 26 June, 2018, the *European Union (Withdrawal) Act 2018* came into force upon the signature of the British Monarch, Queen Elizabeth II. Under the bill, the UK would withdraw from the EU at 23:00 on 29 March, 2019.

⊙ Theresa May's resignation

Theresa May announced on 24 May, 2019, that she would step down as party leader on 7 June after failing to resolve the Brexit impasse and under pressure from within her party. Theresa May went to Buckingham Palace on 24 July to formally submit her resignation to the Queen following the announcement of a new Conservative leader. She was succeeded as Prime Minister by Boris Johnson, the new Conservative leader and former Foreign Secretary and Mayor of London. Teresa May would remain a backbencher in the House of Commons in her constituency of Maidenhead.

⊙ Boris Johnson and Successors

**Boris Johnson** was elected leader of the ruling Tories on 23 July, 2019, and took over from Theresa May as Britain's new Prime Minister the following day. In his first

speech as Prime Minister, Johnson promised that the UK would leave the EU on 31 October, 2019 with or without a deal. The British government spent £2.1 billion in making preparations for Brexit on 31 October, which included mass advertising.

On 13 December, 2019, the results from the general election indicated that the British Conservative Party won more than half of the total seats in Parliament and Boris Johnson would remain Prime Minister.

Numerous scandals hitting his standing in the polls, including accusations of using donor money inappropriately to pay for a refurbishment of his Downing Street home and ordering MPs to vote in such a way that would protect a colleague who had breached lobbying rules, Johnson agreed to step down on 7 July, 2022, but hoped to stay on until the autumn, when the Conservative Party chose a replacement. His reputation was also damaged by the resignation of his second ethics adviser in less than two years. Johnson's departure marked a remarkable downfall for a prime minister who was seen as having political superpowers, with an appeal that transcended traditional party lines.

**Liz Truss** on 6 September, 2022 as the new Prime Minister replaced Boris Johnson but only 45 days to 20 October, 2022, followed Margaret Thatcher and Theresa May to become Britain's third female premier. She was previously Secretary of State for Foreign, Commonwealth and Development Affairs from 15 September, 2021, appointed Minister for Women and Equalities on 10 September, 2019 and elected as the Conservative MP for south west Norfolk in 2010.

**Rishi Sunak** became Prime Minister on 25 October, 2022 — leader of the Conservative Party who was previously appointed Chancellor of the Exchequer from 13 February, 2020 to 5 July, 2022 and Chief Secretary to the Treasury from 24 July, 2019 to 13 February, 2020.

### Labour in Power

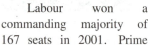
⊙ Tony Blair

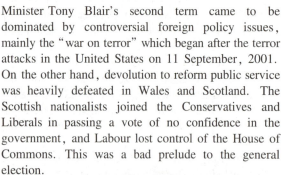

**Tony Blair** was elected the 51st Prime Minister in 1997, which ended the 18-year period of the Conservative in power. Tony Blair became the youngest Prime Minister in Britain in the 20th century. He was the first Labour Prime Minister serving for three terms.

Labour won a commanding majority of 167 seats in 2001. Prime Minister Tony Blair's second term came to be dominated by controversial foreign policy issues, mainly the "war on terror" which began after the terror attacks in the United States on 11 September, 2001. On the other hand, devolution to reform public service was heavily defeated in Wales and Scotland. The Scottish nationalists joined the Conservatives and Liberals in passing a vote of no confidence in the government, and Labour lost control of the House of Commons. This was a bad prelude to the general election.

On the whole, Blair did better in the following aspects. In politics, Prime Minister Blair promoted the programme of devolution, put emphasis on the reform of public service, and contributed to the peace agreement in Northern Ireland. In economy, the Blair government adopted a series of measures to keep the national economy growing steadily and to sustain a lower rate of unemployment and inflation. Widespread British unease about the European single currency obliged Prime Minister Tony Blair, who was keen on the project, to stay out. The "euro" was launched as an electronic currency used by banks, foreign exchange dealers, big firms and stock markets in 1999. Euro coins first hit the streets of the 12 "**Euro zone**" countries on 1 January, 2002. In international affairs, the Blair government advocated participating in the integration of Europe, consolidating the relations with America, and improving the relations between the European Union and Russia. However, following America's decision and dispatching troops against Iraq resulted in the loss of Labour reputation and capacity in office.

In 2005, Labour won with a substantially reduced majority. Blair served as Prime Minister for the third term. Nonetheless, he quickly announced his intention not to stand for a fourth term. In 2007, his successor, Chancellor of the Exchequer Gordon Brown assumed office as Labour Prime Minister after Blair's resignation.

⊙ Gordon Brown

On 27 June, 2007, **Gordon Brown**, the Labour leader, took over the office as the 52nd Prime Minister. He was a little similar to Mrs. Margaret Thatcher in the leadership. Brown is the best political partner of the ex-Prime Minister Tony Blair, but different from him in personality. In order to keep an image of being eloquent, witty and humorous, Brown invited joke writers to write some funny stories for him to tell so as to improve his personal charm. In diplomacy, Brown declared to keep the policy against Iraq and Afghanistan; while in domestic policies, he advocated various reforms to keep economy increasing smoothly.

> ❓ **Question for discussion:**
> 
> Britain has long been in the control of the two major political parties, each having held majority and minority positions. Compare the style of the Labour Party with that of the Conservative Party in power.

### Relations with China

British-Chinese relations refer to the interstate relations between China and the United Kingdom. Both countries were allies during World War II, and are members of the UN. In 1950, Britain recognised the People's Republic of China as the government of China. In 1972, the ambassadors of Britain and China signed the Joint Declaration, which normalised the diplomatic relationship between the two countries. Ten years later, Margaret Thatcher came to visit China for the first time as a British in-service Prime Minister. In 1984, the Sino-British Joint Declaration was signed on the status of Hong Kong, and then Queen Elizabeth II, as the British head of state, had a visit to China for the first time in October 1986.

The cooperation between China and Britain is fruitful in many aspects. The amount of the bilateral trade has increased by three to four times. Up to now, Britain is the second largest trade partner of China in European Union, and its investments in China rank first among European countries. In addition, frequent communication between the Chinese people and the British people has laid a solid foundation for future relations. More and more Chinese students are studying in Britain, and the number of Chinese-English learners has exceeded that of the native English speakers. Britain and China cooperate with each other as members of the UN to deal with various problems ranging from organised crimes to ecological variety, from illegal immigration to life-long education, and from issues in the information industry to the reformation of legal and financial system. Therefore, the British-Chinese relations are going smoother and better, especially in the satisfactory settlement on the status of Hong Kong and the fight against terrorism.

⊙ Return of Hong Kong to China in 1997

The transfer of sovereignty of Hong Kong from the United Kingdom to the People's Republic of China (PRC), often referred to as "The Handover", occurred on 1 July, 1997. The event marked the end of British rule and the return of sovereignty of Hong Kong to China.

The handover ceremony was held at the new wing of the Hong Kong Convention and Exhibition Centre in Wan Chai on the night of 30 June, 1997. The principal British guest was the Prince of Wales who read a farewell speech on behalf of the Queen. The newly elected Prime Minister of the United Kingdom, Tony Blair, and the departing Hong Kong Governor Chris Patten also attended.

Representing China were the President of the People's Republic of China, Jiang Zemin, and Tung Chee-hwa, the first Chief Executive of the Hong Kong Special Administrative Region of the People's Republic of China. This event was broadcast on several television and radio stations across the world.

After more than 150 years of British rule, Hong Kong was eventually returned to Chinese control in 1997. Under the "One Country, Two Systems" policy, Hong Kong retained its own legal system, currency, customs policy and immigration laws for a minimum of 50 years after the handover. This would be considered a miracle in the world diplomatic history.

⊙ China-UK relations after 1997

Britain and China succeeded in transferring sovereignty of Hong Kong in 1997, which set an example for peaceful resolution of the historical problems between countries.

In 1998, Premier Zhu Rongji and Prime Minister

Tony Blair of the United Kingdom exchanged successful visits, and issued the China-UK Joint Statement which announced the establishment of comprehensive partnership between the two countries. In October, 1999, at the invitation of Queen Elizabeth II, President Jiang Zemin paid the first state visit by a Chinese head of state to the UK, which turned out to be a great success. The visit laid a significant foundation for the development of Sino-British relations in the new century.

In return for the British Queen's visit, President Jiang Zemin visited Britain in 1999. This was also the first visit of a Chinese president to Britain, which promoted the development of relations between China and Britain. In January 2008, Prime Minister Gordon Brown travelled to China for a formal visit in response to the invitation of Chinese Premier Wen Jiabao, and the bilateral relations between Britain and China was further deepened and developed. In 2013, at the invitation of Premier Li Keqiang, Prime Minister David Cameron paid an official visit to China from 2 to 4 December. In 2015, Xi Jinping visited the United Kingdom from 19 to 23 October after Chinese Premier Li Keqiang's visit between 16 and 19 June, 2014, which made Xi Jinping the first Chinese President to visit the United Kingdom since 2005 and the second Chinese state leader to visit the UK. In 2018, Prime Minister Theresa May arrived in China with the largest business delegation ever. Her government was taking on an overseas trip as she sought to put her Brexit troubles aside and make progress on boosting British trade. Britain and China have different social systems, values as well as national situations, but share widespread common interests.

⊙ Economic and trade relations

Britain has been the second largest trade partner of China among the EU countries. Statistics from the Chinese side show that in the year of 2019, the Sino-British trade volume reached US $95.68 billion, 4.2% higher than that of the same period of the previous year, of which China's export and import volume stood at US $30.18 billion and US $65.5 billion, a growth rate of 6.5% and 3.2% respectively over the same period in 2018. By December, 2019, the bilateral trade volume had approximated US $95.68 billion, 4.2% higher than that of the same period of the previous year.

Actual British investment in China has been the largest among the EU countries. By October 2001, the UK had invested in 3013 projects in China, with a real input of about US $9.62 billion. The UK has provided China four government loans since 1986, totaling 855 million pound (approximately US $1.37 billion). The Sino-British Economic and Trade Joint Committee was established in 1996, and three sessions have been held. China-UK Investment Partnership was established in 2001. In June, 2019, the Tenth Session of China-UK Financial Dialogue was held in Beijing.

⊙ Cultural exchanges

The two countries have experienced active cultural exchanges and frequent visits by art troupes in recent years. Performance teams from China Symphony Orchestra and Central Nationalities Orchestra in 1998 and the gala night "Bravo China" jointly sponsored by China Central TV Station and Shanghai TV Station in August 2000 were well-received in the UK. During the state visit to Britain by President Jiang Zemin in October 1999, the exhibition Buried Treasures as well as Masterpieces from Shaanxi Province was held in the British Museum. On the other hand, artists from the British Royal National Theatre and the Royal Academy of Music visited China respectively in 1998, and Britain's Royal Ballet visited China in May 1999. In 2000, the exhibition of the British sculptor Henry Moore's work was held in Beijing for the first time.

⊙ Educational exchanges

Britain is one of the earliest among European countries to join China in creating academic relationships. The Gansu Basic Education Program was initiated in 1998; the Sino-British Conference of University Vice-Chancellors and Principals has been held yearly in Beijing or London since 1997; CERNET (China Educational Research Network) and JANET (Britain's Joint Academic Network) were linked in 1998. In addition, about 110 to 150 British volunteers come to teach in less developed areas of China every year. Statistics indicated that over 170,000 Chinese students have studied in Britain since 2017. The other way around, over 35,000 self-sponsored British students have studied in China since 1980. Programmes under implementation include Sino-British Scholarship Exchanges and British Chevening Scholarship Scheme for China administered by the Foreign and Commonwealth Office and the Sino-British Friendship Scholarship Fund Scheme. In July 1999, the Chinese delegation led by the Minister of Education Chen Zhili paid a visit to the UK, during which the two countries signed the Joint Statement on Educational Cooperation. During the visit by British Secretary of State for Education and Employment David Blunkett in June 2000, the two countries signed the China-UK Framework Agreement on Educational Cooperation.

⊙ Scientific and technological cooperation

In addition to the Agreement on Scientific and Technological Cooperation between the two governments signed in November 1978, over 20 agreements or memorandums have been signed by relevant departments or institutions of the two countries ever since, covering such fields as basic research, environmental protection, health, agriculture, meteorology, space and aviation. The Amendment to the Protocol on Scientific and Technological Cooperation between the two governments was signed in September 1998. When Prime Minister Tony Blair visited China in October 1998, an announcement was made that the two governments would invest 600,000 pounds to establish the China-UK Scientific and Technological Research Fund. In November, 1999, the Chinese delegation of Science and Technology paid a visit to Britain, during which the China-UK Joint Committee on Scientific and Technological Cooperation reconvened and the minutes of the meeting were recorded, reflecting the aim to promote exchange and cooperation in the fields of science and technology between the two countries.

⊙ Military exchanges

China and Britain exchanged military attaches at the end of 1972. The British Chief of the Defense Staff Nell Cameron paid an official goodwill visit to China in April 1978 at the invitation of the Chinese Ministry of Defense. The Chinese Minister of Defense Zhang Aiping visited Britain in September, 1986 and signed officially with the British Secretary of State for Defense the Memorandum of Understanding on Co-operation and Defense Equipment between the People's Republic of China and the United Kingdom of Great Britain and Northern Ireland. Since then, the Assistant Chief of the Defense Staff, the Chief of Defense Intelligence, and the Chief of the Defense Staff Field Marshal Peter Inge visited China successively in 1996. Other main visits to China on Britain's part include those by Vice Admiral McNally, Commandant of the Royal College of Defense Studies in September 1998, Admiral Michael Boyce, the First Sea Lord in March 1999, General Charles Guthie, Chief of the Defense Staff in October 1999, British Defense Secretary Hoon in June 2000, Admiral Nigel Essenhigh, Chief of Navy Staff and First Sea Lord, Marshal Sir Peter Squire, Chief of the Air Staff and Commodore Mark Kerr of the Royal Naval College in 2001. British Ships Missile Escorter Cornwall and Destroyer New Castle visited Shanghai and Qingdao in 2000.

On the other hand, major visits on the Chinese part include those by Chief of the General Staff of the People's Liberation Army Fu Quanyou in March 1997, Air Force Commander Liu Shunyao in March 1999, Vice Chairman of the Central Military Committee, State Councilor and Defense Minister Chi Haotian in January 2000, Navy Commander Shi Yunsheng in April 2000, Director of Armament Department of People's Liberation Army Cao Gangchuan in June 2000 and Director of General Logistics of the People's Liberation Army Wang Ke in 2001. The Chinese Navy fleet paid its first visit to the UK in September 2001.

With the rapid growth of the economy, China becomes stronger and more influential. David Cameron, Theresa May and Boris Johnson paid special attention to the relation with China. The China-British relationship is greatly improved in many issues of the world.

### ? Questions for discussion:
1. Prime Minister Thatcher was well-known as an "Iron Lady" both in domestic and international affairs. Could you give some examples to support this label?
2. What's the current relationship between Hong Kong and Britain? What's the effect of the return of Hong Kong to China on Britain?

## Exercises
### Ⅰ. Fill in the blanks.
1. World War I from _____ to _____ was actually a combat between two _____ groups for a fresh division of the world.
2. Thatcher was the _____ woman to serve as the British Prime Minister, nolding the office from _____ to _____.
3. In 1915, the Triple Alliance turned into the _____ after the departure of Italy.
4. Tony Blair was the first _____ Prime Minister serving for _____.
5. The "euro" was launched as an electronic currency used by banks, foreign exchange dealers, big firms and stock markets in _____. Euro coins first hit the streets of the 12 "Euro zone" countries on 1 January, _____.
6. British forces contributed to the initial US military strikes against the Islamic fundamentalist _____ regime in _____.
7. The separation of the Sinn Fein Party resulted in various violence cases, which made IRA an image of _____.
8. On 31 July, 2007, the British Royal Irish Constabulary was dismissed as a response to the declaration of the _____ to give up military equipment, which indicated the _____ of the 38-year military conflicts in Northern Ireland.
9. Prime Minister _____ narrowly escaped the blast by Irish Republican Army terrorists of the Grand Hotel Brighton during the Conservative Party conference.
10. Mrs. Margaret Thatcher visited China and signed the _____ with Deng Xiaoping on 19 December, 1984.

### Ⅱ. Define the following terms.
1. the second Middle-East War
2. Thatcherism
3. the Irish Republican Army
4. the Falklands War
5. the Sino-British Joint Declaration

### Ⅲ. Multiple choice.
1. At the beginning of the 20th century, France, _____ and America grew up into strong competitive matches for Britain in the world.
   A. Italy           B. Germany
   C. Russia          D. Japan
2. Following America and _____ resulted in the loss of Labour reputation and capacity in office, which made Blair resign in 2007.
   A. dispatching troops against Iraq
   B. the terror attacks in the United States on 11 September, 2001
   C. the Scottish Nationalists joining the Conservatives and Liberals
   D. the failure of devolution
3. In 1907, Britain, France, and _____ made a rival pact known as the Triple Entente.
   A. Russia          B. Japan
   C. Italy           D. America
4. Germany became a fascist nation, followed up by _____.
   A. Italy           B. Hungary
   C. Austria         D. Italy and Japan
5. Britain and France respectively declared a war against Germany in September _____ when Germany invaded Poland. Thus World War II burst out.
   A. 1938            B. 1937
   C. 1939            D. 1935
6. In 1945, Berlin was surrounded by the _____ army. The surrender of Germany ended the war in Europe.

A. Russian   B. French
C. British   D. American

7. The surrender of _____ marked the end of anti-facist World War II.
   A. Italy   B. Germany
   C. Japan   D. Austria

8. Despite significant opposition at home, the British government gave military support to the controversial United States-led invasion of _____ in 2003.
   A. Iran   B. Iraq   C. Egypt   D. Sudan

9. In _____, Britain recognised the People's Republic of China as the government of China.
   A. 1950   B. 1972   C. 1984   D. 1986

10. Three men blew themselves up on London underground trains, while a fourth exploded his bomb on a double-decker on 7 July, _____. Fifty-two people were killed and more than 700 injured.
    A. 2002   B. 2003   C. 2004   D. 2005

## IV. Translate the following terms into English.

1. 三国同盟
2. 三国协约
3. 巴黎和会
4. 法西斯国家

## V. Answer the following questions in a few sentences.

1. What's the effect of World War I on Britain?

2. How is the cooperation between China and Britain in the recent 30 years?

**Mini-task:**

Over time, Britain has attached more importance to its relationship with China and China's influence on world politics, economy and culture. For example, many secondary schools in Britain begin to offer Chinese classes, and a number of universities set up Confucius Institutes for native students to popularize Chinese culture. Please search for the information about the Confucius Institutes in Britain as well as in other countries.

# VOLUME TWO

# THE UNITED STATES
# OF
# AMERICA

# Chapter One  Geography and Population

*The United States of America is gradually becoming the representative of Western countries after World War II. Before going into this chapter, select some information about the following items through any resource available.*
1. *What are the differences between America and Britain in climate?*
2. *Since America is considered as a "melting pot", try to list its ethnic groups as many as possible.*

## Part One  Names and Position

The official name of America is the United States of America, often shortened to the United States, or just to America, the USA., the U. S. and the US.

The United States is a constitutional federal republic comprised of a federal district (Washington, D. C.) and fifty states, two of which — Alaska and Hawaii — are separated from the continental United States. Alaska, the largest state of the United States, is to the northwest of the continent. It touches the **Pacific Ocean** on the south and the **Arctic Ocean** on the north, with Canada to its east and Russia to the west across the **Bering Strait**, while Hawaii, the youngest and the smallest state of the United States, lies in the Central Pacific Ocean 3,200 kilometers from mainland America.

Mainland America is situated in the southern part of North America, mainly within the northern temperate zone. The north of the country shares more than 6,000 kilometers of land boundary with Canada, which runs along the 49th parallel in the west and then goes across the four of the five Great Lakes, ending at the Atlantic Coast. The boundary between America and Canada is open and undefended.

America's southern land neighbor is Mexico, with which it shares a common boundary of some 3,000 kilometers, starting from the mouth of the Rio Grande River, continuing through the lower reaches of the river and ending at the Pacific Seashore. The American government has established some checkpoints along its border with Mexico with the purpose of preventing drug traffickers and illegal immigrants from stealing into America.

On the west of mainland America is the Pacific Ocean, across which the United States trades its products for goods from the Far East. On the east of the country lies the Atlantic Ocean which witnessed large numbers of European immigrants sailing to their land of opportunities. The Atlantic is still the most important sea route from America to Europe and the Middle East.

The total area of America is about 9.371 million square kilometers, which makes it the fourth largest country in the world. Its mainland covers a distance of some 4,500 kilometers from east to west and about 2,700 kilometers from south to north. The United States of America has a long coastline of 22,680 kilometers, which makes it one of the countries with the longest coastlines in the world.

## Part Two  Geographical Features

The landform of the United States is divided into three major regions according to its geographical features: the eastern part, the central part and the western part.

### The Eastern Part

The eastern part is made up of the highlands formed by the **Appalachians** and the **Atlantic coast**. The Appalachian Mountains divide the eastern seaboard from the Great Lakes and the grasslands of the Midwest. The Appalachian Mountains holds one sixth of the national territory on the continent. These mountains are relatively low with an average altitude of only 800 meters above sea level. The highest peak in the Appalachians is **Mount Mitchell** (2,037 meters) in North Carolina. The mountains run about 2,000 kilometers from northeast to southwest and are gradually replaced by the coastal plain and finally stretch to the Atlantic, forming a number of fine deep-water harbors. Partly because of this geographic condition, America's foreign trade first developed in the northeast.

To the east of the Appalachians lies the Atlantic coast, also known as the **Eastern Coastal Plain** which begins from the south of New York City, includes the entire peninsula of Florida in the south and merges with the wide **Gulf Plain**. It is where the first European immigrants arrived and established the 13 original states. Broad in the south, the coastal plain narrows towards the north. Though not large in size, this area is rich in water resources and is the origin of many rivers running into the Atlantic Ocean, such as the **Connecticut River**, the **Hudson River**, the **James River**, and so on. Today, it is famous not only for its advanced industry but also as America's political and cultural center.

## The Central Part

The central part, also called the **Central Plains**, is made up of the large area between the Appalachians on the east and the **Rocky Mountains** on the west. It covers a distance of about 2,000 kilometers from east to west, taking up nearly half of America's landmass on the continent. It stretches from Canada on the north to the Gulf of Mexico on the south. This region is known as the "**Barn of America**" for its large size and rich soil.

The western part of the Central Plains is the "**Great Plains**". The whole territory, slightly rising from east to west, is covered with rich prairie grass, but no trees. The flat, fertile prairie land of the Great Plains is bordered by a highland region along its southeastern part and even today this area is still cattle country.

## The Western Part

The western part consists of high plateaus and mountains formed by the Great Cordillera Range, extending from Canada through the western part of the United States to Mexico and further south. From east to west, this mountain system is composed of the Rocky Mountains, the **Sierra Nevada Mountains**, the **Cascade Ranges** and the **Coast Ranges**. The whole area holds one-third of the country's territory on the continent.

The Rocky Mountains, at the western edge of the Great Plains, known as "**the backbone of the continent**", stretch from the Canadian border in Montana and Idaho through Wyoming, where they are met by a vast plateau named the Wyoming Basin and continue into New Mexico. The area to the west of the Rocky Mountains is dominated by the rocky Great Basin and deserts such as the Mojave.

The Rocky Mountains is the Continental Divide in North America. Nearly all the rivers in the United States originate from the Rocky Mountains. It is also famous for its varied scenery. The U.S. government has established 62 national parks to protect the environment and foster tourism.

One of the most famous is the **Yellowstone National Park** situated in the northwestern part of Wyoming. Established in 1872, the park got its name from the yellow rock lining the Yellowstone River. It is the oldest national park in the world and contains the largest wildlife preserve in the United States. Covering about 9,000 square kilometers, the Yellowstone National Park has thousands of hot springs and geysers. **Old Faithful** is the most famous geyser in the park, erupting 106 – 185 feet in the air every 90 minutes.

Between the Rocky Mountains and the Sierra Nevada and the Cascade Range are plateaus. This region consists of three parts — the **British Columbia Plateau**, the **Great**  **Basin and Range region**, and the **Colorado Plateau**. The British Columbia Plateau is a vast and dry region and it contains the Great Salt Lake. The

Colorado Plateau is a lofty tableland cut by deep gorges. The largest and best known is the **Grand Canyon** of the Colorado River, now an attraction known as the **Grand Canyon National Park**. The Great Basin and Range region lies between the Colorado and the British Columbia Plateau. It is featured by short, rugged mountain ranges separated by desert basins, including a desert named **Death Valley**, covering 1,408 square kilometers. It is 225 kilometers long, 6 to 26 kilometers wide. There are 550 square meters below sea level, which is the lowest place with the highest temperature in the Western Hemisphere. It got the name because many adventurers died of starvation and thirst in the valley during the gold rush.

Along the Pacific Coast are the Coast Ranges. Between the Coast Ranges and the Sierra Nevada Mountains and the Cascade Mountains are two great valleys. The south one is **Central Valley**, situated in California and to the north, **Willamette Valley**. Many fresh fruits are produced in these two valleys and shipped to the U.S. markets.

> **? Questions for discussion:**
> 1. What are the major geographical features of the U.S.?
> 2. What are the similarities and differences between the U.S. and China in geography?

## Part Three    Climate

Because of its large size and wide range of geographic features, nearly every type of climate can be found in the United States. The climate is temperate in most areas, tropical in Hawaii and southern Florida, polar in Alaska, semi-arid in the Great Plains, desert in the Southwest, Mediterranean in Coastal California and arid in the Great Basin. Extreme weather is not uncommon — the states bordering the Gulf of Mexico are prone to hurricanes and most of the world's tornadoes occur within the continental United States, primarily in the Midwest's Tornado Alley.

### Features of Climate

Generally speaking, America has four features in terms of its climate.

(1) Most of the country belongs to the typical temperate continental climate. It's mainly because America is walled between the Appalachian Mountains and the Rocky Mountains, free from any influence from the two oceans, but the air can go freely from the north to the south.

(2) America has a variable climate. Owing to its large size and variable landforms, America has different climates in different districts, such as the temperate continental climate, the temperate maritime climate, the semi-tropical climate, etc.

(3) The temperature varies from one region to another. The temperature becomes higher in the south because these areas are nearer to the tropical south.

(4) The rainfall is different in states. Generally speaking, the east is wet and the west dry. Some regions even become deserts, except for the Pacific coastal regions.

In the eastern part of the United States, although it has dry seasons, the rain is enough to support crops. The total annual rainfall in most parts of New England is over 1,000 millimeters and 2,000 millimeters in the southeastern America.

But in the Midwest, the annual rainfall is lower in the west, generally between 500 to 1,000 millimeters, so that much land relies on irrigation for production. To the west further, the climate becomes much drier, with the annual rainfall below 500 millimeters, especially the southern desert area with that below 250 millimeters.

In the western part of the country, especially the west of the Rocky Mountains, the climate condition is sharply different. On the western slopes of the Mountains, that is, the Cascade and the Sierra Nevada Mountains, it catches the largest share of the rain coming from the ocean and the annual rainfall amounts to over 1,500 millimeters. But after crossing these mountains, air masses become warmer as they go down the mountain slopes and as they retain much of moisture, rain becomes rare. As the air masses move up the Rocky Mountains, they become colder again and produce rainfall.

Hawaii receives abundant rainfall with annual rainfall about 3,500 to 4,000 millimeters, and on some slopes against the wind, the rainfall can reach up to 12,000 millimeters. It is one of the rainiest regions.

### Factors Influencing Climate

Many factors besides latitude influence the climate in the United States. Perhaps the most important forces are the Atlantic and Pacific Oceans, the Gulf of Mexico and the Great Lakes. These great water regions contribute to mild temperatures and great amounts of rainfall in their surroundings.

Ocean currents also affect the climate for most parts of the United States. New England is affected by Cold Labrador Current so the weather is cool. Gulf Stream influences the southeastern part of the country, causing a warm climate. In the Pacific Coast, the southern part is influenced by Cold California Current and the weather is mild.

The western mountains have great influence on the climate of the west of the United States. The Sierra

Nevada and the Cascade Ranges hold back the moisture from the inland regions. Besides, because there are no mountains in the Midwest to hold back the cold air from Canada and the warm air from Mexico, the temperature in this region changes greatly.

In addition, the size of the country, various landforms and the great expanse from north to south, all these features lead to various types of climate.

> **? Questions for discussion:**
>
> Since the United States covers nearly all climate conditions, such as temperate climate, tropical climate, polar climate, semi-arid climate, desert climate, Mediterranean climate and arid climate, etc., what influences does the climate have on the daily life of the Americans in different parts of the country? Give some examples from the perspective of food, transportation, the way of life, and so on.

## Part Four  Natural Resources

The United States is rich in natural resources and ranks first among all countries in reserves of water, forests, and minerals.

### Waters

The United States enjoys abundant fresh water. Except for some dry areas in the west, the country for the most part receives more than enough rainfall for agriculture. Besides, rivers and lakes provide advantages for irrigation, transportation, and power generation. In the United States, there are four international rivers: the St. Lawrence River in the northeast, Columbia River in the northwest, Rio Grande River and Colorado River in the southwest. Among these rivers, the first two rivers are shared with Canada, the other two with Mexico.

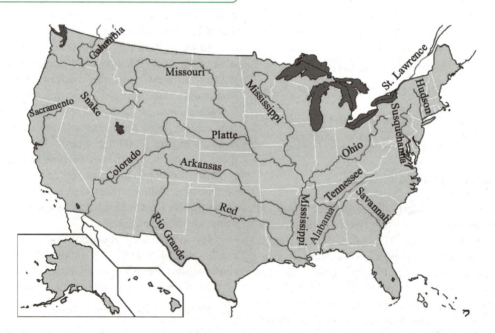

Water has played an important role in America's development. There are numerous fertile valleys through which many rivers flow, such as the Mississippi, the Hudson and the Rio Grande. The early development of agriculture and industry largely relied on vast water resources.

⊙ Mississippi River

The **Mississippi River**, often called the "**Father of Waters**" and "Old Man River", is the longest and the most important river in the United States. It flows from its northwestern source in the Rockies to the Gulf of Mexico, with a length of about 6,262 kilometers and a drainage area of 3,225,000 square kilometers. Nearly all the rivers in the west of the Appalachian Mountains and in the east of the Rockies empty into this large river. The Mississippi River has many tributaries, among which the Missouri and the Ohio are two of the largest ones.

The Missouri River, the largest tributary, with a length of about 3,726 kilometers, flows from the Rockies in Montana and empties into the Mississippi River from the west. It runs through the dry west and the river water is deep brown because it contains a large amount of topsoil.

The Ohio River, running some 2,100 kilometers, originates from the Great Lakes in the northeast and reaches Mississippi River in the southwest. It flows through the rainy east and the water is clear.

⊙ **Hudson River**

The Hudson River is one of the most notable rivers to the east of the Appalachians, because New York stands at its estuary. With a length of 507 kilometers, it provides passage from the Great Lakes through the Erie Canal to the Atlantic. It was once one of the most important and busiest rivers in the United States. It got its name in 1609 when a British man named Hudson first discovered this river.

⊙ **Rio Grande**

The Rio Grande River, about 3,030 kilometers long, flows south from the Rocky Mountains in southern Colorado through New Mexico to Texas, then turns southeast and empties into the Gulf of Mexico. It is a boundary river between Mexico and the United States. Now the two countries have made agreements to share the water resource and have built irrigation and flood control projects on the river, from which both countries have benefited a lot.

⊙ **The Great Lakes**

The **Great Lakes** are a collection of freshwater lakes located on the Canada — United States border in eastern **North America**, consisting of Lakes Ontario, Erie, Huron, Michigan and Superior. These lakes cover an area of about 245,660 square kilometers, up to 100 meters deep, with 72% of this area belonging to America and 28% owned by Canada. Of the five lakes, only **Lake Michigan** completely belongs to America, the other four are shared with Canada. As the largest fresh water lake group in the world, the Great Lakes hold 21% of the world's fresh water, with recognition as the "Mediterranean in American Continent". All the five lakes are interconnected, flowing through the St. Lawrence River and finally into the Atlantic.

The five lakes slope upward from east to west. **Lake Erie** is over 100 meters higher than **Lake Ontario** and the steep water flow gives birth to the famous **Niagara Falls** with a width of 1,240 meters.

Today rivers and lakes of America supply 63% of the fresh water for daily life and for irrigation and 93% of the fresh water is used for electric power. From the early days, the rivers have been an important means of transportation through which goods are shipped from one place to another.

## Forests

When the first European colonists arrived, they found half of America covered with trees, with dense forests stretching from the Atlantic coastline to the **Midwest**. In fact, the early settlers cultivated their lands around countless stumps left after the trees were cut down.

Even today about 33% of the land area in the United States is forest land, which is concentrated mainly in three areas: the area along the northwestern coast of the Pacific, the area in the south and the area in the north. The greatest virgin forests, which provide protection for wildlife, are in the northwestern states of Washington and Oregon. To protect wildlife, especially the national bird Bald Eagle, also classified as a hawk, the American government has forbidden lumbering in many places.

## Minerals

The United States is rich in minerals and some rank first among capitalist countries: coal, natural gas, iron ore, oil and other metals. But now some have to be imported to meet the industrial demand. It also abounds in lead, copper, gold, silver, aluminum and tungsten.

America abounds in coal reserves. Among its 50 states, 36 states have rich coal resources. Coal reserves are mainly to be found in the Appalachians, the Central Plain and the Rockies. Additionally, in the northern part of the country, the Pacific coast and Alaska, coal reserves have also been found. Today coal is mainly used to produce electricity and chemicals. About 24% of America's electricity comes from coal. America also exports coal to other countries, mainly Japan and European countries.

America has a large reserve of iron, most of which is in the areas near **Lake Superior**. The second largest iron reserve region is near Birmingham. However, because of its large consumption, America has to import iron ore from other countries.

America was once the largest oil-producing country in the world. Most of the oil reserves are in the southwestern part of the country and along the coast of the **Gulf of Mexico**. Texas, Louisiana and Oklahoma produce more than half of the country's total, while Texas once produced about one-third of the total. Alaska and California are also rich in oil. Today the largest oil-producing state is Oklahoma. With only 5% of world population, America needs up to 30% of oil consumption. The large consumption has required America to import oil from Mexico,

England, Venezuela and the Middle East. America has rich offshore oil resources, but to provide strategic reserves and protect the ocean environment, the Congress does not allow exploring it.

America was once rich in silver and gold. In 1848, gold was found in a stream in California. The news quickly spread across the continent and caused the so-called **gold rush**. But the gold ore there was soon exhausted and the Chinese translation of San Francisco — "old gold mountains" was born. To seek gold, miners went to the Rockies. Surprisingly, they discovered many other mineral veins. Tin ore was found in the Black Hills of South Dakota and a large deposit of silver, lead, and copper was found in Montana. Today the largest open-pit copper mining center is at Bingham, Utah.

All these natural resources provide a solid base for American industry. Although it has to import many materials to further develop its industry, America has the largest home market served by rich natural resources among the developed capitalist countries.

Today America is facing serious problem in availability of minerals. Soon after World War II, America had to import many raw materials from other countries. Many non-renewable resources have been used up because of excessive explorations and large consumption. Now the government is trying its best to find resources available to meet their industrial demand.

> **? Questions for discussion:**
> 1. To some extent, the U.S. is rich in water resources, though the west is dry and has even become desert. For example, the Mississippi River has many branches. Try to find out the route of these branches, and their contribution to the development of the country in agriculture and industry.
> 2. In modern times, oil plays a vital role in industrialized countries. But it is non-renewable energy resource, so how does the American government cope with this problem?

## Part Five  The People

In 2019, the population of the United States estimated by the **U.S. Census Bureau** was 329,065,000, including the estimated 12 million illegal immigrants. The birth rate was 1.7%, 30% below the world average, while higher than any European country except Albania and Ireland. In 2017, 88,847,550 immigrants were granted legal residence. Mexico has been the leading source of new U.S. residents for over two decades. Since 1998, China, India and the Philippines have been among the top four sending countries every year. The United States is the only industrialized nation in which large population increases are projected.

| Region of birth | Population | Percent |
|---|---|---|
| Total | 39,956 | 100.0 |
| Africa | 1,607 | 4.0 |
| Asia | 11,284 | 28.2 |
| Europe | 4,817 | 12.1 |
| Latin America and the Caribbean | 21,224 | 53.1 |
| Mexico | 11,711 | 29.3 |
| Other Central America | 3,053 | 7.6 |
| South America | 2,730 | 6.8 |
| Caribbean | 3,731 | 9.3 |
| Northern America | 807 | 2.0 |
| Oceania | 217 | 0.5 |

(Source: U.S. Census Bureau, American Community Survey, 2010.)

### Immigration to America

As a nation composed of immigrants, the United States received 4.5 million immigrants from 1990 to 1994, and the number had reached 37.9 million by 2007, nearly one eighth of the nation's total population, and most of them were from Asia and Latin America.

Actually, the first immigrants were European explorers who arrived in North America more than 400 years ago. Spanish colonists came first and established a few outposts in what is now Florida during the 1500s, and then a French colony was founded. In 1607, Britain established its first colony, **Jamestown**, in what is now Virginia and gradually founded 13 colonies. Some other European countries also planted their colonies along the Atlantic coastline in North America. Since the arrival of the immigrants, the native Indians were driven into barren desert regions, the so-called "**Indian Reservations**", and lived a disadvantageous life. By 1780, three-fourths of the Americans were of English or Irish origin.

Most of the early immigrants came to America for economic and social reasons like religious persecution, political unrest, famine and unemployment. During the **American Civil War** (1861–1865), immigrants who would serve in army were granted with land.

After the Civil War, more immigrants came due

to the improvement of economy. With the native Americans' fear of threat to their culture and influenced by the growth of racialism, the Congress passed the ***Chinese Exclusion Act*** in 1882. Immigrants from other Asian countries were also refused. In 1892, American government set up a special port of entry on Ellis Island in New York Harbor to prevent undesirable people from getting into America.

After World War I, with the growth of nationalism in America, the Congress passed the ***Reed-Johnson Immigration Act*** in 1924. The act set limits on the number of people permitted to immigrate to America each year. This number was determined by the population from each country already living in America. In 1965, the Congress passed a new immigration law, under which, a person's country of origin was not a consideration. Permits are based on individual applications within overall annual limits set by the Congress.

Now restrictions of legal immigrants still exist and the number is to be determined by the Congress. The maximum annual number for each country is 20,000. Permits are granted on the basis of a priority system. The most popular applicants are the unmarried children of American citizens. The second are spouses and unmarried children of resident aliens (immigrants with green cards). The third group are people with special skills. Others have little possibility of getting the permit. In addition, America also accepts people known as "refugees". The practice began after the end of World War II.

The new law has changed the immigration pattern. Before 1964, over 80% of immigrants came from Europe and Canada, while today they are mainly from Asia and Latin America.

## Composition of Population

The population is unevenly distributed. About 83% of the population lives in the country's 363 metropolitan areas. In 2006, 254 incorporated cities and towns in the United States had populations over 100,000, nine cities had more than 1 million residents, and four international cities including New York City, Los Angeles, Chicago and Houston had over 2 million. The United States has fifty metropolitan areas with population greater than 1 million. Of the fifty fastest-growing metro areas, twenty-three are in the West and twenty-five in the South.

### ⊙ The Caucasians

The Caucasians, the majority of Americans, are immigrants or descendants of immigrants from European nations, most of whom believe in Christianity.

The United States was formed from the 13 British Colonies established by Britain before 1700. Most of the early immigrants from Britain, the so-called **White Anglo-Saxon Protestants** (WASP), were repelled from their homeland because they rejected the Church of England and demanded freedom of religious belief.

New England was mainly populated by freedom-loving Puritans in the colonial time, so it earned the name of the "cradle of American liberty". In 1620, some English Puritans founded the Plymouth colony in Massachusetts and they signed the Mayflower Compact, the beginning of a new system — self government based on equality and democracy instead of one-man rule. They held the first **Thanksgiving Day** celebration to thank God for their harvest.

Because of intermarriage with white people, the majority of African Americans have white admixture and white people also have African ancestry.

Now the Caucasians are considered as the wealthiest and most influential in the United States. One reason is that the mainstream culture of the United States is primarily WASP in character. The Caucasians play a dominant role in the United States of America, not only in daily life but also in politics. Although Obama is the first African American president in the history of the United States, the status and role of the Caucasians in the country is unchanged.

### ⊙ African Americans

African Americans are the largest minority in the United States with the population of 46,800,000 in 2017, accounting for about 13.2% of the total population of the United States. The first African Americans were brought to North America as slaves in 1619. Later on, more slaves were shipped into North America as labor force, especially in the south. They were treated as property and deprived of any human rights. The miserable life is vividly described in the novels ***Uncle Tom's Cabin*** and ***Roots***.

Nowadays, African Americans' situation is much better and black Americans and white Americans have equal rights in many areas. No area of human activity can be legally closed to blacks. In 1983, the first African American astronaut traveled in space aboard the space shuttle. In 1986, more than 5,000 African Americans were elected to be government officials. African Americans began to gain social status by their

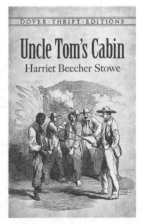

contributions to the development of the country.

But African Americans are still not satisfied with present conditions: poor all-black areas in cities, lower income and poor education resource. It is a problem that needs time to solve.

⊙ The Hispanics

The term **Hispanic** was first adopted in the United States by the administration of Richard Nixon and has since been used in local and federal employment, mass media, academia, and business market research. It has been used in the U.S. Census since 1980. Due to the widespread use of "Latino", the government adopted this term as well in 1997 and it was used in the census in 2000.

Hispanics refer to Spanish-speaking people from Latin America. The population growth of Hispanic and Latino Americans has been a major demographic trend. By 2019, Hispanics and Latinos constituted 17.4% (57.5 million) of the total population of the United States, becoming the second largest ethnic group after non-Hispanic White Americans, while in 2006, Hispanics accounted for 14.8% (around 44.3 million) of the national population. From July 1, 2005 to July 1, 2006 the Hispanic growth rate was 3.4% — higher than any other minority group in the United States, actually three and a half times the rate of the nation's total population (at 1.0%).

Between 2000 and 2010, the population of the Hispanics increased by 43%. Much of this growth is from immigration. Before Donald Trump built the wall, there were about 600,000 illegal immigrants in the United States every year.

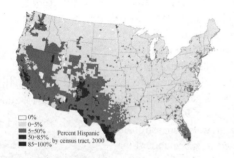

Hispanics and Latinos, with large population, played an important role in president election.

The largest group among the Hispanics is Mexican-Americans, also known as Chicanos. As the land neighbor of the United States, Mexicans are generally trying to enter the United States legally or illegally. Most of them are concentrated in the southwest, primarily California, Texas, Arizona, Nevada and New Mexico. Most of those who enter the U.S. work as manual laborers due to insufficient education and skills.

⊙ The American Indians

The Indians were the original inhabitants of the continent. Some 25,000 years ago, the forefathers of the Indians came to the continent from Asia by crossing the Bering land bridge which later became the Bering Strait. When Columbus first landed in the New World in 1492, he thought he had reached India, so he called the natives Indians and the name has been misused ever since.

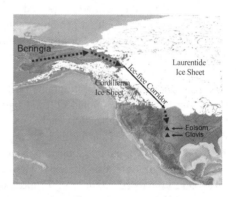

Most Indians lived in Central and South America, with only over one million in North America. They were all red-skinned and dark-haired.

The earliest Americans lived on hunting. Because larger animals became scarce as they moved to the south, they had to hunt smaller animals and eat plants for food. They began to raise and eat sunflower seeds and corn about 3,000 years ago.

The Indians had their own social structure and civilization before the Europeans came. They lived in tribes and the smallest unit was a clan with kinship as its basis. Individualism was forbidden and everything was shared by all.

⊙ Chinese-Americans

There are about 5.5 million Chinese immigrants and their descendants living in the United States today. Most of them entered America during the period from 1850 to 1880, with only 500 working as gold miners in 1850, but the number had increased to 300,000 by 1882. Chinese workers played an important role in rail construction in California in the 1860s. Chinese laborers did the most difficult work with the lowest pay. As California Governor Stanford put it in the letter to President Johnson in 1865:

"...*Without the Chinese laborers, it will be impossible to complete the western section of the national project (railway) within the time limit laid*

*down by the Act of Congress."*

But after the finish of gold rush and railway construction, the Chinese workers became unemployed and had to do low-paid jobs, which enraged American workers, for they were fighting for higher pay. In 1882, the Congress passed the *Chinese Exclusion Act*. Under this law, Chinese immigrants were not permitted to enter for ten years. Moreover, in 1902, the Congress decided to stop Chinese immigration for an indefinite period. It was not until 1943, after China became an ally to the United States, that the *Chinese Exclusion Act* was rescinded.

Chinese-Americans proved to be industrious and intelligent and some of them were very successful in the United States. They have found high-paid jobs in universities, hospitals and engineering firms. Up to 2018, nine Chinese-Americans had won the Nobel Prize.

⊙ Jewish-Americans

According to the Jewish Agency, in 2017 there were 14 million Jews worldwide, 0.3% of the current estimated world population, 6.3 million of whom lived in Israel, 5.7 million in the United States and the remainder were distributed in communities of varying sizes around the world.

Jews have made contributions in a broad range of human endeavors, including science, arts, politics, business, etc. The number of Jewish Nobel Prize winners (approximately 189 in all) is far out of proportion to the percentage of Jews in the world's population.

The United States is a nation of over 100 ethnic groups and each has some unique characteristics that make them different from others, so America is known as a "**melting pot**".

Today most ethnic groups have been assimilated and lost much of the distinctiveness of their culture. But Asian immigrants prefer to retain their cultural characteristics. Some ethnic groups still suffer from economic and social problems. Although racial discrimination has been outlawed, covert discrimination still exists in some places.

> **❓ Questions for discussion:**
>
> In order to maintain a balanced population, the U.S. government has made a series of laws about immigration. Try to search for the relevant information through the U.S. government website about the qualifications people should have to settle in the U.S.

## Exercises

### Ⅰ. Fill in the blanks.

1. The U.S. is bordered by _____ on the north and by _____ and the Gulf of Mexico on the south.
2. On the west of America lies the _____ Ocean. On the east of America lies the _____ Ocean.
3. The _____ part is made up of the highlands formed by the Appalachian Range.
4. The western part of the Central Plain is also called the "_____ _____".
5. The two main tributaries of the _____ River are the Missouri River and the Ohio River.
6. The two youngest states are _____ in the northeastern part of America and _____ in the Central Pacific.
7. Most of the inhabitants in the U.S. are of _____ origin.
8. Most of America belongs to _____ type of climate.
9. America extends _____ kilometers from east to west, and _____ kilometers from north to south. Its coastline runs as long as _____ kilometers.
10. About _____ of America is covered with forests.

### Ⅱ. Define the following terms.

1. the Central Plains

2. the Mississippi River
3. the Great Lakes
4. the *Chinese Exclusion Act*
5. melting pot

### Ⅲ. Multiple choice.

1. Most Americans lived in _____.
   A. city areas          B. countryside
   C. mountain areas      D. river valleys
2. The first immigrants in American history came from _____.
   A. England and Germany
   B. England and Ireland
   C. England and the Netherlands
   D. England and Spain
3. The _____, the backbone of the North American continent, is also known as the Continental Divide.
   A. Appalachians
   B. Rockies
   C. Blue Ridge Mountains
   D. Great Smokies
4. The major Hispanic groups in the United States are _____.
   A. the Mexicans
   B. the Puerto Ricans and Cubans
   C. the Mexicans and the Puerto Ricans
   D. the Mexicans, Puerto Ricans and Cubans
5. The United States is _____.
   A. the largest country in the world
   B. the second largest country in the world
   C. the third largest country in the world
   D. the fourth largest country in the world
6. Recently most of the immigration to the United States has been from _____.
   A. Asian countries
   B. Asian and Hispanic countries
   C. Eastern European countries
   D. former Soviet republics
7. The Mississippi, which is sometimes called the _____, has played a vital role in the history of the United States.
   A. "Old Man River"
   B. "Moon River"
   C. "Old Father River"
   D. "Mother of the United States"
8. Many early Chinese immigrants worked in the mining industry, especially in the _____.
   A. gold mines         B. silver mines
   C. coal mines         D. copper mines
9. *Uncle Tom's Cabin* and *Roots* are two novels which give a vivid description of the miserable life of the _____.
   A. early settlers     B. Puritans
   C. native Indians     D. black slaves

### Ⅳ. Translate the following terms into English.

1. 温带海洋性气候
2. 美国谷仓
3. 黄石国家公园
4. 淘金热
5. 感恩节

### Ⅴ. Answer the following questions in a few sentences.

1. What are the advantages contributed by the favorable position of the United States for its rapid development?

2. What are the climate features of America?

3. Why is the Mississippi River very important in America?

4. What are the reasons for Asian-Americans' success?

### Mini-tasks:

1. The Great Lakes are the largest freshwater lakes in the United States. However, with the development of the national economy, especially the application of new technologies and machines, the Great Lakes have encountered severe ecologic challenges. Search for information about the ecologic changes of the Great Lakes in history.

2. Energy is a necessity to a nation, especially to a developed industrialized nation. Traditional energy resources, such as coal and oil, are non-renewable and will be soon used up at the pace of current consumption. What kinds of new energy can be employed in the United States? You can answer it with the consideration of America's position, environment and technology.

3. Group discussion:
The Great Lakes belong to both Canada and the United States. A series of actions had been taken by both governments to protect the Lakes, but have produced unsatisfactory results. How can the two governments improve the condition of the Lakes, while not damaging benefits of the two countries?

# Chapter Two　Government and Politics

*The federal government of the United States is the central government entity established by the United States Constitution, which shares sovereignty over the United States with the governments of the individual U. S. states. Think about the following items before going into this chapter:*
1. *What is the structure of the U. S. government?*
2. *How do the branches of the government cooperate with each other in making laws and policies?*
3. *How is the president elected? What qualifications should the presidential candidates have?*

The **American Dream** is liberty and equality. People have paid high price to pursue and protect this ideal since the first immigrants arrived on the continent. Even today people are still concerned with the problems of liberty and equality, because they are the basis of the American values. The United States is the world's oldest surviving federation and is a constitutional republic, in which majority rule is tempered by minority rights protected by law. It is fundamentally structured as a representative democracy, though U. S. citizens residing in the territories are excluded from voting for federal officials.

## Part One　Government Principles

The political system of the United States of America is established on the basis of three main principles: **federalism**, the **separation of powers** and **respect for the Constitution**, and the rule of law. The three main branches of government are separate and distinct from one another.

In the American federalist system, citizens are usually subject to three levels of government, federal, state, and local. The federal government deals with foreign affairs and matters of general concern to all the states. The states have the basic functions of providing law and order, education, public health and most of the things concerning everyday life. The local governments' duties are commonly split between county and municipal governments.

The government is regulated by a system of **checks and balances** defined by the **American Constitution**, which is the basis of American laws and a social agreement for the people of the United States. Under the principle of checks and balances, the federal government is divided into three branches — the executive, the legislative and the judicial. Each branch can check or block the action of the other branches. They are in balance and no branch can act to be more powerful than the other two branches. In almost all cases, executive and legislative officials are elected by popular vote of citizens in district. There is no proportional representation at the federal level and very rare at lower levels. Federal and state judicial and cabinet officials are typically nominated by the executive branch and approved by the legislature, though some state judges and officials are elected by popular vote.

The **Federal Constitution**, adopted in 1787, came into effect in 1789 and is the first comparatively complete written constitution. It outlines the structure of the national government and is the fundamental law of the land.

## Part Two　The Federal Government

### The President

The President is the chief executive officer and the head of state and takes the **White House** as the official presidential residence located in Washington, D. C. The President is not elected by direct vote, but by an indirect Electoral College system in which the determining votes are apportioned by the state. He receives advice and assistance from his Cabinet formed by department heads, also called secretaries. According to the Constitution, the President should be born in the U. S. territory and at least thirty-five years old. He can only serve one or two successive terms of four years each. As the most prominent public person in America, the President is known as the **First Citizen**, his wife being the **First Lady**.

The President really has enormous power. He appoints government officials, including ambassadors, judges and department heads with the consent of the Congress. With the approval of the Senate, he can appoint the U.S. **Secretary of State** who is the official spokesperson of the U.S. foreign policy and responsible to the President. He has the authority to decide the American foreign policy and make treaties with foreign countries once he gets the approval of the Congress. However, when he makes executive agreements with foreign governments he does not need any congressional approval. As **commander-in-chief** of the United States Armed Forces, he is entitled to send and receive diplomatic officials. The President plays an important role in making laws. He can propose legislation, but laws can be put into effect only when approved by **two-thirds** of the Senate. All the bills passed by the Congress must be signed by the President before becoming law. Because the **Justices** of the Supreme Court are appointed by the President, he can check the judicial branch. He is also the head of the whole nation. But his powers are not unlimited and most of them are shared with and moderated by the other two branches of the administration.

According to the law, every natural-born American citizen not less than 35 years old has right to participate in election. But, in fact, only candidates nominated by the two major parties can win the general election.

The election process in the United States is rather complex, even an American citizen can be puzzled sometimes. The general election can be divided into three steps: **primary election**, **party conventions** and the campaign for the **general election**.

The first step is primary election. Both parties hold their conventions to elect delegates. In fact, early before primary election, every aspirant for presidential candidacy begins his personal campaign for the delegate elected by his party members.

The second step is that the elected delegates cast their votes for presidential candidates in their party's national conventions, nominating a president and a vice-president. The number of delegates from each state is equal to that of its senators and representatives in the Congress. That is, there are altogether 538 presidential delegates in the country, 535 for the states and 3 for the District of Columbia (without seats in the Congress). If the candidates of a party for delegates in a certain state receive a majority of the total vote, then the party is entitled to have all the electoral votes of that state, even though a presidential candidate recieves only slightly more than electoral votes of that state. This system is known as the **"winner-take-all" principle**. If there are three or more candidates and none of them receives more than half votes, the President will be chosen by the House of Representatives among the top three candidates. In this case, the voting is by states, each state counting as one vote.

The third step is national wide campaign and ballot held in November. To win voters' support, candidates tried every means like TV, radio, newspaper, door-to-door-visit, public speech, and so on to convince the voters that he is more competent to solve the current and future problems than his rival.

### The Congress

The Congress is the law-making and the supreme legislative body of the United States of America. It consists of two houses with equal powers: the **Senate** and the **House of Representatives**.

The Senate has 100 members with each state having two senators. The term of office is six years, with one-third of the Senate seats up for election every two years. A senator must be over 30 years old, and have been an American citizen for at least nine years and a resident in the state in which he or she is seeking elective office. The head of the Senate serves as the vice-president of the United States.

The Senate is vested with special powers not enjoyed by the House. It has the power to ratify or reject proposed treaties with foreign countries and important nominations to government offices proposed by the President. It has the sole power to hear charges filed by the House against high-level officials for alleged wrongdoings and to find them guilty.

The House of Representatives, with the Speaker as its head, currently the leader of the majority party in the House, has a permanent membership of 435. The seats of each state depend on its population. The members of the House are called representatives or Congress members. They must be at least 25 years old, have been an American citizen for no less than seven years and residents in the states from which he is elected. Representatives are elected every two years, but with no limitation on the number of terms. Elections are in November of even-numbered years.

But the Constitution provides that each state should at least have one representative in **Congress**. The House has some exclusive powers that are not enjoyed by the Senate, such as the impeachment power and the initiation of revenue bills.

The annual session of **Congress** begins on January 3 each year. The outstanding characteristic is that the vice-president is the **ex officio** president of the Senate while the House of Representatives chooses its own speaker.

The Congress has many functions: to regulate commerce with foreign countries, to collect taxes and pay the debts, and to raise armies and pay for them. The major function of **Congress** is to make federal laws. A bill becomes a law after it is introduced and passed in **Congress** and signed by the President.

Any member of **Congress** has right to introduce a bill and most bills are introduced in the House of Representatives. The most important public bills are often introduced at the request of the President or involve major problems with which legislators are especially concerned.

When bills come into being, they are immediately sent to an appropriate legislative committee which deals with the subject of the bill. The committees conduct inquiries and examine each new bill proposed. Then committees and sub-committees hold public hearings, at which people may argue for or against a policy. After the bill gets the approval of the two Houses of **Congress**, it goes to the White House for presidential action.

The President may approve the bill and sign it, then it automatically becomes a law. The President can veto the bill if he disapproves of it. In this case, two-thirds of each House of **Congress** must approve the bill before it can still become a law.

According to the Constitution, the President may be removed from the office if he is impeached and found guilty. If the House of Representatives get a "bill of impeachment" with sufficient evidence and approval of two-thirds of its membership, a trial will be held in the Senate. If two-thirds of the Senate votes that the President is guilty, he will be removed from office. But the impeachment is designed only to remove an unfit official from his office, with no other punishments involved.

### The Supreme Court

The Supreme Court is the most important judicial body and is the only court created by the Constitution. It is the highest court in the United States with the sole right to interpret the Constitution and review laws to see whether they are in agreement with the Constitution. The Supreme Court is composed of one **Chief Justice** and eight associate justices. The nine justices are appointed for life terms by the President and take office with the consent of the Senate. They can be removed through impeachment if they violate the law.

The decisions made by the Supreme Court are final unless the Constitution is amended or the Supreme Court itself changes the decisions. All the lower courts should follow the rules of the Supreme Court. The Supreme Court has the jurisdiction over issues involving foreign citizens, governments and cases in which the federal government itself is a party. Under the principle of judicial review, the Supreme Court can determine whether acts passed by **Congress** or actions taken by the President are in agreement with the Constitution. It is entitled to nullify any actions of **Congress** and the President by declaring them unconstitutional.

Under the Supreme Court, there are thirteen federal courts of appeals and 94 federal district courts and both types are created by the Congress. According to the Congress, a smaller state forms one district of its own and a larger one may have four districts. The **American Court of Appeals**, a higher court than the district court, reviews the cases from a district court. It makes the final decisions except those reviewed by the Supreme Court. State judges are not appointed for life but elected for limited terms.

> **Question for discussion:**
> Although the U. S. government system is completely different from that of the U. K., the rights given to the American President are similar to the powers of the British Prime Minister. What are these similarities and differences?

### Notable Government Agencies

⊙ The Federal Bureau of Investigation (FBI)

The Federal Bureau of Investigation (FBI) is the primary investigative department of the **Department of Justice**, serving as both a federal criminal investigative body and a domestic intelligence agency. At present, the FBI has investigative jurisdiction over violations of more than 200 categories of federal crimes. The motto of the bureau is "Fidelity, Bravery, Integrity", corresponding to the "FBI" initials.

The headquarters of FBI is located in Washington, D.C. It has 59 sub-offices, over 400 resident agencies throughout the nation and more than 50 international offices in the U.S. embassies worldwide.

The FBI was established in 1908 as the Bureau of Investigation (BOI) and the name was changed to the Federal Bureau of Investigation (FBI) in 1935. The mission of the FBI is "to protect and defend the United States against terrorists and foreign intelligence threats, to uphold and enforce the criminal laws of the United States and to provide leadership and criminal justice services to federal, state, municipal, and international agencies and partners".

The director of the FBI is appointed by the President of the United States. He must be confirmed by the Senate and serve ten-year terms. The director is responsible for the day-to-day operations at the FBI. Along with his deputies, the director ensures that cases and operations are handled correctly. The director is also in charge of making sure the leadership in any one of the sub-offices is manned with qualified agents. Before the **Intelligence Reform and Terrorism Prevention Act** was passed in the wake of the terrorist attacks on September 11, 2001, the director would brief the President on any issues that arise from within the FBI. Since then, the director has been reporting to the Director of National Intelligence (DNI) who in turn reports to the President.

All employees of the FBI require a Top Secret (TS) security clearance, and in many instances, employees need a higher level — Top Secret clearance. In order to get a security clearance, all candidates must pass a series of **Single Scope Background Investigations** (SSBI), conducted by the **Office of Personnel Management**. Special Agents candidates have to pass a **Physical Fitness Test** (PFT). The personnel are subject to random drug tests. There is also a polygraph test personnel have to pass, with questions including possible drug use.

After potential special agent candidates are cleared with TS clearance and a non-disclosure agreement is signed, they are sent to take the training facility located on **Marine Corps Base Quantico** in Virginia. After spending approximately 21 weeks at the Academy, qualified candidates successfully graduate and are placed all around the country and the world, depending on their areas of expertise. Professional support staff work for one of the support buildings of the FBI. However, they can be transferred to any place for any length of time if they are in urgent need at one of the sub-offices or resident agencies.

⊙ The Central Intelligence Agency (CIA)

The Central Intelligence Agency (CIA) is a civilian intelligence agency of the United States government. It is the successor to the **Office of Strategic Services** formed during World War II to coordinate espionage activities among the branches of military services.

The primary function of the CIA is collecting and analyzing information about foreign governments, corporations, and persons in order to make suggestions to public policymakers. Prior to December 2004, the CIA was literally the central intelligence organization for the government. The *Intelligence Reform and Terrorism Prevention Act of 2004* created the office of the Director of National Intelligence (DNI) who took over some functions of the government and the Intelligence Community that had previously been under the CIA.

The current the CIA still has a number of functions in common with other countries' intelligence agencies — collecting and analyzing intelligence. The headquarters of the CIA lies in the community of Langley in Virginia, a few miles west of Washington, D.C. along the Potomac River.

> **? Questions for discussion:**
>
> The CIA and the FBI have been well known by all the people around the world through movies and TV series. Try to search for information about the following items.
> 1. The roles the CIA and the FBI had played in the 2008 U.S. presidential election.
> 2. Their cooperation in guaranteeing the national security.

## Part Three  State and Local Governments

The **state government** also consists of three branches: the executive headed by the state governor, the state law-making body and the state courts. The state government is supreme within the sphere of its reserved powers. It has power to pass the state laws and levy taxes to cover state expenditures and maintain the state police force. The state governor and the members of the state legislature are elected by the residents of the state without any participation of the federal government. The laws vary from state to state because they are usually made by a state law-making body in areas without federal laws.

Local governments created by state government vary greatly in the form of organization. There are two types of local governments: territorial governments and corporate governments. A territorial government has jurisdiction in a certain area like a county or a school district. A corporate government, founded on the basis of the charter granted by the state government and serving as a local constitution of a university, a city or a town, has the authority to exercise some home rules, without interference from the state government.

**Counties** are the major units of local governments in most states, but their size and power differ greatly. Counties perform many functions like law enforcement, providing schools, welfare and collecting taxes. But the county government does not have a dominant officer and the decisions are made under the principle of "one man one vote". Nearly all the practical work is done by the county clerk, a popularly elected administrative officer. His duty ranges from supervision of elections to death records.

**Towns** are mainly used to designate local self-governing units under the state in New England. They are equivalents to counties and cities of other states. The city is a municipal corporation chartered by the state. A township is a subdivision of the county outside New England, which is common in the Midwest.

> **? Question for discussion:**
>
> Different from the federal government, local governments are given some rights that the federal government does not have. Discuss the rights and powers that the local governments have and give some examples to support each point.

## Exercises

**I. Fill in the blanks.**
1. There are _____ voting members in the House of Representatives.
2. There are _____ judges in the Supreme Court of America.
3. The balance is always kept among the three branches of the power of the government and this is called the "System of _____ and _____".
4. The _____ determines the government and divides the power of the government into three branches.
5. The official presidential residence is the _____ _____.
6. The American Congress is made up of two houses: the _____ and the House of _____.
7. The head of the House of Representatives is called the _____.
8. According to the _____, the President should be a citizen born in the U.S. territory.
9. The two main parties are the Democratic and the _____ Party.
10. American presidents are elected every _____ years.

**II. Define the following terms.**
1. checks and balances
2. American Constitution
3. the White House
4. the First Lady
5. the "winner-take-all" principle

**III. Multiple choice.**
1. The political system of the U.S. is based on the following except _____.
   A. federalism
   B. the constitutional monarchy
   C. separation of powers
   D. respect for the constitution
2. The U.S. Federal Government is composed of the following except _____.
   A. the legislative
   B. the standing committee

C. the judicial
D. the executive

3. The members in the Senate must be at least _____ years old and those in the House of Representatives _____ years old.
   A. 40, 30  B. 30, 26  C. 30, 25  D. 40, 25

4. If the President wants to put a treaty into effect, he has to get the approval by two-thirds of the _____.
   A. Senate           B. Cabinet
   C. Congress         D. Supreme Court

5. The number of Congress members from each state varies depending on _____.
   A. the size of the area
   B. the number of the population
   C. the tradition
   D. the wealth

6. The Federal Government and the state governments are supposed to _____ each other.
   A. guide
   B. control
   C. keep independence from
   D. help

7. The origin of the American party system can be traced to _____.
   A. the struggle between the Royalists and revolutionaries in the War of Independence
   B. the constitutional debate between the Federalists and the anti-Federalists
   C. the struggle between those who upheld slavery and those who opposed slavery
   D. none of the above

8. The Constitution of the United States provides that _____ shall be president of the Senate.
   A. the Secretary of State
   B. the Chief Justice
   C. the President
   D. the Vice President

9. When the President of the U.S. signs an act passed by the Congress into law, it still can be cancelled if _____.
   A. the lower federal court decides that it goes against previous laws
   B. the Supreme Court decides that it goes against previous laws
   C. the lower federal court decides that it is unconstitutional
   D. the Supreme Court decides that it is unconstitutional

## IV. Translate the following terms into English.
1. 参议院
2. 众议院
3. 司法部门
4. 听证会
5. 总统大选

## V. Answer the following questions in a few sentences.
1. What are the functions of the Congress?

2. What is a federal system?

3. How do the Americans elect Congress members?

### Mini-tasks:

1. The Vice-President is the second-highest executive official of the government. As the first candidate in the U.S. presidential line of succession, the Vice-President would become president upon the death, resignation, or removal of the President, which took place nine times in the U.S. history. Read the documents about the U.S. history, which nine Vice-Presidents became president on the death, resignation, or removal of the President? As the Vice-President, what roles does he or she play in the government and the country?

2. Comparison:
The day-to-day enforcement and administration of the federal laws is in the hands of the various federal executive departments, created by the Congress to deal with specific areas of national and international affairs. The heads of the 15 departments, chosen by the President and approved with the "advice and consent" of the U.S. Senate, form a council of advisers generally known as the President's "Cabinet". The Cabinet plays a vital part in presidential decision making and policy formulation. Make a comparison between the American Cabinet and the British Cabinet, what similarities and differences do they have in function and power?

# Chapter Three  Economy and Major Cities

*The economy of the United States is the largest national economy in the world in both nominal value and purchasing power parity. In the past 240 years, the United States has grown into a huge, integrated, industrialized economy making up over a quarter of the world economy. Try to answer the following questions before reading this chapter.*
1. *As an industrialized country, what is the economic structure of the U. S. ?*
2. *What measures did the U. S. government take to promote economic development?*

## Part One  Economic Profile

The United States has a capitalist mixed economy, which is fueled by abundant natural resources, well-developed infrastructure and high productivity. According to the International Monetary Fund, the United States GDP of $21. 34 trillion (2019) constituted 24. 8% of the gross world product at market exchange rates and 15. 18% of the gross world product at purchasing power parity (PPP). With the largest national GDP in the world, it was slightly less than the European Union combined at purchasing power parity in 2006. The country ranked eighth in the world in nominal GDP per capita and fourth in GDP per capita at PPP. In 2008, seventy-two percent of the economic activities in the U.S. came from consumers.

The rapid development of the U.S. economy can be attributed to many factors: First, the New World with its rich mineral resources and fertile farm land provided an ideal place for the early European immigrants to carry out their democratic experiment. Second, the vast territory, ample natural resources and good climate proved to be a major advantage for economic development. The U. S. also has extensive coastlines on both the Atlantic and Pacific Oceans, as well as on the Gulf of Mexico. Rivers flow from far within the continent and the Great Lakes provide additional shipping access. These extensive waterways have helped to fuel the country's economic growth over years and helped to bind America's 50 individual states together into a single economic unit. Third, America can provide the necessary labor force to meet the demands of a growing economy. The continuous influx of immigrants not only provides human resources but also helps to reduce the cost of labor, because wages are low. Fourth, America's labor force possesses various advanced skills. Workers have a strong work ethic and are willing to experiment and advocate new technology.

The U.S. economy maintains a high level of output per person, a stable overall GDP growth rate and high levels of research and capital investment funded by both national and foreign investors.

## Part Two  Economic System

The United States is the largest developed industrialized country with strong economy and advanced technologies. The economic system is principally privately owned and often known as **free enterprise system** in which private firms make the majority of the microeconomic decisions while being regulated, to some extent, by the government. Everyone is free to start an enterprise. The law protects American people's right to "life, liberty and pursuit of happiness". Possession of property is a means of pursuing happiness.

The United States is a **monopolized capitalist** — its economy is marked by concentration and monopolization of production. Large corporations are the dominating force in the economic life. Although capitalism may cause social problems, such as unemployment and disparity in people's income, American people still embrace free enterprise with the belief of equity to opportunity. At the same time, small businesses also play a remarkable role and the government has, to some extent, always been involved in ensuring the economic health.

Private business in America can be divided into two types according to their size: giant corporations and small businesses.

### The Giant Corporations

**Corporations**, a group of people authorized to act as an individual for a certain purpose, are very important organizations in American society. The vast American economy depends increasingly on the vigor and effectiveness of its large corporations, supplying goods and services on a national or multinational scale. Economic power is concentrated, to some extent, in the hands of these massive corporations. With less than 2% of all businesses, they generate about 90% of all business income of the United

States.

Some corporations are privately owned and their stock is not for sale to the general public. However, most corporations raise capital mainly by selling stock. The most striking feature of a large corporation is its great number of stockholders, who are, in fact, owners of the corporation. Nevertheless, a common stockholder does not participate in management. Effective control is in the hands of a board of directors elected by stockholders themselves. A president or chief executive officer is appointed to make managing operations, except policy.

Corporations, creating millions of jobs and large part of federal government revenues, are pillars of American economy. When a big corporation meets with trouble or even goes bankrupt, it will trigger a chain reaction: Many workers are forced out of jobs, related businesses will be closed down and the stock market will be impacted.

Most giant labor-intensive corporations are multinational firms. They established their subsidiaries in the countries with lower labor cost. These subsidiaries are responsible for the production of component parts or even finished goods in order to reduce production costs.

### The Small Businesses

Generally, there are two forms of small businesses: **proprietorships** started and managed personally by single owners or single entrepreneurs, and **partnerships** in which two or more people share the risks and rewards of a business. Small businesses, large in number, represent about 98% of all businesses. It is easy for people to start a small business in America, but they have to face intense competition and be guided by operation of market principles. Many start, but more fail every year.

Small businesses, with its production on a small scale and in local or regional market, are mostly retail and service providers. Small as they are, they play an important role in the U. S. economy. Nearly one-third of the U. S. labor force is employed in this sector and a large proportion of the Gross National Product comes from small businesses.

The government provides help for small businesses because they absorb surplus labor force. For example, small businesses are given advice and financial help for their expansion and modernization. Besides, joint corporations often shift less profitable and small-scale production to small businesses. These considerations make development of small businesses possible in America.

### Role of Government in Economy

Government plays an indispensable role in the development of national economy now. But before 1890, the government refused to intervene in the production and distribution of the goods. People believed generally that the natural economic order was the ideal economic pattern and could produce maximum well-being for all people. However, with further development and concentration of the industrialized base, competition became intense and many businesses began to abuse the nonintervention policy.

In the years following the **Great Depression**, the U. S. devised a complex system to stabilize prices for agricultural goods, which tended to fluctuate wildly in response to rapid changes in supply and demand. A number of other industries — trucking and, later, airlines — successfully sought regulations by themselves to limit the so-called harmful price cutting. The Congress passed a series of laws to prevent big businesses who attempted to monopolize manufacturing, distribution and price of goods from collaborating with each other. Traditionally, the government sought to prevent monopolies such as electric utilities from raising prices beyond the level that would ensure reasonable profits. At times, the government has extended economic regulatory control to other kinds of industries as well.

After World War II, the function of the government continues to expand because of increasing international competition. Since the 1970s, the government has also exercised control over private companies to achieve social goals, such as improving the public's health and safety or maintaining a healthy environment. Americans now generally believe that the government should be responsible for the overall development of the economy and the well-being of all people. The government has put regulations and control over private enterprises to ensure fair competition and to protect the public, and branches of the government have attempted to spur economy and fight inflation and recession by various means, like establishing safety standards, regulating production as well as improving working conditions.

> **Questions for discussion:**
> 1. What are the advantages and disadvantages of the economic structure of the United States?
> 2. During the 2008 economic crisis, how do the components of the national economy interact with each other to prevent a further rise of unemployment rates?

## Part Three   Structure of Economy

The United States is the largest industrial country

in the world and the manufacturing and service industries are especially important for the growth of its economy.

## The Primary Industries

The United States is the world's richest agricultural nation because of its vast areas of fertile soil, moderate climate and a large diversity of landscapes. The country produces all kinds of agricultural products. Although agriculture accounts for just less than 1% of GDP, the United States is the world's top producer of corn and soybeans. The country's leading cash crop is marijuana, despite federal laws making its cultivation and sale illegal.

The postwar American agriculture has been characterized by the decline of the family farm and an increase in mechanization. Consequently, less population is engaged in agriculture, but farm productivity has grown at a high rate.

American farmers receive federal crop-price support and farm credits to maintain a stable economic environment. Besides, farmers benefit from federal programs providing rural electrification, crop insurance and other services.

The United States is the largest corn producer in the world, accounting for nearly 50% of the world's total production. The **Corn Belt** is mainly located in the Midwest. At the same time, half of pigs and one-third of meat cattle are reared in this area because of the product — corn.

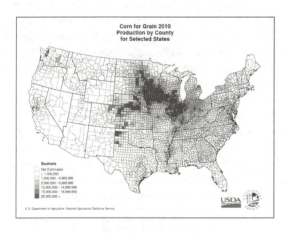

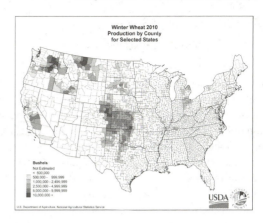

Wheat is the most important food crop in the United States. The **Wheat Belt** is mainly in the western part of the great Central Plain including the north and south Dakota, Kansas and Oklahoma.

Rice is also a largely exported product, second to Thailand. Today, rice is grown in the coastal region of the South where, more than one hundred and fifty years ago, the predominant cash crop was cotton. The center of cotton has shifted to the Mississippi Valley, Texas and the Central Valley of California.

Also, the United States grows many kinds of fruits in the area of Pacific Coast, especially California. Beef and dairy products are indispensable components of the American diet. Cattle production is widespread throughout the United States.

## The Secondary Industries

The United States is a leading manufacturing power in the world with a yearly industrial output of $3,900,000 million (2019). The U.S. manufacturing is highly diversified and technologically advanced. Main industries are petroleum, steel, motor vehicles, aerospace, telecommunications, chemicals, electronics, food processing, consumer goods, lumber and mining. The total value of manufacturing output ranks first in the world. The traditional pillar industries are steel-making, automobile and military industries. The total manufacturing industry employs about one-sixth of America's workers and produces 11% of the annual GDP.

Steel-making used to be the most important industry. Although it has long been in stagnation and faces many difficulties today, the United States is still one of the biggest steel-making countries in the capitalist world and has the most advanced technology.

The automobile industry makes up 5% to 6% of the Gross National Product (GNP). The three biggest giants in this industry are **General Motors**, **Ford** and **Chrysler**.

Military industry contributes greatly to the rapid growth of the economy. Nowadays, countries spend a lot to build up a strong national defense. With advanced technology and knowledgeable experts, the United States produces first-class weapons and machines. Consequently, America has become a large exporter of military equipment and earns substantial profit.

Labor costs are much higher in the United States than in most other countries. To reduce production costs, most big corporations make investments abroad. Today it is hard to find products entirely made within the United States.

### The Tertiary Industries

Service industry is the largest sector of the U. S. economy in terms of output and employment. It consists of many different organizations and industries, ranging from hospitals to scenic resorts to automobile repair shops. These various industries provide jobs and positions for American people to lower unemployment and increase GDP. Growth in economy is based on the stable financial supports, so banking and financial businesses mainly operated by private businesses make up an important part of the service industry. The U. S. banks receive money as deposits from both individuals and companies and then make loans to governments, businesses and private individuals, from which the banks make a profit in terms of interest changed.

The United States has a large insurance industry. In addition to providing insurance, these companies also offer many other services, like deposit accounts, mutual funds, etc.

As the largest productive nation in the world, the U. S. heavily relies on foreign trade to sustain its economic development. However, the U. S. share of the world trade has declined in recent years. The leading export products are industrial, electrical, transportation and communication equipment, tobacco products, chemicals and so on.

Tourism is another important sector of the service industry. The diversity of landforms makes the United States a natural, fantastic scenic spot which attracts a continuous flow of visitors both at home and abroad.

Transportation-related businesses are even more important to America than to other nations. The United States has a vast landmass and people are scattered over the land. In addition, American people like to move from place to place, thus the nation got the nickname "**a nation on the move**" or "**a nation on the wheels**". As a result, the United States has a large transportation system. Large railroad network, air transport system and water transportation provide great convenience for transporting goods.

Approximately 39% of personal vehicles owned

by Americans are vans or light trucks. The average American adult (including all drivers and non-drivers) spends 55 minutes behind the wheel every day, but bicycle usage is minimal. The civil airline industry is entirely privatized, while most major airports are publicly owned. The five largest airlines in the world all belong to the United States.

> **? Question for discussion:**
>
> A nation's political power depends mainly on its industry and military forces. Discuss what roles American industry plays in the economic development.

### Part Four  Imports and Exports

The United States plays the most significant role in the world in terms of international trade. It is the largest importer and third largest exporter of goods, though its exports per capita are relatively low. Mexico, Canada, China, Japan and Germany are its top trading partners. The leading export commodity is electrical machinery, while vehicles constitute the leading import.

As the epicenter of world trade, the United States enjoys leverage that many other nations do not. For instance, the United States is the top export market for almost 60 trading nations. Many businesses compete for a share in American market. In addition, America occasionally impose economic sanctions in different regions of the world.

Since the United States is the world's leading importer, many U. S. dollars are widely in circulation. The stable economy and fairly sound monetary policy have led to faith in the U. S. dollar as the world's most stable currency.

In order to fund the **national debt** (also known as public debt), the United States relies on selling treasury bonds to people both at home and abroad. Much of the money generated for the treasury bonds came from U. S. dollars with which consumers used to purchase imports in the United States.

## Part Five   Energy

The United States energy market is 101.113 Quadrillion Btu per year. Energy consumption per capita is 7.8 tons of oil equivalents per year, compared to Germany's 4.2 tons and Canada's 8.3 tons. In 2019, 37% of the nation's energy came from petroleum, 11% from coal, and 32% from natural gas. The remainder was supplied by nuclear power and various renewable energy sources. The United States is the world's largest consumer of petroleum. For decades, nuclear power has played a limited role compared with many other developed countries. Recently, applications for new nuclear plants have been filed.

In 2009, President Barack Obama and President Hu Jintao established the U. S.-China Clean Energy Research Center to facilitate joint research and development of renewable energy technologies.

The **U. S.-China Energy Cooperation Program** (ECP) was underscored by both presidents in an official joint statement during President Obama's visit to China in the same year. Today, more than 90 organizations from the U. S. and China joined in ECP.

## Part Six   Current Problems

The economic system of the U. S. is mainly privately owned, so individuals have rather great freedom to explore opportunities, to do experiments and to create profit for working organizations. The federal government, to some extent, intervenes and regulates the development of the economy. However, the government has not yet been able to develop a proper and effective way to solve the persistent problem of poverty.

Major economic concerns in the U. S. include national debt, external debt, entitlement liabilities for retiring baby boomers who have already begun withdrawing from their Social Security accounts, corporate debt, mortgage debt, a low saving rate, falling house prices, a weakening currency and a large current account deficit. In 2006, the U.S. economy had its lowest saving rate since 1933.

As a nation with advanced technology and developed industries, the United States needs access to raw materials to meet the demands of production. It is heavily dependent on foreign sources for many essential primary materials, such as tin, manganese, crude petroleum, nickel and bauxite. Many industries are built on an expectation of having a continuous supply of essential raw materials.

In addition, affected by the ongoing worldwide COVID-19 pandemic and China-U. S. trade war, America suffered a great loss. With high unemployment and high price of goods, Trump and Biden urged economic recovery.

> **? Question for discussion:**
> As a leading importer and exporter, what kinds of goods does America export to China, and what does America import from China?

## Part Seven   Major Cities

### Washington, D. C.

**Washington**, **D. C.**, the nation's capital, is situated on the banks of the **Potomac River** between the two states of Maryland and Virginia. The District of Columbia was named after Christopher Columbus who discovered the continent. The city itself was named after George Washington, the first president of the United States of America. Washington, D. C., the first city specially planned and built as a national capital, was laid out by the French architect, Pierre L'Enfant, in 1791. It is considered one of the most beautiful capitals in the world.

Washington is the seat of the U. S. government. Here we can find the White House — the official presidential residence and the nation's most popular tourist attraction, the **Capitol** — the seat of the Senate and the House of Representatives, the **Pentagon** — the center of the military establishment and the headquarters of the Federal Bureau of

Investigation, and so on.

As a leading cultural center, Washington boasts numerous museums, theaters and centers of interest. The most famous are the **Washington Monument**, the **Lincoln Memorial**, the **Jefferson Memorial**, the **Kennedy Theater** and the **Library of Congress**.

## New York City

**New York City**, the largest city and home of the United Nations, is located in New York State. It is the commercial and financial center of the United States. The city is composed of five boroughs: **Manhattan**, the Bronx, Queen's, Brooklyn and Richmond, covering an area of 789 square kilometers with a population of 8,537,673.

Manhattan, famous for its massive skyscrapers, is the smallest but best-known among the five boroughs. The **Empire State Building** has 102 stories, with 380 meters in height. The **World Trade Center** had 110 stories and was 419 meters high, but was destroyed on September 11, 2001. Famous stages and motion picture theaters are mainly located around **Broadway** in Midtown which includes the famous **Times Square**.

New York is the largest seaport in America. Nearly 40% of U.S. foreign trade passes through its port. Near the gate of New York Harbor, there is a small island called Liberty Island and on this island stands the **Statue of Liberty** given by French as a gift and remains the most important landmark of New York.

New York City is the business and financial center of the world. Many leading joint corporations place their headquarters in New York. **Wall Street** is America's financial center. The famous **New York Stock Exchange** is diagonally across the street.

New York is also the home of various industries like machinery manufacture, chemical production, textiles, garment industry, and electronics industry.

In New York City we can also find Chinatown, the **Fifth Ave** and more than 100 colleges and universities. Examples are **New York University** — the nation's largest private university and **Columbia University** — the oldest, wealthiest, and most famous institution of higher education in New York.

### Boston

**Boston** is on a small peninsula in the middle of Massachusetts' Atlantic Coast, a little over 320 kilometers northeast of New York City. It is a fine natural harbor and one of the largest seaports in the United States. The city was founded in 1630 and is one of the earliest major cities settled by English Protestants.

Boston has three major industries: financial services, health care industry and high-technology. There are many universities and colleges in Boston area, such as **Harvard University**, **Yale University** and **Massachusetts Institute of Technology** (MIT).

### Los Angeles

**Los Angeles** is the largest city in the state of California and the second largest in the United States. Often nicknamed the **City of Angels**, Los Angeles is the seat of Los Angeles County, the most populated and one of the most diverse counties in the United States. In 2015, Los Angeles ranked the seventh in a list of the world's most economically powerful city pruduced by *The Atlantic*, ahead of Shanghai and Toronto, but behind New York and London.

Los Angeles, first founded by a Spanish explorer in 1542 and turned over to the United States of America in 1846, is located in southwestern California and on the Pacific Coast. The city has a two-season climate: summer and winter. Summer is usually hot and dry and winter is always wet and mild for most of the precipitation arrives in winter.

Los Angeles is an important center of industry, commerce and communication. The Los Angeles metropolitan area employs 30% of California's

workforce and generates nearly one-third of the value of goods manufactured in the state. Since the first American movie was made in Los Angeles in 1908, the city has remained the film center of the United States. **Hollywood** is a world-famous film producing center.

### San Francisco

**San Francisco** is located on the central part of the California shoreline. The city covers the tip of a 50-kilometer peninsula in Northern California, with the Pacific Ocean on the west and the San Francisco Bay to the north and east.

The city is the birthplace of the **United Nations Organization** which was first founded here in 1945.

In the San Francisco area, food-processing and shipbuilding are the main industries. In addition, it has the largest Chinese settlement in the United States of America.

> **? Group presentation:**
>
> As world-wide communication capabilities have developed, world-class cities have been well known by people around the world. Divide the class into several groups, and make a presentation about one city that you like.

---

## Exercises

### I. Fill in the blanks.

1. The economic system of the United States is known as _____ because everyone is free to start an enterprise.
2. Private business in America can be divided into two types according to their size: _____ and _____.
3. Giant corporations account for less than _____ of all businesses, but they generate about _____ of all business income of the United States.
4. There are two forms of small businesses: _____ and _____.
5. The small businesses are mostly _____ and _____ providers.
6. The South's leading industries are those that make use of the _____ supply of natural resources and _____ materials.
7. Washington, D.C., the capital of the U.S., is situated on the _____ River banks.
8. _____ is a symbol of American theater and world-class entertainment.
9. The world-famous Harvard University is in _____.
10. In the United States, _____ is a leading commercial crop in the South.

### II. Define the following terms.

1. monopolized capitalist
2. corporations
3. proprietorships
4. Space City of the U.S.A.
5. free enterprise system

### III. Multiple choice.

1. The following are the factors that have contributed to the development of the U.S. economy EXCEPT _____.
   A. the vast space and resources of the land
   B. the ideals of freedom and economic opportunity
   C. English as its national language
   D. hard work by the people
2. _____ is the largest city and the chief port of the United States.
   A. Washington, D.C.
   B. Los Angeles
   C. San Francisco
   D. New York City
3. Washington, D.C. is named after _____.
   A. the U.S. President George Washington
   B. Christopher Columbus
   C. both George Washington and Christopher Columbus
   D. none of them
4. The United States is the world's largest consumer of _____.
   A. coal
   B. nuclear power

     C．gas              D．petroleum
5. The United States produces as much as half of the world's _____.
     A．wheat and rice     B．cotton
     C．tobacco           D．soybeans and corn
6. The total value of manufacturing output ranks _____ in the world.
     A．first             B．second
     C．third            D．fourth
7. Hollywood, the center of American movie industry, is closest to _____．
     A．Los Angles        B．Chicago
     C．New York         D．Washington
8. The financial, manufacturing and transportation center of the United States is _____．
     A．New York         B．Washington, D. C.
     C．Philadelphia      D．Chicago
9. _____, with the nickname of "Space City of U.S.A.", is administered by the National Aeronautics and Space Administration (NASA).
     A．Detroit           B．Houston
     C．Los Angeles      D．San Francisco
10. The Midwest is America's most important _____ area.
     A．agricultural
     B．industrial
     C．manufacturing
     D．mining industry

## IV. Translate the following terms into English.
1. 纽约证券交易所
2. 百老汇
3. 自由女神像
4. 联邦调查局
5. 第五大街

## V. Answer the following questions in a few sentences.
1. Please list some factors which contribute to the fast development of American economy.

2. What kind of economic system does the United States have?

3. What role does the U. S. government play in developing national economy?

4. Why is manufacturing important in the U. S. ?

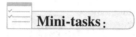 

**Mini-tasks:**

1. Presentation: As the capital of the United States, Washington, D. C. is a national center for historic sites and museums, arts, national and international media, and sports, as it is home to five major professional men's teams. Make detailed travel guidance for foreigners in PPT form.

2. As the home base of Hollywood, Los Angles is known as the "Entertainment Capital of the World", leading the world in creation of motion pictures, television production and recorded music. In Hollywood, many historic Hollywood theaters are used as venues and concert stages to premiere major theatrical releases and host the Academy Awards. It is a popular destination for nightlife, tourism and is home to the Hollywood Walk of Fame. Hollywood is also a district of Los Angles. Although it is not the typical practice of the city of Los Angeles to establish specific boundaries for districts or neighborhoods, Hollywood is a recent exception.

    Movies made by Hollywood always get high recognition and are often considered as top-level works. Besides, movie stars take working for Hollywood as the highest honor in their career lives. Numerous movie directors and stars have achieved success and made their dreams to be an actor or actress come true here. Which movie and movie star do you like? Make a brief description and comment on it.

# Chapter Four  Education and Social Life

*Education in the United States is mainly provided by the public sector, with control and funds from three levels: the federal, state, and local. America has compulsory education, but the three levels are different. Find out in which part they are different through the Internet, movies, books, documents, and so on.*

## Part One  American Education

The United States does not have a unified national educational system. American public education is operated by state and local governments and regulated by the **American Department of Education** through restrictions on federal grants. However, education has been greatly respected throughout the American history. Even before the revolution, several outstanding colleges had been founded. Americans believe that education is indispensable to becoming a qualified citizen. In order to promote the proper development of the nation, each citizen should receive a quality education as much as possible. The fourth president, James Madison once said: "Knowledge will forever govern ignorance."

Each state has its own laws on education. Some laws are similar while others are different. American schools highly value the "learning by inquiry and doing" approach and Americans pay more attention to practical skills than pure theory. Children are required in most states to attend school from the age of six or seven (generally kindergarten or first grade) until eighteen (generally the end of high school) while some states allow students to leave school at sixteen or seventeen. About 12% of children are enrolled in parochial or nonsectarian private schools, over 2% of children home-schooled. The United States has many competitive private and public institutions of higher education, as well as local community colleges of varying quality with open admission policies. The basic literacy rate is approximately 99%. The United Nations assigns the United States an Education Index of 0.97, making it the twelfth-best in the world.

### Elementary and Secondary Education

In America, most state schools offer ten years of education and some twelve. Many children begin their school education at the age of six and usually graduate from high school at eighteen. Children of five years old have to attend kindergarten for one year in many states.

There are two kinds of elementary and secondary schools in the United States: **public schools** and **private schools**. Public schools are supported by taxpayers and children can study there without any charge. Private schools are run by churches and other organizations. Children who study there have to pay tuition fees, but the teaching quality is generally more consistent and much better.

Without national curriculum in the United States, the subjects in elementary and secondary schools vary from state to state except for basic subjects.

After pupils finish elementary and middle school education, they go to high schools automatically without any entrance examinations. The high school students have to take 17.5 units of course work on average. Each unit equals about 120 hours of class in one subject. Students who want to go to university usually have to take 20 units.

In most high schools, except for general education, one can also take part in vocational training to pursue their interests or a specific occupation on condition that prerequisite units have been completed successfully.

### Higher Education

States and large cities operate their own universities, colleges and other institutions of higher learning. The term "college" refers to an institution requiring a secondary school certificate for admission and colleges offer only undergraduate courses. A college may or may not be a part of a university. A university may have many branches. In the United States, there are public and private universities and colleges. **Public universities** make up nearly 47% of the total and they receive financial assistance from the government. **Private universities**, open to all, are operated by religious and other organizations. But the academic programs are similar in both public and private universities.

Private universities and colleges are generally smaller in size and population but more numerous than public ones. As some prestigious private institutions don't enjoy tax support, the students have to pay a high tuition.

There are three types of institutions of higher

education in America.

A two-year college, serving as a bridge connecting secondary schools and universities, is called a "community college", most of which are established and controlled by public authorities.

A four-year college which is smaller than a university with smaller classes is often called a "liberal arts college" or a "college of arts and science". Commonly, the four-year colleges offer degrees of the **Bachelor of Arts** (BA) and the **Bachelor of Science** (BS).

A university, more comprehensive and complex than any other higher educational institutions, usually consists of many colleges and its curriculum is broader and deeper. Besides, many universities have one or more professional schools and pursue a variety of research activities in various fields.

About one-third of American high school graduates receive higher education. To gain admission to universities, applicants should take the **Scholastic Aptitude Tests** (SATS). First-year students of prestigious universities are usually chosen on the basis of the following aspects: **high school records**, **recommendations** from their high school teachers, **performance on SATS**, and **impressions** made during interviews at the university.

In 2014, 47.97% of enrolled students graduated from college in four years. Forty-five percent of students completed their undergraduate requirements in six years at the same college they first enrolled in.

One of the measurements for an undergraduate in academic progress is credit hours earned. One credit usually equals one hour of class lecture or two or three hours of experiments per week for a semester (about 16 weeks).

It is commonplace for students to earn money not only on vacation but also often in their spare time during the term. Even students from relatively wealthy families take part-time jobs in restaurants or supermarkets. Students often get funds for their tuition and living expenses. More importantly, part-time jobs can cultivate self-reliance.

Many students are very interested in students' organizations which play an important role in university life. Each student union election is taken seriously and each member has to obey the rules of the union.

> **? Questions for discussion:**
> As is known, education in the West is different from that in the East, think about the following questions:
> 1. What advantages and disadvantages does America's education system have?
> 2. What is America's educational concept?
> 3. What can we learn from their educational system?

## Part Two  Employment and Social Welfare

### Employment in America Today

Labor force and their productivity help determine the health of American economy. Throughout its history, the United States has experienced steady growth in labor force. Shortly after World War I, most workers were immigrants or their immediate descendants from Europe, or African Americans who were mostly slaves, or slave descendants. In the early 20th century, many Latin Americans immigrated, followed by large numbers of Asians because of removal of nation-origin based on immigration quotas. The promise of high wages brings many highly skilled workers from around the world to the United States.

Labor mobility is important for the capacity of economy to adapt to changing conditions. When immigrants flooded into labor markets on the East Coast, many workers moved inland, often to farmland waiting to be employed. Similarly, economic opportunities in industrial northern cities attracted African Americans from southern farms in the first half of the 20th century.

In 2019, 157.56 million people were employed with earnings, of which 80% worked in full-time jobs. The majority were employed in the service sector. For approximately 126 million people, health care and social assistance are the leading field of employment. About 10.5% of American workers are unionized, compared to 30% in Western Europe. The U.S. ranks number one in the ease of hiring and firing workers, according to the **World Bank**. Between 1973 and 2003, a year's work for an average American grew by 199 hours. As a result, the United States maintains the highest labor productivity in the world. However, it no longer leads the world in productivity per hour as it did from the 1950s to the early 1990s and workers in Norway, France, Belgium, and Luxembourg are now more productive.

The United States ranks third in the World Bank's Ease of Doing Business Index. Compared to Europe, U.S. property and corporate income taxes are generally higher, while labor and, particularly, consumption taxes are lower.

### Types of Social Welfare

The United States started its social welfare system in the 1930s and has extended it ever since. The modern American believes that the government is responsible for the welfare of every citizen and everyone is entitled to get help if he has lost his job through no fault of his own. The United States can hardly be called a welfare state when compared with European countries, where half of the workers' income comes from pensions and social benefits. However, the expenditure on social welfare programs in the United States is also very large. The government's expenditure on social welfare programs has far outstripped that on military.

Government provides a "Safety Not" for individuals who cannot or will not adequately care for themselves. **Social Security**, financed by a tax on employers and employees, accounts for the largest portion of Americans' retirement income. The first systematic arrangements for Social Security were made by the *Social Security Act of 1935* attempting to deal with the effects of the Depression at that time: It provided old-age and unemployment insurance, living allowances for mothers and children and assistance for the poor. Today, anyone who works has to pay proportional income taxes until retirement age, which can be divided into seven grades: 10%, 15%, 25%, 28%, 33%, 35%, and 39.6% of the wages or salary. At the appropriate retirement age, workers are entitled to receive a monthly Social Security payment. Disabled workers and their children can also receive support payments. In addition, people whose income is below the poverty line can also receive monthly welfare payments.

One of the greatest misfortunes in the United States is to fall ill. Hospital costs are surprisingly high. To solve this problem, the United States set up a mixed system of private and government responsibility for health care. According to the plan, the individual has to pay a monthly fee to the health insurance company. Once he is ill, the company will pay most major medical costs, subject to certain conditions.

The **Medicare program** restricted to the disabled and the elderly (62 years of age for women and 65 for men) is completely financed by the government. In many states, the government maintains institutions for the mentally ill or people with severe disabilities. Although Medicare pays the major share of the cost of any illness requiring hospitalization, it does not offer adequate protection for long-term illness or mental illness. Many people subscribe to private insurance companies for personal coverage.

The federal government provides **food stamps** to help poor families obtain food and the federal and state governments jointly provide welfare grants to support low-income parents with children. Food stamps are a special stamp equivalent to cash with which the poor can buy food at any store. School breakfast and lunch programs are financed by the government to provide free meals for school children from low income families. Public housing programs financed by the government provide apartment buildings to people with low income.

Many of these programs, including Social Security, trace their roots to the New Deal programs of Franklin D. Roosevelt, the U.S. president from 1933 to 1945.

Many other assistance programs for individuals and families, including Medicare and **Medicaid**, began in the 1960s during President Lyndon Johnson's (1963–1969) War on Poverty. Although some of these programs encountered financial difficulties in the 1990s and various reforms were proposed, these programs continued to get strong support from both of the American major political parties. Critics argued, however, that providing welfare to unemployed but healthy individuals actually created dependency rather than solving problems. Welfare reform legislation (the *Personal Responsibility and Work Opportunity Act*) passed in 1996 under President Bill Clinton (1993–2001) and a Republican Congress requires people to work, search job, enter training, or receive education as a condition of receiving benefits and imposes federal limits on how long individuals may receive payments.

> **? Group discussion:**
> Compared with developing countries, America has a more effective social welfare system. Could you give some examples about its social welfare in different states and their roles in people's daily life through TV reports, newspapers and other resources available?

## Exercises

### Ⅰ. Fill in the blanks.

1. American public education is operated by _____ and _____.
2. Formal education in the United States consists of elementary, _____ and _____ education.
3. The fourth U. S. president, _____ once said, "Knowledge will forever govern ignorance."
4. The value of American schools is "_____".
5. About _____ of children are enrolled in parochial or nonsectarian private schools.
6. In America, most state schools offer _____ years of education and some _____.
7. There are two kinds of elementary and secondary schools in the United States: _____ and _____.
8. Without _____ in the United States, the subjects in elementary and secondary schools vary from state to state except some basic subjects.
9. The first systematic arrangements for Social Security were made in _____.
10. The modern Americans believe that _____ is responsible for the welfare of every citizen and everyone is entitled to get help if he has lost his job through no fault of his own.

### Ⅱ. Define the following terms.

1. food stamps
2. public schools
3. private schools
4. college
5. the Medicare program

### Ⅲ. Multiple choice.

1. The functions of institutions of higher education in the U. S. are _____.
   A. research and teaching
   B. teaching and degree awarding
   C. professional training, teaching and public service
   D. teaching, research and public service
2. Most of the colleges and universities in the U. S. are located _____.
   A. in only 5 or 6 states along the Atlantic coast
   B. in the South
   C. in states with a large population
   D. along the Atlantic and Pacific coasts
3. The typical organizational pattern for elementary and secondary schools in the United States is that of _____.
   A. classified schools   B. vocational schools
   C. graded schools   D. public schools
4. The expenditure in American public schools is guided or decided by _____.
   A. teachers   B. students
   C. the headmaster   D. boards of education
5. Which of the following statements about American education is wrong?
   A. Elementary and secondary education in America is free and compulsory.
   B. Private schools are financially supported by religious or nonreligious private organizations or individuals.
   C. There are more public colleges and universities than the private ones.
   D. Credits taken at community colleges are normally applicable to requirement for a four-year bachelor's degree.

### Ⅳ. Translate the following terms into English.

1. 学生能力测试
2. 社会保障
3. 学士学位
4. 社保法案
5. 世界银行

### Ⅴ. Answer the following questions in a few sentences.

1. What is the general view of the Americans on education?

2. What are some of the characteristics of American education?

3. What is the social welfare of the U. S. A. ?

### Mini-tasks:

Harvard University is a private university located in Cambridge, Massachusetts and a member of the Ivy League. Established in 1636 by the colonial Massachusetts legislature, Harvard is the oldest institution of higher learning in the United States and currently comprises ten separate academic units. It is also the first and oldest corporation in the United States.

Harvard has the second-largest financial endowment of any non-profit organization (behind the Bill & Melinda Gates Foundation), standing at $26 billion as of September 2009. Harvard is consistently ranked at the top as a leading academic institution in the world by numerous media and academic rankings.

1. As an academic and research university, Harvard

University makes a set of rules and requirements for new learners and students in school. Applications from foreign students for Harvard are especially difficult. Select relevant information about requirements and examinations to study in Harvard University for foreign students.

2. Compared with Britain's famous universities — Cambridge University and Oxford University, what similarities and differences do they have in educational concepts, curriculum arrangements, graduation qualifications and intelligence requirements?

■ VOLUME TWO  The United States of America

# Chapter Five  History

## Part One  The Thirteen Colonies and the War of Independence

> In the very beginning, the United States only had 13 colonies, which were established by Great Britain. To gain familiarity with the history of the U.S., try to answer the questions as follows:
> 1. How was the New World discovered?
> 2. What are the names of the first 13 colonies which contributed to the establishment of America?
> 3. Why did the colonies decide to unite together and revolt to win their independence?

The first known inhabitants of the modernday United States territory are believed to have arrived from sometime prior to 15,000 years ago by crossing the Bering land bridge into Alaska. Solid evidence of these cultures settling in what would become the U.S. is dated to at least 14,000 years ago. It was said that Chinese may have arrived on the American Continent some 4,500 years ago and recorded it specifically. Some descriptions about the Five Lakes and the Mississippi region are found in the Chinese book *Shan Hai Jing*. In the 5th century, Chinese Buddhists were reported to have set foot on Mexico traveling along Alaska. In addition, a Fusang country in the Chinese book *Liang Shu* was viewed highly similar to the present-day Mexico in terms of location and custom.

Columbus' men, Spain's navigators, were the first documented people of the Old World to land on the territory of the United States when they arrived in Puerto Rico during their second voyage in 1493. Juan Ponce de León, who arrived in Florida in 1513, is credited as being the first European to reach modern-day U.S. territory, although some evidence suggests that John Cabot might have reached what is presently New England in 1498.

### Columbus Discovering the New World

**Christopher Columbus** (1451-1506), born in Genoa, Italy, went to Portugal in 1476. He believed that the earth was round, but he also thought the earth was much smaller than it is. In time, **Queen Isabella** of Spain supported and paid for Columbus' voyage.

On August 3, 1492, Columbus set sail with three ships: the Nina, the Santa Maria and the Pinta. He and his sailors overcame countless difficulties and finally on October 12, they landed at San Salvador. Convinced he had arrived in Asia, an area the Spanish referred to as the Indies, Columbus called the local

people "Indians" and named the island the West Indies. Columbus made three more voyages between 1493 and 1504, and on his third voyage in 1498, he discovered the mainland of South America for the first time. He died in 1506, never realizing that he had discovered a new continent.

Another important figure in the process of the discovery of the New World was **Amerigo Vespucci**, an Italian navigator. He drew the conclusion in 1500 that a new continent rather than Asia had been discovered. The proposal to name the new continent America was first put forward by the German geographer Martin Waldseemuller. The proposal was accepted and the name of America gradually came into use and became known as the New World, while Europe was seen as the Old World.

The discovery of the New World was of great importance. Not only did it widen people's horizons, but it opened up fresh ground for the rising bourgeoisie. It promoted commerce, sea navigation and industry and paved the way for early capitalism.

> **? Question for presentation:**
> During the voyage of Columbus, there were many interesting stories and hardships. Search for some detailed information about this voyage via documents and books, then make a presentation about your findings.

### The Founding of the Colonies

⊙ Spanish and French colonization

After the discovery of the New World, the

European powers sent many explorers to the new continent and they began to compete with each other for territory in the New World.

Spanish explorers came to what is now the United States beginning with Christopher Columbus' second expedition. The first confirmed landing in the continental United States was by a Spaniard, **Juan Ponce de León**, who landed in 1513 on a lush shore he christened La Florida.

Within three decades after Ponce de León's landing, the Spanish became the first Europeans to reach the Appalachian Mountains, the Mississippi River, the Grand Canyon and the Great Plains. In 1540, **De Soto** undertook an extensive exploration of the present U. S. and, in the same year, **Francisco Vázquez de Coronado** led 2,000 Spaniards and Mexican Indians across the modern Arizona-Mexico border and traveled as far as central Kansas. Other Spanish explorers also came onto the land successively.

The Spanish created the first permanent European settlement in the continental United States at St. Augustine, Florida in 1565. Later Spanish settlements included Santa Fe, San Antonio, Tucson, San Diego, Los Angeles and San Francisco. Most Spanish settlements were along California coast or **Santa Fe River** in New Mexico.

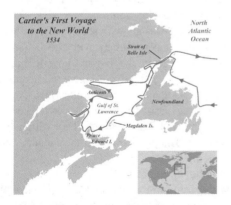

New France was the area colonized by France in North America during a period extending from the exploration of the St. Lawrence River by **Jacques Cartier** in 1534, to the cession of New France to Spain and Britain in 1763. In 1712 (before the *Treaty of Utrecht*), the territory of New France once extended from Newfoundland to the Rocky Mountains and from Hudson Bay to the Gulf of Mexico. The territory was divided into five colonies, each with its own administration: Canada, Acadia, Hudson Bay, Newfoundland and Louisiana.

⊙ The First Thirteen Colonies

Most of the early Spanish explorers and colonists were driven by desire for wealth and glory. Not finding riches, the Spanish turned to agriculture. But in 1588, the Spanish were soundly defeated by the English navy. The English began to settle in the New World.

English colonies in America were divided into three kinds: **royal colony**, **proprietary colony** and **charter colony**. Most of the colonies, such as New York, New Jersey, were royal colonies, in which the king himself appointed the governor.

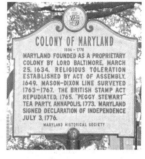

Proprietary colonies, such as Pennsylvania and Maryland, were colonies founded by individuals in which the governors were appointed by the proprietors and granted by the king. Charter colonies were established by charter or permit, given by the monarch to a group of merchants.

The first successful English colony in North America was established on James River at Jamestown by the Virginia Company of London in 1607. The first group of 104 colonists were not financially successful, and unfortunately, most of them died of hunger and illness. Later, they settled the problem of subsistence by growing corn and got a harvest. They expanded their territory to make more profit, but colony was defined by a severe labor shortage that gave birth to forms of non-free labor, such as slavery and **indentured servitude**, and by a British policy of benign neglect that permitted the development of an American spirit distinct from that of European founders. The first colony languished for decades until a new wave of settlers arrived in the late 17th century and established commercial agriculture based on tobacco. King James I encouraged foreign expansion as a way of easing religious disputes and economic distress in England. Between the late 1610s and the Revolution, the British shipped an estimated 50,000 convicts to its American colonies.

One of the conflicts between Native Americans and English settlers was the **Powhatan Uprising** in Virginia in 1622, in which Native Americans killed hundreds of English settlers. The largest conflict in the 17th century was **King Philip's War** in New

England.

The **Plymouth Colony** was established in 1620. The area of New England was initially settled primarily by Puritans who established the Massachusetts Bay Colony in 1630. The Middle Colonies, consisting of the present-day states of New York, New Jersey, Pennsylvania, and Delaware, were characterized by a large degree of diversity. The first English settlement south of Virginia was the Province of Carolina, with Georgia Colony the last of the thirteen colonies established in 1733. Methodism became the prevalent religion among colonial citizens after the First Great Awakening, a religious revival led by a preacher Jonathan Edwards in 1734.

The colonies of other nations came under the control of Great Britain one after another. In 1776, there were thirteen British colonies in that part of America, which later became the first thirteen states of the United States. They were Virginia, Massachusetts, Maryland, Rhode Island, Connecticut, New Hampshire, Delaware, North and South Carolina, New York, New Jersey, Pennsylvania and Georgia.

## The Early Immigrants

The early settlers in 13 colonies were from different European countries, mainly from England, with different reasons. Those from England became known as the White Anglo-Saxon Protestants (WASP).

⊙ The Pilgrims

Religious disputes in England were one of the reasons causing people to flee to America. The Anglican Church persecuted not only the Catholics but also the Protestant extremists, like the Puritans.

In 1620, a ship named Mayflower with 102 passengers sailed from England to the New World. The Pilgrims, constituting nearly half of the passengers on Mayflower, were the first Puritans to settle in North America. They had suffered greatly in England because of their religious beliefs. Now they were heading for Virginia where they hoped to worship as they pleased.

Unfortunately, Mayflower ran into storms in the Atlantic and the ship was blown off. The Pilgrims, instead of arriving in Virginia, landed on the sandy coast of Cape Cod.

Far from Virginia, they decided to set up their own government. They reached an agreement called the **Mayflower Compact** which was signed by all adult male passengers on the ship. They would elect their own leaders and make laws. It is the first time that colonists had planned to govern themselves.

In fact, the Pilgrims were now in "Plymouth", a place John Smith had explored and named some years before. There was a clearing in the land and a permanent English settlement in New England.

Nearly half the Mayflower's passengers died in the first icy winter and some became sick. The food they had brought was almost used up. Those who had survived signed a peace treaty with the Indians. The Pilgrims learned from the Indians how to hunt wild turkey and deer, and how to plant corn and catch fish. They had a harvest of corn in the summer of 1621. On the last Thursday in November, they celebrated the first **Thanksgiving Day** with a feast to thank God for His protection and the Indians who had helped them.

⊙ Other Immigrants

With virgin soil and resources, the New World attracted many people hoping to become rich quickly and poor people suffering from illness, hunger or debt. Most of the poor went to America as **indentured servants** — people who couldn't afford ship tickets promised to serve for a period of usually seven years in return for the passage across the Atlantic. They could be sold like slaves, and could be free if they survived the indenture period, but many died before they regained freedom.

There were also a large number of convicts among the early settlers. In this thinly-populated wild world, labor meant wealth. The colonial companies and merchants persuaded the English government to transport convicts to America. This took a burden off the English government and gave cheap labor to the colonies. After serving their term, these convicts would become free men with their own land.

> **? Question for discussion:**
> Thanksgiving Day, the last Thursday in November, is an important holiday to Americans. But how did it come into being and what's the significance of it? Search for information about the origins of other holidays, such as Easter, Halloween and April Fool's Day.

### Relations Between England and the Colonies

The colonies founded and granted by the English Monarch were still regarded as English subjects. But for most of the 17th century, the English government was busy with domestic problems — the English Bourgeois Revolution reached its climax with the execution of Charles I, and failed to formulate a well-founded and consistent policy for the colonies.

Each colony made full use of this opportunity to develop and followed its own plan. As the colonies grew in population and wealth, they relied less on England for food, clothing and protection.

However, to take more profits out of its colonies, England exercised increasingly strict policies on the colonial people. The English government passed a series of trade regulations known as the *Navigation Acts* between 1651 and 1696. According to these acts, goods shipped to the colonies must be from England. If not, the colonies had to pay a heavy tax on their imports. This aroused the resistance of the colonists.

### Conflicts Leading to Armed Revolution

Former English colonies became British colonies as the Kingdom of Britain was founded in 1707.

By 1733, British settlers had occupied the Atlantic Coast while France controlled Canada, Louisiana and the entire watershed of the Mississippi River. But a series of conflicts between the British and the French culminated in the **French and Indian War** (1754 – 1763) in which Britain, with its American colonial allies, emerged victorious. France ceded Canada and the Ohio territories east of the Mississippi River to Britain in 1763 under the *Peace Treaty of Paris*.

The British government was in debt after the war with France, so the government continued to strengthen its control over 13 American colonies.

In 1763, the King of Great Britain and King of Ireland, **George III** and his Prime Minister, **George Granville** made three important decisions: raising the import taxes and taxing more goods; closing the frontier to further settlement and placing an army of 20,000 men in America to "protect" American colonies. Two years later, the **Stamp Act** was also carried out by English Parliament. According to this act, stamp paper must be used for all legal documents, pamphlets, newspapers and other articles. People of the colonies grew indignant with the *Stamp Act* and rose to oppose it. When the time came for the law to go into effect and stamps to be sold, nobody sold them and no one bought them.

With the suggestion of Massachusetts, delegates were chosen from nine of the colonies to hold a **Stamp Act Congress** in New York in 1765, protesting against the Act and declared that the colonies could not be taxed by anybody except their own colonial assemblies. Parliament heeded their protests and repealed the *Stamp Act*. However, it enforced the **Quartering Act**, enacted taxes on tea and other goods. When the colonists refused to obey, the British sent soldiers to Boston.

Soon all British taxes were removed except that on tea, which aimed at reminding the colonies that Parliament had right to tax them. In 1773, "Boston Tea Party" broke out. The British government allowed the East India Company to sell its tea to the colonies free of import duty, which enraged the colonial merchants. They strongly protested this unequal treatment. On the night of December 16, a group of men disguising as Indians destroyed the tea cargo in Boston Harbor.

As a punishment on Boston people, English Parliament passed five bills in the spring of 1774. First, the **Boston Port Bill** closed the harbor. Second, town meetings could not be held without the prior written approval of the governor. Third, a new act permitted the quartering of troops in private homes. Fourth, the king would appoint the Council elected by the House. Fifth, the Ohio River region was assigned to Quebec and this limited the westward expansion of New England. These acts, generally known as the "**five intolerable acts**", aroused much stronger indignation within all the colonial people, who immediately went into action by sending money and various supplies to the Boston people.

### The First Continental Congress

In September 1774, representatives from 12 colonies (no representatives from Georgia) met in Philadelphia "to consult upon the present unhappy state of the colonies". It was the first meeting of the **Continental Congress**. Most delegates of this congress decided to support the city of Boston and break with Britain. The Congress issued a call for a boycott of trade, including both imports and exports, between the colonies and Britain. The Continental Congress drew up the **Declaration of Rights and Grievances** that requested protection of rights of the colonies from **George III**.

The declaration was rejected by English Parliament. By the end of 1774, conflicts between the colonies and Britain had become unavoidable because the British Government seemed unwilling to make any significant concessions. The Continental Congress agreed to raise a volunteer army, including radical opponents

of English rule and members of the **Sons of Liberty**, to protect the colonies if Britain used force to break the boycott. It was said that the volunteers could be ready to fight in only one minute, so they were nicknamed minutemen.

### The First Armed Clash

The first armed clash occurred in Boston area on April 19, 1775. When General **Thomas Gage**, Governor of Massachusetts, learned that the colonial revolutionaries were removing weapons and munitions from the arsenal in a small town of **Concord**, he ordered the British troops to take away the guns and supplies that the colonists had stored. The town got the news once the British troops left Boston.

In **Lexington**, Massachusetts, American minutemen were forced to withdraw after shots broke out, while at Concord, farmers shot back at British troops who were defeated and retreated to Boston that night.

The news of fighting at Lexington and Concord flew across the 13 colonies. Within 20 days all the 13 colonies witnessed a general agitation against the British troops and officers. On March 23, 1775, Patrick Henry called for independence at the convention of Virginia. His closing words "give me liberty, or give me death" became the call for colonists to pursue freedom and independence.

### The Declaration of Independence

**The Second Continental Congress** was held in

Philadelphia in May 1775. The colonists had not yet decided to break away from Britain. However, they realized they needed a regular army to defend themselves against British troops. The congress decided to take charge of the troops around Boston and to appoint George Washington as the commander. This showed that the Americans had made up their mind to fight for their freedom and independence.

However, the British government didn't give in. The congress then appointed a committee of five members, including Thomas Jefferson, Benjamin Franklin, and John Adams, to draw up the **Declaration of Independence**. This declaration would announce to the world that the colonies meant to become a free and independent nation.

After three weeks' discussion, the committee worked out the famous document which was formally adopted on July 4, 1776, a day celebrated each year as **Independence Day** or **National Day** in the United States, although the states were at that time still dependent entities and not yet formally bound in a legal union. The Declaration of Independence was signed by representatives from all the colonies. The new nation was dedicated to principles of republicanism, which emphasized civic duty and a fear of corruption and hereditary aristocracy.

The Declaration made the struggling people believe that they should be independent and have right to enjoy liberty. As a result, they decided to go ahead to gain their independence by war. The Declaration not only had a great influence on the course of the war, but also had a far-reaching influence on the world history.

### The War of Independence

⊙ Process of the war

**The War of Independence** started in 1775 and ended in 1783, lasting nearly eight years.

At the beginning of the war, the colonies were not in a favorable position. Firstly, there was a sharp contrast in military strength between England and America. America's total population was only about 3 million while England had about 10 million. Secondly, their supplies were not enough for a long-time war while England was the strongest country at that time. England had the most advanced navy but the colonies nearly had nothing. The Americans, however, knew they were fighting a just war, so their morale was high.

Throughout 1775 and 1776, George Washington and his army met many problems. On one hand, the supplies were not enough; on the other hand, the states were more concerned with defending their own territory than sending their men to join the troops commanded by **General Washington**. The army still lacked the strength to repel major attacks of the English troops. As a result, the colonial army lost several battles.

In the spring of 1777, the British took the offensive with three armies. One led by **General Burgoyne**, advanced from Montreal along Lake Champlain to the Hudson Valley in New York. He met resistance everywhere on his way and was finally defeated in Saratoga by General Horatio Gates. This victory was a turning point for the Americans. It saved New York State and the whole of New England. Furthermore, it persuaded the French to join the war against Britain.

Americans could not win their independence entirely on their own. Foreign help was in need. Experienced soldiers from Germany and Poland served as officers in the Continental Army. The greatest help came from France. The French government sent an army of 6,000 soldiers together with a fleet of ships.

In 1778, the French army captured the British ships on their way to North America. This made it hard for the British to get fresh troops and supplies.

In the summer of 1781, the British troops decided to concentrate their efforts on Virginia — the largest and most centrally located colony. **Cornwallis**, a British general, moved his army to Yorktown surrounded by water on three sides. The French fleet broke the blockade set up by the British navy along the Atlantic coast and cut off the British supply line. George Washington drew most of his forces to Virginia. By October, the British troops had been trapped and had no way to escape. At Yorktown, on October 19, 1781, Cornwallis surrendered to George Washington.

After the surrender of Cornwallis at Yorktown, a peace negotiation was held and the final treaty was signed in Paris, which went into effect in 1783. The United States of America had won its independence.

⊙ Significance of the war

The American War of Independence was of great historical importance and influence. It marked a new beginning in American history and showed the world that a just cause will sooner or later win out while the unjust cause will surely lose. The victory of the Americans greatly influenced and encouraged the people in the colonies ruled by other nations in the possibilities of independence and promoted the national liberation struggle of other colonies in the world.

### ? Questions for discussion:

1. What caused the relations between Britain and the colonies to become worse and what led to the wars between them?
2. What was the influence and impact of the First Continental Congress on the British government as well as the colonies?
3. Try to search for relevant information about the Declaration of Independence.
4. What's the reason for the success of the War of Independence?

## Exercises

### I. Fill in the blanks.

1. It was _____ who first discovered the America in 1492.
2. The English colonies in America were divided into three kinds: _____, _____ and _____.
3. The first English colony was _____.
4. In 1620 some English Puritans sailed to Plymouth on a ship called _____.
5. Lexington Fire was the _____ of the War of Independence.
6. The War of _____ broke out in 1775 and ended in 1783.
7. On July 4, 1776, the document called the Declaration of _____ was accepted by the American Congress.
8. The American War of Independence shows that a _____ nation can defeat a _____ one.

### II. Define the following terms.

1. royal colony
2. proprietary colony
3. charter colony
4. the *Stamp Act*
5. indentured servant

### III. Multiple choice.

1. The history of the U. S. is generally agreed to have begun in _____.
   A. 1620   B. 1607   C. 1776   D. 1619
2. The following states are among the first thirteen colonies except _____.
   A. Maryland       B. South Carolina
   C. Delaware       D. Colorado
3. The First Continental Congress was held in _____ in September 1774.
   A. Philadelphia   B. Boston
   C. New York       D. Washington, D. C.
4. The battle of _____ marked the turning point of the War of Independence.
   A. New York       B. Saratoga
   C. Bunker Hill    D. Lexington
5. On October 19, 1781, the British General Cornwallis and his 7,000 men surrendered at _____.
   A. Yorktown       B. Boston
   C. Charleston     D. Saratoga
6. The Declaration of Independence was drafted by _____.
   A. James Madison
   B. Thomas Jefferson
   C. Alexander Hamilton
   D. George Washington
7. The important decision made at the Second Continental Congress was _____.
   A. the establishment of a continental army under the command of George Washington
   B. the adoption of the Constitution
   C. an appeal to the British king
   D. A and B

Ⅳ. **Translate the following terms into English.**
1. 《五月花号公约》
2. 《巴黎和约》
3. 《印花税法》
4. 自由之子
5. 独立宣言

Ⅴ. **Answer the following questions in a few sentences.**
1. Why did the early settlers come to America?

2. What were the causes of the War of Independence?

3. What was the significance of the War of Independence?

4. What is the Boston Tea Party?

| Part Two | **Appearance of the American Constitution and Territorial Expansion** |

*Although the 13 states won their independence, they were not united and closely organized. To make some rules for the new country, the 13 states first drew up their Articles of the Confederation in 1781 which marked the foundation of the United States of America. Subsequently, the Constitution was created and published and has been the guiding light of the government with amendments until now. Before reading the following text, differentiate the Confederation from the Constitution and explain why the Confederation was replaced by the Constitution.*

### The Confederation and the Constitution

The period from 1783 to 1789 was extremely important in the American history. After the War of Independence, Americans faced the situation of bringing into existence their country and government.

Near the end of the war, a committee was appointed to draw up a constitution to stipulate the governance of the United States. The committee produced the **Articles of the Confederation** which was accepted by all the states in 1781. Thus the United States was officially founded.

The Articles of the Confederation was unusual in many ways. First, it provided for no king. To avoid troubles with King George Ⅲ, the drafters decided to have a republic. Second, while the Articles created a central government in the form of Congress, the emphasis was still on state powers. Third, the Articles of the Confederation was a written constitution for the United States, which is the first written one in the world.

The Articles of the Confederation gave too little power to the central government. To protect their victory, prominent persons met to discuss the problems facing the nation. Attempts to outline and press reforms culminated in the Congress called the **Constitutional Convention** in Philadelphia, Pennsylvania on May 25, 1787. Fifty-five delegates from all the states except Rhode Island attended the Convention. George Washington was elected Chairman of the Convention.

However, as the Convention proceeded, the delegates found that it was impossible to solve the problem by only following the Articles of the Confederation. With the proposal of **James Madison**, known as "**Father of the U.S. Constitution**", the delegates began to secretly draw up a  new constitution because they had not been empowered by the states. The work of writing the Constitution was completed on September 17, 1787, which later became the **Constitution Day** in the United States.

The delegates agreed to the structure of the new government: The central government was divided into three branches checking and balancing each other, the executive, the legislative and the judicial; a system of federalism that guaranteed every state a republican government was adopted; the new government should be given adequate power.

Many problems were solved through compromise, like the allocation of seats in the Congress between the large states and the smaller ones. After a long and heated argument, a final agreement was reached. The Congress should be made up of two houses: the House of Representatives and the Senate. Each state would have an equal number of Senators while the number of representatives would be based on state population.

When the Constitution was placed before the people of the 13 states, it was supported by one group of people, headed by **Alexander Hamilton**, called the **Federalists**, while it also met strong opposition from another group, headed by Thomas Jefferson, known as the **Anti-federalists**.  The Anti-federalists, mostly small farmers and people with debts, criticized the draft Constitution for its limits of state power and individual's rights. After a long struggle, the first ten amendments, known as the *Bill of Rights*, were put into the Constitution in 1791.

The *Bill of Rights* offers protection of human rights and ensures that the Constitution guarantees freedom of religion, speech and the press, the right to keep and bear arms, the right against unreasonable searches and arrest, and the right against self-incrimination. The *Bill of Rights* helps to avoid arbitrary violations of human rights by the government.

According to the U.S. Constitution, the country's powers were separately given to the federal government and the states. The powers given to the federal government are known as delegated powers listed in the Constitution. All the powers not listed in the Constitution are reserved for the states. The states could pass state laws to deal with issues concerning people's living on condition that the laws do not contradict the federal laws.

The Constitution was the first constitution written in modern sense, because there was no written constitution at that time, even in Britain. It rejected one-man rule and carried out the principle that the government should serve the people.

> **? Questions for discussion:**
> 1. After the War of Independence, the American government set a series of rules to help the development of the unoccupied areas. What rules did the government make to attract people to cultivate those areas?
> 2. Under what condition was the Constitution made? What significance did it have to the country?

### Washington as the First President

After the making and adoption of the Constitution in 1788, the nation started a new government and New York was chosen as the temporary capital. **George Washington** — a renowned hero in the American Revolutionary War, commander-in-chief of the Continental Army and President of the **Constitutional Convention** — was elected the first president of the United States by a unanimous vote under the new U.S. Constitution which came into effect on April 30, 1789.

After his inauguration, Washington set up his Cabinet in which Thomas Jefferson was appointed Secretary of State dealing with foreign affairs, Alexander Hamilton as Secretary of the Treasury, Henry Knox as Secretary of War and Edmund Randolph as Attorney General. Besides, President Washington appointed the federal judges and set up the federal judicial system. The Federal Supreme Court consists of one chief justice and eight associate justices.

During Washington's administration, Hamilton proposed four plans. One was to place an excise tax on whiskey in order to meet financial needs of the federal government, which met strong opposition and led to the **Whiskey Rebellion** in 1794, that is, settlers in the Pennsylvania counties protested against a federal tax on liquor and distilled drinks. It was the first serious test of the federal government, but was successfully put down. The incident showed the strength of the federal government and proved federal authority in every part of the United States.

The second plan was to establish a national bank. The idea also caused heated debates. Opponents led by Jefferson feared that a strong central government could only benefit the wealthy class at the expense of small farmers. Besides, the Congress and the President were not entitled such power by the Constitution. Supporters led by Hamilton argued that the Congress and the President had such power because the power was implied in constitutional language as the Congress had the power "to make laws which shall be necessary and proper". In the end, Washington accepted the proposal, and Jefferson was so angry that he resigned his position as Secretary of State.

The different interpretations of the Constitution led to the emergence of party politics. Jefferson's supporters became known as the **Democratic Republicans**, forefather of the present-day Democratic Party and Hamilton's supporters as Federalists.

The third plan was to pay the public debt and the fourth plan proposed that the government assume debts of the states. The rich southern states supported the proposal on condition that the northern states agreed to establish the national capital in the south. Washington chose the capital site at the mouth of the Potomac River named the **District of Columbia** and placed it under the direct control of the U. S. Congress.

President Washington gave priority to economic development. When the French Revolution took place, he followed a neutral policy and refused to give a hand even though France had helped America win its independence. His neutral policy caused public dissatisfaction, but promoted rapid development of the nation.

As the first president of the United States, Washington was committed to the principles set out in the Constitution and abided by the law. After serving as President for eight years, he announced his resignation from the presidency in his farewell address, which was published in the newspaper *Independent Chronicle* on September 26, 1796. In his address, Washington settled the benefits of the federal government and the importance of religion and morality while warning against foreign alliances and the formation of political parties. After his retirement, he returned to Virginia without taking a pension and died there in 1799. He set a good example for limiting the presidential terms of office and was praised by the Americans as "the first man in peace, the first man in war".

### John Adams

**John Adams**, Jr., the eldest of three brothers, was born on October 30, 1735, in Braintree, Massachusetts. Adams's birthplace, North Braintree, became the town of Quincy, Massachusetts in 1792 and is now part of **Adams National Historical Park**. As one of the most influential Founding Fathers of the United States, John Adams served as the second president (1797–1801), after being the first Vice-President (1789–1797) for two terms.

Adams came to prominence in the early stages of the American Revolution. As a delegate from Massachusetts to the Continental Congress, he persuaded the Congress to adopt the Declaration of Independence in 1776. As a representative of the Congress in Europe, he was a major negotiator of the eventual peace treaty with Great Britain and chiefly responsible for obtaining important loans from Amsterdam.

He played a minor role in the politics of the early 1790s and was re-elected in 1792. Washington seldom asked Adams for advice on policy and legal issues during his tenure as Vice President. The subsequent vice presidents were also generally not powerful or significant members of their president's administrations until after World War II.

When Adams became the President, he realized that he needed to protect Washington's policy of staying out of the French and British war. After the *Jay Treaty*, the French became angry and began seizing American merchant ships trading with the British, which became known as the "**Quasi-War**". On one hand, Adams sent a commission to negotiate with France; on the other hand, he urged the Congress to expand navy and army in case of diplomatic failure. In 1798, Adams signed the *Alien and Sedition Acts* into law to protect the United States from enemy aliens and to prevent seditious attacks from weakening the government.

As President, Adams followed Washington's lead in making the presidency the example of republican values. Stressing civic virtue, he was never implicated in any scandal.

In 1799 the death of Washington weakened the Federalists, as they lost the man who symbolized and united the party. In the presidential election of 1800, Adams and his fellow Federalist candidate, Charles Cotesworth Pinckney, went against the Republican candidates Jefferson and Burr. In the end, Adams lost narrowly to Jefferson by 65 to 73 electoral votes. Just before his loss, he became the first president to occupy the new, but unfinished president's Mansion on November 1, 1800.

Causes of his defeat were distrust of him by "High Federalists" led by Hamilton, the popular disapproval of the *Alien and Sedition Acts*, the popularity of his opponent, Thomas Jefferson, and the effective politicking of Aaron Burr in New York State, where the legislature was shifted from Federalist to Democratic-Republican on the basis of a few wards in New York City controlled by Burr's fellows.

After Adams was defeated for re-election, he retired to Massachusetts. He and his wife Abigail Adams founded an accomplished family line of politicians, diplomats, and historians now as the Adams political family. His achievements have received greater recognition in modern times.

On July 4, 1826, the 50th anniversary of the adoption of the Declaration of Independence, Adams died at his home in Quincy. His last words are often quoted as "**Jefferson lives**", although only the word "Jefferson" was clearly intelligible. Adams was unaware that Jefferson, his compatriot in their quest for independence, once a great political rival, later a friend and correspondent, had died a few hours earlier on the very same day.

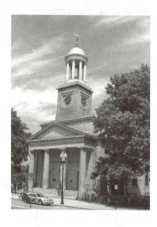

His crypt lies at the **United First Parish Church** (also known as the Church of the Presidents) in Quincy. Until his record was broken by Ronald Reagan in 2001, he had been the nation's longest-living president (90 years, 247 days) holding the record for 175 years. The record is currently held by former President Gerald Ford who died on December 26, 2006 at 93.

## The Administration of Thomas Jefferson

**Thomas Jefferson** was elected the third president in 1801. He was the first president inaugurated in the city of Washington and was the principal author of the Declaration of Independence (1776) and one of the most influential Founding Fathers for his promotion of the ideals of republicanism in the United States. During his presidency, great changes took place in almost every aspect in the United States.

Soon after he took the oath of office, Jefferson abolished the *Sedition Act*. He cut expenses in every department, lowered taxes, and reduced the army and navy.

In 1803, Jefferson successfully bought Louisiana from Napoleon who was then at war and needed more funds. It was first claimed by Spain and in 1800 was ceded to France.

The **Louisiana Purchase** was regarded as one of Jefferson's great achievements, for it doubled the country's territory. Consequently, the Mississippi River system came completely under the control of America. Cheap water transportation greatly influenced the agricultural and industrial production and many big cities sprung up in this area.

In March 1809, Jefferson left the presidency and James Madison was elected President.

Jefferson was a very important statesman in the American history. He chose the direction towards which the country should develop and his concept of equality and democracy had great influence on American values.

### ? Questions for discussion:

1. France once offered great help in the American War of Independence; accordingly, what policy did America take regarding the French Revolution, and why?
2. As the third president of America, Jefferson achieved great success in promoting progress of the country. Search for the information about what measures were taken to develop the country in the period of President Jefferson.

## The War with Britain Between 1812 and 1814

James Madison, the fourth president of the country, together with his predecessor Jefferson and the following president James Monroe shared similar viewpoints. They were all Democratic Republicans from Virginia. So the term **Virginia Dynasty** was later used to refer to the 24 consecutive years of their presidencies.

After James Madison was elected to be the President, he met a serious situation abroad. Relations with the British Empire were tense and a second war seemed inevitable.

Because of the higher pay and better working conditions of American sailors, many British seamen deserted and signed on American ships. The British troops then began to search American ships for British deserters. When the American ships refused to be searched, they were fired upon, which enraged the Americans.

After the purchase of Louisiana, the younger generation was eager to add Canada (controlled by Britain) to the north of the United States. As frontiersmen pushed deeper and deeper into Indian Territory in the west, wars with Indians broke out. Many Indians fled into Canada for protection.

At that time, Britain was at war with France. Relying on its large navy, the British government blocked all coastal trade between France and the neutrals, including America, which made it impossible for American farmers to export their farm products to France. The Congress, therefore, had to declare war against Britain on June 18, 1812.

Because of the great contrast in strength, many Americans, especially big bankers and merchants in New England, did not support the war. The Americans made attempts to invade Canada but failed. Still, the American warships' winning a battle on Lake Erie by defeating an British fleet encouraged the Americans and restored their confidence.

In August 1814, the British occupied the New York City and Washington, D. C. and the residence of the President was burned. The war lasted for more than two years without decisive victory for either country. On January 8, 1814, the *Treaty of Ghent* was signed. Officially ending the war, the treaty essentially resulted in the maintenance of the status quo ante bellum. However, crucially for the U. S., some native American tribes had to sign treaties with the U. S. government in response to their losses in the war. During the later course of the war, the Federalists held the Hartford Convention in 1814 over concerns that the war would weaken New England. They proposed seven constitutional amendments meant to strengthen the region politically, but once the Federalists delivered them to Washington, D. C., the recent American victories in New Orleans and the signing of the *Treaty of Ghent* undermined the Federalists' arguments and contributed to the downfall of the party.

The Second War with Britain has been called the Second War of Independence because of its great influence on the American history. It showed to the world that America had the ability to defend its sovereignty. Besides, the war united Americans and confirmed the importance of the Union and a strong government.

After the war, the United States was completely free from British control, resulting in a period of rapid development.

## The Monroe Doctrine

After the second war with England, America witnessed rapid economic development. However, some European colonies in South America began to revolt and started independence republics, like Mexico and Brazil. Some European countries formed a group seemingly to help America settle the revolutions. To defend America's interest, **James Monroe**, the fifth president of the United States,

carried out his new policy, known as the **Monroe Doctrine**, in 1823. The major points are as follows:

Any foreign interference with independent America would be an unfriendly act.

Any further colonization by foreign powers in the New World would be forbidden.

The United States ought not to interfere with any existing colonies in the New World.

The United States ought not to be involved in the affairs of European countries.

The Monroe Doctrine was adopted in response to fears of America and Britain about Russian and French expansion into areas of the Western Hemisphere. It was not until the Presidential Administration of Teddy Roosevelt that the Monroe Doctrine became a central tenet of American foreign policy. The Monroe Doctrine was then invoked in the Spanish-American War as well as later in the proxy wars between the United States and Soviet Union in Central America. It also had given essentially developing nations support from the United States and warned the powers in Europe to steer clear of far western affairs.

## Jackson and Spoils System

**Andrew Jackson** was elected President in 1828. Due to favor of agricultural development and the westward movement, farmers and frontiersmen supported him. Like Jefferson, Jackson preferred equality and simplicity. During his presidency, he stayed in touch with common

people and was considered as the first man in the White House to truly represent the common people. Also, he was the first American president who employed the power of veto in the process of making law.

In 1830, the Congress passed the **Indian Removal Act**, which authorized the President to negotiate treaties that exchanged Indian tribal lands in the eastern states for lands west of the Mississippi River. This established Andrew Jackson, a military hero and President, as a cunning tyrant in dealing with native populations. The act resulted most notably in forced migration of several native tribes to the West, with several thousand Indians dying on route, and the Creek Indian violent opposition and eventual defeat. The *Indian Removal Act* also directly caused the ceding of Spanish Florida and subsequently led to many Seminole Wars.

Jackson was also famous for his **spoils system**, the practice of appointing officials on the basis of political affiliation or personal relations without considering their merit and fitness for office. He put several hundred of his supporters into public office replacing federal employees soon after he became President.

> ### ? Questions for discussion:
> 1. During his administration, Adams advocated trade with Britain which even made France angry, because Britain was strong enough and it could offer great help in the development of America. However, during the period from 1812 to 1814, fierce wars between Britain and America broke out. Try to search out the reasons from the perspective of territory and business.
> 2. The spoils system was one of the actions Jackson took during his presidency. Make comment on the content of the spoils system by group discussion and cooperation through resources available.

### The Mexican War

Jackson favored the westward territorial expansion and the frontiersmen continued to move west causing Indians to be driven to the so-called "**Indian Reservations**". However, frontiersmen's aggressiveness did not stop; they still wanted to further expand their territory.

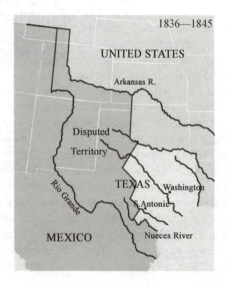

Texas, a territory controlled by Mexico in 1835, was the prelude to the Mexican War. The Americans living in Texas declared independence from Mexico and founded the Republic of Texas on March 1, 1836. President Jackson and many southerners had wanted to acquire Texas.

In 1845, the U. S. Congress brought Texas to the Union. Mexico soon protested. In May 1846, the American government sent troops to the border region between Texas and Mexico and war broke out. In September 1848, the capital of Mexico was occupied by American troops. The Mexican government was forced to capitulate. In February 1848, the war came to an end with the signing of an unequal treaty — ***Treaty of Guadalupe Hidalgo***. According to the treaty, America got nearly half of Mexican territory, including California and New Mexico at the price of $15 million. The territory of the United States now reached to the Pacific Coast.

### The Westward Movement

The purchase of Louisiana and the annexation of Texas doubled the territory of the United States. The vast land provided opportunities for people to become wealthy. As early as the 1820s, a flood of new immigrants from Europe came to the United States and the stream of immigration continued in the subsequent decades.

⊙ Causes of the Westward Movement

There are many reasons underlying the Westward Movement.

First, people living in the crowded Northeast were very poor and wished to live a better life. With the influx of more settlers, they were dissatisfied with the situation in the east and hoped to find a favorable environment to seek their fortune. Moreover, countless workers lost their jobs and farmers lost their land because of land speculation, so the newcomers, landless farmers and jobless workers ventured to the Wild West in hope of being wealthy.

Second, people moving west had an easy access to cheap land. Settlers could buy a large piece of land at a very low price. In fact, during the Westward Movement, many people did not have enough money to buy land; unlawful occupation of land was a common practice. They believed that the vast land should belong to anyone who occupied and cleared it. Officials sent by the government to survey territory were always challenged by these people.

Third, new inventions and constructions contributed to the Westward Movement. In 1815, Americans successfully made the first steamboat that could navigate the Mississippi and other rivers. In 1833, the first railroad was built in South Carolina. Meanwhile, new machines were invented and factories were set up one after another. These caused shortage in labor forces, attracting more people from Europe to the United States.

⊙ Effect of the Westward Movement

The Westward Movement greatly enhanced development of the national economy. It helped to narrow the gap between the rich and the poor. With massive influx of new settlers, people began to promote social equality. All white men gained the right to vote even if they did not own property or pay taxes, a circumstance completely different from before.

With the development of democracy, changes were also made in election practices. After 1824, presidential candidates were selected by party members from all states rather than nominated by Congressional caucus. The President represented the wishes of most people and common people had more "say" in things concerning national affairs.

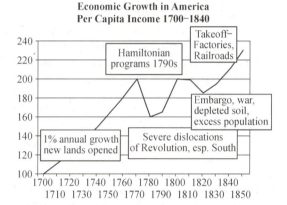

In addition, debtors were no longer put in prison but were helped by lenders. The practice of hanging criminals in the public was also banned. America was making great progress in every aspect.

> **Questions for discussion:**
>
> The Westward Movement was one of the largest population immigration in the history of the United States. What caused the Westward Movement? What did the movement bring for the country, especially the common people?

---

# Exercises

## I. Fill in the blanks.

1. The last war between the United States and Britain was fought between _____ and 1814.
2. In 1803, the United States purchased Louisiana from _____.
3. The Constitution Convention lasted _____ weeks from May to September, _____.
4. The Constitution drawn up at the end of the Independence War is called the _____ of the Confederation.
5. The bourgeois democratic personages headed by Thomas Jefferson, were opposed to the Constitution. They were called _____.
6. The people, headed by John Hamilton, who supported the Constitution of 1787, were called _____.
7. The war with England between 1812 and 1814 was called the Second _____ of _____.
8. The first great tide from 1840 to 1860 in America was the _____ Movement.
9. According to the treaty with Britain, the new nation had an area of some _____ square kilometers with a population of about _____ million.
10. _____ was praised by the Americans as "the first man in peace, the first man in war".

## II. Define the following terms.

1. the *Bill of Rights*
2. the Constitutional Convention
3. the spoils system
4. the Monroe Doctrine
5. the Westward Expansion

## III. Multiple choice.

1. Which of the following statements is true?
   A. The Louisiana was taken from Britain as a result of the War of 1812.
   B. The Louisiana Territory was ceded to the United States by France.
   C. The Louisiana Territory was purchased from Spain.
   D. The Louisiana Territory was purchased from France.
2. As a result of the U.S.-Mexican War, nearly _____ of the entire territory of Mexico was lost.
   A. 1/4   B. 1/2   C. 1/3   D. 1/5
3. The second president John Adams adopted a high-handed policy which was called _____ to protect the United States and its government.
   A. the "Intolerable Acts"
   B. Un-American Activities
   C. the *Alien and Sedition Act*
   D. *Jay Treaty*
4. Ten amendments introduced by James Madison in 1789 were added to the Constitution. They are knows as _____.
   A. the Articles of Confederation
   B. the *Bill of Rights*
   C. the Civil Rights
   D. Federalist Papers

5. The following were the founding fathers of the American Republic EXCEPT _____.
   A．George Washington  B．Thomas Jefferson
   C．William Penn       D．Benjamin Franklin
6. It was _____ who advanced four plans which met bitter criticisms from many people.
   A．Alexander Hamilton
   B．Thomas Jefferson
   C．George Washington
   D．John Adams
7. _____ was the first American president who was inaugurated in the city of Washington.
   A．John Adams
   B．Thomas Jefferson
   C．James Madison
   D．George washington
8. The War with England between 1812 and 1814 happened during the administration of President _____.
   A．James Madison
   B．James Monroe
   C．John Adams
   D．Thomas Jefferson
9. The Purchase of Louisiana Territory in 1803 from France _____.
   A．increased the American territory by one third
   B．increased the American territory by half
   C．almost doubled the size of the United States
   D．almost tripled the size of the United States

Ⅳ．**Translate the following terms into English.**
1. 威士忌反抗
2. 哥伦比亚特区
3. 分肥制
4. 购买路易斯安那
5. 印第安保留区

Ⅴ．**Answer the following questions in a few sentences.**
1. What were the consequences of the War of 1812?

2. What was unusual about the Articles of Confederation?

3. What plans did Hamilton propose during the administration of Washington?

4. List some main points of the Monroe Doctrine.

5. What were the causes of the Westward Expansion?

## Part Three   The United States During and After the Civil War

*The slavery system was one of the reasons for the Civil War. Slaves' miserable life was read and understood. The great work "Uncle Tom's Cabin" gives a vivid description about slaves' life and fate. Read the novel and get a general idea about slaves' life and the country at that time.*

### The American Civil War

● Background of the Civil War

In the middle of the 19th century, white Americans in the North and the South were unable to reconcile the fundamental differences in their approach to government, economy, society and African American slavery. War between the North and the South took place from 1861 to 1865. The **American Civil War** was the bloodiest war people in the United States had ever fought. Three main causes led to the breakout of the war.

One is different economic systems in the North and the South. The capitalist economy in the North developed rapidly, mainly based on industrial production, while the South, with vast level land, needed slaves as cheap labor force working for the plantations growing cotton and tobacco.

The slavery problem existing in the South was another cause. **Black slavery** began in English-American colonies soon after the first permanent settlement was founded in Virginia. The slaves solved the problem confronting the colonists — short supply of labor, because farming was the basic industry at the beginning. They were mainly shipped from African countries and could be sold freely. Slavery became common both in the North and the South.

After the Revolution, the northern states no longer needed slaves because the North did not have much level land. But slaves in the South continued to be treated inhumanely and viewed as property of he owners. The miserable life caused slaves to fight for freedom, but they were cruelly suppressed, which further intensified the dispute about slavery between the North and the South.

The dispute over black slavery was the main cause of the Civil War. The Westward Movement and industrial development intensified the conflict over slavery.

Before the Civil War, some important political changes took place. During the middle fifties, the Whig Party formed during Jackson's day broke up and a new party was set up, known as the **Republican Party** that opposed slavery. Later on, the southern Whigs became the **Democratic Party** who supported slavery. Thus the two-party system was established.

Because of disagreement on slavery, the relations between the South and the North was increasingly intense. When **Abraham Lincoln** was elected President in 1860, the southern states held meeting to leave the Union and set up a new country. It was a critical situation for President Lincoln who had the responsibility to work out a proper solution to the problem.

⊙ Progress of the Civil War

The Civil War began on April 12, 1861 when Confederate **General Pierre Beauregard** opened fire upon **Fort Sumter** on the edge of Charleston Harbor in the Confederate state of South Carolina, where a small band of federal troops were stationed.

The news of the attack shocked the whole country. Lincoln had to prepare for the war. He realized the importance of European trade to the South, so his first action was to blockade the southern ports to cut off their supplies. Lincoln issued a call for 75 thousand soldiers to join the Union Army. Meanwhile, the President of the South, or the Confederacy raised 100 thousand soldiers.

There was great contrast between the North and the South in terms of strength. The North had 23 states with a population of about 22 million while the South had only 11 states with a population of about 9 million, including 3.8 million slaves. The North controlled two-thirds of the national wealth while the South was poor in finance. But the South had its own advantages. The battleground was in the southern territory, so they were familiar with the environment and close to the local sources of supply. It also had fine officers and soldiers.

On July 21, 1861, the first major battle took place on a stream called Bull Run and the Union was defeated.

In 1863, the situation became worse for the Union in the east when General George McClellan led the army. Because he was slow to attack, the Union troops were defeated and forced backward.

In the west, the Union won a series of victories. They first broke a long Confederate line in Tennessee and then took the port of Memphis on the Mississippi River. **General Ulysses S. Grant** pushed slowly but steadily southward. On July 4, 1863, the strongest Confederate army surrendered.

The war continued for two more years with the South steadily retreating. On April 9, 1865, the southern troops commanded by **General Robert E. Lee** surrendered at Appomattox, Virginia. The war ended in failure for the South. Based on the 1860 census figures, 8% of all white males aged from 13 to 43 died in the war, including 6% in the North and an extraordinary 18% in the South.

During the war, President Lincoln issued the famous **Emancipation Proclamation** on September 22, 1862. It provided that all the slaves in the seceding states were freed or given opportunity to join the Union Army. The declaration of Emancipation Proclamation greatly mobilized the northern populace and the Union Army launched a series of successive attacks.

⊙ Significance of the Civil War

The American Civil War was a significant revolutionary war, which brought the slavery system to an end in the United States and united the nation once again. Abolition of slavery paved the way for further capitalist development. The broad masses played a very important role in the progress and victory of the war.

> ❓ Question for group work:
>
> The famous Emancipation Proclamation was one of the great achievements during the Civil War. Search for the relevant information about its principal author, the content and effects.

### After the Civil War

The victory of the North in the Civil War protected the integrity of the United States as an indivisible nation. But the abolition of slavery and equal chance for everyone were not perfectly achieved. Negroes had neither gained full civil rights politically nor gained an economically better life. Slave owners never gave up their hope for the restoration of slavery.

After the constitutional abolition of slavery, the Congress sought to carry out a program of Reconstruction in the southern states devastated by the war and burdened with heavy debt. Most southern whites resented the Reconstruction program because of interest conflict.

On April 15, 1865, **Andrew Johnson** became the President. He began to carry out a series of policies against the blacks. The southern whites regained control of the state governments. They passed laws to segregate whites and blacks in public places. Segregation was also enforced by  terror. By the end of the 19th century, the system of segregation had become stricter. Moreover, strict segregation in public transportation, theaters, sport, schools and even cemeteries became lawful in the South. The blacks were deprived of all the rights and maltreated by most whites.

After the Civil War, another upsurge of westward movement appeared in the United States. New immigrants and people from the whole country went to explore the western half of the United States, partly because the Congress passed the *Homestead Act* in 1862. According to the law, anyone who was either the head of a family, 21 years old, or a veteran of 14-day-service in the U. S. armed forces, or who was a citizen or intended to be a citizen could get 65 acres of land in the public domain. There frontiersmen could still strive for the goal of individualism and rough equality. After the gold rush was over in California in the 1850s, many people went to the Rocky Mountain regions and many farmers dispersed into other regions to found new farms. **The Wild West** was soon settled.

## Economic Development

### Reconstruction

Reconstruction took place for most of the decade following the Civil War. During this era, the "**Reconstruction Amendments**" were passed to expand civil rights for African Americans. Those amendments included the Thirteenth Amendment which outlawed slavery, the Fourteenth Amendment that guaranteed citizenship for all people born or naturalized within the U. S. territory and the Fifteenth Amendment that granted the vote for all men regardless of race. While the *Civil Rights Act of 1875* forbade discrimination in the service of public facilities, the Black Codes denied blacks certain privileges readily available to whites. In response to Reconstruction, the **Ku Klux Klan** (KKK) emerged around the late 1860s as a white-supremacist organization opposing black civil rights. Increasing hate-motivated violence from groups like the Klan influenced both the *Ku Klux Klan Act of 1870* that classified the KKK as a terrorist group and a Supreme Court decision in 1883 nullifying the *Civil Rights Act of 1875*. Reconstruction ended after the disputed election between Republican Rutherford B. Hayes and Democratic Samuel J. Tilden in 1786. Hayes won the election and the South soon re-entered the national political scene.

### Features of economic development

After the Civil War, the United States witnessed a rapid economic development in every aspect. By the end of the 19th century, it had become the most powerful industrial country in the world. Two features were shown in its development patterns.

The first feature was mechanization. Science and new inventions made great contribution to economic development. The telegraph cable was laid across the Atlantic Ocean and telephones provided rapid flow of information. Newly-invented machines, such as typewriters, cash registers, threshing machines, reaper-threshers and automatic wire binders, were extensively applied in industry and agriculture and their production value increased by dozens of times. The new machines also helped to release labor forces for other occupations. In addition, with the application of new machines, construction of public facilities and transportation system proceeded rapidly. By the early years of the 20th century, six transcontinental railroads running through the country from east to west had been built.

The second feature was the appearance of **monopoly businesses**. Monopolies began to appear in the United States after the Civil War. As more businesses were being set up, competition became more and more acute. Small businesses began to merge into larger businesses in order to survive competition and be profitable. As a result, big businesses controlled the industrial processes from raw materials to the sale of finished goods. Most of the national wealth was in the hands of big businesses, even the U. S. government turned to them for help when facing financial problems. However, the fast growth of monopolies by big businesses caused new problems.

⊙ Effects of economic development

Because of the rapid economic development and monopolization, distinct classes began to come into existence in the society. Owners of big businesses, or millionaires with investment in agricultural equipment, mining, commerce and real estate made up the wealthy upper class.

As to people who were neither the richest nor the poorest, in 1889 *The Century Dictionary* introduced the phrase "middle class" to describe them for the first time in the United States. Traditionally, American culture favored the middle class. The middle class' way of life encouraged both personal ambition and an abiding interest in the common good.

Another effect of economic development and monopoly was the sharp rise in prices. As the only suppliers, big monopoly businesses raised the prices of their goods. On the other hand, they lowered the price of raw materials supplied by small businesses and farmers.

The application of newly-invented machines pushed laborers to work faster and harder. Those who did simple, repetitive tasks with simple skills could easily be replaced by more skilled workers.

These problems pushed literary works into the period of realism. Many famous works were created by progressive novelists.

By the end of the 19th century, the American industrial production and per capita income had exceeded those of all other nations except Great Britain. In response to heavy debts and decreasing farm prices, farmers joined the Populist Party. Later, an unprecedented wave of immigration served both to provide labor for the American industry and to create diverse communities in the previously undeveloped areas. Abusive industrial practices led to successive violence of the labor movement in the United States.

## Social Reforms During Industrialization

Rapid development of industry and concentration of wealth led to the social reform. Although the social economy was prosperous, it was hard to neglect the shady business practice corruption in the government and poverty in the cities. Because of the event of meatpacking, all the people, including notable figures, demanded reforms.

Many farmers joined in the struggle for reform. Because of high production costs and a shrinking market, farmers were united in seeking effective redress from the government. They also sought government intervention in the economic development. The government was petitioned to increase the volume of money in order to allow prices of farm products to rise. Other demands were a national system to provide loans to farmers, an eight-hour workday and government ownership of railroads.

Industrial workers joined, too, seeking increase in wages, improvement of working conditions and restriction of child labor.

The voice of people forced the government to regulate public transportation and build public utilities. Many states, to satisfy the demands of residents, also made suitable regulations, such as protecting female workers, limiting working hours and so on.

Woodrow Wilson, elected as President in 1912, supported the reform movement by carrying out a reform program known as "**New Freedom**". In his program, income tax was introduced to distribute social wealth, antitrust laws were toughened and workers were entitled to strike for higher wages and better working conditions.

### ❓ Question for discussion:

Any nation could be destroyed by war, America was not an exception. Although the Civil War contributed in uniting the country, it also brought heavy debts and damages to the people. Economic development became an urgent task for the American people. As a post civic war country, how did America develop its economy as rapidly as possible, by relying on itself or asking help from others?

## The Growth of U.S. Imperialism

In the second half of the 19th century, the United States began its rise in international power with substantial population and industrial growth at home and numerous military adventures abroad, including the Spanish-American War. The rapid concentration of capital and emergence of monopolies showed that the U.S. capitalism had grown into full-fledged imperialism in every aspect.

### ⊙ The war with Spain

The United States was covetous of Cuba and the Philippines, which were then still controlled by Spain. In 1895, Cuba started the war of independence. At the beginning of 1898, serious disorder broke out in Havana, Cuba. The U.S. warship *Maine*, sent to protect American citizens and property, was sunk in Havana Harbor. With approval of the Congress, the U.S. President **William McKinley** declared war on Spain on April 29, 1898. The fighting went on for ten weeks with the main battlefields being in the Philippines and Cuba.

In December 1898, the representatives of Spain and the United States signed the *Treaty of Paris* to end the war. Spain ceded Cuba and Puerto Rico to the U.S. and sold the Philippines to the United States for 20 million dollars. The United States controlled the Philippines until it won its final independence on July 4, 1946.

The war with Spain was the first imperialist war for reshaping the world map. The United States began to turn into an imperialist power.

### ⊙ Aggression against China

The Sino-American relations can be traced back to the early 19th century when trade developed between the two countries. In 1900, the Congress passed the **Open Door Policy** requiring China to grant equal trading access to all foreign nations. But by the 1900s, the major European powers had controlled important regions of China. To protect its own interests in China, the United States made an agreement with other foreign countries to ensure that every country had equal and impartial access to trading with China.

With a large number of merchants and missionaries pouring into China, waves of anti-foreign aggression spread across many parts of China. Finally, this situation caused the uprising of Yihetuan; called the **Boxer Uprising** by the Westerners. Several foreign missionaries were killed. With the pretext of protecting their citizens and property, the Eight-power Alliance invaded China. The Qing government was defeated and forced to sign the inequitable treaty — the **Boxer Potocol**. China paid 450 million dollars to the foreign allies, among which America received 24 million dollars, and authorized foreign troops to control the railroad section from Tianjin to Beijing.

### ❓ Questions for discussion:

1. If it is strong or powerful enough, what would a country do? What would it deliver to the people, not only to its own but to the world's population?
2. How do we understand the word "imperialism" from the perspective of America?

## Exercises

### Ⅰ. Fill in the blanks.

1. The War between the North and the South from _____ to _____ is called the American Civil War.
2. The President during the American Civil War was _____.
3. During the Civil War, Lincoln issued the _____, which declared the abolition of the slavery system.
4. The _____-American War broke out in 1898.
5. During the Civil War, Lincoln took two important measures, one was the _____ _____, the other was the _____ _____.
6. By the end of the _____ century, the U.S. had become the most powerful country in the world.
7. With the passage of the military *Reconstruction Act* in March, 1867, the power of Reconstruction of the south passed from the President to _____.
8. The most notorious society which mainly persecuted the blacks was _____ _____.
9. Monopoly began to appear in the United States after the _____ _____.

### Ⅱ. Define the following terms.

1. "New Freedom"
2. Emancipation Proclamation
3. monopoly businesses

4. Open Door Policy

### III. Multiple choice.
1. Even after the abolition of slavery, organized or individual discrimination was practiced against _____.
   A. Chinese Americans
   B. American Indians
   C. Japanese Americans
   D. African Americans
2. The first American president to be elected from the Republican Party was _____.
   A. Thomas Jefferson   B. James Monroe
   C. James Madison      D. Abraham Lincoln
3. The Ku Klux Klan was the most notorious terrorist society which persecuted the _____.
   A. blacks             B. Indians
   C. progressive people D. Chinese
4. Which of the following may NOT be President Wilson's achievements in his program of New Freedom?
   A. Making loans available to farmers at low rates.
   B. Adopting an income tax.
   C. Regulating trusts by stating clearly the unfair business practices.
   D. Regulating railroad prices and their rebates.
5. In the 1900s, with the development of industry and the extension of railroad network, there was a _____ in the United States.
   A. fast growth of population
   B. rapid growth of military power
   C. fast growth of labor unions
   D. rapid growth of cities

### IV. Translate the following terms into English.
1. 共和党
2. 民主党
3. 《解放宣言》
4. 重建计划
5. 《巴黎和约》

### V. Answer the following questions in a few sentences.
1. Why did the Civil War break out?

2. What is the effect of the Civil War?

3. What are the examples of U.S. foreign expansion after the Civil War?

## Part Four  The United States During and After World War I

*World War I was a disaster for nearly all the people in the world. Even winning nations had paid a lot. Think about the questions as follows:*
1. *What role did America play in the war?*
2. *What policies did the American government take in the war? Why?*
3. *What did America get from the war?*

### World War I

The First World War broke out on July 28, 1914 and ended on November 11, 1918, lasting for more than four years.

The United States did not enter the war when the war broke out. **President Woodrow Wilson** declared U.S. entry into World War I in April 1917. During the first three years of the war, the United States still clung to its traditional isolation and took a neutral policy, and it made huge profits by selling munitions to the allies. But later, the situation changed and to protect its interests, America had to enter the war.

Several important factors led the United States to enter the war.

First, Germany, relying mainly on submarine warfare to fight against Britain, announced that it would sink all the ships to England, regardless whether the ships were for commercial or war purposes. This action greatly threatened and decreased the American trade.

The second factor was the influence of pressure groups. Before America entered the war, it had received a series of orders from Britain and its allies for products. American bankers had provided a large number of loans for Britain. Should Britain be defeated, American bankers and businessmen would suffer a great financial loss. Hence, America's strength would be weakened and Germany would become the strongest power threatening America.

The third factor was that after more than two years of fighting, both sides had become war weary. It was a good opportunity for America to enter the war.

The fourth factor was the **Zimmerman Note.**

Zimmerman, the German Foreign Minister, wrote a letter to the Mexican government and was intercepted by Britain. America was enraged and made the letter public. To prevent America from entering the war against it, Germany tried to persuade Mexico and Japan to declare war on America. If Mexico helped Germany win, Mexico would be able to regain its territory lost in 1848.

With the support of most Americans, the U. S. President Wilson asked the Congress for a declaration of war against Germany in April, 1917. America's strong economy provided great help for the allies and in 1918, the war ended with a victory of the allies.

⊙ The *Treaty of Versailles*

In January 1919, a peace conference was held in Paris. The U. S. President Wilson proposed a Fourteen Points program for a new world order. The main points included free trade without tariffs, reduction of armies, freedom of the seas, new relationships between countries and organization of a general **League of Nations** to preserve world peace. In fact, his real attempt was to establish a dominate position for America in the world order. Naturally, his proposals met with a strong opposition and most of his proposals were not included when the *Treaty of Versailles* was signed on June 28, 1919. Only the League of Nations was organized but under the control of Britain instead of America. Because the treaty failed to establish preeminence in the world order, the U. S. Congress refused to ratify the treaty and the United States did not join the League of Nations.

### American Red Scare

World War I caused great losses to both sides. America played a decisive role in ending the war, causing America to be self-confident and more suspicious to foreign ideas. After World War I, the U. S. grew steadily in stature as an economic and military world power. The aftershock of **Russia's October Revolution** resulted in real fears of communism in the United States, leading to a three-year **Red Scare**.

In May 1919, many mail bombs were sent to prominent Americans, especially high-ranking officials. Conservatives concluded that Communists were trying to subvert the United States. This view caused the Red Scare. Conservatives tried every means to look for Soviet accomplices. The Supreme Court made a series of decisions which helped Conservatives to search for dangerous aliens. During that period, no one would claim to be Communist and anyone who showed any sign of support for Communism would be arrested.

In January 1920, more than 4,000 suspected Communists were arrested across the country and the Red Scare subsided at the end of 1920.

### Changes of America After World War I

In 1920, the manufacture, sale, import and export of alcohol were prohibited by the Eighteenth Amendment to the United States Constitution. The **Prohibition** encouraged illegal breweries and dealers to make substantial amounts of money selling alcohol illegally. The Prohibition ended in 1933 as a failure. Additionally, the KKK reformed during that decade and had gathered nearly 4.5 million members by 1924. And the U. S. government passed the *Immigration Act of 1924* restricting foreign immigration. During most of the 1920s, the United States enjoyed a period of unbalanced prosperity: Farm prices and wages fell, while industrial profits grew. The boom was fueled by a rise in debt and an inflated stock market.

⊙ Industrial progress

Soon after World War I, the U. S. industry progressed rapidly due to improvements in science and technology. During World War I, many new machines were invented and applied in the war. After the war, these machines were refitted and applied into industrial production. New inventions appeared, such as assembly lines for automobile manufacturing invented by **Henry Ford** and airplane production based on the "**Flyer**" invented by Wright brothers. The most fundamental invention was the improvement of generators which made electricity become the power source of most industries instead of coal. New inventions led to great increases in profits. To protect American products from foreign competition, the American government imposed high protective tariffs on imported goods through federal legislation. Moreover, big businesses were more loosely controlled and soon came to dominate the national pillar industries. Big businesses controlled the national wealth and production again. However, the income of common Americans did not increase as quickly as the productivity did. Besides, because of the extensive application of new machines, higher level skills were required and many workers with only simple skills lost their jobs.

### ⊙ Changes in culture

With the development of national economy, cultural change also took place in the 1920s. The feature of the new culture was advertising and installment buying. It favored a belief in pleasure, consumption and individualism.

Many factors led to the appearance of a new culture. First, the institution of five-day workweek and increases in wages gave Americans more free time. Also, modern technology made work less time-consuming. This led Americans to look for new ways of entertainment and relaxation. Accordingly, consumerism appeared. Businesses used various advertisements to attract people's interest in products and services. Music, radio, sports, and games became great sources of pleasure and enjoyment for people.

Popular music, especially jazz, played an important role in new culture movement. It was an expression of freedom and individual rights by musical improvisation and a way people expressed themselves and their emotions. So Jazz attracted both the blacks and the whites. The popularity of jazz led to the development of communication technology. The first permanent network of radio stations, the **National Broadcasting Company** (NBC) was established in 1926.

Second, the image of women was changing. According to the 19th Amendment of the Constitution passed in 1920, women were granted right to vote, to attend schools and to have a job. They could pursue interests in fashion and imitate characters seen in movies.

Third, individualism pervaded. Young people became representatives of fashion, with college students in the majority. Middle class families sent their children to college in order to meet the requirements of the developing economy. Students also required "freedom in thought and action" when they were in college.

However, the rapid growth of new culture did not satisfy every American. Some conservative Americans thought supporting cultural change was to abandon traditional values. And, the blacks said the changing culture didn't remove the inequalities that existed in the society.

### ⊙ The Lost Generation

**The Lost Generation** referred to some young artists who felt disappointed with the society after World War I. They shared something in common: being confused and losing direction in life, going to Europe with the belief that industrialization had made work boring, and criticizing consumerism and similar recreational pursuits.

Several factors contributed to the emergence of the Lost Generation. One was the *Treaty of Versailles* which disappointed Americans. A second factor was the influence of the Great October Revolution which took place in Russia in 1918. A third one was the Red Scare spread by the conservatives in the United States due to the Great October Revolution. In addition, the negative effects of the Prohibition and corruption also caused idealistic young people to lose heart and become aimless in their lives.

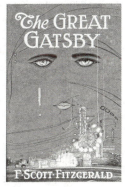

> **❓ Questions for discussion:**
> 1. Although American industry and economy developed rapidly after World War I, people's lives were not improved accordingly, but even got worse, especially for the blacks and labor workers. Could you list some problems appearing in this period?
> 2. As to the younger generation, living in a well-developed country did not mean a better life, why? What were their reactions to the new country?

### The Great Depression

**The Great Depression** from 1929 to 1933 was the longest and most severe period of financial crisis the United States had ever experienced.

Economy of the United States appeared prosperous in the 1920s, but this prosperity was not based on a solid foundation. To make more profit from European countries through trade, the U. S. government raised the prices of agricultural products and encouraged farmers to expand production. However, European countries could not import much American goods due to high prices. Also, America would not recall the loans given to European countries who had suffered great loss during World War I. What's more, banks invested much money in stock market or made large loans to investors. Last but not least, rapid increase in productivity was far beyond the slow growth in wages. American workers did not have the purchasing capacity to support the economic growth.

The direct cause of the Great Depression was a severe crash in the New York Exchange on October 24, 1929, known as "**Black Thursday**". Hopes of becoming rich failed, many people owned nothing and people with loans could not repay their debts. Rich people withdrew their money from banks and some began to hoard gold. Many banks closed.

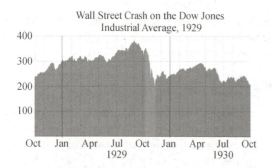

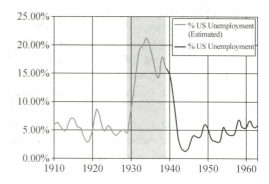

People were left with nothing because of banks' collapse and they could not buy anything, including food. In turn, factories and companies could not sell their products and went bankruptcy. Many farmers lost their land because of debts. Others even refused to harvest their ripe crops because the price of farm products was so low that it would not cover the cost of harvesting them.

The depression in every aspect put countless people out of work and made them homeless. Suffering from hunger and unemployment, they had to "travel" everywhere looking for a job or a meal. It was said that 17 million people lost their jobs in 1933. On the other hand, plenty of "extra" goods were destroyed. For example, milk was poured into rivers and cattle were killed and thrown away.

### President Roosevelt's "New Deal"

**Franklin Roosevelt** was elected President in 1932 during the period of the crisis. He was the only president served more than two terms (four times) in American history. Roosevelt was empowered by the Congress to save the nation. He carried out a program of social and economic reforms from 1933 to 1941, known as **New Deal**.

Soon after his inauguration, the Congress passed many laws proposed by Roosevelt. To cope with economic crisis, the government was granted the power to interfere with financial business through the *Emergency Banking Act*. Some banks reopened under its help and companies resumed business operations.

To create new job opportunities for the unemployed and to increase consumption, the prohibition was repealed and many public projects were launched. Furthermore, to raise the price of farm products, farmers were asked to destroy crops or plant grass on the farmland, which could reduce agricultural production.

He also initiated such social programs as social security, paying pensions to the old, the unemployed and the injured.

Roosevelt's government created a new foreign policy. Efforts were made to maintain foreign markets and conquer new ones under the concept of the "**Good Neighbor Policy**".

Although the New Deal did not end the Great Depression, it helped Americans survive the worst economic crisis in the history of capitalism. People were granted freedom of speech and expression, freedom of religion, the freedom from want and fear. Most importantly, it increased government involvement in the nation's economic life and had great influence on people's concept of the role of government.

> ❓ **Questions for discussion**:
> 1. The Great Depression became a block to the country, and it even pushed the country backward. What caused the Great Depression?

2. "New Deal" did not completely solve the problems caused by the Great Depression, but it provided some help in people's lives. What did it bring to the Americans?

## Exercises

### Ⅰ. Fill in the blanks.
1. World War I broke out on July 28, _____ and ended on November 11, _____, lasting for about four years.
2. Franklin Roosevelt's program for the Great Depression was called _____.
3. At the beginning of World War I, the United States pursued a policy of _____.
4. The _____ _____ Conference in 1919 was in fact a meeting to divide the spoils and re-divide the old colonies.
5. The new culture was based on _____ and characterized by advertising and _____.
6. The Russian Communist Revolution of 1917 terrified Conservatives in the United States and caused the _____.
7. The New York Stock Market crash of 1929 marked the beginning of _____.

### Ⅱ. Define the following terms.
1. the Lost Generation
2. Black Thursday
3. the Great Depression
4. Four Freedoms

### Ⅲ. Multiple choice.
1. American women did not have voting right until the adoption of the 19th Amendment _____.
   A. in the late 19th century
   B. under President Wilson
   C. under President Theodore Roosevelt
   D. in the 1920s under President Harding
2. _____ was the only American president who was re-elected three times in succession.
   A. Theodore Roosevelt
   B. George Washington
   C. Franklin D. Roosevelt
   D. Thomas Jefferson
3. The goal of Roosevelt's New Deal was _____.
   A. to save the American economic and political system
   B. to change the American economic system
   C. to weaken monopoly interests in America
   D. to nationalize banks and financial institutions in America
4. In World War I, _____ was not one of the defeated nations.
   A. Germany          B. Austro-Hungary
   C. Ottoman          D. Russia
5. After a period of prosperity (1920 – 1929), government involvement in economy increased _____.
   A. during the Great Depression
   B. after World War I
   C. after World War II
   D. during the Cold War
6. In 1918, President _____ issued the "Fourteen Points".
   A. Woodrow Wilson
   B. William H. Taft
   C. Theodore Roosevelt
   D. Warren G. Harding
7. Which statement is NOT true about the Great Depression in the 1930s?
   A. Billions of dollars of paper profits were wiped out within a few days.
   B. Misery and personal sufferings were widespread.
   C. Many lost their land and other properties because of foreclosures.
   D. The stock market crash was the beginning of long economic recovery.
8. A typical example of American intolerant nationalism from 1919 to 1920 was _____ that exaggerated the danger of Communism.
   A. McCarthyism      B. the Ku Klux Klan
   C. the Red Scare    D. Desegregation

### Ⅳ. Translate the following terms into English.
1. 国际联盟
2. 红色恐怖
3. 俄国十月革命
4. 禁酒令

### Ⅴ. Answer the following questions in a few sentences.
1. List some factors that contributed to the appearance of the Lost Generation.
2. What was the policy pursued by the American government at the beginning of World War I?
3. What were the contents of the New Deal?
4. What contributed to the emergence of the new culture?

## Part Five  The United States During and After World War II

*World War II was another disaster for people around the world. Before going into the text, collect the relevant information about World War II and think about which country received greatest benefits from the war and what did it lose?*

### World War II

⊙ America entering the war

At the beginning of the war, America kept its neutrality toward the war. Because American people were still bitter about World War I, they supported America's neutral policy.

However, as the war went on, the situation seemed to pose a future threat to America.

In 1939, to control oilfields and cut off China's only transportation line through Burma with the outside world, Japan did not invade the Soviet Union but went south. In July 1941, Japan invaded Indo-China, which enraged the American government. In retaliation, the U.S. government froze Japanese assets in America and refused to export raw materials essential for Japan's military industry. To solve the problem of materials and prevent America from entering into the war, Japan adopted a deceptive diplomacy. While the Japanese government was pretending to seek a compromise, on December 7, 1941, several Japanese planes launched a surprise attack on the United States naval base at **Pearl Harbor**, Hawaii. It was Sunday and the Americans at the base were enjoying their weekend. The United States suffered great losses. On the following day, Franklin D. Roosevelt successfully urged a joint session of the Congress to declare war on Japan, calling December 7, 1941 "a date which will live in infamy". Four days after the attack on Pearl Harbor, Nazi Germany declared war on the United States, drawing the country into a two-theater war. Subsequently, the whole world was dragged into the war.

After the Pacific War broke out, there were two war arenas in the world. One was the European arena and the other was the Pacific arena. The United States, together with Britain, China and other countries fought against Japan in the Pacific arena. The Soviet Union joined the U.S. and its allies in the fight against Germany in the European arena.

Upon entering the war, the United States and its allies decided to concentrately fight Hitler in Europe, while maintaining a defensive position in the Pacific until Hitler was defeated. The first step was to establish a large air force presence in Britain to concentrate on bombing raids into Germany. Their air force suffered great losses until the introduction of the P-51 Mustang as a long range escort fighter for the bombers.

Japan captured a large part of China and soon other countries and some of British islands. However, the situation changed when the main force of Japanese fleet was destroyed in the Midway Island Battle in June 1942. On June 6, 1944, American and British armies landed on the beaches of Normandy, opening a western front to attack Germany. They entered Germany across France, while the Soviet Union advanced from the east, ultimately capturing Berlin, Germany's capital. Germany surrendered on May 8, 1945. Hitler committed suicide.

However, the Japanese refused to surrender. On August 6 and 9, 1945, America dropped two atomic bombs in Japan. And Russia declared war on Japan on August 8, 1945. On August 14, Japan surrendered and World War II ended.

During the war, a series of agreements were reached by the allies. On November 22, 1943, Roosevelt and Churchill met with Chiang Kai-shek at Cairo and agreed that Japan should give back to China all it gained from China, including Taiwan. The Yalta Conference was held in February, 1945, attended by Roosevelt, Churchill and Stalin, ending with the agreement that the Soviet Union would

declare war on Japan within three months after Germany surrendered on condition that the independence of Mongolia was recognized and the Soviet Union could control China's Dalian City and the railway from Dalian to Russia.

⊙ Consequences of the war

World War II was enormously destructive. More than 36 million people were killed and millions more were left homeless. Under its program of racial extermination, with respect to Jews, Germany practiced atrocities in concentration camps on a large scale.

After the war, the global power was balanced between the U.S.S.R. and the U.S.A. Germany was divided into four sections held respectively by Britain, France, the U.S. and the Soviet Union. Years later, Germany was reunified when East Germany and West Germany were combined.

The war was an anti-fascist war. After the war, many countries became socialist or democratic. Many colonies won their independence.

> ❓ **Questions for discussion**:
> What policies did the American government take in the war? Did they differ from those in World War I? Try to explain it from the perspective of the people and the government.

### Cold War and America's Containment

Soon after World War II, the world entered the period of **Cold War**, completely different from "hot war", because it involved international tensions without actual bloodshed and casualties. The Cold War ended in 1989 when the Berlin Wall was broken down and Germany was reunited.

Although World War II had not ended, the conflicts between the United States and the Soviet Union became more and more obvious and acute. The root cause of the conflicts was different views about the world order after the war. America, having increased in strength during the war, was determined to build an America-oriented world order, open foreign markets for its capital and products, and decrease the domination of the Soviet Union in Eastern Europe, while the Soviet Union, concerned with its own security and the capitalist challenge to the communist system, took a firm decision to maintain its control over Eastern European countries.

After the war ended, the contention between the two countries intensified because of disagreement on the new world order. Socialism advocated by the Soviet Union could not peacefully coexist with capitalism. So both the two countries began to make military preparations against each other. The containment policy became the U.S. official policy to the Soviet Union during the Cold War until 1989.

In the spring of 1947, President **Harry S. Truman** proclaimed his foreign policy, known as the **Truman Doctrine**. It marked the beginning of the Cold War period, as it promised to give military and economic aid to European countries and governments fighting against domination by the Soviet Union.

When Stalin successfully put Eastern Europe behind the "**iron curtain**", America shifted its attention to Western and Southern Europe where conflicts were also evident. It realized that an impoverished Europe filled with despair could easily lead to an anti-America movement and endanger the Western system and its values. So in 1947, the U.S. Secretary of State George Marshall proposed a massive aid program, known as the **Marshall Plan**, to help rebuild the destroyed Europe. The Plan offered economic assistance to any European country who would act as the plan required. By early 1952, America had paid out 13 billion dollars as its contribution to the reconstruction and development of economies in Western European countries.

**Berlin Blockade** also happened during the Cold War. In 1948, West Berlin was completely isolated by the Soviet Union in an attempt to force it to join the Soviet sector. To hold back the expansion of the Soviet Union, however, the United States and many other countries delivered goods and services to West Berlin by a massive air lift. The United States,

Canada and ten European countries organized the **North Atlantic Treaty Organization** in April 1949 which aimed to help each other should any country become involved in war. The Soviet Union removed its blockade of West Berlin in May 1949.

## The Korean War

**The Korean War** was a military conflict between the North Korean and South Korean regimes, with major hostilities lasting from June 25, 1950 until an armistice was signed on July 27, 1953.

After defeating China in the Sino-Japanese War of 1894 to 1895, the Japanese forces remained in Korea, occupying strategically important parts of the country and exploiting the Korean people. At the end of World War II, forces of both the Soviet Union and the United States occupied the peninsula in accordance with an agreement put forth by the United States government to divide the Korean peninsula into North Korea and South Korea along the thirty-eighth parallel.

When South Korea and North Korea tried to achieve national unification by war, the Korean War broke out (June 25, 1950). By September 1950, the North Korean troops had occupied most of South Korea, including its capital. The American troops, confined to an area at the southern tip of the Korean Peninsula, launched an amphibious landing at Inchon and the North Korean army were defeated and retreated backward. The American troops, across the thirty-eighth parallel, continued northward to the Yalu River. In response to an appeal by North Korea, in October, China entered the war. In November, the American troops were overwhelmed by the Chinese Volunteers and withdrew to the south of the thirty-eighth parallel.

In 1953, the two sides agreed to sign an armistice agreement and the war ended. However, up to now, they have not signed a peace treaty and the two governments still view the thirty-eighth parallel as the boundary.

The war was described as a false war with false enemies at a wrong place in an improper time and was considered to be the **Forgotten War**. After the war, the number of American soldiers doubled and the expenditures on the military greatly increased, because of the realization that the threat of war existed everywhere. The Korean War was the only war that the United States lost in its history.

## McCarthy Era

Due to the failure in the Korean War and Americans' concern about socialism, Republican Senator McCarthy advanced an anti-communist challenge in the U.S. with the claim of a so-called communist name list. The anti-communism movement became known as **McCarthyism**.

McCarthyism is a term describing the intense anti-communist suspicion in the United States in a period that lasted roughly from the late 1940s to the late 1950s. This period is also referred to as the **Second Red Scare** and coincided with the increasing fears about communist influence on American institutions and espionage by Soviet agents.

During this period many thousands of Americans were accused of being communists or communist sympathizers and became the subject of aggressive investigations and questioning. Many of them suffered from unemployment and even imprisonment.

American people were enraged by McCarthy's actions and became dissatisfied with the American government, especially the President. In December 1954, the Senate censured McCarthy for his illegal actions and falsehoods. His political career came to an end and McCarthyism was over. In May 1957, McCarthy died of disease caused by overdrinking.

Since the time of McCarthy, the word "McCarthyism" has entered American lexicon as a general term for a variety of distasteful practices: aggressively questioning a person's patriotism, making poorly supported accusations, using accusations of disloyalty to pressure a person to adhere to conformist politics or to discredit an opponent, subverting civil rights in the name of national security, and so on.

## Cuban Missile Crisis

**The Cuban Missile Crisis** was a confrontation between the United States, the Soviet Union and Cuba during the Cold War. Following the Berlin Blockade, the crisis is considered as one of the major confrontations of the Cold War and as the moment in which the Cold War came closest to a nuclear war.

Soon after the **Cuba Revolution**, Cuba became the major focus of the Kennedy administration. With the fear of American invasion in Cuba, shortly after routing the **Bay of Pigs Invasion**, Cuba Governor Castro declared Cuba a socialist republic, established formal relations with the Soviet Union and began to modernize Cuba's military.

The United States feared any country's adoption of communism or socialism and that a Latin American country openly allied with the Soviet Union was considered as unacceptable. As a punishment, John Kennedy first engaged Operation Mongoose, a series of covert operations against Castro's government in late 1961, and then launched an economic embargo against Cuba in 1962.

Facing this situation, Cuba turned to the Soviet Union for help. Considering the political and military atmosphere, together with the fear that the Americans might invade Cuba, **Khrushchev** agreed to supply missiles to Cuba in April 1962. On one hand, he kept in touch with Kennedy and promised to remain neutral; on the other hand, he secretly transported and installed nuclear missiles under Soviet control in Cuba, seeking to avoid discovery of America. By late July, more than sixty Soviet ships had secretly arrived in Cuba, carrying military materials and experts.

The climax of the crisis began on October 15, 1962, when the United States reconnaissance photographs taken by an American spy plane revealed missile bases being built in Cuba. Deceived by the Soviet Union, the enraged American government assembled all its military resources preparing for the war. Another world war was on the verge of breaking out.

To protect its military strength, Khrushchev began to search for compromise. After much deliberation between the Soviet Union and the United States, Kennedy agreed to remove all missiles set in Turkey on the border of the Soviet Union in exchange for Khrushchev removing all missiles in Cuba. The Cuba Missile Crisis ended peacefully on October 28, 1962.

The Cold War narrowed the gap between the United States and the Soviet Union on military strength. America realized that the Soviet Union also had advanced missiles. But for Cuba, it was a partial betrayal by the Soviets, because decisions on how to resolve the crisis had been made exclusively by Kennedy and Khrushchev and certain issues of interest to Cuba were not addressed. On the other hand, Cuba continued to be protected from invasion by the Soviet Union.

> **? Group work:**
>
> During the Cold War, the relations between communist countries and capitalist countries became tense. A series of rules and measures that blocked the intercommunication were set up accordingly. List the rules and measures that the United States and the Soviet Union made and took to each other.

## John Kennedy and New Frontier

**John Kennedy** was inaugurated in January 1961 and was assassinated in November 1963. He carried out his own policy known as **New Frontier** symbolizing the American spirit of exploration and vigor.

During his presidency, he paid more attention to the problems concerning with common people and their lives, such as the national welfare, poverty, employment and housing. Besides, he established the Peace Corps in 1961 and sent American volunteers to provide help for other nations' development including Latin and Central American countries. But, many conservatives opposed his policy, arguing that it would increase federal financial burden.

When the Soviet Union sent its first man into the space, Americans were shocked. President Kennedy pledged that the United States would send a man onto the moon and return him safely to the Earth before the end of the decade. In the following years, America greatly increased its expenditures on education and scientific research.

In July, 1969, Neil Armstrong stepped out of Apollo II spacecraft onto the moon for the first time in the history of human beings. The United States achieved victory in space race and maintained its leading position in science and technology.

## Demands for Reform

America was filled with various protests and demands for reforms after World War II. Generally, there were three categories: the Civil Rights Movement, the Women's Movement and the Youth Movement.

### ⊙ The Civil Rights Movement

Throughout American history, blacks were a large minority but a subjugated one. Lincoln proclaimed the emancipation of black slaves in 1863, but not much progress had been made and they were still at the bottom of the society. Especially in the South, they suffered from discrimination in education and employment.

The Civil Rights Movement referred to the blacks' fighting for equal rights with the whites. It emerged at the end of World War II and reached a climax in the 1960s. The blacks together with students protesting against segregation demanded equality in higher education and freedom of choice in seating on buses.

An outstanding leader of the Civil Rights Movement was **Martin Luther King**, a Baptist clergyman. The movement actually started in 1955. A black woman named Rosa Parks was arrested for violating the city law because she refused to give her seat to a white man on the bus in the town of Montgomery, Alabama. Her arrest sparked a protest movement led by Martin Luther King who later set up a boycott of the bus lines. In 1956, the Supreme Court declared Alabama's segregation laws unconstitutional.

Then Martin Luther King turned to Birmingham, the most racist city in the South. There he organized the blacks fighting for jobs and freedom. The *Civil Rights Act* was passed in 1964 during Johnson's presidency.

In history, nearly all movements involving racial change were achieved through violence. By contrast, Martin Luther King advocated nonviolent tactics. Although he succeeded in his speech for freedom, he was assassinated in Memphis, Tennessee on April 14, 1968.

### ⊙ The Women's Movement

Women were considered as inferior to men and had a low status in society at that time. With the progress of the Civil Rights Movement, there came the Women's Movement. They opposed discrimination in jobs and demanded equal pay for equal work. They required establishment of child-care centers so that they could have more time and energy to work outside and pursue their own dreams. They also called for free abortion and freedom to do things as they liked.

### ⊙ The Youth Movement

Young people always played an important role in social activities, either good or bad. Young people joined in the movements for various reasons, and it was related with both internal and external problems.

Because of the extended wars, Americans were burdened with increased national deficit, and young people lived a lower standard life. Political scandals often appeared in the newspapers. All these made young people doubt their traditional culture and the values they had learned.

Young people became dissatisfied with the government and demanded social reform. As too much power was controlled by a small group of elite, young people advocated that all American people should participate equally in making economic and political decisions. College students especially called for real freedom of speech provided in the Constitution. As the movement went on, people gradually protested America's involvement in the Vietnam War. The antiwar movement came to a climax in 1970 and the government had to send troops to suppress rioting.

Young people became discontented, so they separated themselves from the society, denied traditional values, refused to obey authority, and followed their own style. One group, **Hippies** was the radical representative of the **counterculture**.

The Youth Movement exerted some influence on the society. Colleges became more democratic: more minority students were allowed into universities and students enjoyed more freedom on campus. Most importantly, the Youth Movement led to a quick ending of the American involvement in the Vietnam War.

### The Beat Generation

During World War II, America experienced fullscale development, especially in economy. People's income continued to rise after the war. **Materialism** came into people's life. They tried to buy all kinds of consumer goods and live for their personal desires. On the other hand, the influence of the war still existed. People who criticized the government policy would be considered as communist or supporters of communism. Opposition to strict social rules gave rise to **the Beat Generation**, first in San Francisco.

The Beat Generation referred to the members of the American writers of the 1950s, who tried to separate themselves from society. Calling for spiritual rediscovery, they looked for various kinds of social freedom such as long hair, mini-dresses, casual sex and rock music, etc. **City Lights Bookstore** in San Francisco and **East Village** in New York City were two cultural centers of the Beat Generation.

 **Group discussion:**
Find out the detailed information about Kennedy's assassination.

### The Vietnam War

The Vietnam War lasted from November 1, 1959 to April 30, 1975. The war was fought between the communist **Democratic Republic of Vietnam** (North Vietnam), supported by its communist allies, and the **Republic of Vietnam** (South Vietnam), supported by the United States. It was a long-time suffering for the American involvement in Southeast Asia.

When the Vietnamese Communists and nationalists fought against French in Indo-China after World War II, American President Truman sent military aid to France. However, France was defeated and withdrew from Southeast Asia in 1954. The U.S. President **Dwight D. Eisenhower** sent American advisers and aids to help set up a pro-America government in South Vietnam.

In August 1963, two American destroyers on the sea were reported being attacked by North Vietnamese ships. American President Johnson, regardless of his promise of not sending soldiers to Vietnam, ordered air strikes against North Vietnamese naval bases. In 1965, the first American combat unit was sent to South Vietnam.

People in America opposed to the war and demanded American withdrawal, so Johnson was in a difficult position and finally gave up re-election.

**Richard Nixon**, the 37th President and Johnson's successor, made efforts to improve the relations with socialist countries, especially the supporters of North Vietnam, such as China and the Soviet Union.

Nixon continued to bomb, on a large scale, many cities in North Vietnam. In 1973, a peace treaty was finally signed after a lengthy bargaining between the United States and North Vietnam. At the same time, almost all U.S. troops left Vietnam. In 1975, communist forces assumed control of South Vietnam. The North and South parts of Vietnam were reunified in 1976 thereafter.

The war and the failure of the United States had a major impact on U.S. politics, culture and foreign relations. Americans were deeply divided over the U.S. government's justification for and conduct of the war. Opposition to the war formed the basis for the counterculture Youth Movement of the 1960s.

The war exacted a huge human cost as well. Approximately 360,000 U.S. soldiers were killed or wounded and nearly $686 billion (in constant dollars, FY 2008) were expended.

### The Watergate Affair

The Watergate Affair was also called **Watergate Scandal** or Watergate Break-in. Watergate was a building complex in Washington, D.C., where the break-in occurred. It is a general term for a series of political scandals during the presidency of Richard

Nixon that resulted in the indictment of his several closest advisors and the ultimate resignation of President Nixon himself on August 9, 1974.

Attempting to discover what the Democrats were planning to do for Nixon's re-election, five men broke into the Democratic National Committee headquarters at the Watergate Hotel complex in Washington, D. C. on June 17, 1972 but were arrested on the spot.

Investigations were conducted initially by the FBI and then later by the Senate Watergate Committee and the House Judiciary Committee. The press revealed that this burglary was just one of many illegal activities authorized and carried out by Nixon's staff and those loyal to him.

President Nixon and his staff decided to cover up the break-in as early as six days after it occurred. However, adequate evidence suggested that Nixon had a tape recording system in his offices, revealing his participation in the break-in.

With impeachment in the House of Representatives and conviction in the Senate, Nixon resigned on August 9, 1974, becoming the only U. S. President who resigned from office. His successor, Gerald Ford, issued a pardon for any federal crimes Nixon may have committed while in office.

### ❓ Question for discussion:

President Nixon was one of the supporters for the Vietnam War. Explain why the president advocated the war in spite of the common people's violent protest against it. Is it against the belief of the country?

### Present America

⊙ Jimmy Carter

**Jimmy Carter**, the recipient of the Nobel Peace Prize of 2002, served as the 39th President of the United States from 1977 to 1981. Prior to becoming president, Carter served two terms in the Georgia Senate and as the 76th Governor of Georgia from 1971 to 1975.

The day he took his oath of the office in 1977, he fulfilled a campaign promise by issuing an Executive Order declaring unconditional amnesty for Vietnam War Era draft evaders. In his inaugural address he said: "We have learned that more is not necessarily better, that even our great nation has its recognized limits, and that we can neither answer all questions nor solve all problems."

His first steps in the White House were to reduce the size of the staff by one third and order Cabinet members to drive their own cars. As president, Carter created two new cabinet-level departments: the Department of Energy and the Department of Education and signed into law a major **Civil Service Reform**, the first in over 100 years.

In 1973, during the Nixon Administration, the **Organization of Petroleum Exporting Countries (OPEC)** reduced supplies of oil available to world market, partly due to deflation of the dollars they were receiving and partly due to America's sending arms to Israel during the **Yom Kippur War**. The U. S. government imposed price controls on gasoline and oil following the announcement. In respond to the problems caused by the crisis, Carter established a national energy policy that included conservation, price controls, and new technology. Foreign oil imports were reduced by 50% from 1977 to 1982.

Carter was one of the first presidents to address the topic of gay rights. He opposed the **Briggs Initiative**, a California ballot measure that would have banned gays and supporters of gay rights from being public school teachers. He has stated that he "opposes all forms of discrimination on the basis of sexual orientation and believes there should be equal protection under the law for people who differ in sexual orientation".

Carter continued the policy of Richard Nixon to normalize relations with the People's Republic of China by granting it full diplomatic and trade relations but not with Taiwan (though both sides continued to trade and the U. S. unofficially recognized Taiwan through the *Taiwan Relations Act*). According to the Joint Communiqué and the Shanghai Communiqué, the United States acknowledged the Chinese position that there is only one China and Taiwan is a part of

China. Beijing acknowledged that the American people would continue to carry on commercial, cultural, and other unofficial contacts with the people of Taiwan.

The final year of carter's presidency was marked by several major crises, including serious fuel shortages and the **Soviet invasion of Afghanistan**. In the 1980 presidential election, Democratic Carter was defeated by Republican Ronald W. Reagan.

After leaving office, Carter and his wife founded the **Carter Center**, a non-governmental, not-for-profit organization that works to advance human rights. He has traveled extensively to conduct peace negotiations, observe elections and advance disease prevention and eradication in developing nations. He is also a key figure in the **Habitat for Humanity Project**. In 2019, Carter was the oldest living former president with the age of 94.

⊙ Ronald Wilson Reagan

**Ronald W. Reagan** (1911 – 2004) was the 40th president of the United States (1981 – 1989). His start in politics occurred during his work as a spokesman for **General Electric** (GE). Originally a member of the Democratic Party, he switched to the Republican Party in 1962.

President Reagan's first term was mainly on economic recovery and growth. As president, Reagan implemented new political initiatives as well as economic policies, advocating a limited government and economic noninterference philosophy. After surviving an assassination attempt and ordering military actions in Grenada, he easily won the election for a second term in 1984.

Reagan's second term began at the end of the Cold War, as well as the revelation of the Iran-Contra affair. The President made an arms race with the Soviet Union by strengthening its military. Despite his rejection of détente, he negotiated with Soviet General Secretary Mikhail Gorbachev to shrink both countries' nuclear weapons. Reagan left office in 1989 and in 1994 the former president disclosed that he had been diagnosed with Alzheimer's disease. He died ten years later at the age of ninety-three.

⊙ George Herbert Walker Bush

**George H. W. Bush** (1924 – 2018), was the 41st American president from 1989 to 1993. Before his presidency, Bush held a multitude of political positions, including the Vice President and the Director of the CIA.

Bush took office at a period of changes in the world. The fall of the **Berlin Wall** and the collapse of the Soviet Union came early in his presidency. Early in his term, Bush faced the problem of national debt, amounting to $220 billion in 1990. Dedicated to curbing the deficit to maintain the leadership in the world, he began an

effort to persuade the Congress to act on the budget. Republicans insisted on cutting government expenditures, while Democrats wished to raise taxes, which placed Bush in trouble.

In the struggle with the Congress, Bush was forced by the Democratic majority to raise taxes. As a result, many Republicans felt betrayed because Bush had promised "**no new taxes**" in his campaign of 1988. Because of various complicated reasons, at last, Bush accepted the Democrats' demands for higher taxes and more expenditure, which alienated him from Republicans and gave way to a sharp decrease in popularity.

During his second year in office, Bush was told by his economic advisors to stop emphasizing the economy, as they believed that he had done everything necessary to ensure his re-election. But in the middle of 1992, unemployment rate reached up to 7.8%, the highest since 1984. In September 1992, the Census Bureau reported that 14.2% of all Americans lived in poverty. In addition, he operated the "Desert Storm" on Iraq, which obsessed him later. He lost the presidential election to Democrat Bill Clinton in 1992.

⊙ William Jefferson Clinton

**William Jefferson Clinton** served as the 42nd president of the United States from 1993 to 2001. His birth name was William Jefferson Blythe III and then he adopted his step-father's name. Clinton was born in the period after World War II and is known as the first **Baby Boomer President.** Clinton is the second president impeached and was subsequently acquitted by the Senate on perjury and obstruction of justice charges.

Shortly after taking office, Clinton signed the *Family and Medical Leave Act of 1993*, which required large employers to allow employees to take unpaid leave for pregnancy or a serious medical condition.

One of the most prominent items during Clinton's presidency was the result of a task force headed by Hillary Clinton, a healthcare reform plan aiming at achieving universal coverage through a national healthcare plan.

Though initially well-received in political circles, it was ultimately doomed by well-organized opposition from conservatives, the American Medical Association and the health insurance industry. However, despite his party holding a majority in the Congress, because of lacking coordination within the White House, the effort to create a national healthcare system ultimately died under heavy public pressure. It was the first major legislative defeat of Clinton administration.

Two months later, after two years of Democratic Party control, the Democrats lost control of the Congress in the mid-term elections in 1994, for the first time in forty years.

The application of the federal death penalty was expanded to include crimes not resulting in death, such as running a large-scale drug enterprise, by Clinton's ***Omnibus Crime Bill*** in 1994. During Clinton's re-election campaign he said, "My 1994 Crime Bill expanded the death penalty for drug kingpins, murderers of federal law enforcement officers, and nearly 60 additional categories of violent felons."

Clinton administration launched the first official White House website on October 21, 1994. With three more versions, the final edition was launched in 2000. The White House website was part of a wider movement of the Clinton administration toward web-based communication.

The media and prominent Republicans raised a controversy over Clinton's relationship with **Monica Lewinsky**, a 22-year-old White House intern, resulting in the Lewinsky scandal on January 21, 1998. For the belief Clinton lied about his relationship with Lewinsky in a sworn deposition in the Paula Jones lawsuit, the Republican-controlled House voted to impeach Clinton in 1998. Subsequently, Clinton was not convicted by the Senate.

Clinton enacted the ***Digital Millennium Copyright Act*** on October 21, 1998, the first significant amendment to the ***Copyright Act*** since 1976. It provided a framework for sound recording copyright owners and recording artists to seek public performance royalties under statute, which proved to be a landmark achievement for the recording industry.

Clinton became the first president to visit Vietnam in November 2000 since the end of the Vietnam War. Clinton remained popular with the public throughout his two terms as the President, ending his presidential career with a 65% approval rating, the highest end-of-term approval rating of any president since Dwight D. Eisenhower. Clinton also oversaw a boom of U. S. economy. Under Clinton, the United States had a projected federal budget surplus for the first time since 1969.

### George Walker Bush

**George W. Bush**, the 43rd president of the United States from 2001 to 2009, is the first son of former president George H. W. Bush. In a close and controversial election, Bush was elected to the Presidency in 2000 as the Republican candidate, receiving a majority of the electoral vote but narrowly losing the popular vote.

As President, Bush's main policies have largely focused on foreign policy and economy. He enacted large tax cuts and the ***No Child Left Behind Act***. His presidency saw a national debate on immigration. After terrorist attacks on September 11, 2001, Bush announced a global war on terrorism and ordered an attack of Afghanistan in the same year and an attack of Iraq in 2003.

Facing opposition in the Congress, Bush held town hall-style public meetings across the country in 2001 to increase public support for his plan about a $1.35 trillion tax cut program — one of the largest tax cuts in U. S. history. Bush argued that unspent government funds should be returned to taxpayers. With reports of the threat of recession, Bush argued that such a tax cut would stimulate economy and create jobs. By 2003, the economy had showed significant signs of improvement.

In 2008, America encountered severe economic crisis, consisting of a housing market correction, a sub-prime mortgage crisis and declining value of the dollar. To ease the situation, Bush signed a $170 billion economic stimulus package to improve the economy by sending tax rebate checks to Americans and providing tax breaks for struggling businesses.

After his re-election in 2004, Bush received increasingly heated criticism. During his two terms he had both the highest and the lowest domestic Gallup poll approval ratings of American presidents, which ranged from around 90% immediately after terrorist attacks of 2001 to 28% in June 2008.

### War against terrorism

After the collapse of the Soviet Union, the United States lost its strongest rival and also lost directions on how to develop the country and the role America would play in a changing world.

Later the two political parties believed they should protect their security and interests first and decided to carry out "**New World Order**" **program.**

Under the program, America successfully defeated Hussein's invasion of Kuwait in **Gulf War** in 1990. However, in August 1998, the U. S. embassies in African nations of Kenya and Tanzania were bombed, which made the United States launch a war against Islamic fundamentalist terrorists headed by **Osama bin Laden**.

On September 11, 2001, the United States was attacked by Islamic terrorism. The attacks were a series of coordinated suicide attacks by al-Qaeda upon the United States. Nineteen Islamist terrorists affiliated with al-Qaeda hijacked four commercial passenger jet airliners. The hijackers intentionally crashed two of the airliners into the Twin Towers of the **World Trade Center** in New York City, killing everyone on board and many others working in the building. The hijackers crashed a third airliner into the Pentagon. The fourth plane crashed into a field near Shanks ville in rural Somerset County, Pennsylvania, failing to reach Washington, D. C. 2,974 people died in the attacks, excluding the 19 hijackers. All the people died in the attacks were citizens except 55 military personnel at the Pentagon.

In response to the attacks, the United States launched a war on terrorism, attacking Afghanistan to depose the Taliban, who had harbored al-Qaeda terrorists, and enacting the ***U.S.A. Patriot Act.*** Many states also strengthened their anti-terrorism legislation and expanded law enforcement powers.

The damage to the Pentagon was cleared and repaired within a year and the Pentagon Memorial was built on the site. However, as to rebuilding the World Trade Center site, there were various controversies over possible designs, the pace of construction, security concerns, and so on.

⊙ War against Iraq

**Iraq War**, also known as **Oil War**, was a conflict beginning on March 20, 2003. A multinational coalition, including the United States, the United Kingdom, Australia and other nations, invaded Iraq.

Many reasons led to the invasion. At first, the United States argued that Iraq possessed **weapons of mass destruction** (WMD) posing threat to the security and interests of the United States, Europe and the other nations in the Middle East. Then some U. S. officials accused **Saddam Hussein** of harboring and supporting Al-Qaeda. Other reasons for the invasion stated by officials included Iraq's financial support for the families of Palestinian suicide bombers, Iraqi government human rights abuses and a desire to spread democracy in the Middle East. Though the claims were supported by many countries, no firm evidence was found.

After the war broke out, Iraqi military was soon defeated. President Saddam Hussein escaped but was captured in December 2003 and hanged in December 2006. After the initial invasion, conflicts between Iraqi forces and coalition forces took place from time to time.

On April 9, 2008, Iraqi government declared that Iraqi security forces were capable of discharging their responsibilities and the U.S. troops should be pulled out as the situation allowed, which was refused by the U. S. President Bush.

In late 2008, the U. S. and Iraqi governments approved a Status of Forces Agreement. The pact establishes that U. S. combat forces would withdraw from Iraqi cities by June 30, 2009 and that all U. S. forces would be completely out of Iraq before December 31, 2011. The pact required criminal charges for holding prisoners over 24 hours and a warrant for searches of homes and buildings that were not related to combat. U. S. contractors working for U. S. forces would be subject to Iraqi criminal law, while contractors working for the U.S. State Department and other U.S. government agencies may retain their immunity from arrest.

On December 14, 2008, U. S. President George W. Bush signed the security pact with Iraq. In his fourth and final trip to Iraq, the President met with Iraq's Prime Minister and observed that more work was to be done.

On January 1, 2009, the United States handed control of the Green Zone and Saddam Hussein's presidential palace to Iraqi government in a ceremonial move described by the country's Prime Minister as a restoration of Iraq's sovereignty. Iraqi Prime Minister Nouri al-Maliki said he would propose "January 1" as declared national "Sovereignty Day".

"This palace is the symbol of Iraqi sovereignty and by restoring it, a real message is directed to all Iraqi people that Iraqi sovereignty has returned to its natural status." al-Maliki said.

After taking office, the 44th United States President Barack Obama announced that the U.S. combat mission in Iraq would end by August 31, 2010. A "transitional force" of up to 50,000 troops tasked with training the Iraqi Security Forces, conducting counterterrorism operations and providing general support may remain until the end of 2011, the President added on February 27, 2009.

### ⊙ The global financial crisis of 2008

The financial crisis of 2008 had been called by leading economists the worst financial crisis since the Great Depression of the 1930s. Many attributed to the crisis, including the failure of pillar businesses, declines in consumer wealth and consumption capacity, a significant decline in economic activities, and so on.

Beginning with failures of large financial institutions in the United States, the crisis rapidly evolved into a global credit crisis, deflation and sharp reductions in shipping resulting in a number of European bank failures and declines in various stock indexes, and large reductions in the market value of equities and commodities worldwide.

The Bush government proposed legislation to purchase about $700 billion of "troubled mortgage-related property" from financial firms in hopes of improving confidence in the mortgage-backed securities markets and the financial firms participating in it. After a series of heated discussions, hearings and meetings among legislative leaders, in the end, a revised compromise version was approved by the Senate.

The financial crisis has made great impact on the society of the United States. Under the influence of crisis, unemployment rate was rising and consumer prices got higher and higher. Nearly every aspect of social life changed more or less.

The United States presidential election of 2008 was held on November 4. Democrat **Barack Obama** won decisively, defeating Republican candidate, John McCain. In the last few months of the election campaign, particularly after the outbreak of economic crisis, the main themes shifted from foreign and domestic matters to domestic policy and the economy.

It was the 56th consecutive quadrennial United States presidential election. Selected electors from 50 states and the District of Columbia voted for the President and the Vice President of the United States on December 15, 2008. The votes were tallied before a joint session of the Congress on January 8, 2009,

thus making the projected electoral votes official. Obama received 365 electoral votes, and **McCain** 173.

For the first time in history, both major party nominees were sitting Senators: Republican candidate John McCain (Arizona) and Democratic candidate Barack Obama (Illinois). The 2008 election marked the first time since the election of John F. Kennedy in 1960 that a sitting Senator was elected President of the United States. It was also the second time in American history, after the election of John F. Kennedy and Lyndon B. Johnson in 1960, that both the successful presidential and vice-presidential candidates (Barack Obama and Joe Biden) were sitting Senators. With their victory, Biden, the longest-serving Senator in history (served for 36 years) became the Vice President. He was also the first Vice President since Lyndon B. Johnson in 1960 being re-elected to the Senate, easily winning his seventh terms.

To cope with financial crisis, the Obama government took a series of measures. Obama signed into law the ***American Recovery and Reinvestment Act of 2009***, a $787 billion economic stimulus package aiming at helping the economy recover from the deepening worldwide recession. The act, being distributed over the course of several years, included increasing federal spending for health care, infrastructure, education, various tax breaks and incentives, and directing assistance to individuals.

In March, Obama's Treasury Secretary took further steps to manage the financial crisis, including introducing the Public-Private Investment Program which contains provisions for buying up to $2 trillion in depreciated real estate assets. *The New York Times* noted that "investors reacted ecstatically, with all of the major stock indexes soaring as soon as the markets opened". Obama intervened in the troubled automotive industry, renewing loans for General Motors and Chrysler Corporation to continue operations while reorganizing both companies. He also signed into law the **Car Allowance Rebate System**, known colloquially as "*Cash for Clunkers*" bill, on August 7, 2009.

Early in the second half of 2009, the U.S. economy expanded at a 2.8% annual pace, which proved that the stimulus package helped stop the economic downturn. Various economists have credited the stimulus package with helping to create economic growth. However, unemployment rate has continued to rise to 10.1% (the highest in 26 years) and "underemployment" rate rose to 17.5%. In mid-November, Obama expressed his concerns that excessive deficit spending could cause the economy to slide into a "double dip" recession.

⊙ **Barack Hussein Obama II**

Barack Obama was the 44th president the United States from 2009 to 2017. He was born in Honolulu, Hawaii, becoming the first president born outside the continental United States. He is also the third president from Illinois, the first two being Abraham Lincoln and Ulysses S. Grant. (Ronald Reagan was born in Illinois, but when elected he had been in California for decades, where he was a former governor.) Obama, having a white mother and a Kenyan father of the Luo ethnic group, is the first African American president. He was awarded Nobel Peace Prize in 2009.

On March 11, 2009, Obama created the White House Council on Women and Girls, concerning about the welfare of American women and girls. He also established the White House Task Force to protect students from sexual assault through a government memorandum on January 22, 2014, concerning about sexual assault on college and university campuses throughout the United States.

Obama appointed two women to serve on the Supreme Court in the first two years of his presidency. He nominated Sonia Sotomayor in 2009 to replace retiring Associate Justice David Souter, which madener the first Supreme Court Justice of Hispanic descent, and nominated Elena Kagan in 2010 to replace retiring Associate Justice John Paul Stevens, bringing the number of women sitting simultaneously on the Court to three for the first time in American history.

Health care reform was a key campaign promise and a top legislative goal. The Affordable Care Act (ACA) was signed into law on March 23, 2010. The Act includes health-related provisions, most of which took effect in 2014, including expanding people's Medicaid eligibility, offering businesses incentives to providing health care benefits, prohibiting denial of coverage and denial of claims based on pre-existing conditions, establishing health insurance exchanges, prohibiting annual coverage caps, and support for medical research.

On January 16, 2013, one month after the Sandy Hook Elementary School shooting, Obama signed executive orders regarding gun control. He urged the Congress to ban military-style assault weapons, introduce background checks on all gun sales, pass a ban on possession and sale of armor-piercing bullets, introduce harsher penalties for gun-traffickers, especially unlicensed dealers who buy arms for criminals and approve the appointment of the head of the federal Bureau of Alcohol, Tobacco, Firearms and Explosives for the first time since 2006. On January 5, 2016, Obama announced new executive actions extending background check requirements to more gun sellers.

Early in his presidency, Obama moved to bolster U.S. troop strength in Afghanistan. He announced an increase in U.S. troop in February 2009. In October 2015, the White House announced a plan to keep U.S. Forces in Afghanistan indefinitely in light of the deteriorating security situation.

In 2009, the Obama administration went ahead increasing nuclear weapons production. But in November 2013, the Obama administration made negotiations with Iran to prevent it from acquiring nuclear weapons. Negotiations reached a deal which was announced on July 14, 2015. The deal, titled the "Joint Comprehensive Plan of Action", saw the removal of sanctions in exchange for measures that would prevent Iran from producing nuclear weapons. While Obama hailed the agreement as being a step towards a more hopeful world, the deal drew strong criticism from Republican and conservative quarters, and from Israeli Prime Minister Benjamin Netanyahu. On May 27, 2016, Obama became the first sitting American president to visit Hiroshima, Japan, 71 years after the U.S. atomic bombing of Hiroshima. Accompanied by Japanese Prime Minister Shinzō Abe, Obama paid tribute to the victims of the bombing at the Hiroshima Peace Memorial Museum.

⊙ **Tea Party Movement**

The **Tea Party Movement** is a United States conservative political movement emerging in 2009 and opposing to government taxation and spending. It originated in libertarian anti-tax protests but grew dramatically during the presidency of Barack Obama.

The events are in protest of President Barack Obama, the federal budget and the stimulus package. They opposed the increase in the national debt and objected to possible future tax increases. The name "Tea Party" is a reference to the Boston Tea Party with an attempt to evoke images and slogans from the American Revolution. The movement eventually became the Taxpayer March on September 12, 2009, in Washington, D.C.

⊙ *Travel Promotion Act of 2009*

The ***Travel Promotion Act of 2009*** was a law proposed to charge non-American tourists staying less than 90 days in the United States with a fee of $10. The Electronic System for Travel Authorization could be used as web-based interface to obtain credit card data of foreign tourists. The money collected from travelers would be spent for advertising to attract tourists. Harry Reid supported the bill because his constituency had shown a decline in visitor numbers.

The reactions of the European Union were harsh and suggestions of a similar fee had been raised on grounds of Reciprocity.

⊙ Donald Trump

**Donald Trump**, born in New York on June 14, 1946, defeated Democratic former Secretary of State Hillary Clinton in the presidential election of 2016 and took the oath of the office to be the 45th president of the United States on January 20, 2017.

The Trump administration made great progress in cutting taxes, toughening trade policies, increasing diplomatic and military layout, relaxing financial regulation through legislation, and signing executive order and personnel appointment, among which tax reform is the biggest highlight of his early achievements.

During his campaign, Trump promised to cut taxes for middle-class workers and families and businesses. In April 2017, the White House unveiled a brief outline that would slash corporate taxes to 15% from the then 35%, cut the number of individual income tax brackets from 7 to 3, abolish estate tax and double tax-free income. In September, the Trump administration unveiled a detailed plan for tax reform that was broadly consistent in content, with exception of a reduction in the top corporate tax to 20% from 15% as outlined in April. On December 22, 2017, Trump signed the **Tax Cuts and Job Act**. The law took in effect in January 2018.

Financial deregulation has been a central agenda of the Trump administration. On May 25, 2018, Trump signed the **Economic Growth, Regulatory Relief, and Consumer Production Act**, the first major adjustment to 2010 Dodd-Frank Financial Regulation Law. The bill has been relaxed on the assets of less than $10 billion in the bank transactions, lending and capital aspects of regulatory requirements, and regulations of assets under $250 billion no longer participating in the federal's stress tests annually, and not submitting to the federal reserve the approval of "living wills" after bankruptcy. The two acts were set up to prevent economic crisis.

After taking the office, Trump abolished the Affordable Care Act (ACA) signed by Obama, which led to people's opposition and demonstration. The new plan proposed was approved by the House but rejected by the Senate. On October 12, 2017, Trump signed an executive order "Promoting Healthcare Choice and Competition Across the United States", paving the way for the eventual repeal of ACA.

Trump retreated many organizations and groups, which was criticized by people at home and abroad. On January 23, 2017, Trump signed an executive order to quit the Trans-Pacific Partnership (TPP) Agreement. In June, he announced that the U. S. would stop relationship with the non-binding Paris Agreement, and the process began on November 4, 2019. In October, he claimed the U. S. withdrawal from the United Nations Educational, Scientific, and Cultural Organization (UNESCO), which was in effect on January 1, 2019. In May and June 2018, the U. S. withdrew from Iran nuclear deal and the United Nations Human Rights Council. In October, Trump signed a memorandum to start the process of quitting the Universal Postal Union. In April 2019, it was announced that the United States would withdraw from the Arms Trade Treaty, and from the Intermediate-Range Nuclear Forces Treaty (INF) in August.

On May 22, 2020, President Trump announced that the United States withdrew from the Open Skies Treaty due to alleged Russian violations. Early in October 2019, the plan started. NATO allies and partners, especially Ukraine, were against the move, fearing it would license Russia to reduce further or ban overflights, thus preventing them from learning Russian military movements.

On May 29, 2020, President Trump announced plans to withdraw the U. S. from the World Health Organization (WHO). Early in time, he announced that his administration would halt funding to the WHO. Funds previously earmarked for the WHO were to be held for 60 to 90 days pending an investigation into WHO's handling of the COVID-19 pandemic, particularly in respect to the organization's purported relationship with China. The announcement was immediately criticized by world leaders including the Secretary General of the United Nations António Guterres, the German Foreign Minister Heiko Maas, and African Union Chairman Moussa Faki Mahamat.

⊙ Government shutdowns

The United States federal government shutdown amounted to 35 days from December 22, 2018 to January 25, 2019. It was the longest U. S. government shutdown in history, and the second federal government shutdown involving furloughs during the presidency of Donald Trump. The shutdown stemmed from an impasse over Trump's demand for $5.7 billion in federal funds for a U. S. - Mexico border wall which he had promised in his presidential campaign.

⊙ Trump's border wall (Mexico-United States barrier)

After Trump took office in 2017, he began attempting wall construction along the Mexican border by using existing federal funding, but due to the significant cost, the actual construction did not begin at that time. Trump's insistence that he would veto any appropriations bill that did not fund wall construction led to the shutdown of the federal government.

In September 2019, Trump claimed to build 450 – 500 miles of new wall by the end of 2020. However, only about 76 miles of existing wall had been replaced or reinforced, and no new wall had been completed by November 2019. On January 8, 2020, a federal appeals court granted $3.6 billion for the wall construction. The Pentagon notified the Congress on February 13 that it would divert $3.8 billion from funding for the military's anti-drug activities and the war on terror to building the wall.

⊙ Muslim ban

Muslim ban refers to an executive order titled "Protecting the Nation from Foreign Terrorist Entry into the United States" signed by Trump on January 27, 2017. The order lowered the number of refugees to be admitted into the U. S. in 2017 to 50,000, suspended the U. S. Refugee Admissions Program (USRAP) for 120 days, suspended the entry of Syrian refugees indefinitely, directed some cabinet secretaries to suspend entry of those whose countries do not meet adjudication standards under U. S. immigration law for 90 days, and included exceptions on a case-by-case basis. The Department of Homeland Security (DHS) lists these countries as Iran, Iraq, Libya, Somalia, Sudan, Syria, and Yemen. More than 700 travelers were detained, and up to 60,000 visas were "provisionally revoked".

The order provoked widespread condemnation and protests and resulted in legal intervention against the enforcement of the order with some calling it a "Muslim ban" because President Trump had previously called for temporarily banning Muslims from entering America and because all the affected countries had a Muslim majority.

⊙ Influence of the China-US trade war

The **China-United States trade war** is an ongoing economic conflict between China and the United States because of trade tariffs and barriers on China in 2018. The Congressional Budget Office (CBO) explained tariffs reduce U. S. economic activity in three ways: consumer and capital goods become more expensive; business uncertainty increases, thereby reducing or slowing investment; and other countries impose retaliatory tariffs, making U. S. exports more expensive and thus reducing them.

The trade war caused turbulence in the stock market. The Dow Jones Industrial Average dropped continually, especially on the day Trump informally ordered American companies to immediately seek alternatives to doing business in China. By the end of 2019, stock markets had risen due to the agreement between the United States and China to sign the first phase of a trade deal.

Analysts speculated that the trade war could affect the 2020 United States presidential election, as tariffs have negatively affected farmers, an important constituency for Trump.

⊙ COVID – 19 pandemic

The COVID – 19 pandemic, also known as the coronavirus pandemic, is an ongoing pandemic of coronavirus disease, caused by severe acute respiratory syndrome coronavirus. The WHO declared a Public Health Emergency of International Concern on January 30, 2020 and a pandemic on March 11. By June 19, 2020 more than 8.45 million cases had been reported in more than 188 countries and territories, resulting in more than 452 thousand deaths and more than 4.13 million recovered.

⊙ Joe Biden

**Joe Biden** was inaugurated as the 46th president of the United States on January 20, 2021. He defeated incumbent Donald Trump, becoming the first candidate to defeat a sitting president since Bill Clinton defeated George H. W. Bush in 1992. At 78, he is the oldest elected president, the first from Delaware, and the second Catholic. He was once as Vice President serving as an adviser to Obama and a vocal supporter of his initiatives.

On December 13, 2022, Biden signed into law the Respect for Marriage Act. The act formally repealed the federal Defense of Marriage Act (1996), which had defined marriage as a legal union between one man and one woman and had permitted states to refuse to recognize same-sex marriages performed in other states.

Among Biden's goals in foreign policy were to repair frayed relations with several U. S. allies, to cooperate in global efforts to ameliorate climate change, and, in general, to return the United States to a position of global economic and political leadership. Biden had also promised during his campaign that he would withdraw all remaining U. S.

troops from Afghanistan, finally ending nearly 20 years of U. S. military involvement in the country during all phases of the Afghan War, the longest military conflict ever fought by the United States. Besides, it seems that relations between the U. S. and China are on a "dangerous" path with "no trust" on either side, since tensions between the U. S. and China have been rising over the years, ranging from trade and tariffs to tech rivalry.

After the outbreak of **the Russia-Ukraine war** on February 24, 2022, the United States and its Western countries, on the one hand, imposed massive blockade and sanctions on Russia, and on the other hand, provided weapons aid and economic support to Ukraine. As Biden do have complicated strategies to hit Russia a double blow by using the Ukrainian government, it is stated that the Russia-Ukraine war rooted in US policy towards Russia.

⊙ The Retreat of American Troops from Afghanistan in 2021

On October 7, 2001, the United States launched an air strike against Afghanistan in the name of "anti-terrorism" and launched the war in Afghanistan. Over the past 20 years, more than 2,000 US soldiers have died and more than 20,000 US soldiers have been injured in the Afghan war, at a cost of more than $2,000 billion.

In April 2021 Biden announced a withdrawal of all U. S. troops by September 11—an extension of the May 1 withdrawal deadline negotiated with the Taliban by the Trump administration in 2020. By early August, after Biden had advanced the withdrawal deadline to August 31, the Taliban had begun to take military control of several Afghan provinces, and soon thereafter the Afghan capital, Kabul, was captured and the national government collapsed. Chaos ensued as the airport in Kabul was flooded with desperate Afghan refugees seeking to flee the country on American evacuation flights. During and after the withdrawal, the Biden administration was criticized by Republican and some Democratic leaders for having misjudged the strength and resolve of both the Taliban and the Afghan government and security forces.

? **Group presentation:**
1. What policies did American president Obama take against terrorism?
2. What was Obama's attitude to the Iraq War?
3. What measures did Obama take to cope with the 2008 economic crisis?
4. What is Trump's "America first"?

### Relations with China

The present China-American relations are complex and multi-faceted with the United States and the People's Republic of China (P. R. C.) being neither allies nor enemies. Generally, the American government does not regard the Chinese as an adversary, but as a competitor in some areas and a partner in others. At the same time, it is acknowledged that the nature of China-American relations will be a major factor in determining the fate of the world in the 21st century.

Throughout history, the China-American relations have experienced normal and tense states.

In July 1971, **Henry Kissinger**, on his way to Pakistan, feigned illness and did not appear in public for one day. He was actually on a top-secret mission to Beijing to establish relations with the government of the P. R. C. On July 15, 1971, **President Richard Nixon** announced that he had accepted the invitation to visit the P. R. C.

This announcement caused immediate shock around the world. In the United States, some anti-communists stood against the decision, but public opinion supported the move. In 1972, President Nixon visited the People's Republic of China, marking the first official visit of a president in recent history of the United States. From February 21 to 28, 1972, President Nixon traveled to Beijing, Hangzhou and Shanghai. As the conclusion of his trip, the U. S. and the P. R. C. issued the **Shanghai Communiqué**, a statement of their respective foreign policy views. In the Communiqué, both nations pledged to work toward the full normalization of diplomatic relations. The U. S. acknowledged the P. R. C. position that there is only one China and that Taiwan is a part of China. The statement enabled the U. S. and the P. R. C. to temporarily set aside the "sensitive topic (Taiwan) obstructing the normalization of relations" and to open trade and other contacts.

In May 1973, in an effort to establish formal diplomatic relations, the U. S. and the P. R. C. established the United States Liaison Office (USLO) in Beijing and a counterpart Chinese office in Washington, D. C. In the years between 1973 and 1978, distinguished Americans such as David K. E.

Bruce, George H. W. Bush, Thomas S. Gates, and Leonard Woodcock served as chiefs of the USLO with the personal rank of Ambassador.

President Gerald Ford visited China in 1975 and restated America's interest in normalizing relations with Beijing. Shortly after taking office in 1977, President Jimmy Carter again reaffirmed the aims of the Shanghai Communiqué. One year later, the two governments declared that the United States would establish diplomatic relations with the People's Republic of China at ambassadorial level on January 1, 1979. The China-American relations became normalized. Deng Xiaoping's visiting Washington, D. C. in January 1979 initiated a series of important and high-level exchanges which continued until the spring of 1989. The invitation resulted in many bilateral agreements, especially in the fields of scientific, technological and cultural interchange as well as trade relations. Since early 1979, the United States and China have initiated hundreds of joint research projects and cooperative programs under the Agreement on Cooperation in Science and Technology, the largest bilateral program.

As a consequence of high-level and working-level contacts started in 1980, the communications between the two countries broadened to cover a wide range of issues, including political-military questions, global and regional strategic problems, United Nations and other multilateral organization affairs, and so on.

In 1981, regardless of the former communiqués, America sold weapons to Taiwan, which led to the crisis of China-American relations. The Chinese government strongly protested America's action. Secretary of State Alexander Haig visited China in June 1981 with an attempt to resolve Chinese questions about America's unofficial relations with Taiwan. After eight-month negotiations, on August 17, 1982, the two countries issued the **U. S. -P. R. C. Joint Communiqué**, in which the United States stated it would gradually reduce the level of arms sales to Taiwan and China took it as a fundamental policy to strive for a peaceful resolution to the question of Taiwan.

In 1996, the China-American relations improved, with increased high-level exchanges and progress on numerous bilateral issues, including human rights, nuclear nonproliferation and trade. President Jiang Zemin visited the United States in the fall of 1997 and the two sides came to a consensus on implementation of their agreement made in 1985 on Peaceful Nuclear Cooperation as well as a number of other issues. President Clinton visited the People's Republic of China in June 1998. He traveled extensively in China's mainland and had direct interaction with the Chinese people including live speeches and radio shows, allowing the President to convey firsthand to the Chinese people a sense of American ideals and values.

With the efforts of both governments, the China-American relations were turning better until the Chinese embassy in Belgrade was bombed by an American B-2 bomber in May 1999, with three Chinese journalists dead, many people wounded and the building destroyed.

After the incident, enraged Chinese, especially students, held demonstrations against the American government and other European countries. To settle the incident, the two governments reached an agreement. American President Clinton apologized to the Chinese government for the incident and promised to pay for the damaged embassy. Not until the end of 1999 did the China-American relations gradually come to recovery, but the exchange between the heads of two governments ceased.

Shortly after the bombing of Chinese embassy in Belgrade, an American reconnaissance plane collided with a Chinese fighter jet scrutinizing the American observation activities on Chinese territory 110 miles away southeast of Hainan Island on April 1, 2001. The reconnaissance plane made an emergency landing on Hainan Island despite extensive damage, but Chinese fighter jet crashed with its pilot, Wang Wei, killed. It was widely believed that the reconnaissance plane was conducting a spying mission on the Chinese Armed Forces before the collision.

Another anti-American demonstration was staged following the incident. The Chinese government insisted that the American government stop any scouting activities along the Chinese seacoast and make a formal apology. The U.S. Ambassador Joseph Prueher delivered a letter to Tang Jiaxuan, Foreign Minister of China, that is, the so called "letter of the two sorries" — sorry for the loss of Chinese pilot and sorry for American plane entering China's airspace and landing without approval of the Chinese government. American pilots were sent back to America after eleven days' being held in China, but the U. S. aircraft was not permitted to depart for another three months.

The crash incident harmed China-American relations.

China-American relations changed completely following the terrorist attacks in 2001. The Chinese government offered strong public support for the war on terrorism and contributed $150 million of bilateral assistance to Afghan reconstruction following the defeat of the Taliban. Shortly after terrorist attacks, the U.S. and the P.R.C. commenced a counterterrorism dialogue, with the third round of the dialogue held in Beijing in February 2003.

Terrorist attacks greatly changed the nature of discourse in America: China was not the prime security threat, but the Middle East. The war on terrorism made it a priority for the U.S. to avoid potential distractions in East Asia.

Taiwan continues to be a volatile issue, but one that remains under control. American policy toward Taiwan has involved emphasizing the **Four Noes and One Without**. On occasion the United States rebuked Chen Shui-bian for provocative pro-independence rhetoric. However, in 2005, the People's Republic of China passed an anti-secession law which stated that the P.R.C. would be prepared to resort to "non-peaceful means" if Taiwan declared formal independence. Many critics of the P.R.C., such as the Blue team, argued that China was trying to take advantage of the U.S. war in Iraq to assert its claims on Taiwan Island.

In September, 2009 a trade dispute emerged between China and the United States which came after the U.S. imposed tariffs of 35 percent on Chinese tire imports. The Chinese Commerce Minister accused the United States of a "grave act of trade protectionism" and China was taking the dispute to the World Trade Organization. Additional issues were raised by both sides in subsequent months.

American President Barack Obama visited China from November 15 to 18, 2009, discussing economic issues, concerns over nuclear weapons proliferation, and the need to act to stem climate change. During the visitation, the two governments reached some agreements and the China-American relations stepped into a new stage.

After Trump took the office, he overhauled the US policy toward China in the name of "fairness, mutual benefit" and "result oriented". The focus of his efforts to restructure China-US relations is to reshape the framework and connotation of the relationship, with economic and trade as the starting point and comprehensive efforts in diplomacy, security, politics, culture, and other fields.

The reconstruction of economic and trade relations included two aspects: One was to expand American commercial interests in China, and the other was to limit the growth of Chinese power. Trump began setting tariffs and other trade barriers on China in 2018, which led to the ongoing China-United States trade war.

In 2019, Trump successively signed the *Hong Kong Human Rights and Democracy Act*, and the *TAIPEI Act*, which seriously interfered in China's internal affairs. The China-US relationship has been victimized and became tense again.

United States China talks in Alaska were held on March 18 in 2021, lasting two days. The talks took place at the Captain Cook Hotel in Anchorage, Alaska. The Chinese representatives accused the United States of using military force and financial means to other countries, abusing its own national security and threatening global trade and of interference in China's internal affairs, while the Americans accused the Chinese of breaking rules and threatening global stability.

On July 26, 2021, Chinese Vice Foreign Minister Xie Feng held talks with US Deputy Secretary of State Wendy Sherman in Tianjin. It was another high-level meeting between China and the United States after their talks in Alaska in March. In the talks, Xie Feng proposed two lists to the United States. One is a list of asking the US to correct its wrong China policies, words and deeds, and the other is a list of key cases that China is concerned about. Meanwhile, China has put forward the "four stops", that is, "immediately stop interfering in China's internal affairs; stop harming China's interests; stop stepping on the red line and playing with fire provocations, and stop engaging in bloc confrontation under the guise of values". To manage differences between the two sides and prevent China-US relations from slipping further or even getting out of control, China's Foreign Minister Wang Yi put forward three basic requirements to the U.S., which are also China's three bottom lines.

On July 9, 2022, Wang Yi, Chinese State Councilor and foreign minister, held a meeting with US Secretary of State Antony Blinken in Bali, Indonesia. During the talks, the Chinese representatives pointed out that Sino-US relation has not gone out of difficulties and encountered more challenges due to the problems in the Americans' perception of China, reflecting the deviation of the American's outlook to the world, China, Sino-US history, interests and competition, thus deviating its policy towards China. The Chinese asked the U.S. to seriously take the four lists proposed by China, namely, the list of requesting the U.S. to correct its wrong policies, words and deeds towards China, the list of key cases the Chinese concerned, the list of China-related-acts the Chinese concerned, and the list of cooperation in eight areas between the U. S. and China. Compared with the two lists put forward by the Chinese in Tianjin Talk one year ago, these lists are more detailed. The U. S. proposed "six no's" when introducing its policies towards China, expressing its desire to control risks and cooperate with China. Both sides believe that the dialogue is substantive and constructive, which helps to enhance mutual understanding, reduce misunderstanding and miscalculation, and accumulate conditions for future high-level exchanges between the two countries.

On August 2, 2022, Nancy Pelosi, Speaker of the United States House of Representatives, "visited" Taiwan in spite of China's strong opposition. At the same time, many governments and international organizations around the world issued statements, saying that they adhere to the "one China principle" and oppose the America's actions against China's sovereignty and territorial integrity. From the evening of August 2, the Chinese People's Liberation Army Eastern Theater successively carried out a series of joint military operations around Taiwan Island, conducted joint sea and air performance training in the northern, southwestern and southeastern sea and airspace of Taiwan Island, and conducted long-range live fire in the Taiwan Strait, and organized regular guided fire test in the eastern sea area of Taiwan Island.

On September 20, 2022, the American destroyer "Higgins" and the Canadian frigate "Vancouver" sailed across the Taiwan Strait and were publicly hyped, and the U. S. said that the waterway through which U. S. warships crossed the Taiwan Strait is "international waters". As we all know, Taiwan is an inherent territory of China, and the Taiwan Strait is definitely not the so-called "international waters". What the United States and Canada are doing was a malicious provocation against China!

The Taiwan question is China's core interest, and it is also a very sensitive issue in Sino-US relations. The U. S. should strictly abide by various agreements reached with China, stop "official" exchanges with Taiwan, stop selling weapons and equipment to Taiwan, and avoid damaging bilateral relations and destabilizing the Taiwan Strait.

### ❓ Group discussion:
1. What policies did the American government take for and against China in different periods of history?
2. What policies did Obama take as to China? Did they have any changes?
3. What's the effect of the three Sino-US talks?

## Exercises

### Ⅰ. Fill in the blanks.
1. Counterculture in the 1960s was a movement of _____ against the moral values, the aesthetic _____ and the personal behavior.
2. During World War Ⅱ, the leaders of the United States, the Soviet Union and Britain met at _____, _____ and _____ conferences.
3. Japanese bombers, on the morning of December 7, 1941, suddenly showered bombs on the American fleet and military installations at _____, Hawaii.
4. On September 1, 1939, one week after _____ and Hitler's German government signed their _____, World War Ⅱ broke out with the Germany invasion of Poland.
5. On December 15, 1978, the U. S. and the China governments announced that the United States would establish diplomatic relations with the People's Republic of China at _____ level on January 1, 1979.
6. _____, also known as the Oil War, is an ongoing conflict which began on March 20, 2003.
7. George W. Bush's main policies have largely focused on _____ and the _____.
8. _____ became president at the end of the Cold War, and, as he was born in the period after World War Ⅱ, is known as the first Baby Boomer President.

### Ⅱ. Define the following terms.
1. counterculture
2. the Axis powers
3. Lend-Lease Bill
4. McCarthyism
5. New Frontier

### Ⅲ. Multiple choice.
1. The New Frontier and War on Poverty were put forward respectively by _____.
   A. Eisenhower and Kennedy
   B. Johnson and Nixon
   C. Johnson and Kennedy
   D. Kennedy and Johnson
2. President Nixon decided to resign because he _____.
   A. refused to hand over the White House tapes to court
   B. was tired of political struggle in Washington, D. C.
   C. came to see that most probably he would be impeached

D. was deserted by the Republican Party
3. In 1972, U. S. President _____ visited China, which led to the establishment of U. S. diplomatic relations with China in January 1979.
   A. Ronald Reagan    B. Richard Nixon
   C. Jimmy Carter     D. Gerald Ford
4. The best-known speech made by Civil Rights leader Martin Luther King is _____.
   A. "Guess who?"
   B. "I have a dream"
   C. "United we stand, divided we fall"
   D. "First in war, first in peace, first in the hearts of his countrymen"
5. During World War II, the Axis powers were mainly made up by _____.
   A. Germany, France and Japan
   B. France, Japan and Britain
   C. Germany, Italy and Britain
   D. Germany, Italy and Japan
6. _____ was an actor before he became the President.
   A. Ronald Reagan
   B. Abraham Lincoln
   C. Herbert Hoover
   D. Jimmy Carter
7. The two fighting sides in World War II were _____.
   A. the Allies and the Axis (powers)
   B. the Axis and Holy Alliance
   C. the Central Powers and the Allies
   D. the Alliance and the Entente
8. The program of 1947 that America would offer its money supplies and machinery to any European nation that wished to participate in was called _____.
   A. Eisenhower Doctrine
   B. Marshall Plan
   C. Truman Doctrine
   D. McCarthyism

## IV. Translate the following terms into English.
1. 北大西洋公约组织
2. 古巴导弹危机
3. 水门事件
4. 越南战争
5. 冷战

## V. Answer the following questions in a few sentences.
1. What impacts did the Vietnam War have on American society?

2. Why did America change its foreign policy in World War II?

3. What is the main content of Johnson's "Great Society" program?

### Mini-tasks:

1. In order to manage the financial crisis domestically, the Obama government made a series of laws and acts to protect and promote the development of economy; on the other hand, it tried to attract foreign capital and receive loans from other countries. The Obama government was opposed by people both at home and abroad. Several marches in the country showed that increasing taxes put greater burden on people, and a set of trade barriers made other countries unsatisfied. Talk about the management measures the Obama government had made. To what extent, in what way, can these measures bring benefits to the common Americans?

2. The 2009 Nobel Peace Prize was awarded to U. S. President Barack Obama "for his extraordinary efforts to strengthen international diplomacy and cooperation between peoples". Obama is the first U. S. president to receive the award during his first year in office (at eight and a half months, after being nominated less than a month in office). The Norwegian Nobel Committee announced the award on October 9, 2009, citing Obama's promotion of nuclear nonproliferation and a "new climate" in international relations fostered by him, especially in reaching out to the Muslim world. Discuss what contribution Obama made to the peace of the country and the world.

# VOLUME THREE

# THE COMMONWEALTH OF AUSTRALIA

# Chapter One  Geography and Population

> *Famous for its beautiful scenery, Australia attracts millions of tourists around the world. Try to get some information about Australian geography and tourist attractions and offer some advice to the potential tourists.*

## Part One  Position

Australia, with full official name as the **Commonwealth of Australia**, is a country in the Southern Hemisphere comprising the mainland of the world's smallest continent, the major island of Tasmania, and numerous other islands in the Indian and Pacific Oceans. To the Europeans, Australia is at the end of the world. That is why Australia is popularly known in the West as "the **Land Down Under**". Australia is surrounded by the **Tasman Sea** and the Pacific Ocean to the east, by the Indian Ocean to the west, by the **Coral Sea**, the **Arafura Sea** and **Timor Sea** to the north, and the Southern Indian Ocean and the **Great Australian Bight** to the south. Its neighbouring countries are **Indonesia**, **East Timor** and **Papua New Guinea** to the north, the **Solomon Islands**, **Vanuatu** and **New Caledonia** to the northeast and **New Zealand** to the southeast.

Australia is the world's sixth largest country and the only single country occupying an entire continent. Australia has a total 36,735 kilometres of coastline (excluding all offshore islands) and claims an extensive Exclusive Economic Zone of 8,148,250 square kilometres (excluding the Australian Antarctic Territory).

## Part Two  Geographical Features

The island continent is featured by landscape variety. The geographical structure is generally divided into three regions: the **Eastern Highlands**, the **Central Eastern Lowlands** and the **Great Western Plateau**.

### The Eastern Highlands

The Eastern Highlands, better known as the Great Dividing Range, is Australia's main watershed. It extends as an almost unbroken series of plateaus from northern Queensland, to the eastern coast of Australia.

The northern part of the Highlands is generally low and vast and grows higher to the south. In the middle part, there are many highlands. **Mount Kosciuszko**, 2,228 metres, is the highest mountain on the Australian mainland, while **Mawson Peak** on the remote Australian territory of Heard Island is taller at 2,745 metres.

The Great Dividing Range is the main dividing range in Australia. Rivers that flow down the eastern slope empty into the Pacific Ocean and rivers that run down the western slope flow to the Central Lowlands providing irrigation for the fertile soil. The **Great Barrier Reef**, the largest coral structure in the world, lies a short distance off the northeast coast. There lies the **Murray River**, the longest in Australia, which extends about 2,589 kilometres and flows into the sea in **South Australia**.

### The Central Eastern Lowlands

The Central Eastern Lowlands refers to the great **lowland belt** between the Eastern Highlands and the Great Western Plateau. The average elevation in this region is about 150 metres, and is even 12 metres below sea level in Lake Eyre area. **Lake Eyre** is regarded as the largest lake in Australia, but it is a parttime lake, because most of the time the lake is empty. This lowland region is occupied by the **Great Artesian Basin**, which consists of sedimentary rocks holding water entering the wetter Eastern Highlands and is well-known for its fertile farmland and pastureland.

### The Great Western Plateau

The Great Western Plateau, covering nearly two-thirds of Australian territory, is made up of ancient rocks. The land in this region is flat with elevation of only 300 metres.

Generally speaking, Australia is considered as the flattest, lowest and driest continent country and is the only continent where people can get to the top of the highest mountain by car. In addition, the world's two largest mountains are located in Australia. Mount Augustus in Western Australia is the largest and Uluru in central Australia ranks second.

## Part Three  Climate

### Features of Climate

The most significant feature of climate in Australia is high temperature. Climate in northern Australia, with a tropical climate and the annual temperature above zero, is very hot. It may snow or freeze only in mountain peaks in winter. The northern part of the country is covered with vegetation consisting of rainforest, woodland, grassland and desert.

Climate in central west is very dry. Two-thirds of the country suffers from drought and some areas even become deserts or semi-deserts due to the lack of rainfall and rivers. Climate in southeast and southwest is temperate. Southern coastline, with abundant rainfall, becomes the place of residence for most people.

### Factors Influencing Climate

The climate is significantly influenced by ocean currents, including the El Niño southern oscillation, which is correlated with periodic drought, and the seasonal tropical low pressure system that produces cyclones in northern Australia.

Several factors contribute to the hot and dry climate of Australia.

First, the continent is located in the Torrid Zone which is the hottest and driest area in the world. Second, Australia is a flat continent and there are no high mountains which can hold back the clouds from the ocean and provide cool and wet weather. Third, most part of the country is far away from ocean, so wet clouds can hardly reach into the inland.

## Part Four  The People

Although Australia has a vast territory, the total population is about 25.44 million in July, 2019. The indigenous population, mainland Aborigines and Torres Strait Islanders, makes up 2.8% of the total population in 2019. Indigenous Australians suffer from higher rates of imprisonment and unemployment, and lower levels of education. Life expectancies for indigenous males and females are 14.8 years lower than those of non-Indigenous Australians.

Others are immigrants and their descendants. Most of the Australians are descendants of colonial-era settlers and post-Federation immigrants from Europe. For generations, the vast majority of both colonial-era settlers and post-federation immigrants came almost exclusively from the British Isles and people of Australia are still mainly of British or Irish ethnic origin.

Australia's population has quadrupled since the end of World War I, spurred by an ambitious immigration programme. Following World War II and by the year of 2000, almost 5.9 million of the total population had settled in the country as new immigrants, that is, nearly two out of every seven Australians were born overseas. Most immigrants are skilled, but the immigration quota includes categories for family members and refugees. In 2006, the five largest groups of Australians born overseas were from the United Kingdom, New Zealand, Italy, Vietnam, and China. Following the abolition of the White Australia policy in 1973, numerous government initiatives have been established to encourage and promote racial harmony based on a policy of **multiculturalism**. From the year of 2018 to 2019, more than 239,600 people immigrated to Australia, mainly from Asia and Oceania. Australia opens its doors to about 300,000 new migrants in 2008 and 2009 — it is the highest level since the **Immigration Department** was created after World War II. People from different countries and cultures brought with them different ways of life, languages, religions, food and customs, which has characterised Australia as a multicultural society in which people can keep their own cultures.

In common with many other developed countries, Australia is experiencing a demographic shift to an aged society, with more retirees and fewer people of working age. In 2004, the average age of the civilian population was 38.8. A large number of Australians live outside their homeland.

Since it was once a colony of Britain, people in Australia and Britain share more similarities than differences. Australia is one of the most urbanized countries in the world, with 80% of Australians living in the suburbs of coastal cities and towns, while other parts of the country thinly populated because of shortage of water and food.

### ❓ Questions for discussion:

1. With the worsening of global warming, what changes has Australia gone through in climate, compared with past decades?
2. The Australian government made a set of laws and acts to encourage immigration to Australia in order to maintain a balanced population. What requirements should people meet and what qualifications should they have to be citizens of Australia?

---

## Exercises

### I. Fill in the blanks.

1. To the Europeans, Australia is at the end of the world. That is why Australia is popularly known in the West as "_____ _____ _____ _____".
2. Australia is the _____ continent in the world with an area of some _____ million square kilometres on the Indo-Australian Plate.
3. Australia is generally divided into the following three topographical regions: _____, _____ and _____.
4. _____ is the highest mountain on the Australian mainland, although _____ on the remote Australian territory of Heard Island is taller at 2,745 metres.
5. _____ is the longest river in Australia.
6. _____ is regarded as the largest lake in Australia, but it is a part-time lake, because most of the time the lake is empty.
7. The people of Australia are still mainly of _____ or _____ ethnic origin.

### II. Define the following terms.

1. the Land Down Under
2. Great Dividing Range

### III. Multiple choice.

1. Australia has always been a continent with few people mainly because _____.
   A. Australia is too far away from Europe
   B. Australia is the least mountainous and the flattest of the world's continents
   C. Australia is separated from the rest of the world by seas
   D. most of the continent is hot and dry
2. With regard to its size, Australia is _____ country in the world.
   A. the third largest
   B. the fourth largest
   C. the fifth largest
   D. the sixth largest
3. Although Australia has a large area, _____ of the continent is desert or semi-desert.
   A. one-third          B. two-thirds
   C. half               D. more than half
4. In Australia _____ has the country's richest farmland and best grazing land.
   A. the Great Western Plateau
   B. the Eastern Highlands
   C. the Central Eastern Lowlands
   D. the Outback
5. Which of the following statements about Australia is NOT true?
   A. It lies south of the equator.
   B. It is the world's smallest continent.
   C. It is the flattest and lowest continent.
   D. It is the continent that contains more than one country.
6. _____ is Australia's main watershed where short, swift rivers flow into the Pacific Ocean.
   A. The Great Western Plateau
   B. The Great Dividing Range
   C. The Central Eastern Lowlands
   D. The Nullarbor Plain
7. In recent years Australian governments have encouraged people with different ethnic backgrounds to keep their own cultures. This policy is called _____.
   A. assimilation
   B. integration
   C. multiculturalism
   D. alienation

### IV. Translate the following terms into English.

1. 大堡礁
2. 低地带

3. 艾尔湖
4. 多元文化主义

V. **Answer the following questions in a few sentences.**
1. List several factors contributing to the hot and dry climate of Australia.

2. What kind of life do Indigenous Australians live?

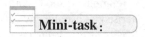

Mini-task:

Australia has many natural tourist attractions, such as the Great Barrier Reef, Uluru (Ayers Rock), the Snowy Mountains, and Kakadu National Park.

Search for some information about these or other attractions, and introduce them to your classmates.

# Chapter Two   Government and Politics

> The structure of the Australian government is based on the British as well as American models. Review the structure of the American and British governments before going into this chapter, which can help you well understand the following section. Make a comparison among them.

The Commonwealth of Australia, a combination of six colonies, was founded in 1901. The basic structure of the Australian government is based on both the British and American models, but reflects some changes according to national conditions. Generally speaking, the Australian federation has a three-tier system of government: the **federal parliament** and government, six **state parliaments** and governments, and **local government bodies** — the Prime Minister and his Cabinet at federal level is acknowledged the centre of Australian parliamentary power. The Queen of Britain is officially the Queen of Australia and is represented in Australia by the **Governor-General**. The federal political system in Australia consists of three components: the **Legislative**, the **Executive** and the **Judiciary**. But the chief executive is a Prime Minister not a President.

## Part One   Constitution

Differing from Great Britain, Australia has a written constitution which was put into effect once the Commonwealth was founded. The **Constitution** provides for the formation and power of federal government and relations between federal government and state governments.

The written Constitution can be changed only by referendum. In Australia a referendum proposal cannot become law unless it is approved by an absolute majority of electors in a majority of the state, that is, a majority of people and a majority of states. However, the Supreme Court can still raise questions and doubts and has right to veto proposed revisions and to interpret the Constitution.

The Australian Constitution is based on the principle of federalism and the principle of responsible government. In federalism, political functions are divided into two parts: the Commonwealth and the state. In responsible government, the executive authority is vested in a ministry whose members in Australia must be members of the Parliament. All ministers are responsible to the Parliament and for the affairs of their own departments. The central part of responsible government is governed by convention, because the basic rules of responsible government are not clearly stated in the Constitution and the Prime Minister and the Cabinet are not mentioned either in the Constitution.

## Part Two   Parliament

The **Australian Federal Parliament** is modeled on the Westminster system. It consists of the Queen and two Houses of Parliament: the **House of Representatives** (the Lower House) and the **Senate** (the Upper House).

The Australian Federal Parliament is the legislative branch, and has power to make and revise laws. The two Houses in Australia have equal powers except that the Senate cannot propose bills concerning appropriation and taxation, which may be initiated only in the House of Representatives.

Australian Governor-General representing the Queen is appointed by the Queen with the approval of the Prime Minister. He is the commander-in-chief of the defense and empowered to appoint times for holding sessions of the Parliament and to prorogue and dissolve the Parliament. He has the power to ratify the proposed laws passed by both Houses in the Queen's name, and the power to appoint Ministers of State on the advice of the Prime Minister.

The House of Representatives reflects the current opinion of the people at elections, which empowers the House to examine and criticise government action when necessary, with the knowledge that the government must ultimately answer to the people for its decisions.

The House of Representatives now has 150

seats, with each representing a separate electoral division of a state. Seats in the House of Representatives are allocated to states on the basis of population, with each original state entitled at least five seats. Elections for the House of Representatives are held at least every 3 years. The party with majority support in the House of Representatives forms government with its leader being the **Prime Minister**.

The Senate in Australia is an elected house, which is different from that in Britain. Senators are elected directly by the voters. The Senate has functioned as a house of review where the legislation is examined and amendments are suggested. Because of federalism, the Senate is delegated to perform another function: representing the State.

The Senate consists of 76 senators, twelve from each of the six states and two from each of the territories (the Australian Capital Territory and the Northern Territory). Normally, Senators from the states serve a 6-year term, with half of the seats renewed every three years, while territory senators are elected for 3-year terms.

Under the Constitution, the Senate has almost equal powers with the House of Representatives. It can make laws, delay or veto any laws put to it. The Constitution provides a method for solving a deadlock between the two Houses, including a double dissolution. After a bill passed in the House of Representatives is vetoed by the Senate, three months later, the two Houses will be dissolved if the result is the same.

## Part Three    The Judiciary

The Judicial department is the functional department which makes up of the court and judicial system. The Judiciary consists of High Court of Australia, the Federal Court of Australia and the Family Court of Australia. All the states and territories have their own judicial system.

Just like in America, the **High Court**, the final court, is composed of one Chief Judge and six associate judges. It solely has the power to interpret the Constitution.

The Federal Court of Australia was established in 1977. It mainly deals with cases according to federal laws, such as bankruptcy, confined trade activities and appeals proposed by state court.

The Family Court of Australia was established in 1976. Compared with other courts, it, seemingly informal, mainly deals with divorce. It can adjudicate such cases as supporting family members, matrimonial property and the guardianship of children.

> **Question for comparison:**
> The Judiciary structure of Australia is similar to that of America. Make a comparison between them and identify what differences and similarities they have.

## Part Four    Parties

A political party has always been the centre of the federal government since the Commonwealth of Australia was founded in 1901. Generally speaking, there are two major political groups: the **Australian Labor Party** and the Coalition which is a grouping of two parties, the **Liberal Party** and its minor partner, the **National Party**. Independent members and several minor parties, including the **Greens** and the **Australian Democrats**, have achieved representation in Australian parliaments, mostly in upper houses. Voting is compulsory for all enrolled citizens over the age of 18 in each state and territory at the federal level. Enrolment to vote is compulsory in all jurisdictions except South Australia.

### The Australian Labor Party

The Australian Labor Party (ALP) is the oldest of the Australian parties. It was formed in **1891 at the founding of the Commonwealth of Australia**. It is a social democratic party, founded by the trade union movement, representing the urban working class, although it gets increasing support from middle class. Generally, it is a successful political party historically, because it has been in government for 11 terms since 1940 and the latest term was from 2007 to 2013. Its success is partly due to the agreements made with labour unions, and partly due to disagreements within the Liberal Party.

### The Liberal Party of Australia

The current form of the Liberal Party, was set up by R. G. Menzies in 1944. It competes with the Australian Labor Party for political offices. When in government it traditionally governs in a coalition with the National Party.

In federal politics, the Liberal Party, which had held power since the election of 1996 was in opposition after losing the federal election in 2007. However, Liberal won the 2013 federal election and has been in government since then.

Modern Liberalism in Australia is represented in the vast majority by the Liberal Party of Australia, which generally advocates economic liberalism. However, during Liberal governments prior to the Howard Government, the party was quite interventionist in its economic policy and maintained

Australia's high tariff levels. At that time, the Liberals' coalition partner, the National Party, had considerable influence over the Government's economic policies.

Socially, the Liberal Party is a conservative party, although it is called Liberal Party. In recent years, during the Prime Ministership of John Howard, the party moved to a more socially conservative policy agenda, including tough stances on Mandatory detention in Australia and support for the Iraq War.

### The National Party of Australia

Traditionally representing rural voters, it was originally called the **Country Party**, but adopted the name National Country Party in 1975 and changed to its present name in 1982. Federally, in New South Wales, and to an extent in Victoria, it has generally been the minor party in the traditional coalition with the Australian Liberal Party in government and in opposition since the 1940s with the Australian Labor Party. However, it was the major coalition party in Queensland between 1957 and 1989. Since 2008, under the Senate leadership of Barnaby Joyce, the party has moved to the crossbenches and indicated it would be voting independently on their Liberal counterparts.

Traditionally, the leader of the National Party serves as Deputy Prime Minister when the Coalition is in government and as Deputy Leader of the Opposition when it is in opposition. This tradition dates back to the original formation of the centre-right coalition.

In 2003, the party adopted the name **The Nationals** for campaigning purposes, reflecting common usage, but its legal name has not changed. The party's federal parliamentary leader is Michael McCormack since 2016.

> **Question for discussion:**
> The policy of the federal government depends on the political party in office. As the oldest and most successful political party, what policies did the Australian Labor Party take during the period from 1983 to 1996?

## Exercises

### I. Fill in the blanks.

1. The basic structure of Australian government is based on both the _____ and _____ models.
2. The written Constitution can be changed only by _____.
3. The Australian Constitution is based on the principle of _____ and the principle of _____.
4. In responsible government, the executive authority is vested in a _____ whose members in Australia must be members of Parliament.
5. The Australian Federal Parliament is modeled on the _____ system.
6. The two Houses in Australia have equal powers except that the _____ cannot originate "money bills".
7. _____ _____ representing the Queen is appointed by the Queen with the proposal of Prime Minister.
8. The party with majority support in the House of Representatives forms government and its leader becomes the _____.
9. Normally, Senators from the States serve a _____ term, and only half of the seats are put to election every _____ years.
10. _____ _____ _____ _____ is the oldest of the Australian parties.

### II. Define the following terms.
1. federalism
2. Constitution
3. the Australian Federal Parliament
4. the Australian Labor Party
5. the National party

### III. Multiple choice.
1. In Australia, the House of Representatives and the Senate have equal powers except that _____.
   A. the House of Representatives cannot introduce money bills
   B. the Senate cannot introduce money bills
   C. the House of Representatives can pass laws
   D. the Senate can pass laws
2. Federalism is a system of government in which _____.
   A. power is given to a central government which deals with all matters of national interest
   B. power is distributed between two tiers of government, each exercising its allotted powers independent of the other
   C. a central government has no real power and it must depend on the other tier of government
   D. one tier of government must depend on the other tier of government
3. In Australia, the role of the Senate is _____.
   A. to review bills passed by the House of Representatives

B. to introduce "money bills"
   C. to interpret the Constitution
   D. to remove the prime minister from office
4. In Australia, the leader of the majority party or the coalition heads the government as _____.
   A. premier         B. prime minister
   C. chief executive  D. governor-general
5. The Queen of Britain is also head of state of Australia and represented in Australia by the _____.
   A. Governor-General  B. prime minister
   C. commander-in-chief D. chief executive

IV. **Translate the following terms into English.**
1. 首相
2. 总督
3. 公民投票
4. 责任政府
5. 澳大利亚最高法院

V. **Answer the following questions in a few sentences.**
1. What are the differences between Australian and British Constitution?
2. What powers does the Governor-General have?
3. Say something about the Senate in Australia.

📋 **Mini-tasks:**

1. In 2009, Prime Minister Kevin Rudd described the Governor-General as Australia's head of state, announcing an overseas visit by Quentin Bryce by saying, "A visit to Africa of this scale by Australia's Head of State will express the seriousness of Australia's commitment". According to the information above, how should the Governor-General perform duty in diplomatic affairs in order to maintain the country's majesty?
2. In order to register as a political party, an organization must have a constitution outlining the basis of the party and either at least one member in Parliament or 500 members on the electoral roll. Parties may be "deregistered" if they no longer meet these requirements.

**Questions**: How many minor parties are there in Australia? How many minor parties have representation in current parliamentary, and how many representatives does each party have?

# Chapter Three  Education

*Education is of the same or even more importance than industry, military forces and other vital national sectors from the point of the long-term development of a country. Collect current problems existing in Austrilia's education and find out the reasons for them.*

Education in Australia is primarily the responsibility of states and territories. Generally, education in Australia includes **primary education** (primary schools), **secondary education** (secondary schools or high schools) and **tertiary education** (universities and/or TAFE (Technical and Further Education Colleges)). The Australian education system is one of the best in the world, ranking eighth on a worldwide scale.

Schooling is compulsory in Australia between the ages of six and fifteen, depending on the state and date of birth. Post-compulsory education is regulated within the **Australian Qualifications Framework**, a unified system of national qualifications in schools, vocational education and training (TAFE) and the **higher education sector (university)**.

The academic year in Australia varies between states and institutions, but generally runs from late January until mid-December for primary and secondary schools and TAFE colleges, and from late February until mid-November for universities.

## Part One  Primary Education

Primary school education starts at the age of six and lasts for six years. In early education years, the main focus is on the development of basic language and literacy skills, simple arithmetic, moral and social education and some creative activities. In the last years of primary education, students pay more attention to the development of skills learned in earlier years. Courses offered consist of basics, including English, mathematics, social studies, science, music, sport and art. There are also optional courses in the field of industry, technology, religion and commerce.

In the Northern Territory, the primary school often include a pre-school. In Western Australia, primary schools often include two pre-school years. The Northern Territory introduced middle schools for Grade 7 to 9 and High School for Grade 10 to 12, which began in 2007. Australian Capital Territory, South Australia and Tasmania have a "Grade 13" for students wishing to take extra time to develop their skills before tertiary education.

There is no national policy on the provision of pre-school education. Pre-schools are usually run by local councils, community groups or private organizations except in the Northern Territory and Queensland where they are run by the Territory and State Governments respectively. Pre-school is offered to three-to five-year-old children, although attendance varies widely from 50% in New South Wales to 93% in Victoria.

## Part Two  Secondary Education

**Government schools** educate about two-thirds of Australian students, with the other third in independent schools, a proportion rising in many parts of Australia.

Government schools run by the local state or territory government are free, with the majority of their costs provided by the relevant government and the rest by voluntary levies and fundraising. Most Catholic schools are run by either local parish or state's **Catholic Education Department**, or by both. **Independent schools**, non-Catholic, non-government schools, including schools operated by religious groups and secular educational philosophies such as Montessori, enroll about 14% of students. Some independent schools charge high fees. Government funding for independent schools often comes under criticism from the Australian Education Union and the Australian Labor Party. Regardless of whether schools are government or independent, they are required to adhere to the same curriculum frameworks. Most school students, be they in a government or independent school, usually wear uniforms. There are varied dress codes, but some schools do not require uniforms at all.

All government schools can be divided into two categories: **open schools** and **selective schools**. The open schools accept all students from areas the government defined. Selective government schools mostly cater for academically gifted students (usually the top 5%), although some schools focus on performing arts and sports. Almost all selective schools are in New South Wales, except for a few in other areas.

Selective schools are more prestigious than open schools and generally achieve better accomplishments in graduation exams. Entrance to selective schools is often highly competitive and these schools cover a large geographical area.

## Part Three  Tertiary Education

**Tertiary education** in Australia is made up of universities and other higher education institutions (called higher education providers), including Colleges of Advanced Education and Technology and Further Education. A higher education provider is a body that is established or recognised by or under the laws regardless of the Commonwealth, a State or Territory. The provider has to get approval from the Australian Government before the students can receive assistance from the Australian Government under the *Higher Education Support Act of* **2003** (*HESA*). Providers are subject to quality and accountability requirements. In 2020, the Australian higher education system consisted of 42 universities, of which 40 were public institutions and 2 were private.

A higher education provider is a university, self-accrediting provider, or non-self-accrediting provider.

Universities generally have high academic achievements, focusing on research work and awarding a full range of degrees, including the doctorate. University courses are based on credit system and students can graduate after they get required credits for compulsory and optional courses.

The non-self-accrediting higher education providers form a very diverse group of specialised, mainly private, providers that range in size and include theological colleges and other providers that offer courses in areas such as business, information technology, natural therapies, hospitality, health, law and accounting.

> **❓ Questions for discussion:**
>
> What are the differences between government schools and independent schools? Why do more and more students prefer to attend independent schools?

## Exercises

### Ⅰ. Fill in the blanks.

1. Education in Australia is primarily the responsibility of _____ and _____.
2. Education in Australia is _____ up to an age specified by legislation.
3. In the Northern Territory, primary schools often include a _____.
4. Pre-schools are usually run by local councils, community groups or private organizations except in _____ and _____ where they are run by the Territory and State Governments respectively.
5. Pre-school is offered to _____ to _____ -year-old children, although attendance numbers vary widely from 50% in New South Wales to 93% in Victoria.
6. School is compulsory in Australia between the ages of _____ and _____, depending on the state and date of birth.
7. Australian Capital Territory, South Australia and Tasmania have a "_____" for students wishing to take extra time to develop their skills before tertiary education.
8. In 2020, the Australian higher education system consisted of _____ universities, of which _____ were public institutions.
9. _____ education in Australia is made up of universities and other higher education institutions.

### Ⅱ. Define the following terms.

1. post-compulsory education
2. government schools
3. tertiary education
4. academic year
5. selective schools

### Ⅲ. Multiple choice.

1. _____ in Australia is relatively unregulated, and is not compulsory.
   A. Pre-school          B. Primary school
   C. Secondary school    D. Tertiary school
2. The Australian education system is one of the best in the world, ranking _____ on a worldwide scale.
   A. 8th    B. 7th    C. 6th    D. 9th
3. All government or state schools can be divided into two categories: _____.
   A. open and selective    B. public and private
   C. open and private      D. selective and public
4. Which kind of school charges fees?
   A. public school         B. government school
   C. private school        D. selective school

5. The academic year in Australia generally runs from _____ until _____ for primary and secondary schools and TAFE colleges.
   A．late February, mid-November
   B．late January, mid-December
   C．late February, mid-December
   D．late January, mid-November

Ⅳ. **Translate the following terms into English.**
1. 技术与继续教育学院
2. 独立学校
3. 选择性学校
4. 支持高等教育法
5. 高等教育机构

Ⅴ. **Answer the following questions in a few sentences.**
1. What is a higher education provider?

2. What is the Australian education system?

**Mini-task:**

Monash University is a public university based in Melbourne, Australia. It is Australia's largest university with around 56,000 students and 15,000 staff. Monash University is a member of the "Group of Eight", a group composed of some of the most research-intensive universities in Australia. It was recently ranked 75th and 58th of the world's top universities by the Times Higher Education and QS World University Rankings respectively in 2020.

The university is named after the prominent Australian general Sir John Monash. One of his most well-known statements is inscribed along a walkway between the Robert Blackwood Hall and Performing Arts Centre at the Clayton campus: Adopt as your fundamental creed that you will equip yourself for life, not solely for your own benefit, but for the benefit of the whole community.

The University's motto is *Ancora imparo* (Italian), meaning "I am still learning", a saying attributed to Michelangelo.

Try to search for more information about the university.

# Chapter Four  Economy and Major Cities

*Economy is the most vital factor that determines the status and strength of a nation. Generally speaking, people in Australia are better off, compared with those in many other countries. Think about the question: What are the advantages of the Australian economic structure in promoting people's standard of living?*

Australia's emphasis on reforms is often taken as a key factor to the continuing strength of the economy. From the early 1980s on, both major political parties, the Australian Labor Party and the Liberal Party of Australia, have played an instrumental role in the modernisation of the Australian economy. In 1983, when Prime Minister Bob Hawke was in office, the Australian dollar was floated and prudent financial deregulation was undertaken. But in the early 1990s Australian economy fell into recession with government debt soaring to $96 billion which was successfully paid off in full between 1996 and 2007 by the Liberal Government led by Prime Minister John Howard and Treasurer Peter Costello. During the period from 1996 to 2007, **goods and services tax** (GST) was introduced in order to encourage the level of savings amongst lower income earners. In addition, to combat the substantial reduction in consumption for low income earners and oppose to higher government expenditure, **income taxes** were lowered in exchange for the introduction of the goods and services tax. This economic strategy, in accordance with principles of individual liberty, choice, freedom, initiative and enterprise, has led to an unprecedented economic prosperity with continuous economic growth, moderate inflation and low unemployment.

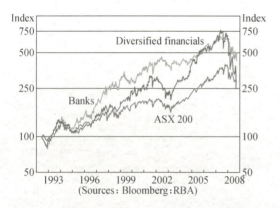

In April 2020, 12,418,700 people were employed with unemployment rate being 6.2%. The country ranked eighth in **Human Development Index** in the United Nations in 2019 and fourth in **Quality of Life Index** in 2019 by Numbeo, world's largest cost of living database. The focus on export has underpinned a significant increase in terms of Australia's trade during the rise in commodity prices since the start of the century. The growth rate of economy was 2.9% from 2017 to 2018, with gross export rising 7.9%, and gross import rising 9%.

## Part One  Structure of Economy

### Agriculture

Compared with other countries, Australia is comprised of a vast area and flat land, but in general, it is the driest continent, and only one-fifth of total area receives enough rainfall. Drought is always a threat to its agricultural production. Even though, it produces sufficient food for the native people and immigrants. Although agriculture constitutes only 2.12% of GDP, it contributes substantially to export performance. Wheat and wool are major agricultural export products.

Wheat, the country's leading grain crop, is grown in every state and concentrated in the wheat belts of the southeast and southwest. Nearly eighty percent of the grain is exported to East Asia, the Middle East and the Pacific region.

Pastures and grasses cover much higher rainfall and irrigated areas, which makes livestock account for the largest area of land use in Australia. As the world's leading producer of wool, Australia supplies up to 70 percent of the global total, once bringing it the reputation of "the country riding on the sheep's back".

### Mining Industry

In the past decade, one of the most significant

sector trends experienced by the economy has been the growth of the mining industry, including petroleum. In terms of contribution to GDP, mining industry grew from around 8% in 2006 to 2007, to almost 13.4% in 2016 to 2017.

Rich in natural resources, Australia is a major exporter of minerals, such as iron-ore and gold. It is the largest mineral and metal producer in the world. Over the past few decades, with the rapid increase of export of minerals, Australia now is more often referred to as "the country riding in the mineral cart".

Despite high global demand for Australian mineral commodities, export growth has remained flat in comparison to strong import growth. The discovery of gold caused the so-called "gold rush" period and mineral exports take up a large proportion in the whole. In 1998, Australia accounted for 13 percent of the world's gold production, placing it third in the world rankings after South Africa and the United States. Most of the gold is exported to Singapore, Japan, Switzerland and Hong Kong.

### Service Industries

The service industries, including tourism, education, transportation, communication and financial services, have become the most significant growing component of Australian economy and constitute 66.03% of Gross Domestic Product (GDP). As the single largest component of GDP, growth in service industries has largely been at the expense of the manu-facturing industry, which accounts for around 6% of GDP annually.

Tourism plays the most important role in service industries in terms of Australian economy. With more than 5 million international visitors travelling to Australia every year, tourism has become the largest service export industry. Australian government has attached great importance to the development of tourism industry during the past decades with the Australian Committee on Tourism established as early as 1967. In addition, each state government has tried every means to expand attraction ranges, such as amusement and theme parks, national parks, historic sites and art galleries. The most popular attractions include Queensland's spectacular **Great Barrier Reef**, the **Northern Territory's Kakadu National Park** as well as many famous beach resorts.

### Part Two   Current Problems

One of the current problems that economists are mostly concerned is Australia's large current account deficit. According to the **Australian Bureau of Statistics**, in 2008, the deficit was up to $19.49 billion, resulting from the absence of a successful export-oriented manufacturing industry, a real estate bubble and high levels of net foreign debt owed by the private sector.

As to the financial crisis of 2008, Australia's Treasurer Wayne Swan argued that Australia was in a better position to cope with the crisis than most countries. The **Reserve Bank of Australia** carried out expansionary monetary policy by sharply reducing cash rate which contributed to devaluation of the Australian dollar. Australian dollar was expected to drop in value further because of lower interest rates in the future.

Australian Bureau of Statistics released inflation figures indicating that prices dropped by 0.3% in late December 2008. Even though the country was predicted to avoid a recession, most economists argued that slumping global demand and a possibility of high unemployment would drag the country into its first recession in almost 17 years.

> **? Questions for discussion**:
> What measures did the Australian government take to cope with the problems caused by the financial crisis of 2008? And what is the effect of the crisis on people's life?

## Part Three  Major Cities

### Canberra

"Canberra" comes from an Aboriginal word "Canburry" with the meaning of "meeting place". **Canberra**, the capital of the Commonwealth of Australia, is the political and cultural centre of the country. With a population of over 426,704, it is Australia's largest inland city and located at the northern part of the Australian Capital Territory. The site of Canberra was selected for the location of the nation's capital in 1908 as a compromise between rivals of Sydney and Melbourne. The city was designed by the Chicago architects **Walter Burley Griffin** and **Marion Mahony Griffin**. The design was heavily influenced by the garden city movement and incorporates significant areas of natural vegetation that have earned Canberra the title "Bush Capital". Although the growth and development of Canberra were hindered by the World Wars and the Great Depression, it emerged as a thriving city after World War II.

The city lies within mountains and is bordered by rivers and surrounded by jungle. It is the special position that gives the city the name **"Garden City"**.

As the capital, Canberra is the site of **Parliament House**, the **High Court of Australia** and numerous government departments and agencies. Many social and cultural institutions of national significance, such as the **Australian War Memorial**, the **National Gallery of Australia**, the **National Museum of Australia** and the **National Library of Australia**, are situated in the city.

Canberra has a marine west coastal climate with four distinct seasons. Light snow falls in the city in one out of approximately three winters but is usually not widespread and quickly dissipates. Thunderstorms can occur between September and March, with rainfall maximums in spring and summer.

In February 2004 there were 140 schools in Canberra, among which 96 were operated by the government and 44 were non-government. The two main tertiary institutions are the **Australian National University** (ANU) in Acton, established as a research university in 1946, and the **University of Canberra** (UC) in Bruce. Both universities have campuses interstate and overseas.

By August 2019, the unemployment rate in Canberra had been 3.5%, well below the national unemployment rate (5.2%), with labour shortages reported in some sectors. Due to low unemployment and substantial levels of public sector and commercial employment, Canberra has the highest average disposable income among all Australian capital cities.

### Sydney

**Sydney** is the most populous city in Australia, with a population of more than 5.3 million residents in the Sydney Statistical Division according to the census report of 2019. Inner Sydney was densely populated with 9,301 persons per square kilometre. It is the state capital of New South Wales and was the first British colony in Australia. It was established in 1788 at Sydney Cove by Arthur Phillip, the leader of the First Fleet from Britain.

The urban area of Sydney covered 1,687 square kilometres in 2001. The city locates in a coastal basin, bordered by the Pacific Ocean to the East, the Blue Mountains to the West, the Hawkesbury River to the North and the Royal National Park to the South. The Sydney area is not affected by significant earthquakes. The urban area has around 70 harbours and ocean beaches, bringing the city a nickname, "the Harbour City". The city is famous for the **Sydney Opera House** and the **Harbour Bridge**, and its beaches, such as the famous Bondi Beach. The Opera House, on the edge of Circular Quay and built in 1973, is regarded as Sydney's landmark because of its unique clamshell design. The Sydney Harbour Bridge, built in 1932, combined north Sydney and south Sydney together and once served as the landmark of the city before the Opera House being completed. In addition, the city has hosted

international sporting, political and cultural events, including the British Empire Games in 1938, Summer Olympics in 2000 and the Rugby World Cup in 2003.

Geographically, Sydney extends over two regions: the **Cumberland Plain**, a relatively flat region lying to the south and west of the harbour, and the **Hornsby Plateau**, a sandstone plateau lying mainly to the north of the harbour and dissected by steep valleys. Compared with the southern part of the city, the northern part was slower to develop because of hilly topography and lack of access across the harbour. The Sydney Harbour Bridge was opened in 1932 and linked the northern part to the rest of the city.

Sydney has a temperate climate with warm summers and cool winters and rainfall is spread throughout the year. The weather is moderated by its proximity to the ocean. Rainfall is fairly evenly divided between summer and winter, but is slightly higher during the first half of the year, when easterly winds dominate. But snowfall rarely occurs in the Sydney City area.

Sydney is one of the most multicultural cities in the world and is a major destination for immigrants to Australia. The city is regarded as the most expensive city in Australia, and the 16th most expensive in the world, which was shown in the Economist Intelligence Unit's World Wide Cost of Living 2019 survey.

The largest economic sectors in Sydney, measured by employment, include real estate, business services, manufacturing, and health and community services. Since the 1980s, jobs have moved from manufacturing to the services and information sectors. The Australian Securities Exchange and the Reserve Bank of Australia are situated in Sydney, where ninety banks and more than half of Australia's top companies placed their headquarters. Of the ten largest corporations in Australia (based on revenues), four set headquarters in Sydney.

Sydney is the home to some of Australia's most prominent universities and is the site of Australia's oldest university, the **University of Sydney**, established in 1850. There are five other public universities operating primarily in Sydney: the **Australian Catholic University** (two out of six campuses), **Macquarie University**, the **University of New South Wales**, the **University of Technology, Sydney** and the **University of Western Sydney**. Other universities which operate secondary campuses in Sydney include the **University of Notre Dame Australia** and the **University of Wollongong**.

### Melbourne

**Melbourne**, the state capital of Victoria, is located in the southern part of mainland Australia, on the lower reaches of the **Yarra River** and on the northern and eastern shorelines of **Port Phillip**. It is the second most populous city in Australia, with a population of approximately 5 million (2019 estimated).

As a pastoral settlement, Melbourne was founded by free settlers in 1835, 47 years after the first European settlement of Australia. Thanks to the Victorian gold rush in the 1850s, "Marvellous Melbourne" transformed rapidly into a major metropolis, and the largest and most important city in Australia. At the time of Australia's federation on 1 January, 1901, Melbourne became the temporary seat of the federal government until 1927, when it was removed to Canberra.

Melbourne has a moderate oceanic climate and is well known for its changeable weather conditions. The factors influencing the climate include its flat topography, situation on Port Phillip, and the presence of the **Dandenong Ranges** to the east, and so on. All the factors create weather systems that often circle the bay. The phrase "four seasons in one day" is part of the city's popular culture and observed by many visitors there.

Today, Melbourne is a major centre for commerce, industry and cultural activities. It consistently ranks one of the most livable cities in the world. Figures from the Australian Bureau of Statistics showed that Melbourne had sustained the highest population increase and economic growth rate of any Australian capital city from June 2001 to June 2004.

The city is recognised as a "sporting and cultural

capital" and home to many of most significant national cultural and sporting events and institutions. In addition, Melbourne has hosted many international conferences and events, including the Summer Olympics in 1956 and the Commonwealth Games in 2006. It was the site of the Commonwealth Heads of Government Meeting of 1981 and the G20 summit of 2006.

Since 1997, Melbourne has maintained significant population and employment growth. Substantial international investment has been made in the city's industries and property market. Major inner-city urban renewal has occurred in areas such as **Port Melbourne**, **Melbourne Docklands** and so on.

> **? Group for Presentation:**
> 1. The Sydney Opera House is the landmark of the City of Sydney. Give a description about it as detailed as possible.
> 2. Make an introduction about Melbourne to foreign visitors, including its great events in the history.

---

## Exercises

### Ⅰ. Fill in the blanks.
1. Australia features vast area and flat land, but in general, it is the driest continent, and only ____ ____ of total area receives enough rainfall.
2. Rich in natural resources, Australia is a major exporter of minerals, such as _____ and _____.
3. In the past decade, one of the most significant sector trends experienced by the economy has been the growth of the mining sector, including _____.
4. The city, _____, enjoys a fame of "Garden City".
5. Before Canberra was completed, _____ was used as the workplace of the Commonwealth Australian government.

### Ⅱ. Define the following terms.
1. service industries
2. goods and services tax
3. Garden City
4. Sydney
5. Melbourne

### Ⅲ. Multiple choice.
1. Australia is the world's largest exporter of _____.
   A. wheat         B. wool
   C. meat          D. dairy products
2. The single largest component of Australia's GDP is _____.
   A. agriculture
   B. mining industry
   C. service industries
   D. manufacturing industry
3. Australia, one of the world's developed countries, has become rich through _____.
   A. manufacturing industries
   B. farming and mining
   C. taxing
   D. forestry and fishing
4. Traditionally, Australia has relied heavily on migrants _____.
   A. to build up its labour force
   B. to defend its country
   C. to change its way of life
   D. to improve its living standards
5. Which of the following Australia cities hosted the Summer Olympics in 2000?
   A. Sydney         B. Canberra
   C. Melbourne      D. Perth

### Ⅳ. Translate the following terms into English.
1. 人类发展指数
2. 生活质量指数
3. 商品及服务税
4. 所得税
5. 澳大利亚储备银行

### Ⅴ. Answer the following questions in a few sentences.
1. Say something about the structure of Australian economy.
2. What are the famous structures in Sydney?

> **Mini-task:**
> 1. The Department of Foreign Affairs and Trade (DFAT) in Australia is in charge of advancing the interests of Australia and its citizens internationally. It copes with the Government's policies of foreign relations and makes trade policies. It has six key goals, as stated on its website:
> • To enhance Australia's security;

- To contribute to growth in Australia's economy, employment and standard of living;
- To assist Australian travellers and Australians overseas;
- To strengthen global cooperation in ways that advance Australia's interests;
- To foster public understanding of Australia's foreign and trade policy and project a positive image of Australia internationally;
- To manage efficiently the Commonwealth's overseas owned estate.

Try to search out the information about the department's structure. How do the two parts of the DFAT cooperate with each other?

2. Melbourne, an important tourist destination in Australia, attracts a wide cross-section of visitors for a variety of reasons. Major sporting events hosted by Melbourne have great attraction for large numbers of sports tourists. Other visitors come for the cultural and fashion events including popular sites and events, restaurants, cafes and nightlife. In 2008, Melbourne exceeded Sydney for the first time in terms of money spent by domestic tourists. Collect some materials about tourist attractions as guidance for friends and relatives travelling to Melbourne.

3. Although Victoria is a reasonably safe state by world standards and crime rates in Victoria are the lowest per capita in Australia, a spate of attacks against Indian international students occurred in Melbourne, including several assaults, robberies and stabbings in the year of 2009 and early 2010. Get some materials about the causes of the violence. What impact do the attacks have on the relations between the two countries?

# Chapter Five　History

## Part One　Australia to Federation

> *Nearly all the young countries in the world had the experience similar to the colonies. Australia is not an exception. The natives in Australia suffered a lot after the European settlement. What did the Europeans bring to the natives? Was it good or bad for the natives in the points of history? Try to search for the information from the resources available.*

The history of Australia began with the arrival of Aborigines several thousand years ago, though the first discovery of Australia by European explorers was in 1606, which may be taken as the starting point for the written history of Australia. In 1788, Great Britain began to establish colonies in Australia which led Australia to another important period. Not until 1901 did the colonies in Australia establish the Commonwealth of Australia, ending its history as a colony.

### The Natives in Australia Before 1788

The first human beings on the Australian continent called Aborigines were estimated to settle down between 42,000 and 48,000 years ago, and were possibly the ancestors of the current Indigenous Australians. They might arrive through land bridges and short sea-crossings from present-day Southeast Asia. Originally, the Aborigines lived in three main regions of Australia: the northern coast, the southeast and Tasmania. However, the land between Tasmania and the mainland was inundated. Aborigines on Tasmania were separated from the world, so their tools and way of life were different from that of people on the mainland of Australia.

Aborigines had a good command of knowledge about animals, seasons and agriculture on which they relied to live. Providing them for livings and shaping their religions, land became the centre in the life of the Aborigines. They had strong attachment to plants, animals and waterways of their tribal land. However, unlike Europeans, they did not take the land as private property or tools used to make profits. One person could not become richer or own more than others. They shared whatever the land offered, hunting and gathering only what they needed each day.

The Indigenous Australian population, estimated at 350,000 at the time of European settlement, declined steeply after settlement, mainly because of infectious disease combined with forced re-settlement and cultural disintegration. The removal of children from their families may have contributed to the decline in the Indigenous population, which aroused the heated debate known as History Wars in Australia. Some historians and Indigenous argued that to some extent the removal could be considered to constitute genocide, while some commentators took the view as being exaggerated or fabricated for political or ideological reasons.

### Australia as a Colony from 1788 to 1900

⊙ Discovery of the land

Although British explorer James Cook is often considered as the person who discovered the Australian continent, European explorers were not the earliest visitors to Australia. At least from 1650, every year fishermen from Indonesia came to Australian northern coast, bringing many new skills and tools for the northern Aborigines.

It is assumed that the first Europeans reaching Australia's shores were the Spanish and Portuguese, followed by Dutch and British. Some argued that Portuguese navigators discovered Australia in the 16th century, but no firm evidence was provided.

Records of the discovery of the Australian continent by European expeditions dated back to the early 17th century. Evidence available showed that it was the Dutch who discovered Australia. The first known sight was in 1606 by the Dutch navigator Willem Janszoon, who navigated the **Gulf of Carpentaria**, sighting and making landfall on the western coast of **Cape York Peninsula**. In 1616, another Dutchman, Dirk Hartog, left a pewter plate commemorating his landfall at **Shark Bay** in Western Australia.

The expedition of the Endeavour under command

of British Royal Navy Lieutenant **James Cook** navigated and charted the eastern coast of Australia, making his first landfall at Botany Bay on 29 April, 1770. Cook continued northwards and before leaving put ashore on Possession Island in the Torres Strait off Cape York on 22 August, 1770. Here he formally claimed the eastern coastline discovered for the Crown, naming it **New South Wales**.

On 26 January, 1788, later known as the **Australia Day**, Captain Arthur Phillip raised the Union Jack and formally took possession of the whole eastern half of the continent, from Cape York to Tasmania. These islands included the current islands of New Zealand administered as part of New South Wales. Van Diemen's Land, now known as Tasmania, was settled in 1803 and became a separate colony in 1825. The United Kingdom formally claimed the western part of Australia in 1829. Separate colonies were created from parts of New South Wales: South Australia in 1836, Victoria in 1851, and Queensland in 1859. The Northern Territory was founded in 1911 when it was excided from South Australia which was founded as a "free province", that is, it was never a penal colony. Victoria and Western Australia were also founded "free" but later accepted transported convicts. The transportation of convicts to the colony of New South Wales ceased in 1848 after a campaign by the settlers.

⊙ Reasons of becoming a colony

In the 18th century, the Industrial Revolution, with the growth of factories, machines and manufacturing, brought about great social changes. The populations of London and the industrial north grew larger and people swarmed from rural areas into the cities looking for jobs. Unemployment, overcrowding, homelessness and poverty became the problems faced working class people. To make a survival, people were even forced to steal food, clothing and valuable things.

To protect their interests, middle-class employers and property owners were determined to severely punish criminals. Soon prisons were full and convicts were even imprisoned on the ships in the Thames River near London. The British government had to look for another place to send their convicts. In 1779, a British government committee suggested that new prisons be set up in its colonies in hopes of reducing prison population and criminal rate in Britain. Thus Australia was chosen as a penal colony to receive convicts from Britain. However, some historians argue that Britain wanted to set up a naval base for exploits in the Indian Ocean and the Pacific Ocean to counter other European countries.

⊙ Europeans' influence on the natives

European settlement in 1788 proved disastrous for the Aborigines. The Aboriginal culture and society were completely destroyed because of the conflicts aroused by the settlement. Aborigines were pushed out of their land and lived in the mountain areas or the infertile and dry inland, so they always suffered from hunger. Meanwhile, their tribal life broke down after losing land on which Aboriginal culture was based and Aborigines begging in the white area became dependent on the European settlers.

Aborigines adopted the European habit of drinking, which destroyed many of them. To make it worse, settlers also brought various diseases such as smallpox, measles, flu and venereal diseases, which the Aborigines had no resistance to.

All these, together with the violence between Europeans and Aborigines caused the Aboriginal population to be greatly reduced and put the Aborigines in an unfavourable position ever since 1788.

⊙ Gold rush

The gold rush began in Australia in the early 1850s, in the aftermath of a major worldwide economic depression. When moving from Sydney to the inland, the convicts, explorers and local people first discovered gold in the riverbed in New South Wales and Victoria. In the following years, tens of thousands of immigrants from Great Britain, Ireland, Continental Europe, North America and China arrived in Australia. The population of Australia was about 400,000 in 1850, but in 1862, the population tripled.

In the early years of the gold rush, miners had to pay a high tax for mining licenses, higher than their income. Miners began to fight for democracy and the Eureka Stockade rebellion against mining license fees broke out in 1854, which was an early expression of nationalist sentiment. The flag used to represent it has been seriously considered as an alternative to the Australian flag. The Eureka Stockade rebellion resulted in some reforms in the goldfields. And Queen Victoria introduced voting rights to all men in the late 1850s.

Between 1855 and 1890, the six colonies gained responsible governments respectively, managing most of their own affairs while remaining part of Britain. The Colonial Office in London kept controls of some matters—notably foreign affairs, defense and international shipping.

The gold rush had great effects on the colonies. First, since most of the gold rush immigrants were British and many were middle-class professionals or businessmen, their arrival helped the growth of the middle class in Australia, especially in the cities. Second, the gold rush brought immediate and long-term changes to the economy with more money invested in Australia and increasing trade with Britain. Third, the gold rush also changed people's political and social attitudes. There began a trend towards responsible government in the colonies.

However, the volume of immigrants and gold mining resulted in considerable damage to rivers, valleys and wooded areas due to improper and excessive exploitation.

⊙ Changes from the 1860s to the 1890s

The three decades following the gold rush were a period of rapid and great development in Australia. Considerable changes took place in daily life, work, industry and people's attitudes in cities and countries.

From the 1860s to the 1890s, all major cities expanded, especially Melbourne. It became the financial and commercial centre of Australia with population growing from only 224 in 1836 to 490,000 in 1890, attracting investment from Britain and business people around the country. Melbourne controlled agricultural exports and due to foreign capital, manufacturing and transportation also developed rapidly. However, by the 1890s, the city had faced the problem of the bad smell coming from open drains and sewers and factory pollution. More importantly, in spite of booming economy, large numbers of working class people lived in poverty.

Rural Australia was slowly being opened up. There were more towns and farms, and a network of waterways, roads and railway lines. Small farm owners lived in poverty because of the trouble brought by excessive grazing.

People's attitudes were also changing. By the 1890s, all colonies had made education free, secular and compulsory. Most Australians had been Australian-born by the end of the 1890s and a spirit of nationalism began to develop, although they maintained a strong affection to Britain. Besides, more and more Australians grew to admire Australian writers and painters who depicted Australia, especially the uncultivated regions.

### ❓ Question for discussion:

"Gold rush" was an important period in the history of Australia, which led to great changes around the country. What changes did it bring to people's lives?

## Exercises

### Ⅰ. Fill in the blanks.
1. The history of Australia began with the arrival of _____.
2. It is assumed that the first Europeans who reached Australia's shores were the _____ and Portuguese, whom were followed by the _____ and then the English.
3. Originally, the Aborigines lived in three main regions of Australia: the northern coast, the _____ and Tasmania.
4. In _____, James Cook sailed along and mapped the east coast of Australia, which he named New South Wales and claimed for Great Britain.
5. The original purpose of the foundation of Australia as a colony is to receive _____ from Britain.

### Ⅱ. Define the following terms.
1. History Wars
2. gold rush

### Ⅲ. Multiple choice.
1. In 1788 Australia was settled by the British as a colony founded _____.
   A. to receive free settles
   B. to supply Britain with wool and food
   C. to receive convicts from Britain
   D. to expand Britain's imperial power
2. It is assumed that the first Europeans who reached Australia's shores were _____.
   A. the Dutch
   B. the English
   C. the Germans
   D. the Spanish and Portuguese
3. The first major discoveries of gold, made in _____ ____ in the early 1850s, resulted in gold rush in Australia.
   A. Queensland
   B. South Australia

C. Victoria and Tasmania
D. Victoria and New South Wales

4. The whole eastern half of the Australian continent was formally claimed by the United Kingdom in 1788, as _____ raised the British national flag over that land.
   A. James Cook
   B. Arthur Philip
   C. Willem Janszoon
   D. Dirk Hartog

5. A gold rush began in Australia in the early _____.
   A. 1840s   B. 1850s   C. 1860s   D. 1830s

Ⅳ. **Translate the following terms into English.**
1. 新南威尔士
2. 淘金热
3. 奇妙的墨尔本

Ⅴ. **Answer the following questions in a few sentences.**
1. When did the history of Australia begin?

2. What were the effects of European settlement on the Aborigines?

3. What were the effects of gold rush on the colony?

| Part Two   Australia Since Federation |

*The Commonwealth of Australia was founded after years of planning. Before reading the following, search for the information about its relations with Great Britain and the situation in the country at that time.*

### Founding of Australia-Federation

On 1 January, 1901, the federation of the colonies was achieved after a decade of planning, consultation and voting and the Commonwealth of Australia was born as a Dominion of the British Empire. Sir Edmund Barton was sworn in as the first Prime Minister and the first federal Parliament was inaugurated in Melbourne on 9 May, 1901.

Several reasons led to the foundation of the Commonwealth of Australia. First, people in the colony shared something in common: their British stock, the English language traditions, laws and other features. By the 1890s, most Australians had been born in Australia who held a strong spirit of nationalism and believed that Australians should be the white, British stock. Second, the six colonies realised that it was absurd to have six different approaches to common issues like immigration, foreign policy and national defense. They thought the same immigration policy would be good for their interests. In addition, they were concerned about expansionist interests of France and Germany in the Pacific region. Third, businessmen argued that the commerce and economy within Australia were being weakened because of trade restrictions and tariff barriers at the borders between the colonies. Especially, during the depression of the 1890s, the economy of six colonies suffered a great loss. British reduced their investment in Australia. The situation of Australia can only be solved through their cooperation. Fourth, in the 1880s and the 1890s, organizations acted as pressure groups in the campaign for federation. They demanded a united Australia in which Africans and Asians would be excluded. But federal Australia was still under the control of the United Kingdom. Federation meant Australia was to be an independent country, but in fact, it still relied on Britain, especially in trade and investment. A Governor-General of Australia and a governor in each state were appointed in Britain to represent the British monarch. Britain conducted diplomacy and declared war on behalf of Australia.

### Australia and World War I

World War I broke out on 4 August, 1914. After Britain declared war on Germany, Australia also declared war against it. Prime Minister Joseph Cook said: "If the old country is at war, so we are." At that time, Australian culture was strongly tied with Britain. They modeled their daily lives and the running of their country on British customs and institutions. The similarity and intimacy encouraged many Australians to call Britain "home" and most Australians did not see any contradiction in having dual loyalties, regarding themselves both as

Australians and British subjects.

On 1 November, 1914, the first Australian troops, together with those of New Zealand, were sent out for training. The **Gallipoli Campaign** took place in 1915. The campaign was viewed as a noble defeat. It made Australia not only a country but also an ally with Britain. From 1916 on, ANZAC Day (25 April) has been celebrated and since the late 1920s it has remained Australia's most important holiday.

During World War I, Australia was not attacked by other countries, but the daily life was seriously disrupted. Because of the disagreement on loyalty, conscription and political matters, people were not satisfied with the government.

### Australia and World War II

After World War I, Australians soon adjusted themselves and became optimistic about the future. They were determined to put the war behind them and devote their time and energy to developing their country. In the 1920s, an influx of immigrants arrived in Australia, helping them cultivate the rural areas and develop secondary industry. The country seemed to be prosperous. However, various problems appeared. Poverty and unemployment were serious throughout the whole 1920s. People were still affected by World War I. Moreover, in the middle and northern part of Australia, Aborigines were being killed by whites.

In the late 1920s, Australia suffered a serious economic decline. From 1927 to 1928, the world price of wheat and wool reduced, while the domestic market was too small to pay for overseas loans, which dragged Australia into economic trouble. When the worldwide Great Depression broke out in 1929, Australia had been in serious trouble. Unemployment rate rose to 11% and workers went on strike. From 1934 to 1939, the situation already improved, mainly because the world prices began to go up, and Australian products found overseas market, but the unemployment rate was still as high as 10%.

On 1 September, 1939, Germany invaded Poland. Two days later, Britain and France declared war against Germany. Similar to World War I, Australia entered the war because it had close connection in culture, national defense, trade and economy with Britain. In January 1940, Australian troops were sent to foreign battlefields. In the following two years, cooperating with British troops, they fought against German and Italian troops.

The **Statute of Westminster of 1931** formally ended most of the constitutional links between Australia and the United Kingdom when Australia adopted it in 1942, but backdated it to the beginning of World War II to confirm the validity of legislation passed by the Australian Parliament during the war. The shock of the United Kingdom's defeat in Asia in 1942 and the threat of Japanese invasion caused Australia to turn to the United States as a new ally and protector. In fact, at the very beginning of the war, people in the country did not have any interest in it. After Japan entered the war and attacked Pearl Harbor of America, America and Australia declared war on Japan. Japanese bombers attacked Darwin, the Northern Territory on 19 Febuary, 1942, which united all the Australians. Many women took part in the war providing services for the army. Prime Minister Curtin drew back the troops to protect the country regardless of the disapproval of Britain. Australian and American troops fought against Japanese troops until the end of the war.

During World War II, 33,826 Australian soldiers died and totally 180,864 were wounded. After the war, Australia began full development and entered rebuilding period.

### Australia After World War II

After the war, Ben Chifley took office as Prime Minister. Full employment and social security became the main targets of the government. Rebuilding programmes provided many jobs, but women were expected to stay at home and act as housewives. Some did so, while others joined the working world and found jobs. According to the result of referendum in 1946, the federal government was delegated the right to revise the Constitution, under which the government could offer financial help for widows, children, the unemployed and the sick.

Following World War II, the Australian government proposed a massive programme of European immigration. After narrowly preventing a Japanese invasion and suffering attacks on Australian soil for the first time, Australia must "populate or perish". Under this new policy, thousands of displaced Europeans, including traditional Europeans and southern and central Europeans, migrated to Australia, numbering more than two millions altogether in twenty years. A booming Australian economy stood in sharp contrast to war-ravaged

Europe and newly-arrived migrants found employment in government assisted programmes such as the Snowy Mountains Scheme.

The newly-founded Liberal Party of Australia headed by Robert Menzies dominated much of the immediate post-war era, defeating the Australian Labor Party government of Ben Chifley in 1949. Menzies oversaw the post-war expansion and became the country's longest-serving leader. During the period from 1950 to 1966, manufacturing industries which previously played a minor part in the economy dominated by primary production greatly expanded. People's life was greatly improved and employment was fully carried out, which brought the Australia the reputation "the lucky country".

In the late 1960s and early 1970s, Australia experienced turbulent period in which many problems appeared, such as Australian involvement in the Vietnam War, the relations between Australia and America and conscription. Such problems, to some extent, represented changes in people's values as they looked for answers to a wide range of social problems.

In 1972, Gough Whitlam from the Labor Party became the Prime Minister. He carried out many reforms that represented public attitudes to foreign relations, race relations, women's rights and welfare, one of which was to establish diplomatic relations with China. In the following years, the Labor government cut 25% tariff in order to reduce product price and made industry more competitive. Whitlam introduced a policy of self-determination for Aborigines and a policy of multiculturalism, and abolished race and skin colour as criteria for accepting immigrants into Australia. In addition, Australians took "**Advance Australia Fair**" instead of "God Saved Queen" as the national anthem of Australia, which was another attempt to break away from Britain.

During the depression days of the 1970s, Australia was troubled by economy. Though the governments were trying to change this condition, the problem was not finally resolved.

> **❓ Questions for discussion:**
>
> Soon after the foundation of Australia, World War I and World War II broke out successively. What policies did the government adopt during the two wars? What influences did the war have on the development of the country?

## Present Australia

The final constitutional ties between Australia and the United Kingdom were severed in 1986 with the passing of the *Australia Act*, ending any British role in the government of the Australian states, and ending judicial appeals to the United Kingdom Privy Council. In 1999, Australian voters rejected, by a majority of 54%, a move to become a republic with the president appointed by two-thirds vote of both Houses of the Australian Parliament. To alter the Australian Constitution, an *Act of the Australian Parliament* must occur as well as a referendum, receiving not only a majority of votes across the country, but also a majority of votes in a majority of the six Australian states. The referendum of 1999 did not receive a majority of votes across the country and did not win one of the six Australian states either.

After the election of the Whitlam Government in 1972, there has been an increasing focus on the expansion of ties with other Pacific Rim nations while maintaining close ties with Australia's traditional allies and trading partners. Especially over recent decades, Australia's foreign relations have been driven by a close association with the United States through the *Australia, New Zealand and United States (ANZUS) Security Treaty*, and by a desire to develop relations with Asia and the Pacific, particularly through the Association of Southeast Asian Nations (ASEAN) and the **Pacific Islands Forum**. In 2005, Australia secured an inaugural seat at the East Asia Summit following its accession to the *Treaty of Amity and Cooperation*. In November 2017, Australia was elected to the World Heritage Committee for a four-year term. In December 2019, severe bushfires raged in New South Wales, Victoria, and South Australia, killing more than 20 people, destroying more than 2,000 houses, and forcing tens of hundreds of local people leave their homes. The months-long bushfire resulted in poor air condition and even smog in New Zealand.

### Scott Morrison

**Scott Morrison** was born in 1968 and served as the 30th Prime Minister of Australia from 2018 to 2022. He took office on 24 August, 2018 on his election as leader of the Liberal Party of Australia.

On 1 February, 2019, Morrison opened his official account of Chinese social media WeChat. In the context of Australia's upcoming general election in 2019, Morrison's move is considered to be aimed at attracting Chinese voters. In fact, in order to win the support of Chinese, more and more Australian politicians are turning their attention to WeChat.

Morrison won a second term after leading the Coalition to an upset victory in the 2019 election. Morrison drew near unanimous condemnation for his government's ineffective response to the disaster because many people criticised him for going on a foreign holiday during the Australian bushfire. Later, back from Hawaii, Morrison held a press conference, arguing that his vacation during the bushfire was to fulfill his promise to the children. During the COVID-19 pandemic, Morrison established the National Cabinet, and Australia received praise during 2020 for being one of the few Western countries to successfully suppress the virus, though the slow initial pace of the COVID-19 vaccination rollout was criticised.

On 8 February, 2022, at the beginning of the meeting of the Australian Parliament, both the Senate and the House of Representatives read an apology letter on the long-standing problem of workplace bullying in the Australian Parliament and the government, and Australian Prime Minister Morrison also personally apologised.

In foreign policy, Morrison oversaw the signing of the security pact among Australia, the United Kingdom and the United States and increased tensions between Australia and China. On 8 December, 2021, one day after the United States declared a "diplomatic boycott", Australian Prime Minister Scott Morrison also announced that Australia would not send officials to participate in the 2022 Beijing Winter Olympics under the pretext of the so-called "human rights" issues. Morrison offered logistical support to Ukraine as part of the international effort against Russia in the wake of the 2022 Russian invasion of Ukraine.

In the 2022 Australian federal election, Morrison was defeated by Anthony Albanese from the Labor Party, making him the first prime minister since John Howard to serve a complete term in office. Following the loss, Morrison announced that he would step down as leader of the Liberal Party, with Peter Dutton being elected unopposed to replace him.

### Anthony Albanese

**Anthony Albanese** has been leader of the Australian Labor Party since 2019. He defeated Scott Morrison in the 2022 Australian federal election and served as the 31st and current prime minister of Australia on 1 June.

Albanese is the first Italian-Australian to become Prime Minister, the first Australian prime minister to have a non-Anglo-Celtic surname, and—along with 14 other Commonwealth prime ministers—is the last to serve under the reign of Queen Elizabeth II. Albanese's first acts as prime minister included updating Australia's climate targets in an effort to reach carbon neutrality by 2050, and supporting an increase to the national minimum wage.

On 24 May, 2022, Albanese flew to Japan to participate in the "Quadrilateral Security Dialogue" meeting with U.S. President Joe Biden, Indian Prime Minister Narendra Modi and Japanese Prime Minister Fumio Kishida. At the meeting, Albanese explained the important topic of "climate change" and said that his government would seek to take stronger action in reducing carbon emissions. He also committed his new government to the goals of the Quad.

On 21 June, NATO Secretary General Stoltenberg invited Albanese by the phone to participate in the NATO Summit to be held in Madrid, Spain, to discuss security threats facing the Pacific region from 29 to 30 June as a NATO Asia-Pacific partner. This will be the first time that Australian leaders have participated in the NATO Summit. After the Summit, Albanese travelled to Ukraine to meet with President Volodymyr Zelenskyy, making him the first Australian prime minister to make a diplomatic visit to Ukraine. Albanese pledged a further $100 million in aid to assist with the ongoing Russo-Ukrainian War.

On 29 August, Australian Prime Minister Albanese delivered his inaugural 100th-day speech at the National News Club, mainly introducing the ruling direction of the Labor Party in the next term of office. Its priorities include cleaner and cheaper energy sources, better skills and training, cheaper childcare services and the revitalisation of the local manufacturing industry, which were promised during the election. In his speech, Albanese accused the previous government, saying that it only focused on short-term political manipulation rather than long-term solutions. Therefore, the Labor government has been cleaning up the mess of the previous government since the election.

### Relations with China

While the economic relations between China and Australia have improved significantly to the benefit of both nations, Australia under the previous Howard Government has appeared reluctant to pursue closer political ties with China and has maintained the role of what critics have named "America's Sheriff" in the Asia-Pacific Region.

The election of Kevin Rudd as the Prime Minister of Australia has been seen as favorable to Sino-Australian relations, notably in view of the fact that he is the first Australian Prime Minister speaking fluent Mandarin and that closer engagement with Asia is one of the "Three Pillars" of his foreign policy.

In 2004, Rudd, who at that time was the Shadow Minister for Foreign Affairs, had delivered a speech in Beijing entitled "Australia and China: A Strong and Stable Partnership for the 21st Century".

On 1 January, 2009, Vice Premier Li Keqiang visited Australia and signed a joint statement, which is the first time that the basic principles and important consensus of developing bilateral relations have been fixed in the form of a joint statement since the establishment of diplomatic ties.

In June 2010, Kevin Rudd resigned and Julia Gillard became the nation's first-ever woman Prime Minister.

In April 2013, Chinese President Xi Jinping met with Australian Prime Minster Julia Gillard, and the two sides agreed to build a strategic partnership and set up the China-Australia Annual Prime Ministerial Meeting mechanism.

In 2014, Chinese President Xi Jinping paid attention to the incident of Malaysia Airlines Flight MH370 and talked with Australian Prime Minister Tony Abbott over phone.

From 2019 to 2022, China-Australia relations have experienced significant setbacks in political, economic, military and cultural exchanges. In May 2022, Albanese said Australia's relationship with China would remain "a difficult one".

On 8 July, during the G20 Foreign Ministers' Meeting, Australian Foreign Minister Huang Yingxian met with Chinese Foreign Minister Wang Yi. Wang Yi sincerely put forward suggestions on the development of China-Australia relations, namely, "four insists" — Australia insists on China as a partner; Australia insists on its ground not being dominated by third parties; Australia insists on the principle of seeking common ground while reserving differences and insists on building a positive and pragmatic social public opinion base.

Australian Foreign Minister Huang Yingxian responded at the first time, saying that Australia is willing to treat the relationship between China and Australia with mutual respect. Australia has no intention to contain China, let alone expand the differences between China and Australia. Although there are differences in China-Australia relations, it is more in the interests of both sides to stabilise the bilateral relations.

However, shortly after the Sino-Australian Foreign Ministers' Meeting, Australian Prime Minister Albanese suddenly stated harshly to China that the Australian government will only respond to matters related to national interests and will not pay attention to the suggestions put forward by China.

From Albanese's words, it is not difficult to see that the Australian government is still reluctant to repair China-Australia relations, but this does not mean that all the Australians think so. At least, people of insight like Huang Yingxian still want to seek cooperation with China.

In this regard, China demonstrated its diplomatic spirit that a country should have, that is, tolerance, pragmatism and cooperation. The Spokesperson of the Ministry of Foreign Affairs of China said sincerely to Australia that China was willing to continue trade cooperation with Australia, to improve China-Australia relations, and tried to remove the obstacles currently between the two countries, so that China and Australia can return to normal relations early.

During the United Nations Conference in 22 September, 2022, Wang Yi and Huang Yingxian met once again. They had a frank and constructive talk, and the relationship between China and Australia is to witness a turning point, China willing to improve trade relations with Australia in spring 2023.

> **? Question for discussion:**
>
> With the Sino-American relations being improved after World War II, the relationship between Australia and China changed accordingly. How about the political relations between the two countries in recent years and the trend of development in the future?

## Exercises

### I. Fill in the blanks.

1. In the 1950s, there was a boom in Australia's economy and people's living standard was high, so Australia was called "the _____ _____" in that period.
2. In World War II, Australia declared war on Japan immediately after Japan bombed the U.S. naval base at _____ _____.
3. In _____ Australia secured an inaugural seat at the East Asia Summit following its accession to the *Treaty of Amity and Cooperation*.
4. Gough Whitlam carried out many reforms after he won the election, one of which was to establish diplomatic relations with _____.
5. After World War II, full employment and _____ were chiefly government's main targets.

### II. Define the following terms.

1. Gallipoli Campaign

2. the lucky country

## III. Multiple choice.

1. In Australia, 25 April is known as _____.
   A. Australia Day   B. Independence Day
   C. Anzac Day       D. ANZUS

2. Under the Whitlam Government "God Save the Queen" was replaced by _____ as Australia's national anthem.
   A. "Waltzing Matilda"
   B. "Click Go the Shears"
   C. "Advance Australia Fair"
   D. "My Country"

3. When did the third wave of migration begin in Australia?
   A. After World War I.
   B. During World War II.
   C. After World War II.
   D. After the Vietnam War.

4. There is a continuing debate in Australia about _____.
   A. whether Australia should join the EEC (now European Union)
   B. whether Australia should remain a monarchy or become a republic
   C. whether Australia should develop its own manufacturing
   D. whether Australia should build its own defense

5. The main British nature of Australian society has been challenged since the third wave of migration because _____.
   A. many new migrants are unskilled workers
   B. many new migrants are not used to the Australian way of life
   C. many new migrants come from the non-English-speaking world
   D. many new migrants feel rejected in Australia

6. As far as Australian culture is concerned, the history of Australia can be divided into the following phases with the exception of _____.
   A. the period of the original culture of Aboriginal people
   B. the period of the dominant British culture
   C. the period of Asian culture
   D. the period of a multicultural society

7. During the 1990s, many Australians called for their nation to become a republic with _____.
   A. a president replacing the British monarch as head of state
   B. a prime minister replacing the Governor-General as head of government
   C. a Governor-General replacing the British monarch as head of state
   D. a president replacing the Governor-General as head of government

8. After the outbreak of World War I, Australia followed Britain's lead and declared war on _____.
   A. Japan   B. Turkey   C. Italy   D. Germany

## IV. Translate the following terms into English.
1. 雪山计划
2. 幸运的国家
3. 枢密院
4. 太平洋岛国论坛
5. 威斯敏斯特规约

## V. Answer the following questions in a few sentences.
1. When did the Commonwealth of Australia come into being?

2. What reforms did the Whitman Govern

### Mini-task:

Australia has become a target of a number of ongoing international disputes. Australia's role in the 2003 Invasion of Iraq without UN sanction has caused a great deal of protest. In 2006, there was a tension in Australia's relations with Indonesia over the release of Abu Bakar Bashir as well as Australia's recent decision to grant temporary protection visas to 42 West Papuans, after which Indonesia's ambassador was recalled. There were also minor tensions between the two countries in 2004 to 2005 when Schapelle Corby was imprisoned for 20 years for possessing 4.2 kilograms of marijuana.

Another foreign relations dispute came to light when, on 12 September, 2006, the Australian High Commissioner in Honiara, Solomon Islands — Patrick Cole — was labeled *persona non grata* by the Solomon Islands government. The incident marked the beginning of a diplomatic dispute between the two nations, with the Australian federal government and in particular the Prime Minister implementing diplomatic changes including new visa requirements on Solomon Islands diplomats.

Share your opinions with your classmates and try to find out the original reason for it.

# VOLUME FOUR

# CANADA

# Chapter One  Geography and Population

*Canada, as the second largest country in the world, plays an important role in the world's economy, cultures as well as politics. Before going into this chapter, try to get the information about the following items through various resources available.*
1. *Characteristics of geography and climate in Canada.*
2. *Detailed information about one of the rivers or lakes in Canada.*

## Part One  Geographical Features

### Position

Canada is the second largest country in the world with an area of 9,984,670 square kilometres, occupying two-fifths of North America. It extends about 3,200 kilometres northward into the Arctic Ocean and runs about 6,400 kilometres from the Pacific Ocean in the west to the Atlantic Ocean in the east with the longest coastline in the world: 243,000 kilometres. Canada is located to the north of the United States, bordering on Alaska in the northwest and facing the Island of Greenland across **Baffin Bay**. Canada shares land borders of 8,892 kilometres with the United States, but with no defenses for thousands of tourists to pass through every day. In general, the east of Canada is in the hilly belt, and most areas of the south are dotted with basins, while the western areas are mostly mountainous with numerous over-4,000-kilometre peaks.

Canada is a federation composed of ten provinces and three territories; in turn, these may be grouped into the following regions according to their locations: **Western Canada** consists of British Columbia and three Prairie Provinces (Alberta, Saskatchewan, and Manitoba). **Eastern Canada** refers to Central Canada and Atlantic Canada together. The former includes Quebec and Ontario, and the latter involves three maritime provinces (New Brunswick, Prince Edward Island, and Nova Scotia), along with Newfoundland and Labrador. **Northern Canada** is made up of three Territories (Yukon, Northwest Territories, and Nunavut). Provinces have more autonomy than Territories. Each has its own provincial or territorial symbols.

### Landform

Canada has a varied topography. In the mountainous provinces of Eastern Canada, there is an irregular coastline along the Atlantic Ocean and the St. Lawrence Bay. St. Lawrence Plain and the Inland Plain are the major farming land. They are separated by a plateau covered with forest, which originates at Lake Superior and Lake Huron, and extends to the Atlantic Ocean. Boreal forests prevail on the rocky **Canadian Shield**. This plateau has a series of mountains including the Rockies running from north to south. **Mount Logan** is the highest peak in Canada, located in Yukon Territory of northwest Canada. Ice and tundra are prominent in the Arctic and glaciers are visible in the Canadian Rockies and Coast Mountains. The broad Canadian Shield is an area of rock scoured clean by the last ice age, thinly soiled, rich in minerals, and dotted with lakes and rivers. **The Gulf of Saint Lawrence** is bounded by Newfoundland to the north and **the Maritimes** to the south. The Maritimes protrude eastward along the Appalachian Mountain ranging from northern New England in the U.S. and the **Gaspé Peninsula of Quebec**. New Brunswick and Nova Scotia are divided by the **Bay of Fundy**, which experiences the world's largest tidal variations. Ontario and Hudson Bay dominate Central Canada. West of Ontario and the broad flat **Canadian Prairies** spread toward the Rocky Mountains, which separate them from British Columbia.

Canada is full of lakes. Apart from four of the Great Lakes shared with America, Canada also possesses nine lakes with a length of over 161 kilometres respectively and 35 about-80-kilometre-long lakes. Canada by far has more lakes than any other country, occupying 7 percent of the world's freshwater.

Two major rivers in Canada are the **Mackenzie** and the **St. Lawrence**. The Mackenzie River is the longest river in Canada and just secondary to the Mississippi River in America, running 1,650 kilometres between the Canadian Shield and the Rockies in the west and flowing from the Great Slave Lake to the Arctic Ocean. A tributary of the Mackenzie is the South Nahanni River, which is the home to Virginia Falls, a waterfall about twice as high as Niagara Falls. On the other hand, the St. Lawrence River widens into the world's largest estuary before flowing into the Gulf of St. Lawrence. The navigable mileage of the St. Lawrence extends 3,769 kilometres. The Great Lakes feed the St. Lawrence River (in the southeast) where lowlands host much of Canada's population.

According to the landform, Canada can be divided into six regions, which have some overlapping areas: the Atlantic Provinces, the St. Lawrence — Great Lakes Provinces, the Canadian Shield Provinces, the Prairie Provinces, British Columbia Province, the North Provinces and Territories.

The **Atlantic Provinces** are composed of stony hills and barren plains. This region is not fit to develop agriculture, but abounds in potatoes. The irregular Atlantic coastline and the St. Lawrence Bay provide excellent fishing harbours. Tourism industry serves as the economic mainstay in this region because of the beautiful mountains and valleys.

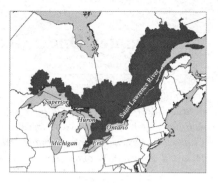

The **Great Lakes-St. Lawrence Provinces** are the most developed region in Canada. This region is enriched by the nearby St. Lawrence River and the Great Lakes, so many European migrants chose to inhabit the region. Nowadays, it has become a denselypopulated area as well as a highly-industrialised region.

The **Canadian Shield Provinces**, occupying almost half of the whole Canada, refer to the stony highlands and Plateau around the **Hudson Bay**. With thousands of lakes and swamps, it is not attractive to inhabitants, but abounds in resources of minerals, water power, and forests.

The sparsely-populated **Prairie Provinces** mainly lie in the North American Plain, which contains smooth and fertile grasslands. It is fit for planting wheat and is rich in oil, gas and coal.

**British Columbia Province** stands on the Pacific coast with three major mountain ranges running through it. These ranges separate the British Columbia Province from other provinces, but provide abundant resources of minerals, rainfalls and forests. It is the second largest producer of hydroelectric power, and forestry serves as its main economic mainstay.

The **North Provinces and Territories** are barren and sparsely populated. Most areas of this region are located to the north of the Arctic Circle, stretching from Alaska to the Atlantic coast. Hills, highlands, rivers and lakes are distributed all over this region, which has a hostile climate but contains plentiful forests, minerals and water power.

### Climate

On the whole, the climate throughout Canada is varied but generally unfavourable. Due to the influence of the westerly belt, most areas of Canada are under the influence of the **continental temperate coniferous climate**, except that the north part belongs to the frigid tundra climate. The moist continental climate influences a wide range from Eastern Canada to the Prairie Provinces. The maritime climate prevails in the southeast of British Columbia, the northern ever-green conifer belt in the sub-arctic area and the warm tundra belt in the polar region. Most areas of Canada are abundant in rainfall with a long and cold winter. But it is not a country that is covered with snow everywhere all the year round. In August, it is as hot and moist in Eastern Canada as in the tropics. The average winter and summer high temperatures across Canada vary depending on the location. Winters can be harsh in many regions of the country, particularly in the interior and the Prairie Provinces which experience a continental climate. The daily average temperature there is near −15℃, but can drop below −60℃ with severe wind chills. In non-coastal regions, snow can cover the ground almost six months of the year (more in the north). The coastal British Columbia is an exception and enjoys a temperate climate with a mild and rainy winter. On the east and west coast, the average high temperature is generally around 20℃, while the average summer high temperature between the coasts ranges from 25℃ to 30℃ with occasional extreme heat in some interior locations exceeding 40℃.

Such a climate is suitable for the growth of maple trees, which makes most of the land covered with maples. Furthermore, Canada enjoys a reputation as a maple-leaf country, and the maple leaf in Canada's national flag reflects Canadians' appreciation of it.

> **Question for discussion:**
> With the global warming, what actions will Canada take to hold back the deterioration of the climate?

## Part Two   Natural Resources

### Minerals

The plentiful natural resources are of great significance to the Canadian economy. Canada is one of the few developed nations as a net exporter of energy. Atlantic Canada has vast offshore deposits of natural gas, and large oil and gas resources are centred in Alberta. The vast Athabasca Oil Sands offers Canada the world's second largest oil reserves behind Saudi Arabia. In Quebec, British Columbia, Newfoundland, Labrador, New Brunswick, Ontario and Manitoba, hydroelectricity is a cheap and clean source of renewable energy.

Canada is one of the world's largest producers of zinc and uranium and a world leader in many other natural resources such as gold, nickel, aluminium and lead. Many towns in the northern part of the country, where agriculture is difficult, were set up because of a nearby mine or source of timber. All the minerals needed in a modern economy can be found in Canada. As a major producer of nickel, zinc and asbestos, Canada also ranks fifth in gold production and twelfth in copper production. It also abounds in silver, iron, aluminium and platinum and is a major world producer of uranium for nuclear power.

The main mineral deposits as well as coal, oil and gas are located in the Canadian Shield, while southern Quebec has the largest deposits of asbestos in the Western Hemisphere. An iron deposit lies in the border between Labrador and Quebec Provinces as well as the north bank of the Siberia Lake. Deposits rich in copper, zinc and silver are found in northern Ontario Province.

It is believed that Canada may possess one of the largest deposits of coal in the world. But the deep coal bed and harsh terrain make development and transportation difficult.

The oil deposit is located in Alberta, which provides two-thirds of oil and four-fifths of gas for Canada. There is a gas pipeline from Alberta to Ontario, stretching over 3,200 kilometres. Another trans-provincial oil pipeline is over 1,120 kilometres from Alberta to British Columbia. These pipelines provide the densely populated areas with gas and oil.

### Waters

Water power is one of Canada's most important

resources. It is found in the St. Lawrence River, the Great Lakes and big rivers in the west, which greatly influenced the settlement and development of territory and industries. The discharge of rivers in Canada takes up almost half of that in the world, while 150 lakes serve as natural conditioners to the rivers, including many inland seas like the Great Bear and the Great Slave Lake. Canada ranks fourth in the production of hydroelectricity in the world, second only to China, Brazil and America.

Canada is one of the countries with the longest coastline. The world-prosperous fishing grounds are situated in the coastal waters of the Pacific and the Atlantic Ocean, which provide basic resources for the Canadian fishery. Today, Canada is the sixth largest exporter of fish and seafood in the world.

### Forests

Forests cover almost half of Canada, producing a great deal of wood and wood products and ranking fifth in world production. The forest belt stretches from the Atlantic to the Pacific Ocean, crossing the Great Plain. Forests provide raw materials for lumbering and papermaking industries. The amount of papermaking in Canada makes up 40% of the total produced in the world, and Canada has become the world's largest producer of newsprint.

Furs are another important resource in Canada. Hunters and fur traders established many settlements in the early times to trap furred animals, such as foxes, minks and beavers.

> **? Question for discussion:**
> With the exploitation of natural resources, an increasing number of the environmental problems have occurred. How does Canada deal with such problems?

## Part Three  The People

Canada is a sparsely populated country with a vast territory. Its population totals over 37,411,000 (2019), about 85% of which is descended from immigrants, mostly from Britain, secondly from France and Asia. There are no long-term residents in about 80% of the whole land. Many areas in the north are covered with dense forests and freezing arctic wasteland. About 80% of the population is estimated to live in big cities near the Canadian — American border, especially in the area between Quebec Province and Lake Ontario.

### Distribution of Population

The population density, 4.1 inhabitants per square kilometre, is among the lowest in the world. The most densely populated area of the country is from Quebec City to Windsor Corridor along the Great Lakes and St. Lawrence River in the southeast. In Eastern Canada, most people live in large urban centres on the flat St. Lawrence Lowlands.

In general, there are four areas with dense population. The first area lies in the towns along the Atlantic coastline, which features agriculture, mining and fishing industries; the second area refers to the cities in the plains, characterised by wheat plantation, cattle rearing and oil mining; the third is in the manufacturing cities in Quebec and Ontario Provinces; the fourth is on the Pacific coastline in British Columbia Province. In addition, most areas to the north of the north latitude 55 degrees are populated by hunters, fishermen, and miners.

### Multinationality

Canada is a **multinational country** in possession of over 100 ethnic groups. The majority of Canadians are descendants of English and French origins. The natives are **Eskimos** and Indians, living in the North Provinces and speaking over 50 languages. English is an official language commonly used in Canada, except for Quebec Province. French, another official language, is commonly spoken by Canadians, especially in Quebec Province.

## Part Four  Culture

### Multiculturalism

The major characteristic of Canadian culture is **multiculturalism.** As a nation of immigrants, Canada has historically been influenced by British, French as well as Aboriginal cultures and traditions, and especially by American culture because of its proximity to America and migration between the two countries. The great majority of English-speaking immigrants to Canada from 1755 to 1815 were Americans from the Lower Thirteen Colonies. They were drawn there by promises of land or exiled because of their loyalty to Britain during the Independent War in America. In view of its ethnic diversity and bilingual framework, Canada's character has been shaped by multiculturalism values, that is, new settlers can introduce their different customs and ways of life to Canada and keep them as they like. Different cultures co-exist but do not overwhelm each other. Each ethnic community can have its heritage acknowledged and retain its identity. Multicultural heritage serves as the basis of Section 27 of the *Canadian Charter of Rights and Freedoms*.

## Bilingualism

Canada has two official languages: English and French. Official bilingualism is fitted by law in Canada, defined in the *Canadian Charter of Rights and Freedoms*, the **Official Languages Act**, and the **Official Language Regulations**; it is enforced by the Commissioner of Official Languages. The population of Montreal and Quebec is mainly French-speaking, with a significant English-speaking community. English and French have equal status in federal courts, the Parliament and all federal institutions. The public has the right to receive federal government services in either English or French, and official language minorities are guaranteed their own schools in all the Provinces and Territories. On the other hand, non-official languages are important in Canada, with over five million people listing one of those languages as a first language. Some significant non-official languages include Chinese (1,204,865 first-language speakers), Italian (407,455), German (404,745), and Punjabi (543,495).

As a multinational country, Canada has been advocating the **bilingual system**. In 1968, Prime Minister Pierre Elliott Trudeau put forward the concept of bilingualism in his proposal of *the Official Languages Bill*, which laid the foundation for the bilingual system in the Canadian federal administration. The bilingual system ensures Canadians know and accept French culture as a distinctive feature of Canadian culture. Most Canadians speak English or French in school or at work, while they speak their own languages at home. So Canadians still keep their own cultures in their ethnic groups. Migrants from different countries remain different in culture, language, religion and lifestyle. Therefore, the Canadian government formulated the multicultural policy in 1971, teaching migrants an official language to help them blend with the society and encouraging them to keep their own cultural heritage.

## Sports

Canada's national sports are ice hockey in winter and lacrosse in summer. Ice hockey is a national pastime and the most popular spectator sport in the country, ever with 1.65 million active participants in 2004. Canada's six largest metropolitan areas — **Toronto**, **Montreal**, **Vancouver**, **Ottawa**, **Calgary** and **Edmonton** — have franchises in the **National Hockey League** (NHL). There are more Canadian players in the league than from all other countries combined. Besides hockey, other popular spectator sports include curling and football; the latter is played professionally in the **Canadian Football League** (CFL). Golf, baseball, skiing, soccer, volleyball and basketball are widely played at youth and amateur levels, but professional leagues and franchises are not widespread.

Canada hosted several high-profile international sporting events, including the 1976 Summer Olympics, the 1988 Winter Olympics, and the 2007 FIFA U-20 World Cup. Canada was the host country for the 2010 Winter Olympics in Vancouver, Whistler and British Columbia.

## Religion

Religion has always played an important part in Canadian history, and churches have been a centre of spiritual and social life for early Canadians. There is no state church in Canada, although Christian values serve as the centre of life in Canada and most people report they are Christians. Originally, religion had a close relation to the educational system in all the provinces, which had educational system separated by religion. But now most Provinces have abolished such a practice. Religion in Canada encompasses a wide range of groups. Therefore, **religious pluralism** is an important part of Canadian culture.

## Part Five    Education

Canada attaches great importance to education. All Canadians receive formal education for at least 10 years because of the increasing complexity of society and technology. A number of schools are set up, funded and overseen by the Canadian federal, provincial and local governments. **Elementary**, **secondary** and **higher education** in Canada belong to the provincial responsibility. There are many variations among provinces with 10 educational systems compatible in Canada, even to the extent that various differences exist side by side in the same province. The Canadian federal government functions as an organisation to appropriate money for each province, to provide various projects to assist students, and to organise and manage the education for minorities.

There are two types of higher education. One refers to **universities** and **university colleges** which can directly grant students degrees. The school year is divided into two terms: the period from January to April and that from September to December. Students

# VOLUME FOUR  Canada

can obtain credits by taking up courses and get graduation certificates and degrees if they meet the requirements. The other type refers to **community colleges** and **vocational colleges** which belong to provincial schools. They aim at the education in professions and trades. Students can get graduation certificates, but cannot obtain degrees.

Canada devotes great amounts of public money to education. There are more than 100 educational institutions for undergraduates and over 200 community universities, of which the tuition fees are lowest in the western world. In addition, Canada carries out **compulsory educational system** for citizens. Education is compulsory up to the age of 16 in all the provinces but Ontario and New Brunswick where the compulsory age is 18. Children of citizens and migrants do not pay tuition fees when receiving primary and middle education in public schools rather than in private schools. Public schools, synonymous with state schools, refer to those funded from tax revenue and most commonly administered, to some degree, by government agencies. According to NBC's 2012 report, Canada is the most educated country in the world. The Program for International Student Assessment shows that Canadian students are well above the OECD average, especially in math, science and reading.

> **? Questions for discussion:**
> 1. What's the purpose of bilingualism in Canada? Is there any relationship between its bilingualism and multiculturalism?
> 2. What's the uniqueness of Canada's educational system?

## Exercises

### I. Fill in the blanks.

1. As the second largest country in the world, Canada extends northward into the _____ Ocean and runs from the _____ Ocean in the west to the _____ Ocean in the east.
2. _____ is the highest peak in Canada, located in the Yukon Territory of northwest Canada.
3. Canada by far has more _____ than any other country and has a large amount of the world's freshwater.
4. _____ Falls is a waterfall about twice as high as Niagara Falls.
5. _____ industry serves as the economic mainstay in the region of the Atlantic Provinces.
6. The _____ Provinces, with thousands of lakes and swamps, abound in the resources of minerals, water power and forests.
7. The sparsely-populated Prairie Provinces mainly lie in the _____ Plain, which contains smooth and fertile grasslands.
8. The North Provinces and Territories are barren and _____ populated. Most areas of this region are located to the north of the _____, and contains plentiful forests, minerals and water power.
9. Most areas of Canada are abundant in _____ with a long and cold winter.
10. As one of the most important resources, water power lies in _____ River, the _____ Lakes and big rivers in the west.
11. The forest belt stretches from the Atlantic to the Pacific Ocean, crossing the _____ and ranking _____ in the world.

### II. Define the following terms.

1. The Great Lakes-St. Lawrence Provinces
2. multiculturalism
3. bilingual system
4. the Prairie Provinces

### III. Multiple choice.

1. The longest river in Canada is _____.
   A. the Mackenzie        B. the St. Lawrence
   C. the Mississippi      D. the South Nahanni
2. The _____ Provinces are the most developed region in Canada.
   A. Canadian Shield
   B. Great Lakes-St. Lawrence
   C. British Colombia
   D. Prairie
3. Canada by far has more lakes than any other country, occupying _____ of the world's freshwater.
   A. 50%    B. 30%    C. 20%    D. 7%
4. _____ serves as the main economic mainstay in British Columbia province.
   A. Hydroelectric power  B. Tourism
   C. Forestry             D. Mining
5. Due to the influence of the westerly belt, most areas of Canada are in the charge of the _____

climate.
　A．continental temperate coniferous
　B．frigid tundra
　C．maritime
　D．continental temperate
6. In Quebec, British Columbia, Newfoundland and Labrador, New Brunswick, Ontario and Manitoba, _____ is a cheap and clean source of renewable energy.
　A．water　　　　　B．oil
　C．gas　　　　　　D．hydroelectricity
7. Canada ranks fourth in the production of hydro-electricity in the world, just secondary to that of _____.
　A．America, Russia and Britain
　B．Russia, America and China
　C．China, Brazil and America
　D．Russia, Britain and Australia
8. Now Canada is the sixth largest exporter of _____ in the world.
　A．corn　B．fish　C．oil　D．timber
9. Now the amount of papermaking in Canada makes up _____ of the total amounts in the world, and Canada has become the largest country producer of newsprint in the world.
　A．30%　B．50%　C．40%　D．60%
10. There is a gas pipeline from _____ to _____, stretching over 3,200 kilometres.
　A．Alberta; Ontario
　B．Alberta; British Columbia
　C．Ontario; British Columbia
　D．British Columbia; Newfoundland
11. Another trans-provincial oil piping is over 1,120 kilometres from Alberta to _____.
　A．Ontario　　　　B．Newfoundland
　C．British Colombia　D．Manitoba

Ⅳ. **Translate the following terms into English.**
1. 滨海诸省
2. 爱斯基摩人
3. 宗教多元化
4. 多民族国家

Ⅴ. **Answer the following questions in a few sentences.**
1. What about the distribution of dense population in Canada?
2. Why is Canadian culture viewed as being inherently multicultural?

Mini-task:

As a sparsely populated country, Canada has long been faced with the problem of a small population. In addition to attracting more people from other countries, Canada carries out a lot of welfare policies to stimulate the population growth. Please search for the information about the preferential treatment the Canadians enjoy.

# Chapter Two  Government and Politics

*As a member of the British Commonwealth, Canada follows Britain in many aspects, especially in the government system. But its political system is still influenced by other countries like America, and has developed its own characteristics. Try to get the information about Canada's politics and find out the similarities and differences between Canada and Britain as well as America.*

## Part One  Political System

Canada is a constitutional monarchy country with the British King/Queen as the head of state, the **Governor-General** as the permanent representative of the British King/Queen and the **Prime Minister** as the head of the government. It is also a parliamentary democracy, featuring federalism that is composed of the **federal government** and provincial governments at a lower level. Therefore, the political community of Canada is actually a mixture of democratic federalism and central-powered constitutional monarchy.

Executive authority is formally and constitutionally vested in the Monarch. However, by convention, the Monarch and the Governor-General play a predominantly ceremonial and a political role, deferring exercise of executive power to the **Cabinet**, which is made up of ministers generally accountable to the elected House of Commons, and headed by the Prime Minister, who is normally the leader of the party that holds the confidence of the House of Commons. Thus, the Cabinet is typically regarded as the active seat of executive power. This arrangement ensures the stability of government, and makes the Prime Minister's Office one of the most powerful organs of the system. However, the sovereign and the Governor-General do retain their right to use the Royal Prerogative in exceptional constitutional crisis situations.

The federal parliament is made up of the King/Queen (represented by the Governor-General) and two Houses: the elected House of Commons and the appointed **Senate**. Each member in the House of Commons is elected by simple plurality in an electoral district, while the Canadian Senate resembles the British House of Lords in the appointment of the Senators, but different from that of America. Canada is a federation with governments at three levels: the federal government, the provincial governments and the municipal governments. Accordingly, elections in Canada can be divided into three levels that have nothing to do with each other. **Federal elections** are held to elect the Prime Minister either once every four years as determined by fixed election date legislation, or triggered by the government losing a confidence vote in the House of Commons (usually only possible during minority governments). Candidates for the Prime Minister are the leaders of various political parties; in **provincial elections**, candidates representing different parties run for the governor of a province; while in **municipal elections**, candidates run for Mayor without representing any political party. Members of the Senate, whose seats are apportioned on a regional basis, are chosen by the Prime Minister and formally appointed by the Governor-General, serving until age 75.

As a member of the British Commonwealth, Canada was established as a federal state and became a dominion in 1867 when the **British North America Act** was passed by the British Parliament. The political system of Canada resembles that of Britain in some aspects, but has its own traits. On the one hand, Canada is a monarchy country. Its head of state is the British King/Queen, who does not live in Canada, but is represented by the Governor-General. On the other hand, Canada is a federation influenced by the American Republicanism. The federal government and the provincial governments have a

definite division of authority when sharing power in some fields. Therefore, the Canadian federalism is based on the British system of government, which contributes to the establishment of a strong central government with power, order and authority. By contrast, the American federalism features checks and balances on the political power, which frequently leads to disputes between the President and the Congress over policies.

Nowadays, King Charles III is the head of state in the British Commonwealth. In Canada, the Governor-General, appointed by the Prime Minister, represents King Charles III to carry out all the Canadian royal privileges. So in theory, the Governor-General serves as the origin of all the authority, but in reality, he only acts on proposals of the Prime Minister and his Cabinet. The Prime Minister is the leader of the party that wins the most seats in the House of Commons and forms the federal government. The Cabinet, chosen by the Prime Minister, consists of senior Members of Parliament from the party in power. Accordingly, the Prime Minister and the Cabinet are responsible to the House of Commons.

The *British North America Act of 1867* laid the foundation for federalism, but did not contribute to a complete Canadian Constitution as a precursor. Most items of the Constitution originated from the basic British acts, common practice and Parliament traditions, which have been revised, added to or abolished in favour of Canadians since 1867. As the Constitution has to adapt to the significant innovation in society, politics, economy and technology, the federal government and the provincial governments will call a meeting to discuss and deal with problems. The Trudeau government made great efforts in this respect as the *Canadian Charter of Rights and Freedom* was passed in 1982.

> **? Questions for discussion:**
> 1. What's the role of the Governor-General and the Prime Minister in Canada?
> 2. What are the similarities and differences in the Parliament between Canada and Britain as well as America?

## Part Two  Parties

Canada carries out the **two-party system** with one party in power at only one time. The leader of the party with the second most seats usually becomes the leader of the Opposition and is a part of an adversarial parliamentary system that keeps the government in check.

It is proved in Canadian political history that if a party frequently wins the election and controls political power for a long time, it will become the major party in power. There are two major federal parties in Canada at present: the **Liberal Party** and the **Progressive Conservative Party**. In addition to these two major parties, many other minor political parties are also prevailing in Canada: the **Unionist Coalition**, the **National Party**, the **New Democratic Party**, the **Green Party**, the **Reform Party** and the **Social Credit Party**. They also possess seats in the House of Commons and play a part in national politics. Since 1900, Liberals have been in power for about 80 years, while the Conservatives' record is about 40 years in government. But neither the party in power nor the opposition party was popular throughout the whole country. For example, the government of Ontario Province has been under the control of the Progressive Conservative Party for 60 years from 1943 to 2003, while the Liberal Party has been in charge of the government of Quebec Province (10 years longer than the Progressive Conservative Party since 1949). The Liberal leader has been the Prime Minister since 6 February, 2015, while the Conservative leader has been the Opposition leader since 2 December, 2015.

However, the political parties in Provinces are not under the control of the federal government party. The provincial parties usually hold a disagreement with the federal party because of regional interests. So voters can support different parties in the federal and provincial elections, which is an important element for Canada to carry out federalism characterised by division of powers. In addition, a member of the federal Parliament cannot serve as a member of the provincial legislature.

## Part Three  Quebec's Problem

As the largest province in Canada, Quebec takes up most of Eastern Canada with an area of 1.54 million square kilometres, which is three times as large as France and seven times as Britain. It abounds in minerals, water power and forests. The St. Lawrence River valley and lowlands lie in the south of Quebec with a dense population. It is the most developed and prosperous area of the country.

However, quite a few revolutions in pursuit of complete independence have been going on in Quebec Province for several decades. Quebec Province differs from other provinces in its own trait of French culture. The majority of the provincial people are French descendants, so Quebec is the largest French-speaking area in North America; French Canadians hold to their own peculiarities in tradition, culture and social system. They have been fighting for the independence of their language and culture since French sovereignty over North America was taken over by Britain in 1763.

In the early 1960s, French Canadians intensely protested disqualification for speaking only French while working in government and big companies. So they believed the only way out was to separate from Canada so as to keep their own identity. The focus of the conflict centred on language, culture and politics. Some advocated the political separation from Canada, while others attempted to solve the problem by adopting terrorism. In order to keep Quebec in Canada, the Canadian government has followed a policy of bilingualism since 1969. Thus, French as well as English serves as an official language in Canada. But in 1976, Quebec elected a separatist government, which was supported by the **Bloc Québécois** and made a commitment to win more autonomy and promote economy. It attempted to adopt a monolingual policy to confront bilingualism. In politics, the Quebec government aimed at increasing its influence on the federation. However, the separatists' efforts to win independence contributed to the growth of nationalism.

Efforts by the Progressive Conservative government of Brian Mulroney to constitutionally recognise Quebec as a "distinct society" collapsed in 1989. Regional tensions ignited by the constitutional debate helped fledgling regional parties like the Bloc Québécois under Lucien Bouchard and the **Reform Party** under Preston Manning in Western Canada, and gain political power at the expense of Progressive Conservatives, who placed fifth in the federal election. The Quebecois is very popular in Quebec Province, demanding special rights and privileges, while the Reform party, with the strongest support in the western provinces, insists on the equality of all the Canadians without any privilege for speaking a different language. The Reform Party expanded to become the Canadian Alliance and merged with the Progressive Conservatives to form the Conservative Party of Canada in 2003. The Conservatives were elected to form a minority government under Stephen Harper in the 2006 federal election. Later that year, Canada's Parliament passed a symbolic motion to recognise the Québécois as a nationality within Canada.

> **? Questions for discussion:**
> 1. Which party is in power in Canada? What's the government's attitude toward the Quebec problem?
> 2. As the largest province in Canada, Quebec is also the birthplace of Canada's history. What advantages does it have to attract the immigrants from all over the world?

## Exercises

### I. Fill in the blanks.

1. Canada is a _____ monarchy country with Elizabeth II as the head of state and _____ as the head of the government.
2. The federal parliament is made up of the King Charles III, _____ and _____.
3. Federal elections are held either every _____ years as determined by fixed election date legislation, or triggered by _____ losing the confidence in the House of Commons.
4. As a member of the British Commonwealth, Canada was established as a federal state and became a _____ in 1867 when _____ was passed by the British Parliament.
5. In Canada, the Prime Minister and the Cabinet are responsible to _____.
6. Most items of the Canadian Constitution originated from _____, _____ and Parliament traditions.
7. As the largest province in Canada, Quebec abounds in _____, minerals and _____.
8. The separatists' efforts in Quebec to win independence contributed to the growth of _____.
9. The government of Ontario Province has been in the charge of the Progressive Conservative Party from 1943 to 2003, while the _____ Party has been in charge of the government of Quebec Province 10 years longer than the Progressive Conservative Party since 1949.
10. Quebec Province differs from other provinces in its own trait of _____ culture.

### II. Define the following terms.

1. the two-party system
2. Quebec's Problem
3. the *British North America Act*
4. the federal parliament
5. federal elections

### III. Multiple choice.

1. _____ is typically viewed to be in the real executive power.
   A. The Prime Minister
   B. The Cabinet
   C. The Governor-General
   D. Elizabeth II

2. Members of the Senate are chosen by _____.
   A. the Queen/King Charles III
   B. the Governor General
   C. the Cabinet
   D. the Prime Minister
3. There are two major federal parties in Canada at present: _____ and the Progressive Conservative Party.
   A. the Liberal Party    B. Unionist Coalition
   C. National Party       D. Green Party
4. _____ is the largest area in North America for speaking French.
   A. British Columbia    B. Ontario
   C. Quebec              D. Yukon Territory
5. In 2003, the government of _____ Province has been in the hand of the Progressive Conservative Party.
   A. Quebec              B. Ontario
   C. British Columbia    D. Alberta
6. The _____ Party, with the strongest support in the western provinces, insists on the equality of all the Canadians without any privilege for speaking a different language.
   A. Quebec              B. Conservative
   C. Reform              D. Liberal
7. The Reform Party merged with the Progressive Conservatives to form the _____ Party of Canada in 2003.
   A. Alliance            B. Green
   C. Liberal             D. Conservative
8. _____ demanded to be granted special rights for being viewed by the Progressive Conservative government as a distinct society.
   A. Quebec              B. Ontario
   C. Yukon Territory     D. Alberta

## IV. Translate the following terms into English.
1. 总督
2. 市县选举
3. 进步保守党
4. 英联邦自治领
5. 自由党

## V. Answer the following questions in a few sentences.
1. What's the difference between Canada and America in federalism?

2. What is the three-leveled elections in Canada?

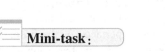 

Prime Minister Stephen Harper stated that Canada's economy would still be encumbered with the global economic crisis despite its recovery. Please search for the information about the consequences of the economic recession in Canada and the Conservative Party's reaction to this crisis.

# Chapter Three  Economy and Major Cities

*Canada has completed its economic transformation, leaping to the top of the developed countries. Try to get the information about the following items from materials available:*
1. *What's the mainstay of economy in Canada?*
2. *How did Canada leap to the top of the world in economy?*

## Part One  Structure of Economy

### Changes and Adjustments

In the past century, the growth of the manufacturing, mining, and service sectors has transformed Canada from a largely agricultural and rural country into a primarily industrial and urban country. As with other first-world nations, the Canadian economy is dominated by the service industry, which employs about three quarters of Canadians. However, Canada is unusual among the developed countries in the importance of the primary sector, with the logging and oil being two of Canada's most important industries.

Canada is a leading industrialised country in the world, which is due to its rich natural resources, the influence of America and the intervention of the federal government in its development of infrastructure. There are three main industry groups in Canada: In 1990, primary industries occupied 10% of Canada's GDP; secondary industries made up 36% of its GDP; while in 2019, tertiary industries amounted to nearly 56.32% of GDP.

**Primary industries** refer to the natural resources industries, which include agriculture, fishing, forestry and mining. Canada is one of the world's most important suppliers of agricultural products, with the Canadian Prairies providing wheat, canola and other grains. Canada is also a producer of raw materials for export markets. As early as in the period of the first Prime Minister from 1867 to 1873, Canada tried to move away from its reliance on exporting raw materials, but failed to develop a strong secondary or tertiary sector. However, it stepped into a period of comparative wealth and growth under the influence of America, as its relationship with Great Britain became weakened at the end of World War II.

**Secondary industries** consist of manufacturing, construction, transportation and communications. As the domestic market for manufacturing products like cars is on a small scale and serves the sparse population in Canada, manufacturers have difficulty in competing with America in production capacity. Canada has engaged in protectionist practices to help stimulate the development of the raw-material processing industry. A sizeable manufacturing sector is centred in southern Ontario and Quebec, with automobiles and aeronautics representing particularly important industries.

**Tertiary industries** comprise trade, finance and public administration. In 1966, the American economy fell into a decline, partly due to the inflation caused by the Vietnam War. This situation had an impact on the trade between Canada and America. Other changes, like the oil crisis of the early 1970s, also greatly affected the Canadian economy. Therefore, the federal government imposed an export tax on shipments to America and began to move toward developing stronger trading relations with Japan and the European countries, rather than be overly-reliant on the United States. As a result, Canada went through an economic recession, and earned the reputation of being rather socialist by means of controlling salary or wages and interfering in the operation of economy. But in 1980, the **National Energy Policy** caused conflicts between the federal government and provincial governments in Western Canada, because the energy industry as a major sector of the Canadian economy was usually under the control of provincial governments, which was in contradiction with the intervention of the federal government. Consequently, the **government interventionism** was gradually replaced by free trade and market economy.

As a member of the **Organization for Economic Co-operation and Development** (OECD), Canada has become one of the world's wealthiest nations with a high per-capita income as well as one of the world's top trading nations. It ranks higher than the U.S. and most western European nations on the Heritage Foundation's index of economic freedom as a mixed market. Since the early 1990s, the Canadian economy has been growing rapidly with low unemployment and large government surpluses at the federal level. Today Canada closely resembles the U.S. in its market-oriented economic system, patterns of production and high living standards. As of October 2019, Canada's national unemployment rate of 5.7% was its lowest in 43 years. Provincial unemployment rates varied from a low of 4.0% in Alberta to a high of 8.8% in Newfoundland and Labrador. According to the Forbes Global 2000 list of the world's largest companies in 2020, Canada had 61 companies on the list, ranking fifth next to the United Kingdom.

The economic integration with the United States has increased significantly since World War II. This has prompted Canadian nationalists to worry about their cultural and economic autonomy in an age of globalisation as American television shows, movies and corporations have become omnipresent. The **Automotive Products Trade Agreement** in 1965 opened the borders to trade in the auto manufacturing industry. In the 1970s, concerns over energy self-sufficiency and foreign ownership in the manufacturing sectors prompted Pierre Trudeau's Liberal government to set up the **National Energy Program** (NEP) and the **Foreign Investment Review Agency** (FIRA). In the 1980s, Brian Mulroney's Progressive Conservatives abolished the NEP and changed the name of FIRA to **Investment Canada** to encourage foreign investment. The **Canada-United States Free Trade Agreement** (FTA) went into effect in 1989 and eliminated tariffs between the two countries, while the **North American Free Trade Agreement** (NAFTA) was put into effect in 1994 with the end of FTA, expanding the free trade zone to Mexico in the 1990s. In the mid-1990s, the Liberal government under Jean Chretien began posting annual budgetary surpluses and steadily paying down the national debt. Since 2001, Canada has successfully avoided economic recessions and has maintained the best overall economic performance in the **G7** (the Group of Seven, an international forum for the governments of Canada, France, Germany, Italy, Japan, the United Kingdom, and the United States). In 2008, due to the impact of the subprime mortgage crisis, Canada encountered an economic recession with the national unemployment rate rising to 8.6%. Around 160,000 full-time jobs and 220,000 permanent jobs were cut in the recession. But Canada's more conservative banking system, the government fiscal surplus before the financial crisis and its long-held policy of reducing public debt made it less vulnerable to the great recession than other G7 countries.

### Agriculture

The cultivated areas cover only 7.4% of the whole land in Canada, but produce agricultural products for the whole country. The main agricultural products contain wheat, grain for raising animals, milk goods and fruits. The Canadian Prairie is the centre of the wheat belt, and the Prairie Provinces specialise in wheat and cereals production, feedstock and cattle.

Eastern Canada is well-known for a variety of agricultural products. Dairy industry is the mainstay of the lowland in Quebec and Ontario Provinces, where big cities offer markets for vegetables and poultry. Potato farming is centred on the infertile lands around the St. Lawrence Bay. And the area on the Pacific Ocean mainly produces fruits and dairy products. Meanwhile, fishery and mining industries are of great importance in this area.

### Manufacturing

Manufacturing industry remains the most significant in the Canadian economy. Food processing takes a leading position in Canada, production of the facilities for transport and communication ranks second, and paper making third. Canada has achieved some notable success in terms of the research and development of advanced technology, such as the nuclear technology for peaceful application as well as the advanced technology in hydroelectricity production and telecommunications. Canada also has a quite innovative aerospace industry, and has contributed to the American space programme by providing a robotic arm to space shuttles.

## Part Two  Current Problems

As a leading country in the world's economy, Canada is transforming its economy from primary to tertiary industries. It is also a major industrialised country in the world with manufacturing industry as a mainstay. Today, about 70.9% of GDP comes from the service industries such as finance, real estate and insurance, which play a key part in the national economy.

As the technology advancing, the labour force in the basic industries is gradually declining with only 1.9% of the population engaging in agriculture, and 2% employed in other basic industries. Most Canadians engage in manufacturing and service industries. In recent years, the rate of unemployment remains higher than other developed countries.

Canada is one of the countries with a high standard of living. However, it has not been able to maintain balanced development in all regions. Ontario and Quebec Provinces produce about 56.7% of GDP with 26% of Canadian territory and a dense population, while primary industries remain most important in northern Canada, owing to the harsh terrain. Geographical isolation has had an effect on the growth of the regional economy to some degree.

However, in recent years, there has been a dramatic drop in agricultural exports which were very important to the Canadian economy in the past. Furthermore, due to the conclusion of the *Free Trade Agreement* and geographical difficulties of western Canada, it has become cheaper in many cases to import foodstuffs rather than produce such items domestically or ship similar products from western Canada.

>  **Question for discussion:**
>
> Confronted with the global economic crisis in 2008 – 2009, how did Canada get out of the financial recession?

## Part Three  Major Cities

### Ottawa

**Ottawa** is the centre of politics and cultures as well as the capital of Canada, situated in the boundaries of Ontario and Quebec Provinces. As the fourth largest city in Canada, Ottawa is a mixture of French and English styles. The unique cultural personality and leisure lifestyle make Ottawa a favourite of Canadians and one of the prominent tourist cities in the world.

Ottawa is one of the coldest capitals in the world. Its average temperature is 6℃, and the cold snowy winter and warm summer take place alternatively. However, no matter how cold it is, Ottawa can provide all the seasonal leisure activities.

Ottawa counts as a city typical of the government economy in the Western world, because all the economic activities are related to government. Tourism is another mainstay of economy in Ottawa. The number of tourists goes far beyond that of its population. Also, the growth of government service industry gradually replaced the traditional industries like timber and paper pulp, which makes Ottawa one of the most desirable cities to live in.

### Montreal

**Montreal** is the second biggest city in Canada with a population of 4,100,000 (2016), located at the intercept of the Ottawa River and the St. Lawrence River. It held the 1967 World Expo and the 1976 Olympic Games. As the largest city in Quebec Province, Montreal has a majority of French Canadians and unique French culture. It is also one of the cities with a long Canadian history, established by Frenchmen about 350 years ago. Therefore, Montreal is characterised by a strong flavour of the European customs. The churches in various styles constitute an attractive cultural miracle and even surpass those in ancient Rome in number.

On the other hand, Montreal is fully modernised. Its industrial production ranks second in Canada. Finance and commerce are developed as well. Tourism is one of the most important industries, and serves as the main source of the regional and national taxes.

With respect to education, there are four universities in Montreal: **McGill University**, **Concordia University**, the **University of Montreal**, and the **University of Quebec.** The former two employ English as the major teaching language, while French is used as the main teaching language in the latter two universities.

### Toronto

**Toronto** is the capital of Ontario Province and the largest city in Canada with a population of over 3 million, located on the Toronto Bay to the north shore of the Ontario Lake. It is the centre of the national transportation and manufacturing industry as well as the centre of culture and industries in Ontario

Province. Its citizens are composed of over 80 ethnic groups, who speak over 100 dialects. The major nationalities are English, French, Italian, Portuguese, and Chinese Canadians.

Toronto is unique in economy, history and geography, serving as an important financial centre and the headquarters of the national organs. **Toronto Stock Exchange** is one of the active stock markets in North America. It is also an important port and the centre of national cultures. Among the 11 universities and institutes, **Toronto University** is the largest institution of higher learning.

### Vancouver

**Vancouver** is a coastal city and major seaport located in the Lower Mainland of southwestern British Columbia. It is the largest city in British Columbia and the Pacific northwest region, ranking as the third largest city in Canada. Vancouver is renowned for its scenery and has one of the largest urban parks in North America — Stanley Park, which enjoys the reputation of the pearl of the Pacific Ocean. With the special landform such as peaks and beaches, it enjoys the mildest climate with a warm winter and cool summer. Vancouver has daily minimum temperatures falling below 0℃ on an average of 46 days per year and below -10℃ on only two days per year. The daily maximum averages 22℃ in July and August, although temperatures sometimes rise above 26℃. The summer months are often very dry, resulting in moderate drought conditions a few months of the year. By contrast, more than half of all winter days receive measurable precipitation. On average, snow falls on only eleven days per year, with only three days receiving six or more centimetres.

The superior geographical position and natural conditions make Vancouver the largest port and an international trade centre in Canada. As an important economic and trade centre between North America and Asia, it wins the title of "the door to the Pacific Ocean". It held the 1986 World Expo, which turned Vancouver into an international metropolis. Besides trade, tourism is another prospering industry.

Vancouver is the cultural centre on the western coastline of Canada. The **University of British Columbia** and the **Simon Fraser University** are the two famous institutions of higher education.

It is also the home to Chinese Canadians that are the majority of immigrants in Vancouver. The Chinatown on Pender Street is the largest in Canada, just second to the Chinatown in America. In addition to English, Chinese is another language to be used in common.

### Calgary

**Calgary** is the largest city in Alberta Province, located in an area of foothills and high plains, approximately 80 kilometres east of the front ranges of the Canadian Rockies. Calgary is well-known as a destination for winter sports and ecotourism with a number of mountain resorts near the city and metropolitan area. Economic activity in Calgary is mostly centred on the petroleum industry; however, agriculture, tourism, and high-tech industries also contribute to the city's fast economic growth. It has a highly developed educational system with the bilingual teaching and a complete educational programme for children. Many big companies provide nursing service for infants. And the **University of Calgary** is well-known in Canada.

Calgary has four distinctive seasons with an average temperature of 22.7℃ in July and -9℃ in January. It is fully modernised with a clean and tidy image. Calgary was ranked the world's cleanest city by Mercer Quality of Living in a survey published in 2007 by *Forbes* magazine.

### Quebec City

**Quebec City** is located in the valley of the St. Lawrence River, on the north shore of the St. Lawrence River near its meeting with the St. Charles River. The region is low-lying and flat. The river valley has rich and arable soil, making this region the most fertile in the province. As the capital of Quebec Province with a flavour of France and a long history, Quebec City is the second largest city in the province and the only city in North America that is listed in the world historical remains. Famous historic sites include churches and castles established in the 17th century, the National Battlefields Park and so on. A high stone wall surrounds the Upper Town of the city, which lies on the top of Cape Diamond promontory. The Plains of Abraham are located near the edge of the promontory. The Lower Town is located at shore level below Cape Diamond promontory.

Quebec City has a humid continental climate characterised by cold and snowy winter, warm and rather humid summer, and ample precipitation throughout the year. As one of the snowiest cities in Canada, Quebec City is almost guaranteed a white Christmas. The prolonged winter season and ample snowfall tends to remind people of establishing the Quebec Winter Carnival. The transitional seasons, spring and autumn, are rather short, although autumn produces spectacular foliage colours. The summer is the sunniest, and paradoxically, the wettest time of year.

### Winnipeg

Located in the prairies of Western Canada, **Winnipeg** is the capital of Manitoba Province and the eighth largest city in Canada. It is a hub of communication, very important in transportation, economy, manufacturing, agriculture and education. It is located in the centre of North America, only 96 kilometres away from the Canadian-American border. As its geographical shape is just like a fork, it is well-known for being called the **Fork City**.

The climate is extreme in Winnipeg which can be counted as one of the coldest cities in the world. It has more rainfall and snowfall than other cities on the plain, but is full of sunshine all the year round.

In addition, there are a number of reception centres for the native inhabitants — Eskimos (also Inuit) in Winnipeg, so Winnipeg is one of the gathering spots for Canadian natives.

> **? Questions for discussion:**
> 1. What's the uniqueness of Ottawa, Toronto and Quebec City respectively?
> 2. What is Vancouver famous for?

## Exercises

### I. Fill in the blanks.

1. The Canadian economy is dominated by the _____ _____ industry which employs about three quarters of Canadians.
2. Canada is a leading _____ country in the world, which is due to its rich natural resources, the influence of America and the _____ of the federal government in its infrastructure.
3. Canada is one of the world's most important suppliers of _____ products, with the Canadian Prairies providing wheat, canola and other grains, and a producer of _____ for export markets.
4. A sizeable manufacturing sector is centred in southern _____ and Quebec, with _____ and aeronautics representing particularly important industries.
5. The *Automotive Products Trade Agreement* in 1965 opened the borders to trade in the _____ industry.
6. In the 1970s, concerns over energy self-sufficiency and foreign ownership in the _____ sectors prompted Pierre Trudeau's _____ government to set up the National Energy Program (NEP) and Foreign Investment Review Agency (FIRA).
7. The *Canada-United States Free Trade Agreement* (FTA) of 1988 eliminated _____ between Canada and America.
8. *North American Free Trade Agreement* (NAFTA) expanded the free trade zone to include _____ in the 1990s.

### II. Define the following terms.

1. the Group of Seven
2. government interventionism
3. North American Free Trade Agreement
4. manufacturing industries
5. the Fork City

### III. Multiple choice.

1. According to the *Forbes Global* 2000 list of the world's largest companies in 2020, Canada had

61 companies on the list, ranking _____ next to Britain.

  A. fifth   B. fourth   C. third   D. second

2. With advanced technology, most of the Canadian labour force engages in _____ and manufacturing industries.

  A. agricultural   B. mining
  C. aerospace   D. service

3. _____ is the centre of politics and cultures as the capital of Canada, situated in the cross of Ontario and Quebec Provinces.

  A. Montreal   B. Ottawa
  C. Vancouver   D. Toronto

4. _____ is another mainstay of economy in Ottawa.

  A. Paper pulp   B. Timber
  C. Tourism   D. Manufacturing

5. As the largest city in Quebec Province, _____ has a majority of French Canadians and unique French culture.

  A. Quebec City   B. Calgary
  C. Ottawa   D. Montreal

6. _____ is the capital of Ontario Province and the largest city in Canada.

  A. Toronto  B. Ottawa  C. Quebec  D. Calgary

7. Vancouver is the largest city in British Columbia and in the Pacific Northwest region, ranking _____ largest city in Canada.

  A. the third   B. the second
  C. the first   D. the fourth

## IV. Translate the following terms into English.

1. 国家能源政策
2. 汽车产品协定
3. 加美自由贸易协定

## V. Answer the following questions in a few sentences.

1. What is the impact of America on Canada in economy?

2. Why did Canada transform its mainstay of economy from the primary industries to the tertiary industries?

**Mini-task:**

Canada is not only a sparsely-populated country with a vast area, but wealthy with abundant natural resources. As the lack of labourers has slowed down the development of its economy, Canada advocates and encourages immigration from around the world. Please search for the information about Canada's immigration policy.

## Chapter Four  History

*Canada is a rising young country as an independent state. Its history and development have been interrelated with those of Britain and America. How did Canada grow from a colony of Britain into an independent country? What role did Britain and America respectively play in the progress of its development? Try to get the information by resorting to various materials available.*

### Part One   Discovery by the European

It is believed that the word "Canada" originated from the native Indians' description of their settlement as "kanata", which was taken as the name of this country by mistake. The European discovery of Canada can be traced back to the end of the 15th century. An Italian Captain and a French navigator played an important role in this discovery. Newfoundland Island and the eastern coast of Canada were discovered by an English expedition under the command of an Italian Captain, who proclaimed the sovereignty over it in the name of Henry VII. This case was five years later than Columbus' discovery of America. But, at that time, the newly-discovered continent was regarded as North China. Throughout the 16th century, fishermen from England, France, Spain and Portugal had been engaged in fishing in the water of Newfoundland. However, it was a French navigator who reached the land of present-day Montreal along the St. Lawrence River in 1535. Although a route to Asia was not found, this discovery paved the way for French fur traders and colonists into Canada.

French explorer Samuel de Champlain arrived in 1603 and established the first permanent European settlements at Port Royal in 1605 and Quebec City in 1608, which set the root for French Canadians. Britain became a rival to France in the settlement of Canada. In 1610, a British explorer named a bay of Central Canada after his own name: Hudson Bay. Later on, he established the British Hudson Company in 1670. In the 17th century, France attempted to expand its colonies in Canada, but failed. A conflict between Britain and France took place over the fishery and fur trade, and consequently, Newfoundland Province, Hudson Bay and Nova Scotia Province fell into the hands of Britain. After the Seven Years' War between Britain and France from 1756 to 1763, France was forced to give up its colonies on North America Continent. From then on, the whole of Canada was under the control of Britain, but the French colonists were allowed to stay in Canada and to keep their own religion and lifestyle.

### Part Two   Colony of Britain

The Englishmen established fishing outposts in Newfoundland around 1610 and colonised the thirteen colonies to the south. A series of four intercolonial wars erupted between 1689 and 1763. Mainland Nova Scotia came under British rule with the **Treaty of Utrecht** (1713); and the **Treaty of Paris** (1763) ceded Canada and most of New France to Britain after the Seven Years' War. However, the first British settlers in Canada were refugees from America, who refused to fight against the British army. They marched toward north and settled in the south near the Lake Ontario, which laid the foundation for English-speaking Canada. The traders from Britain and American colonies gathered around Montreal and soon controlled the fur trade on the St. Lawrence. These Montreal traders were in control of the commerce in Quebec Province, but were not successful in turning Quebec into an English-speaking Province because they were in small numbers. Instead, they agreed to keep French character of Quebec. To avert conflicts in Quebec, the **Quebec Act of 1774** expanded Quebec's territory to the Great Lakes and the Ohio Valley, re-establishing the French language, Catholic faith and French civil law in Quebec on the basis of the British criminal law. The **Constitutional Act of 1791** distinguished Englishmen from Frenchmen by creating Upper Canada where the British settled and Lower Canada populated by the French. During the War of 1812 between the United States and the British Empire, Canada's defense contributed to a sense of unity among the British North Americans. Large-scale immigration to Canada began in 1815 from Britain and Ireland and resulted in the aborted rebellions of 1837. With the **Act of Union** in 1840, Upper and Lower Canada were united again, and established the internal self-government in 1848. Northern America grew stronger as a winner in the American Civil War, and constituted a threat to the British colonies. Therefore, three British colonies were united into a federal union by the **British North**

*America Act* in 1867. Thus the Canadian federal state came into being as a Dominion.

## Part Three  Autonomous Government and the Commonwealth of Nations

Following several constitutional conferences, the **Constitution Act of 1867** brought about the Confederation, creating "one dominion under the name of Canada" on 1 July, 1867 with four provinces: Ontario, Quebec, Nova Scotia and New Brunswick. British Columbia and Vancouver Island (which had united in 1866) and the colony of Prince Edward Island joined this Confederation in 1871 and 1873 respectively.

In 1869 when the first Prime Minister was in power, Canada purchased the central and western area from the Hudson Company and established Manitoba Province. Subsequently, other Prairie Provinces and North Territories were also established and joined the Canadian federation in succession. Apart from the period from 1873 to 1878, Canada had been under the control of the Conservative Party since 1866. Not until in 1896 did the Liberal Party take over political power. In the period of the Liberal Party's governance, the Canadian economy developed rapidly. Agricultural products were transported to Eastern Canada on a large scale, while rapid development of Montreal and Toronto provided industrial products to the farmers in Western Canada. Large-scale mining industries were also developed in northern Ontario, Quebec and British Columbia Province. A number of people began to immigrate from Britain, America and the European Continent.

Prime Minister **John A. Macdonald**'s Conservative Party established a **National Policy of Tariffs** to protect nascent Canadian manufacturing industries. To open the West, the government sponsored the construction of three transcontinental railways (most notably the Canadian Pacific Railway), opened the prairies to settlement with the **Dominion Lands Act** and established the North-West Mounted Police to assert its authority over this territory. In 1898, after the Klondike Gold Rush in the Northwest Territories, the Canadian government created Yukon Territory. Continental European immigrants settled the prairies under Liberal Prime Minister **Wilfrid Laurier**, and Alberta and Saskatchewan became provinces in 1905.

Canada automatically entered World War I in 1914 with Britain's declaration of war, sending volunteers to the Western Front and playing a substantial role in the Battle of Vimy Ridge. The **Conscription Crisis of 1917** erupted when Conservative Prime Minister **Robert Borden** brought in compulsory military service over the objection of French-speaking Quebecers. Great changes followed in Canadian diplomatic relations. The Canadian Navy was established with an attempt to strengthen the government's control over diplomacy. After World War I, Canada won the right to sign the *Treaty of Peace* in 1919, and became a member of the League of Nations.

## Part Four  Independence

In 1931, Canada, along with other British dominions, became a partner nation with Britain and was bound together only by its loyalty to a common Crown. From then on, Canada became a member of the British Commonwealth. But the Great Depression brought economic hardship to the country. In response, the Co-operative Commonwealth Federation (CCF) in Alberta and Saskatchewan presaged a welfare state as pioneered by Tommy Douglas in the 1940s and the 1950s. In addition, Canada declared war on Germany independently as a British ally during World War II under Liberal Prime Minister **William Lyon Mackenzie King** three days after Britain did so. The first Canadian Army units arrived in Britain in December 1939. Canadian troops played important roles in the Battle of the Atlantic, the failed 1942 Dieppe Raid in France, the Allied invasion of Italy, the D-Day landings, the Battle of Normandy and the Battle of the Scheldt in 1944. Canada also provided asylum and protection for the monarchy of the

Netherlands (Holland) during the war after the country was occupied, and the Netherlands credits Canada for its leadership and major contribution to the liberation of the Netherlands from Nazi Germany.

The Canadian economy boomed when manufacturing military material for Canada, Britain, China and the Soviet Union during World War II. In 1945, Canada became one of the first countries to join the United Nations. In 1949, Newfoundland joined the Confederation. Post-war prosperity and economic expansion attracted immigration from war-ravaged European countries. The post-war Canada had a striking development in agriculture and industry with the discovery of deposits of oil and uranium as well as mining of iron.

Under successive Liberal governments of Lester B. Pearson and Pierre Trudeau, a new Canadian identity emerged. Canada adopted its current **Maple Leaf Flag** in 1965. In response to a more assertive French-speaking Quebec, the federal government became officially bilingual with the *Official Languages Act of 1969*. **Non-discriminatory Immigration Acts** were introduced in 1967 and 1976, and official multiculturalism in 1971. Waves of non-European immigration changed the country into a new look. Social democratic programmes such as universal health care, the Canada Pension Plan, Canada Student Loans, the Foreign Investment Review Agency, and the National Energy Program were established in the 1960s and the 1970s; provincial governments, particularly Quebec and Alberta, opposed many of these programmes as incursions into their jurisdictions. Finally, constitutional conferences led by Prime Minister **Pierre Trudeau** resulted in the separation of the Constitution from Britain, putting a Charter of Rights and Freedoms based on individual rights in the *Constitution Act of 1982*. And Canadians continue to take pride in their system of universal health care, their commitment to multiculturalism and human rights.

## Part Five  Present Canada

Nowadays, Canada is a member of the powerful Group of Seven, taking a leading role in developing world's economy and shaping the international system. On the one hand, Canada still has a high standard of living despite lots of inevitable economic problems; on the other hand, Canada has a greater influence on the international issues. For example, it proposed the concept of United Nations peacekeeping force and convinced the international community to put pressure on racial segregation in South Africa, and more recently women's issues and environmental problems have been put on the international agenda with the help of Canada.

It is often assumed that Canada just follows America as a junior partner. Canada began to help American global interests instead of assisting Great Britain in its foreign policy, as Britain lost its status as a world power after World War II. But on the whole, Canadian policy-makers take a pragmatic approach to foreign policy, preferring to work behind the scene to get things done, but willing to lead on certain issues, if necessary. Its participation in dealing with international issues has transformed Canada from a junior partner into a middle power in the world.

① Prime Minister Justin Trudeau

On 19 October, 2015, **Justin Trudeau** led the Liberals to a decisive victory in the federal election. The Liberals won 184 of the 338 seats, with 39.5% of the popular vote, for a strong majority government, a gain of 150 seats compared to the 2011 federal election. On 4 November, 2015, Trudeau officially succeeded Stephen Harper as Canada's 23rd Prime Minister.

Winning the most seats (157) in the 2019 federal election, the Liberals formed a minority government, despite losing the popular vote and receiving the lowest percentage of the national popular vote of any governing party in Canadian history. Justin Trudeau was re-elected as 24th Prime Minister in November 2019.

② Governor General Julie Payette

**Julie Payette** was installed as Canada's 29th Governor-General on 2 October, 2017. Afterwards, she urged Canadians to work together on issues such as climate change, migration and poverty. "Anyone can accomplish anything and rise to the challenge as long as they are willing to work with others, to let go of the personal agenda, to reach a higher goal and to do what is right for the common good. This is exactly what I hope my mandate as the Governor-General will reflect," Payette said. At the Canadian Science Policy Conference the next month, she argued strongly for greater public acceptance of science, saying that too many people believe in astrology, deny climate change, and believe that "maybe taking a sugar pill will cure cancer".

## Part Six  Foreign Relations

Canada and the United States share the world's longest undefended border, co-operate on military campaigns and trainings, and become the largest trading partners with each other. Canada has nevertheless maintained an **independent foreign policy**, most notably maintaining full relations with Cuba and declining to participate in the Iraq War. Canada also maintains historical ties to the United Kingdom and France and to other former British and French colonies through Canada's membership in the Commonwealth of Nations and French-Speaking countries. Canada is noted for having a strong and positive relationship with the Netherlands, which got help from Canada for liberation during World War II, and the Dutch government traditionally gives tulips, a symbol of the Netherlands, to Canada each year in remembrance of Canada's contribution to its liberation.

Canada's strong attachment to the British Empire or the Commonwealth led to its major participation in British military efforts in World War I as well as World War II. Since then, Canada has been advocating multilateralism and making efforts to solve global issues in collaboration with other nations. It joined the United Nations in 1945 and became a founding member of NATO in 1949. During the Cold War, Canada was a major contributor to UN forces in the Korean War and founded the North American Aerospace Defense Command (NORAD) in cooperation with the United States to defend against aerial attacks from the Soviet Union.

Moreover, Canada has played a leading role in UN peacekeeping efforts. During the **Suez Crisis of 1956**, Lester B. Pearson eased tensions by proposing the inception of the United Nations Peacekeeping Force. Canada has served in 50 peacekeeping missions, including every UN peacekeeping effort until 1989 and has maintained forces in international missions in Rwanda, the former Yugoslavia, and elsewhere.

Since 2001, Canada has had troops deployed in Afghanistan as part of the U. S. stabilisation force and the UN-authorised, NATO-commanded International Security Assistance Force. Canada and the U. S. continue to integrate state and provincial agencies to strengthen security along the Canada-United States border through the *Western Hemisphere Travel Initiative*. Canada's Disaster Assistance Response Team (DART) has participated in three major relief efforts in recent years; the two-hundred member team was deployed in relief operations after the 2004 Indian Ocean earthquake in South Asia, Hurricane Katrina in 2005 and the Kashmir earthquake in October 2005.

In February 2007, Canada, Italy, Britain, Norway and Russia announced their funding commitments to launch a $1.5 billion project to help develop vaccines that could save millions of lives in poor nations, and called on other nations to join them. In August 2007, Canadian sovereignty in Arctic waters was challenged following a Russian expedition that planted a Russian flag at the seabed at the North Pole, as Canada has considered that area to be sovereign territory since 1925.

On 1 December, 2018, Huawei Chief Financial Officer Meng Wanzhou, while changing planes at the Vancouver International Airport, was arrested by the Canadian police for extradition to the United States to face charges according to the terms of the extradition treaty between Canada and the United States. U. S. authorities accused Meng of using a Huawei subsidiary, Skycom, to do business in Iran in violation of U. S. economic sanctions against Iran in August 2018.

In the days that followed, Huawei issued a statement saying it was not aware of any wrongdoing by Meng. The Chinese embassy in Ottawa urged U. S. and Canadian authorities to free Meng. China's foreign ministry issued a warning to Canada that there would be consequences if the Huawei executive was not released immediately.

Canadian ambassador John McCallum faced criticism and calls for his resignation on 22 January, 2019 when he told Chinese-language media in Markham, Ontario that he thought Meng had "strong arguments" to make before the courts as her extradition case moved forward, but Canada has a system of extradition treaty, a system of rules of law, which are above the government. On 26 January, Prime Minister Justin Trudeau announced he had accepted McCallum's resignation as Canada's ambassador to China.

On 24 September, 2021, with the great support of Chinese government, a deferred prosecution agreement was reached between Meng Wanzhou with the U.S. government, resolving the U.S. fraud charges against her, which cleared the way for Canada to drop its extradition proceedings. In a media statement issued later in the evening, the federal Department of Justice confirmed that the extradition effort had ended and, "Meng Wanzhou is free to leave Canada."

On 25 September, 2021, Meng Wanzhou arrived in Shenzhen aboard a chartered jet provided by flag carrier Air China in the southern technology hub, where Huawei is based.

### ❓ Questions for discussion:

1. What do you think of Canada in dealing with the international military affairs?
2. What friendly communications does Canada have with China?

## Exercises

### Ⅰ. Fill in the blanks.

1. The European discovery of Canada can be traced back to the end of _____ century.
2. The first permanent European settlements at Port Royal established in 1605 and Quebec City in 1608 set the root for _____ Canadians.
3. In 1763, _____ was forced to give up its colonies in the North America Continent, and the whole Canada was under the control of _____.
4. The Canadian federal state came into being as a _____ with the union of three British colonies in 1867.
5. In 1869 when the first Prime Minister was in power, Canada purchased the central and western area from _____ and established Manitoba Province.

### Ⅱ. Define the following terms.

1. Seven Years' War
2. the Quebec Act
3. French Canadians
4. English-speaking Canada
5. Canada's independent foreign policy

### Ⅲ. Multiple choice.

1. The refugees from America settled in the south to Ontario Lake and laid the foundation for _____ Canada.
   A. French-speaking    B. English-speaking
   C. Italian-speaking   D. Spanish-speaking
2. _____ of 1774 expanded Quebec's territory to the Great Lakes and the Ohio Valley, re-establishing the French language, Catholic faith, and French civil law in Quebec.
   A. The British criminal law
   B. The *Constitutional Act*
   C. The *Act of Union*
   D. The *Quebec Act*
3. _____ of 1791 distinguished Englishmen from Frenchmen by creating English-speaking Upper Canada and French-speaking Lower Canada.
   A. The British criminal law
   B. The *Constitutional Act*
   C. The *Act of Union*
   D. The *Quebec Act*
4. Large-scale immigration to Canada began in 1815 from _____, which resulted in the aborted Rebellions of 1837.
   A. France and Britain
   B. Britain and America
   C. Britain and Ireland
   D. France and Ireland
5. In the period of the _____ Party in power since 1896, Canadian economy was developed rapidly.
   A. Conservative     B. Green
   C. National         D. Liberal

### Ⅳ. Translate the following terms into English.

1. 宪法法案
2. 国家关税政策
3. 联盟法案
4. 自治领土地法
5. 征兵危机

### Ⅴ. Answer the following questions in a few sentences.

1. What's the role of Canada in dealing with international issues?
2. What's the multilateralism of Canada in diplomacy?

 **Mini-task:**

On 2 December, 2009, Canadian Prime Minister Stephen Harper paid a visit to China in response to the invitation of Chinese Premier Wen Jiabao, which was an icebreaking travel in Sino-Canada relationship. Please search for the information about the significance and prospects of this visit in the progress of the relationship between China and Canada.

# VOLUME FIVE

# NEW ZEALAND

# Chapter One  Geography and Population

*New Zealand is well-known for its glorious natural scenery, fresh air and clean environment, serving as a wonderful resort if you enjoy a leisure travel. In addition, New Zealanders are notable for their warmth and hospitality. Try to find out the information about tourist attractions, local customs and practices in New Zealand from various materials available.*

## Part One  Geographical Features

New Zealand is an island country in the southwestern Pacific Ocean comprising two main landmasses, numerous smaller islands and uninhabited isolated islands hundreds of kilometres offshore. The indigenous **Maori** named New Zealand "Aotearoa" which means *The Land of the Long White Cloud* in English. New Zealand is notable for its geographic isolation, situated about 1,600 km (994 miles) southeast of Australia across the **Tasman Sea**, and its closest neighbours to the north are **New Caledonia**, **Fiji** and **Tonga**. New Zealand has a total land area of 268,680 square kilometres, with a long coastline of 15,134 kilometres and extensive marine resources, a little less than those of Italy and Japan, and a little more than the United Kingdom. Mountains and hills take up three-fourths of the entire land area. **New Zealand's Exclusive Economic Zone** is the seventh largest in the world, covering over four million square kilometres, more than 15 times its land area and extending seaward from the low watermark around New Zealand and its offshore islands for fishing areas with a variety of sea species.

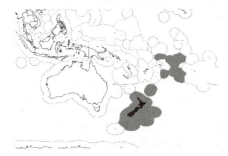

**The North Island** and **the South Island** are the two main landmasses, separated by the **Cook Strait**. Stewart Island is the third largest island to the south of the South Island. The North Island has been formed mostly by volcanoes, and marked by volcanism. Some volcanoes are still active. There is a spectacular cluster of four active volcanoes in the central North Island. The highest mountain in the North Island, named **Mount Ruapehu**, is an active cone volcano with 2,797 metres high, and serves as a major ski area. The famous thermal region contains steam vents, hot pools, bubbling mud and geysers, stretching northeast to the **White Island** in the **Bay of Plenty**.

The South Island is the largest landmass of New Zealand, and more mountainous than the North Island. It is divided along its length by the **South Alps** with the highest peak **Mount Cook** at 3,754 metres. There are 22 peaks over 2,000 metres (10,000 feet) in the South Island. The dramatic and varied landscape of New Zealand has made it a popular location for the production of television programmes and films. The South Alps, a massive mountain chain, runs almost the full length of the South Island. This is also an area of outstanding scenery with many lakes and rivers. The fertile lowlands extend in both islands, though most of the land is about 200 metres above sea level. And plants grow luxuriantly with the moderate climate, abundant rainfall and sunlight.

## Part Two  Climate

New Zealand is in the southern latitudes midway between the Equator and the South Pole with **a maritime climate**. The latitude of New Zealand (ranging from approximately 34°S to 47°S) corresponds closely to that of Italy in the Northern Hemisphere. However, its isolation from continental influences and exposure to cold southerly winds and ocean currents give the climate a much milder character. The climate throughout the country is mild and temperate, mainly maritime, with temperatures rarely falling below 0℃ or rising above 30℃ in populated areas. Conditions vary sharply across regions from extremely wet on the West Coast of the South Island to semi-arid in the **Mackenzie Basin** of inland Canterbury and subtropical in Northland. Of the main cities, Christchurch is the driest, receiving only 640 mm of rain per year; Auckland, the wettest, receives almost twice that amount.

The moderate temperature is partly due to the fact that no part of the country is more than 120 kilometres away from sea. On the other hand, a westerly wind prevails in New Zealand, and many parts of the country have wind and rain because of the mountain backbone. Wellington is the southernmost and windiest national capital city in the world. The west coast of the South Island has one of the highest annual rainfalls in the world.

New Zealand is on the Southern Hemisphere with seasons opposite of the Northern Hemisphere. January and February are the warmest months with average temperatures ranging from 19℃ to 25℃, while July is the coldest month with the average maximum 10℃–15℃.

## Part Three  Biodiversity

Because of its long isolation from the rest of the world and its island biogeography, New Zealand has a distinctive fauna dominated by birds and an extraordinary flora represented by the giant kauri, about 80% of which is endemic, including 65 endemic genera. Its prehuman biodiversity displayed high endemism both in its flora and fauna. But many of them became extinct after the arrival of humans and the mammals they introduced. The remaining vegetation types in New Zealand are grasslands of tussock and other grasses, usually in sub-alpine areas, and the low shrublands between grasslands and forests.

Before the arrival of humans, 80% of the land was forested, while today, the area of forest has been reduced to 30% of the land. It was thought there were no non-marine native mammals. However, in 2006, scientists discovered bones that belonged to a long-extinct, unique, mouse-sized land animal in the Otago region of the South Island. A diverse range of megafauna inhabits New Zealand's forests, including the flightless moas (now extinct), four species of kiwi, the kakapo and the takahe, all endangered because of human action. Unique birds capable of flight includes the Haast's eagle, which was the world's largest bird of prey (now extinct), and the large kaka and kea parrots. Reptiles present in New Zealand include skinks, geckos and living fossil tuatara. There are four endemic species of primitive frogs and only one venomous spider, the katipo, which is rare and restricted to coastal regions. Snakes cannot be found in New Zealand, but there are many endemic species of insects, including the weta, one species of which may grow as large as a house mouse. It is the heaviest insect in the world.

New Zealand has suffered a high rate of extinctions, including the moa species, the huia, laughing owl and flightless wrens. This is due to human activities such as hunting and pressure from introduction of feral animals, such as weasels, stoats, cats, goats, deer and brushtailed possums. Five indigenous vascular plant species are now believed to be extinct, including Adam's mistletoe and a species of forget-me-not.

However, New Zealand has taken the lead in island restoration projects where offshore islands are cleared of introduced mammalian pests and native species are reintroduced. Several islands located near the three main islands are wildlife reserves where common pests such as possums and rodents have been eradicated to allow the reintroduction of endangered species to the islands. A more recent development is the mainland ecological island.

> **? Questions for discussion**:
> 1. What effect will the recent change of the global climate have on the economy in New Zealand?
> 2. What actions has New Zealand taken to refrain from the deterioration of Biodiversity?

## Part Four  The People

New Zealand has a population of 5,002,100 (2020), 70% of which belongs to the European New Zealanders, 17% the native Maori and 15% the Asian New Zealanders. The official language is English and the Maori language. 48.9 percent of the residents are Christians and Catholics.

Although Maori originally inhabited New Zealand in the 14th century, the use of the Maori language as a living, community language has remained in only a few remote areas during the post-war years. Only 4% of the population speak the Maori language. However, the Maori language is currently undergoing a renaissance, in part due to Maori language immersion schools and two Maori television channels. On the other hand, in recognition of the importance of the Maori culture to New Zealand, the language was declared as one of New Zealand's official languages in 1987.

## Part Five  Culture

New Zealand is one of the most recently settled major landmasses. The first settlers of New Zealand were Eastern Polynesians who came here probably in a series of migrations between around 800 and 1300. Over the next few centuries these settlers developed a distinct culture now known as Maori. The population was divided into tribes and subtribes which would cooperate, compete and sometimes fight with each other. At some point a group of Maori migrated to the Chatham Islands where they developed their own distinct Maori culture.

The first Europeans that arrived in New Zealand were Dutch explorer **Abel Janszoon Tasman** and his crew in 1642. The Maori killed several of the crew and no Europeans returned to New Zealand until the arrival of British explorer James Cook who had a voyage of 1768 – 1771. Cook reached New Zealand in 1769 and mapped almost the entire coastline. Following Cook, New Zealand was visited by numerous European and North American whaling,

sealing and trading ships. They traded European food and goods, especially metal tools and weapons, for Maori timber, food, artifacts and water. The potato and the musket transformed Maori agriculture and warfare, although the resulting Musket Wars died out once tribal imbalance in arms had been rectified. From the early nineteenth century, Christian missionaries began to settle in New Zealand, eventually converting most of the Maori population, who had become disenchanted with their indigenous faith as Western culture was introduced.

Much of the contemporary New Zealand culture is derived from British roots. It also includes significant influences from American, Australian and **Maori cultures**, along with those of other European cultures as well as non-Maori Polynesian and Asian cultures in recent years. Large festivals in celebration of **Diwali** and **Chinese New Year** are

held in several of the larger centres. The world's largest Polynesian festival, **Pasifika,** is an annual event in Auckland — the most densely populated city. Cultural links between New Zealand and the United Kingdom are maintained by a common language, sustained migration from the United Kingdom and many young New Zealanders spending time in the United Kingdom on their "overseas experience". The music and cuisine of New Zealand are similar to that of Britain and the United States, although both have some distinctive New Zealand and Pacific qualities.

The European culture serves as the mainstream in New Zealand. The highly democratic political system, superior social welfare, plentiful natural resources, good public order and leisure lifestyle have turned New Zealand into a tourist country.

The Maori culture plays a part in New Zealanders' life. It embraces the language, traditions and customs that make up the rich heritage of the native people. Many Maoris sustain their own unique culture, which enriches the lifestyle of New Zealand. The Maori have also been influenced by Western lifestyle in many aspects, because the Maori culture has undergone considerable changes since the arrival of Europeans; in particular the introduction of Christianity in the early 19th century brought about fundamental changes in everyday life. Nevertheless, the perception that most Maoris now live similar lifestyles to their Pakeha neighbours is a superficial one. In fact, the Maori culture has significant differences, for instance, the marae and the extended family continue to play an important role in communal and family life. As in traditional times, Maoris habitually performed **karakia** to ensure the favourable outcome of important undertakings, but today the prayers are generally Christian. In addition, Maoris still regard their allegiance to tribal groups as a vital part of personal identity, and Maori kinship roles resemble those of other Polynesian peoples. As part of the resurgence of the Maori culture that came to the fore in the late 20th century, the tradition-based arts of **kappa haka** (song and dance), carving, and weaving are now more widely practised, and architecture of the Maori maintains strong links to traditional forms. Maoris also value their connections to Polynesia, as demonstrated by the increasing popularity of **waka ama** (outrigger canoe racing), which is now an international sport involving teams from all over the Pacific.

> **? Questions for discussion:**
> 1. What's the uniqueness of New Zealand cultures?
> 2. Make a comparison between New Zealand cultures and Canadian Cultures.

## Part Six   Education

The New Zealand education is regarded as one of the best systems in the world. It provides compulsory education for New Zealand residents, who can continue to receive education for their whole life. Most of children begin to attend school at the age of 5. The state schools are free of charge in tuition fees, receiving partial funds from government. Adults are encouraged to attend universities or the specialised training courses. Children between the age of 6 and 16 must receive compulsory education, including the primary and secondary education. At primary and secondary school levels, parents have a choice of sending children to state or private schools, and may choose to educate their children at home.

A school year can be divided into three terms, starting in February and ending in December. The first term lasts from February to the first week of May, followed up with a two-week holiday. The second term is from the end of May to the end of August, with a two-or-three-week holiday. The third is from the first ten-day period of September to the end of the school year with a longer summer holiday.

### Primary and Secondary Education

Pre-school education is for children aged from 2 to 4, including kindergartens and early childhood centres. These institutions offer informal pre-school education to children or prepare them to receive formal education.

Primary school education is compulsory for children from 6 to 10 years of age, but most start to attend school on their fifth birthday. In general, after spending two years in the infant classes — Junior 1 and 2, children progress through Standard 1 to 4.

Secondary education is divided into two parts: junior high schools including Form 1 and 2, and senior high schools ranging from Form 3 to 7. At the age of 12 or 13, children can choose one of about 400 secondary schools, most of which belong to state schools with co-educational or single-sex system. However, private schools are often of single-sex systems, usually connected to a religious organisation. They have the same standards of accommodation, staffing, equipment and curriculum as state schools, but most students pay fees for their education.

There are also some residential special schools that provide teaching and other service for children with special educational needs such as the deaf or the blind. And the **Correspondence School** caters for those who cannot attend school because of physical, intellectual, or psychological disabilities, as well as those living in areas too isolated to attend school.

### Higher Education

Higher education in New Zealand comprises universities, polytechnics and colleges of education as well as private colleges. In recent years, a group of private educational institutions have been set up in New Zealand to provide various courses, including the courses for degrees.

There are 19 Polytechnics or Institutes of Technology, all of which belong to state educational institutions. Each Polytechnic has unique characteristics, offering a series of specialised courses for all walks of life and covering a variety of certificates up to degree level. The graduates from these polytechnics are very popular with employers every year. In addition, many Polytechnics provide preparatory courses for overseas students in preparation for their study in New Zealand universities.

New Zealand has 8 universities which have distinguishing features and offer degreed courses recognised in the world. Five of them enjoy historical reputations spanning more than 100 years. Up to now,

New Zealand has not established private universities.

Today, there are two Colleges of Education in New Zealand, and both of them are supported by government, providing short-term or long-term training for teachers as well as educational staff.

Private colleges can become qualified to enroll students after being registered and approved by the **New Zealand Qualifications Authority**. The academic credentials granted by private colleges range from language training, specialised subjects to undergraduate courses as well as post-graduate degrees.

> **? Question for discussion:**
> New Zealand has become a good choice for overseas students. What does New Zealand resort to in order to attract more overseas students?

## Exercises

### Ⅰ. Fill in the blanks.

1. New Zealand is notable for its geographic _____ _____, situated about 1,600 km southeast of Australia across the _____ Sea, and its closest neighbours to the north are New Caledonia, Fiji and Tonga.
2. The two main landmasses refer to the _____ Island and the _____ Island, separated by _____.
3. The North Island has been formed mostly by _____, and the South Island is more mountainous, full of _____ and rivers.
4. The South Island is divided along its length by the Southern Alps with the highest peak _____ at 3,754 metres.
5. The official language in New Zealand is _____ and _____. 48.9% of the residents belong to _____ and Catholics.
6. Eastern Polynesians as the first settlers of New Zealand came to New Zealand between around 800 and 1300 and developed a distinct culture known as _____.
7. New Zealand provides _____ education for New Zealand citizens and permanent residents, who can continue to receive education for their whole life.
8. Universities, Polytechnics and Colleges of Education in New Zealand are financed by _____.
9. Most of secondary schools belong to _____ schools with co-educational or single-sex system.

### Ⅱ. Define the following terms.

1. maritime climate of New Zealand
2. biodiversity
3. the Maori language
4. New Zealand culture
5. Correspondence School

### Ⅲ. Multiple choice.

1. Mountains and hills take up _____ of the whole land area in New Zealand.
   A. one-fourth      B. two-fifths
   C. three-fourths   D. three-fifths
2. The first Europeans that arrived in New Zealand were _____ explorer Abel Janszoon Tasman and his crew in 1642.
   A. British  B. Spanish  C. Italian  D. Dutch
3. British explorer James Cook reached New Zealand in _____ and mapped almost the entire coastline.
   A. 1768   B. 1770   C. 1769   D. 1781
4. Much of the contemporary New Zealand culture is derived from _____ roots.
   A. Spanish  B. British  C. Italian  D. Dutch
5. _____ provide short-term or long-term training for teachers as well as the educational staff.
   A. Colleges of Education
   B. Universities
   C. Polytechnics
   D. Private colleges
6. A school year can be divided into _____ terms in New Zealand.
   A. one   B. two   C. three   D. four

### Ⅳ. Translate the following terms into English.

1. 新西兰特别经济区
2. 库克山
3. 波利尼西亚人

### Ⅴ. Answer the following question in a few sentences.

1. What's the role of the Maori culture in New Zealand?

> **Mini-task:**

New Zealand has been recognised as a good choice for living and travel. It possesses pleasant environment, safe communities, leisure life space and rich food cultures, etc. Please search for the information about New Zealand tourist attractions and various customs and cultures.

# Chapter Two  Government and Politics

> As a member of the British Commonwealth, New Zealand also follows Britain in many aspects. What are the difference and the similarity between New Zealand and Britain in politics? Try to get the information from various materials available.

## Part One  Political System

New Zealand is a constitutional monarchy with a parliamentary democracy. Although it has no codified Constitution, the **Constitution Act 1986** is the principal formal statement of New Zealand's constitutional structure. The Monarch appoints the Governor-General on the exclusive advice of the Prime Minister and is represented by a non-partisan Governor-General in his or her absence. At present, British King Charles III serves as the King of New Zealand, who reigns but does not rule the country. He has no real political influence and his position is essentially symbolic. The political power is held by the democratically elected New Zealand Parliament under the leadership of the Prime Minister who is also the Head of Government.

The Governor-General exercises the Crown's prerogative powers, such as the power to appoint and dismiss ministers and to dissolve the Parliament in accordance with ministerial advice, and in rare situations, the reserve powers to exercise without ministerial advice or even contrary to ministerial advice. The Governor-General also chairs the **Executive Council** which is a formal committee consisting of all ministers of the Crown. Members of the Executive Council are required to be Members of the Parliament, and most are also in the Cabinet. The Cabinet is the most senior policy-making body led by the Prime Minister, who is also, by convention, the Parliamentary leader of the governing party or coalition.

## Part Two  Government

The functions of government departments are more clearly defined as a result of the reform of government affairs. Chief executives and managers are fully responsible for the efficient running of each organisation and the costs of governmental activities are more transparent. Because of the efficient management of the private sectors, a number of former government enterprises have been privatised such as the national airline, telecommunications, railways, insurance and banking companies.

The early European settlers divided New Zealand into provinces, which were abolished in 1876 so that the government could be centralised for financial reasons. As a result, New Zealand has no separately represented subnational entities such as provinces, states or territories, apart from its local government. The spirit of the provinces, however, still lives on, and there are fierce competitions exhibited in sporting and cultural events. Since 1876, the local government has administered the various regions of New Zealand. In 1989, the central government completely reorganised the local government, implementing the current two-tier structure of regional councils and territorial authorities which are constituted under the revised **Local Government Act 2002** (New Zealand). In 1991, the **Resource Management Act 1991** replaced the **Town and Country Planning Act** as the main planning legislation for the local government as well as the first piece of environmental legislation in the world.

## Part Three  Parliament

New Zealand followed Britain, but made some changes in the parliamentary system. Its Parliament is composed of the Governor-General and the Cabinet. The Governor-General is appointed by the Queen, while the Cabinet, formed by the Prime Minister, holds the real power. Since 1950, the Parliament has had only one chamber — the House of Commons or the House of Representatives, which usually seats 120 members. Debates in the Parliament have been transmitted through the national broadcasting station. A referendum can be held on some problems, rather than votes in a party election. In the past 50 years,

the two major parties have been the **Labour Party** and the **National Party**.

The House of Commons produces the Prime Minister who serves as the leader of the major party in power and picks about 20 members to form the Cabinet. Parliamentary general elections are held every three years under a form of proportional representation called **Mixed Member Proportional**. The 2005 general election created an "overhang" of one extra seat occupied by the **Maori Party**, due to that party winning more seats in electorates than the number of seats. Thus the number of Parliament seats adds up to 121.

## Part Four  Election System

The Parliament is constituted through the general election which is held every three years. At present, there are 120 Members of Parliament. Citizens of Maori heritage choose whether to register on the Maori or the General Electoral Roll, and may change their registration at will. From the age of 18, every New Zealand citizen or permanent resident must register on the Electoral Roll and is entitled to vote in elections. The eligible voters can visit polling booths in their electorates, or cast a special vote if they are travelling, sick or overseas. Enrollment is compulsory, but voting is voluntary.

The Parliament election in 1996 was held for the first time under the system of Mixed Member Proportion Representation known as MMPR. Each voter has two votes instead of only one under the previous voting system: One is for a candidate in their electorate, the other for a political party. The party vote decides the number of seats that each party will take in the Parliament. MMPR offers an opportunity for a range of parties to gain seats by achieving at least 5% of the party votes. Since 1996, neither the National nor the Labour Party has held a majority of seats in the Parliament, and New Zealand Government has been a coalition of at least two parties. In 2002, the coalition government was made up of the Labour and the United Future Party. The Prime Minister was the Labour leader, while the Vice-Prime Minister was the United Future leader.

Since 17 October, 2005, the Labour has been in formal coalition with Jim Anderton, the only MP of the Progressive Party. In addition to the parties in formal coalition, the New Zealand First and the United Future Party provide confidence and supply in return for their leaders being ministers outside the Cabinet. A further arrangement has been made with the **Green Party**, which has given a commitment not to vote against the government on confidence and supply. Since early 2007, the Labour has also had the proxy vote of Taito Phillip Field, a former Labour MP. These arrangements assure the government of a majority of seven MPs on confidence votes. The leader of the Opposition is the National Party leader John Key. The ACT and the Maori Parties are also in opposition. The Green, the New Zealand First and the United Future Party vote against the government on some legislation as well.

In addition, the appointment of **public servants** working as the officials for government departments and ministries is independent of the political process in New Zealand. Therefore, public servants remain in their position whenever ministers change in accordance with preference of the party in power.

### John Key

John Key became the Prime Minister following the general election on 8 November, 2008, which signaled an end to the Labour-led government of nine years under Clark. Key launched New Zealand's campaign for a Security Council seat at the UN General Assembly meeting in September 2009. Since 2008, Key has also engaged in Trans-Pacific Partnership negotiations with the United States and other Asia-Pacific economies.

### Bill English

John Key resigned in 2016 and endorsed Bill English as his successor in the resulting leadership election. English was regarded as more socially conservative than his predecessor, John Key, and was sworn in as the 39th Prime Minister of New Zealand on 12 December, 2016.

### Jacinda Ardern

On 19 October, 2017, New Zealand First leader Winston Peters agreed to form a coalition with Labour, making Jacinda Ardern the next Prime Minister. This coalition receives confidence and supply from the Green Party. On 26 October, 2017, Jacinda Ardern officially succeeded English as New Zealand's 40th, and youngest Prime Minister since 1856.

## Part Five  The Judiciary

The highest court in New Zealand is the Supreme Court of New Zealand which was established in 2004 following the passage of the **Supreme Court Act 2003**. The act also abolished the option to appeal to the Privy Council in London. New Zealand's judiciary also includes the Court of Appeal, the High Court, which deals with serious criminal offences and civil matters at the trial level as well as appeals from lower courts and tribunals and subordinate courts.

### Questions for discussion:
1. What's the uniqueness of the election system in New Zealand?
2. Are there any similarities between the public servants in New Zealand and those in China?

## Exercises

### Ⅰ. Fill in the blanks.
1. New Zealand is a _____ monarchy with a parliamentary democracy.
2. New Zealand has no codified constitution and _____ is the principal formal statement of New Zealand's constitutional structure.
3. In New Zealand, the head of state appoints the non-partisan _____ on the exclusive advice of _____.
4. The King/Queen in New Zealand is essentially symbolic. Political power is held by the democratically elected _____ of New Zealand under the leadership of _____, who is the Head of Government.
5. The Parliament in New Zealand is composed of a _____ and the _____, with only one chamber — _____.
6. In the past 50 years, the two major parties in New Zealand have been _____ and _____.
7. Enrollment in New Zealand is _____, but voting is voluntary.

### Ⅱ. Define the following terms.
1. the Executive Council
2. public servants

### Ⅲ. Multiple choice.
1. The current Prime Minister is Jacinda Ardern, the leader of the _____ Party.
   A. Green
   B. Labour
   C. National
   D. Conservative
2. _____ is the most senior policy-making body led by the Prime Minister.
   A. The Cabinet
   B. The Parliament
   C. The Executive Council
   D. The governing party
3. The Parliament is produced through general election which is held every _____ years.
   A. four   B. two   C. three   D. five

### Ⅳ. Translate the following terms into English.
1. 工党
2. 比例代表制
3. 国家党
4. 绿党

### Ⅴ. Answer the following questions in a few sentences.
1. What are the functions of government departments in New Zealand?
2. What's the stipulation of general election in New Zealand?

### Mini-task:

Helen Elizabeth Clark is the first female Prime Minister in New Zealand. She is very similar to the British former Prime Minister Thatcher in political style. Please search for the information about Prime Minister Clark in dealing with the domestic and foreign affairs.

# Chapter Three  Economy

> As a small island country, New Zealand possesses some similarities to Great Britain. After undergoing economic transformation, New Zealand has chosen a way forward reflecting its uniqueness. Try to get the information about its economy through various materials available.

## Part One  Structure of Economy

New Zealand historically enjoyed a high standard of living which relied on its strong relationship with the United Kingdom and the resulting stable market for its commodity exports. New Zealand's economy was also built upon a narrow range of primary products, such as wool, meat and dairy products. High demand for these products such as the New Zealand wool boom of 1951 created sustained periods of economic prosperity. The living standard in New Zealand had ever exceeded that in both Australia and Western Europe before 1973. However, its close economic relationship with the UK came to an end in 1973 with the United Kingdom joining the European Economic Community. During the 1970s, other factors such as the oil crises, undermined development of the New Zealand economy. These events led to a protracted and very severe economic crisis and decline in New Zealand. By 1982, New Zealand came to the lowest in per-capita income of all the developed nations surveyed by the World Bank. Since 1984, successive governments have engaged in major macroeconomic restructuring, transforming New Zealand from a highly protectionist and regulated economy to a liberalised free-trade economy. These changes are commonly known as **Rogernomics and Ruthanasia** named after Finance Ministers Roger Douglas and Ruth Richardson. Another recession began after the 1987 stock market crash and caused the unemployment rate to reach 10% in the early 1990s. Subsequently, the economy recovered and New Zealand's unemployment rate reached a low record of 3.4% in September 2019. Its unemployment rate was the fifth lowest of the 27 OECD nations with comparable data.

The Clark government's economic objectives are centred on pursuing free-trade agreements and building a "**knowledge economy**". On 7 April, 2008, New Zealand and China signed the *New Zealand-China Free Trade Agreement*, the first such agreement China has signed with a developed country. Ongoing economic challenges for New Zealand include a current account deficit of 7.9% of GDP, slow development of non-commodity exports and tepid growth of labour productivity. Therefore, New Zealand has experienced a series of "**brain drains**" since the 1970s, as well-educated young professionals have left permanently for Australia, Britain or the United States. Although the Kiwi lifestyle and family factors motivate some of the expatriates to return, many factors like career, culture and economy tend to be predominant components which keep these people overseas. In recent years, however, a reverse brain gain brought in educated professionals as permanent settlers from poorer countries as well as from Europe.

New Zealand has a modern, prosperous, developed economy with nominal Gross Domestic Product (GDP) of US $202.044 billion (as of 2019). It has a relatively high standard of living with an estimated GDP per capita of US $42,935 in 2019 which is comparable to southern Europe; but it's lower than that of US $47,400 in the United States. Since 2000, New Zealand has made substantial gains in median household income. Along with Australia, it largely escaped the early 2000s recession that affected most other Western countries. New Zealanders have a high level of satisfaction with quality of life as measured by international surveys, despite lower GDP per-head than many other OECD countries. It was ranked twentieth on the **2006 Human Development Index** and fifteenth on the **2005 Economist Worldwide Quality-of-Life Index**. The country was further ranked first in quality of life and fifth in overall prosperity on the **2007 Legatum Institute Prosperity Index**. In addition, the 2007 Mercer Quality of Living Survey ranked Auckland fifth and Wellington twelfth in the world on its list.

New Zealand is one of the wealthiest capitalist countries. Its GDP amounts to 202.044 billion US dollars and ranks forty-ninth in the world. Trade partners of New Zealand are mainly Australia, Japan and America. Since the economic reform of 1984, New Zealand has become an open country with little restrictions on free trade, finances and foreign currency. Today, the service sector is the largest one in economy (71.7% of GDP), followed by manufacturing and construction (22.9% of GDP). Tourism plays a significant role in New Zealand's economy. New Zealand has many sightseeing spots like hot springs, lakes, rivers, glaciers and fiords. As it is well-known as a clean, safe and non-nuclear country, about 3.86 million tourists visited it in 2018. Tourism contributes 10% to New Zealand's total GDP and supports nearly 229,566 full-time equivalent jobs (8.4% of the total workforce in New Zealand). Tourists to New Zealand are expected to increase at a rate of 1.3% annually until 2019.

New Zealand is generally recognised as one of the countries rich in animal husbandry and the largest exporter of wool and mutton as well as cheese in the world. It also has rapidly developed its fisheries, seawater aquiculture, and processing of seaweeds, which is just secondary to tourism and export of vegetables and fruits. In addition, benefiting from its perfect climate, New Zealand produces a variety of wood and wood products. On the whole, the following factors contribute to the development of wood processing in New Zealand: Radiata Pine with short growth period, reasonable prices of energy, skillful manufacturing in wood products, low cost of production and the occupation of Asian-Pacific market.

## Part Two  Export and Import Products

New Zealand is the largest exporter of meat, wool and milk products, but also seriously depends on export of these products. It is a country heavily dependent on trade, particularly in agricultural products. Exports account for around 24% of its output, which is a relatively high figure (around 50% for many smaller European countries). So New Zealand is particularly vulnerable to international commodity prices and global economic slowdowns. Many agricultural products, such as wool, dairy products, apples, pears, eggs, poultry, bees, wheat, potatoes, and tobaccos are exported through trade boards of directors. Apart from the exporting business, these boards have to guarantee the domestic supply of these agricultural products. Its principal export industries are agriculture, horticulture, fishing and forestry. These make up about half of the country's exports. The major export market for New Zealand used to be in western Europe, especially Britain. However, since Britain joined the European Common Market in 1993, New Zealand's export market has been shifted to Australia, Japan, America, South Korea and elsewhere. Its major export partners are China (24.2%), Australia (15.9%), US (9.6%), Japan (6.1%), and the UK (3.0%) (2018). New Zealand also has been growing trade relations with South Pacific countries which enjoy the privilege of free taxes and freedom entering the New Zealand market on the basis of non-bilateral trade. Besides, New Zealand also has a good reputation for offering technical knowledge, especially in agriculture, engineering, forestry and land management. More recently, some New Zealand companies have become successful exporters of electronic products.

By contrast, New Zealand mainly imports industrial materials, basic equipment and consumer goods, which are free of import taxes and come from the following countries: Australia, America, Japan, Britain, German, Saudi Arabia, and Singapore.

### Agriculture

Agriculture has consistently been the main export industry in New Zealand. In 2007, dairy products accounted for 21% ($7.5 billion) of total merchandise exports. Fonterra is the largest dairy cooperative company in the country and controls almost one-third of the international dairy trade. Other agricultural items are meat (13.9%), wood (8.7%), fruit (5.9%) and fishing (3.2%) in 2019. New Zealand also has a thriving wine industry.

Livestock are rarely housed, although sometimes they are fed on small quantities of supplements such as hay and silage, particularly in winter. Grass growth is seasonal, largely dependent on location and climatic fluctuations but normally occurs for 8 to 12 months. Livestock are grazed in paddocks, often with moveable electric fencing around the farm. Lambing and calving are carefully managed to take full advantage of spring grass growth.

Although New Zealand has a reputation for its largest farm and most suitable climate in the world, it has little flat and naturally arable land because many areas are covered with mountains and hills and cannot be fertilised or cultivated by tractor. So scientists and farmers developed a unique approach to pasture management by using aircraft to spread seeds and fertilizer. New Zealand has taken a lead in developing and applying aircraft to agriculture. On the other hand, crops and fruits in New Zealand are competitive because of the low cost of production. They are also healthy without any pollution, given the country's exceptional advantages in climate and soil. Therefore, New Zealand has a great potential in the export of food processing products. New Zealand has become the largest exporter of lambs and mutton as well as dairy products. In recent years, raising deer and goats has been very popular in New Zealand.

### Industry

New Zealand has a complex variety of manufacturing industries, which provides lots of investment opportunities. This is due to the availability of raw materials from both native and foreign sources. New Zealand companies are middle and small in size, devoted to manufacturing light and high value products. The typical manufacturing industries in New Zealand are food and drink, weaving and leather processing, wood products, paper, chemicals, non-metals, and metal products.

### Energy

New Zealand is rich in energy, especially in hydraulic power which can produce 80% of electricity in the country. Most of the hydropower stations are located in the South Island. The electricity generated in the South Island is transported to the densely populated and the industrialised North Island through submarine cables.

Geothermal energy resources are situated in the volcano area of the centre of the North Island. Geothermal electricity is usually applied to heating and cooking.

Coal and gas are of increasing importance. The coal deposits in both the South and the North Islands have been developed to meet the needs of electricity generation and production of iron and steel. In addition, about 350,000 tons of coals are exported to Japan every year. There are four gas deposits in New Zealand. Gas is used as a motive power for automobiles as well as a resource for heating and cooking.

Supply of petrol in New Zealand is inadequate and imported mainly from the Middle East and Southeast Asia, which meets 10% of the national need for energy. With two big oilfields, the proportion of the native resources grows larger in the national supply of energy.

In addition, other resources of energy like solar energy and vegetable oil are being developed and utilised, except nuclear energy. Up to now, New Zealand has not forecast a need for nuclear energy. As most of electricity comes from low-cost coal and water, the energy prices remain considerably low in the world.

### ❓ Questions for discussion:

1. New Zealand is small in area, but listed among the wealthiest countries in the world. What factors contribute to the economic boom in New Zealand?
2. What's the mainstay and the uniqueness of New Zealand's economy?

### Exercises

I. **Fill in the blanks.**

1. New Zealand enjoys the stable market for its commodity _____.
2. New Zealand's economy is built on a narrow range of primary products, such as _____, meat and _____ products.
3. The Clark government's economic objectives are centered on pursuing _____ agreements and building a "_____ economy".
4. Nowadays, the _____ sector is the largest sector in the economy, followed by _____ and construction and the raw materials extraction.
5. New Zealand is generally recognised as one of the countries rich in _____ and the largest exporter of wool and _____ as well as _____ in the world.
6. Its principal export industries are agriculture, _____, fishing and _____.
7. Most of the hydropower stations are located in the _____ Island.

8. New Zealand is rich in energy, especially in _____ power.
9. Petrol in New Zealand is imported mainly from _____ and Southeast Asia.
10. Solar energy and vegetable oil are being developed as resources of energy, except _____ energy.

## II. Define the following terms.
1. Rogernomics and Ruthanasia
2. geothermal energy

## III. Multiple choice.
1. Now the trade partners of New Zealand are mainly _____, Japan and America.
   A. Britain          B. France
   C. China            D. Australia
2. As New Zealand is well-known as a clean, safe and _____ country, its tourism has a great attraction for about 3 million tourists in 2008.
   A. democratic       B. free
   C. non-nuclear      D. developed
3. New Zealand mainly imports _____, basic equipments and consumer goods, which are free of import taxes.
   A. industrial materials
   B. labour force
   C. agricultural products
   D. animal products
4. New Zealand takes a lead in developing and applying _____ to agriculture.
   A. tractor          B. aircrafts
   C. plough           D. sprayer
5. New Zealand companies are of middle and small scale, devoted to manufacturing _____ and valuable products.
   A. heavy            B. electronic
   C. light            D. mechanic
6. Most of the hydropower stations are located in the _____ Island.
   A. uninhabited      B. South
   C. North            D. Stewart

## IV. Translate the following terms into English.
1. 宏观经济调整
2. 新西兰中国贸易协定
3. 人才流失
4. 知识型经济

## V. Answer the following questions in a few sentences.
1. What's the emphasis of the Clark government on the economy in New Zealand?

2. What are the factors influencing the development of wood processing in New Zealand?

Mini-task:

As a well-developed country, New Zealand is open to the immigrants as well as overseas students. In order to stimulate and maintain economic progress, what steps and policies have been taken in New Zealand? Try to search for the information about it.

# Chapter Four  History

> New Zealand has been related to Britain in one way or another since its independence. Try to get the information about the following items from various materials available.
> 1. What role did Britain play in the independence of New Zealand?
> 2. What was the relationship between New Zealand and Britain during the post-war period?

## Part One  The *Treaty of Waitangi* in 1840

Becoming aware of the lawless nature of European settlements and increasing interest in the territory by the French, the British government sent William Hobson to New Zealand to claim sovereignty and negotiate a treaty with the Maori, signing the **Treaty of Waitangi** in the Bay of Islands on 6 February, 1840. As the drafting was done hastily, its interpretation is often the subject of heated debate. The *Treaty* is regarded as a mark of the founding of New Zealand and has been reserved by the Maori as a guarantee of their rights. Hobson initially selected Okiato as the capital in 1840, and then moved the site of government to Auckland in 1841.

Under the British rule, the islands of New Zealand had been part of the colony of New South Wales. In 1840, the number of European settlers particularly from the British Isles increased in New Zealand. At first, the Maori were eager to trade with the European settlers, and many tribes became wealthy. But with the growing number of settlers, conflicts over land arose and led to the New Zealand Land Wars during the 1860s and 1870s. As a result, the Maori lost much land, and the specifics of the European settlements and acquisition of land from the Maori remain controversial.

## Part Two  The Independence of New Zealand

The representative government for New Zealand was set up with the passing of the **New Zealand Constitution Act 1852** by the United Kingdom. And the New Zealand Parliament met for the first time in 1854. As a British colony, New Zealand became effectively self-governing with the grant of responsible government over all domestic matters other than native policy in 1856, but such a power was transferred to the colonial administration in the 1860s. Premier Alfred Domett passed a resolution in 1863 on transferring the capital to a locality in the Cook Strait, apparently due to concern that the South Island could form a separate colony. Commissioners from Australia (chosen for their neutral status) advised that Wellington be suitable because of its harbour and central location, and the Parliament officially set there for the first time in 1865. A notable case in 1893 was that New Zealand became the first nation in the world to grant women the right to vote. In 1907, Britain was forced to accept the independence of New Zealand but claimed New Zealand as a British Dominion. New Zealand was still under the control of Britain in politics, economy and diplomacy. Not until the **Westminster Act** was passed in 1931 did New Zealand obtain complete autonomy as a member of the British Commonwealth. It became a fully independent nation in 1947 when the *Statute of Westminster* (1931) was ratified, although in practice Britain had ceased to play any real role in the government of New Zealand much earlier. New Zealand became more economically dependent, although it became more politically independent; in the 1890s, refrigerated shipping allowed New Zealand to base its entire economy on the export of meat and dairy products to Britain.

As a matter of fact, New Zealand was an enthusiastic member of the British Empire, fighting in the Boer War, World War I and World War II and supporting Britain in the **Suez Crisis**. It was very much a part of the world economy and suffered as others did in the Great Depression of the 1930s. The depression led to the election of the first Labour government, which established a comprehensive welfare state and a protectionist economic policy.

## Part Three  Post-war New Zealand

New Zealand experienced increasing prosperity following World War II. However, some social problems were developing. The Maori had begun to move to the cities in search of work and excitement rather than to keep their traditional rural way of life. A Maori protest movement eventually formed, criticising **Eurocentrism** and seeking more recognition of the Maori culture and they felt the *Treaty of Waitangi* had not been fully honoured. In 1975, a Waitangi Tribunal was set up to investigate alleged violations of the Treaty and historic grievances in 1985. In common with all other developed countries, social developments accelerated in the 1970s and social and political conventions also changed. By the 1970s, the traditional trade with Britain was threatened because of Britain's membership of the European Economic Community. Great economic and social changes took place in the 1980s under the fourth Labour government largely led by Finance Minister Roger Douglas, and commonly referred to as "Rogernomics".

New Zealand has a strong national identity, though it still has a strong colonial legacy. It remains a member of the Commonwealth and maintains close and friendly relations with the United States, but it has developed a very independent trade and foreign policy. New Zealand has been a nuclear-free zone since the mid-1980s, with its armed forces mainly used to keep the peace in the Pacific.

New Zealand's development strategy in the 1980s can be summarised into two parts: "small is beautiful" and "think big". The strategy of "small is beautiful" aims at seeking to enable farms, forestry, fisheries, mining and hydroelectric stations to produce a vast variety of raw materials and energy power that can be processed into products for the outlet or substitute for the inlet by depending on the highly skilled technical workers. The strategy of "think big" involves several key industry sectors and is characterised by the use of the Maori resources such as gas, coal, hydro power and forests for processing and export.

New Zealand is a trade-oriented nation and its successive governments have placed great importance on the development of foreign trade. In the mid-1980s, the new government implemented the economic reform policy to promote trade liberalisation. In the early 1990s, the New Zealand government formulated the development policy of "export-led economic recovery". New Zealand's export trade focus has been shifting to the Asia-Pacific region. At the 1994 APEC meeting, New Zealand strongly endorsed the region's decision to realise trade liberalisation in phase by 2020. In the late 20th century, New Zealand, like Australia, abandoned the post-colonial model of national development in favour of the Anglo-American neoliberal model that became orthodox worldwide.

New Zealand is a typical western developed country where the Chinese language is rapidly spreading. Chinese language education has been introduced into the national education system in New Zealand for a long time. Confucius Institutes have played a good role in the platform and radiation effect. The rapid development of Chinese language education in New Zealand is driven by economic and trade cooperation, joint investment and multicultural society.

### Jacinda Ardern

**Jacinda Ardern** is a New Zealand politician and the 40th prime minister of New Zealand. She was elected leader of the Labour Party in August 2017 and then took the post of prime minister of New Zealand in October 2017. She became New Zealand's youngest and the third female prime minister since 1856. She led New Zealand's Labour Party to victory and remained prime minister in October 2020. In the New Zealand election, Ardern proposed restricting overseas buyers to purchase and invest in New Zealand in response to Auckland property prices, and continuing traditional Labour Party policies such as "taxing the rich", as well as raising taxes on irrigated ranching to combat river pollution and reducing fees for higher education.

On 14 May, 2018, Ardern met with Chinese Premier of the State Council Li Keqiang in Singapore. From 31 March to 1 April, 2019, she visited China at the invitation of Chinese Premier Li Keqiang. And on 5 November, 2021, Ardern had a talk with the President of the People's Republic of China Xi Jinping.

On 8 June, 2020, Ardern lowered New Zealand's pandemic alert status to its lowest level.

Social distancing measures for business, transportation and school activities will be lifted. But she will continue to impose strict border controls, allowing only New Zealand citizens and their immediate family members to enter the country and observe them for 14 days in a government-run quarantine facility.

Jacinda Ardern announced a five-step plan to reopen the country's borders at a press conference on 3 February, 2022. On 11 May, Ardern announced that New Zealand would begin fully reopening its borders as well as reopening its maritime borders to allow foreign cruise ships at the last minute on 31 July, 2022.

## Part Four  Foreign Relations

New Zealand tended to follow the United Kingdom's lead in foreign policy for its first hundred years. Prime Minister Michael Savage proclaimed, "Where she goes, we go; where she stands, we stand" when declaring war on Germany on 3 September, 1939. After the war, however, the United States exerted an increasing influence on its culture and New Zealanders gained a clearer sense of national identity. New Zealand joined with Australia and the United States in the ANZUS security treaty in 1951, and later fought alongside the United States in both the Korea and Vietnam Wars. By contrast, the United Kingdom became increasingly focused on its European interests following the Suez Crisis, and New Zealand was forced to develop new markets after the UK joined the EEC in 1973.

New Zealand has traditionally worked closely with Australia whose foreign policy followed a similar historical trend. Australia is the most important partner of New Zealand in politics, national defense, society and sports, especially in economy. In turn, many Pacific island countries such as **Samoa** have followed New Zealand's lead.

The American influence on New Zealand was weakened by disappointment with the **Vietnam War**, the sinking of the Rainbow Warrior by France, and by disagreements over environmental and agricultural trade issues and New Zealand's nuclear-free policy.

The independent diplomatic policy of New Zealand came into being in the middle 1930s. And diplomatic institutions were set up ten years later. Up to now, New Zealand has established 45 consulates and embassies in 40 countries all over the world.

New Zealand displayed its active participation in a series of international affairs, including trade freedom, environmental protection, military equipment control and armament reduction, etc. In February 1985, New Zealand refused access of nuclear-powered or nuclear-armed ships to its ports. New Zealand became a **nuclear-free zone** in June 1987 and it was the first Western-allied state to carry out the denuclearization through legislation. The ***New Zealand Nuclear Free Zone, Disarmament, and Arms Control Act 1987*** prohibits the stationing of nuclear weapons on the territory of New Zealand and entry of nuclear armed ships into New Zealand waters.

As one of the founding members of the United Nations, New Zealand puts emphasis on each principle of the UN Charter, undertaking the mission of maintaining international peace and security. New Zealand has been active in various wars like the Second Boer War, World War I, World War II, the Korean War, the Malayan Emergency, the Vietnam War, the Gulf War and the Afghanistan War. It has also sent a unit of army engineers to help rebuild Iraqi infrastructure for one year during the Iraq War. As of 2008, New Zealand forces were still active in Afghanistan. It has an assistance plan for overseas development and promotes the development of the South Pacific area through cooperation with other governments and assisting institutions. New Zealand has also joined various multi-national organisations like World Trade Organization, International Money Fund, World Bank, and Organization of Economic Co-operation and Development. It is also a member of the following geopolitical organisations: Asia-Pacific Economic Co-operation, East Asia Summit, Commonwealth of Nations, and the United Nations, and has signed up to a number of free trade agreements, of which the most important are the ***China-New Zealand Free Trade Agreement*** and ***Closer Economic Relations with Australia***.

New Zealand has the longest relationship with Britain, but shares common interests and values with other European countries. The same values and the close contacts in political and economic affairs serve as the base for relations between New Zealand and North American countries. For example, New Zealand has strengthened its relations with Canada because of traditions in common as members of the British Commonwealth.

In recent decades, New Zealand has emphasised developing the relationships with Asian countries because New Zealanders became aware of the importance of East Asia to New Zealand. As a major South Pacific nation, New Zealand plays an active part in APEC as a founding member and has a close working relationship with many Pacific island nations. It continues a political association with the Cook Islands, Niue and Tokelau.

As to relations with China, New Zealand has performed very well. It established diplomatic relations with China in 1972. It was also the first country to recognise the economic position of Chinese market and to negotiate on the question of granting China entrance to WTO. In September 1999, Chinese President Jiang Zemin made a state visit to New Zealand. This was the first time a Chinese head of state visited New Zealand. And New Zealand Prime Minister Clark's visit to China in April, 2001 further enhanced the economic development and cooperation between these two countries.

> **Questions for discussion:**
> 1. Why was New Zealand inclined to strengthen its diplomatic relationships with Asian countries?
> 2. Give some examples to illustrate the interests of New Zealand in participating in the international affairs.

## Exercises

### Ⅰ. Fill in the blanks.
1. The *Treaty of Waitangi* is regarded as a mark of New Zealand's _____ as a nation and has been reserved by _____ as a guarantee of their rights.
2. The Capital of New Zealand was moved to _____ in 1841.
3. By the *Westminster Act of 1931*, New Zealand obtained complete _____ as a member of the British Commonwealth.
4. In 1893, the country became the first nation in the world to grant women the right to _____.
5. The first Labour government in the 1930s established a comprehensive _____ state and a _____ economy.

### Ⅱ. Define the following terms.
1. the New Zealand Nuclear Free Zone
2. relations between New Zealand and Australia

### Ⅲ. Multiple choice.
1. In _____, New Zealand became a British Dominion.
   A. 1840   B. 1841   C. 1907   D. 1931
2. The _____ influence on New Zealand was weakened by the disappointment with the Vietnam War, the sinking of the Rainbow Warrior by France, and by disagreements over environmental and agricultural trade issues and New Zealand's nuclear-free policy.
   A. Japanese          B. Australian
   C. British           D. American
3. In the middle _____, the independent diplomatic policy of New Zealand came into being.
   A. 1920s   B. 1930s   C. 1940s   D. 1950s
4. In _____, New Zealand established diplomatic relations with China.
   A. 1972   B. 1975   C. 1982   D. 1979

### Ⅳ. Translate the following terms into English.
1. 奥克兰
2. 威斯敏斯特法
3. 新西兰宪法法案
4. 亚太经济合作组织

### Ⅴ. Answer the following questions in a few sentences.
1. Briefly describe the relationship between New Zealand and Britain.
2. What are the problems in New Zealand after World War Ⅱ?

> **Mini-task:**
> New Zealand has maintained a friendly relationship with China, and is developing a long-term cooperative partnership with China. It is the first country to sign the bilateral agreement on China's entry into the WTO and to acknowledge China's market economy status. But in which aspects will New Zealand develop a long-term cooperative relationship with China? Please search for the relevant information about it.

# VOLUME SIX

# THE REPUBLIC OF IRELAND

# Chapter One  Geography and Population

*Sharing the island of Ireland with Great Britain, the Republic of Ireland covers various landscapes. Try to get detailed materials about the features of its geography.*

## Part One  Geographical Features

Ireland, officially named as the **Republic of Ireland**, is also called **the Emerald Isle** because of its rich green countryside. The country occupies five-sixths of the island of Ireland which was first partitioned on 7 May, 1921. Located in Western Europe, to the west of **Great Britain**, it is bordered by **Northern Ireland** (part of the United Kingdom) to the north, by the **Atlantic Ocean** to the west, by the **Irish Sea** to the east and by the **Celtic Sea** and **St. George's Channel** to the south and southeast. The strategic location gives it routes on air and sea between North America and northern Europe.

Ireland occupies a total area of 70,280 square kilometres, of which 68,890 square kilometres is land. The country shares a land border with the United Kingdom. The Republic of Ireland has 3,169 kilometres of coastline and it claims a 370-kilometre **exclusive fishing zone** and a **territorial sea** of 22 kilometres.

The **central lowland**, with various landscapes, is the heart of the country. The most significant feature of Irish landscapes remains bogs which occur on all the mountains, cover large areas of the lowlands and are used for peat extraction and production.

The land in the country is mostly level, with a rolling interior plain surrounded by rugged hills and low mountains. There are sea cliffs, hills and low mountains on the west coast. There are no points lower than sea level in the country and the highest point is Carrantuohill, at 1,041 metres.

Ireland's river system is diverse, which produces one of the country's most beautiful sceneries. The streams slowly flow through the central part of the country and into the mouth of the rivers. The longest river in Ireland is the **River Shannon** which is 400 kilometres long and produces a large proportion of electric power for the country.

## Part Two  Climate

The weather of Ireland is described as "mild, moist and changeable". It is not very hot in summer, nor very cold in winter, though it lies in northern latitudes. Its northerly location is offset by the fact that Ireland is washed by the **Gulf Stream**, a warm ocean current that flows from the Gulf of Mexico northward through the Atlantic Ocean, with prevailing winds from the southwest. As a result, it actually has a quite **temperate maritime climate** which does not vary substantially from one season to the next. Summer temperatures usually exceed 30℃ once every decade, though most commonly reach up to 29℃ in summers and freezes occur only occasionally in winter, with temperatures below -6℃ being uncommon.

Precipitation is common, with some parts of the country getting the rain in up to 275 days every year. Nearly 60% of the country receives an average rainfall from 762 millimetres to 1,270 millimetres, more than that in most parts of Britain.

Although small in size, it has distinct climate regions. In the northwest, winter is the longest season with January being the coldest month. The average temperature is below 5℃ in winter and 13℃ to 14℃ in summer. The northwest receives the largest rainfall of the whole country. Sufficient rainfall and warm winter offer suitable environment for plants. In the southwest, it rains nearly every day. Furthermore, the average sunshine time in December and January is only a little more than one hour. In the southeast, the annual rainfall is about 1,000 millimetres and winter is very warm. Generally, climate in this region is very suitable for agriculture. In the northeast, the climate is cooler than that of other regions of the country. Enough rainfall and mild climate produce a region covered by grass. The central lowland gets the smallest rainfall of the country with only about 762 millimetres annually.

## Part Three  Population and Language

In 2007, Ireland experienced the fastest growth of population in Europe. This rapid growth can be said to be due to declining death rates, rising birth rates and high immigration rates.

Ireland's population has increased significantly in recent years. Much of population growth can be attributed to the arrival of immigrants and the return of Irish people (often with their foreign-born children) who emigrated in large numbers in earlier years during periods of high unemployment. In addition, the birth rate in Ireland is currently over double the death rate, which is highly unusual among Western European countries.

According to the Census of Population, the total population of Ireland was 4,813,608 in 2017, with the density of population was about 69.9 per square kilometre. More than 10% of Ireland's population is now made up of foreign citizens. About 50 to 60 thousand overseas Chinese mainly lived in large and medium-sized cities. The single largest group of immigrants comes from the United Kingdom, followed by Poland, Lithuania, Nigeria, Latvia, the United States, China, and Germany. Nearly 90.3% of the population was recorded as having a "White" ethnic or cultural background. 1.3% of the population had a "**Black or Black Irish**" background. 2% of the population had an "Asian or Asian Irish" background. Moreover, the ratio of males to females has declined since 1979, and reached to the lowest of 49.59% to 51.41% in 2016, bur slightly increased since then.

The official languages are **Irish** and **English** which are compulsorily taught in primary and secondary schools, but students may be exempt from the requirement to receive instruction in both languages.

English is by far the predominant language spoken throughout the country. Road signs are usually bilingual, except in Gaeltacht regions, where they are in Irish only.

The legal status of place names has recently been the subject of controversy, since an order was promulgated in 2005 under the *Official Languages Act*. This Act changed the official name of certain places from English back to Irish, despite local opposition and a local plebiscite requesting that the name be changed to a bilingual version. Most government publications and forms are available in both English and Irish and citizens have the right to deal with the state in Irish if they wish so.

According to the 2016 census, nearly 39.8% of the population regarded themselves as competent in Irish. Though no figures were available for English-speakers, it is thought to be almost 100%.

**The Polish language** is one of the most widely-spoken languages in Ireland after English and Irish: there are over 122,515 Polish residents in Ireland surveyed by the 2006 census. Other languages spoken in Ireland include Shelta, spoken by the Irish travellers and a dialect of Scots spoken by the descendents of Scottish settlers in Ulster.

> **? Question for discussion:**
>
> With the increase of population, especially the flow of immigrants, Ireland is gradually becoming a multinational country. What impacts and effects does this phenomenon have on the culture of the country?

## Part Four  Culture

### Religion

Ireland is officially a secular state and the constitution provides that the state is forbidden from endorsing any particular religion. Approximately 78% of the population is **Roman Catholic** and the country maintains one of the highest rates of regular and weekly church attendance in the western countries. However, there has been a major decline in this attendance among Irish Catholics in the past 30 years. Between 2001 and 2009, regular mass attendance declined further from 48% to 40%. A number of theological colleges continue to educate both ordained and lay people.

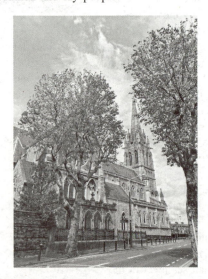

The second largest Christian denomination, the **Church of Ireland**, was declining in number for most of the twentieth century, but recently has experienced an increase in membership, according to the census of 2002. Other large Protestant denominations are the **Presbyterian Church** in Ireland, followed by the **Methodist Church** in Ireland. The very small Jewish community in Ireland also showed a marginal increase in the same period.

The patron saints of Ireland are Saint Patrick and Saint Bridget. According to the census in 2016, the number of people who described themselves as having "no religion" accounted for 10% of the total population. An additional 1,515 people described themselves as agnostic and 929 as atheist. This brings the total nonreligious within the state to 4.5% of the population.

## Part Five    Education

The educational systems are largely under the direction of the government's Minister for Education and Science. Recognised primary and secondary schools must adhere to the curriculum established by authorities empowered to do so.

The **Program for International Student Assessment**, coordinated by the Organization for Economic Co-operation and Development (OECD), currently ranks Ireland's education as the 20th best in the world in science.

Primary, secondary and higher educations are all free in Ireland for all European Union citizens. Schooling is compulsory between ages 6 and 15. The oldest university in Ireland is the **University of Dublin**, of which **Trinity College** is a constituent.

Although a large number of schools in Ireland are run by religious organisations, a general trend of secularism has occurred within the Irish population, particularly in the younger generations. Secular groups tries to eliminate the religious study in the second and sixth grade classes. Children can be excluded from religious study if their parents wish. However, religious studies as a subject was introduced into the state administered **Junior Certificate** in 2001. It is not compulsory and deals with aspects of different religions instead of focusing on one particular religion.

Schools run by religious organisations, but receiving public money and recognition, are not allowed to discriminate against pupils because of religion (or lack of). A sanctioned system of preference does exist, where students of a particular religion may be accepted before those who do not share the ethos of the school, in a case where a school's quota has already been reached.

## Exercises

### Ⅰ. Fill in the blanks.

1. The country is bordered by Northern Ireland (part of the United Kingdom) to the north, by the _____ _____ to the west.
2. The capital of the Republic of Ireland is _____.
3. The weather of Ireland is described as "_____, _____ and _____".
4. It actually has a quite _____ _____ climate which does not vary substantially from one season to the next.
5. The official languages are _____ and _____, which are compulsorily taught in primary and secondary schools.
6. Ireland's oldest university is the _____ _____ _____, of which Trinity College is a constituent.
7. Religious studies as a subject was introduced into the state administered Junior Certificate in _____.
8. Ireland is officially a _____ state, and the constitution states that the state is forbidden from endorsing any particular religion.

### Ⅱ. Define the following terms.

1. Emerald Isle
2. Gulf Stream

### Ⅲ. Multiple choice.

1. Ireland is in the _____ of Great Britain.
   A. east    B. south    C. west    D. north
2. What is Ireland called in Irish?
   A. Irea.    B. Aire.    C. Eare.    D. Eire.
3. Ireland is called the Emerald Isle because of _____.
   A. its unique shape
   B. its connection with Britain
   C. its abundant natural resources
   D. its rich green countryside
4. The most significant feature of Irish landscape is _____.
   A. bogs            B. streams
   C. islands         D. cliffs
5. The population of Ireland is predominantly of _____ origin.
   A. English         B. Celtic

   C. Norman          D. French

6. The longest river in Ireland is _____.
   A. the Liffey River
   B. the Dodder River
   C. the Shannon River
   D. Lough Derg

7. Which statement is NOT true about Ireland?
   A. Ireland is divided into two political units.
   B. Northern Ireland is part of the United Kingdom.
   C. The Republic of Ireland is an independent country.
   D. Ireland is called the Emerald Isle because of its rich deposit of emeralds.

8. In Ireland, the basic ethnic stock is _____.
   A. Celtic         B. Roman
   C. Norman      D. English

9. Ireland has four unusual demographic features. Which of the following is NOT true?
   A. A low birthrate.
   B. A late marriage.
   C. A high proportion of unmarried people.
   D. An excess of females in the population.

## IV. Translate the following terms into English.
1. 绿宝石岛
2. 专属捕鱼区
3. 墨西哥湾暖流
4. 国际学生评价

## V. Answer the following questions in a few sentences.
1. What is largely responsible for the lack of extreme summer heat and winter cold in Ireland?
2. Briefly introduce the position of the Republic of Ireland.

The Gulf Stream, along with its northern extension towards Europe, known as the North Atlantic Drift, is a powerful, warm, and swift Atlantic Ocean current. It originates in the Gulf of Mexico, exits through the Straits of Florida, and follows the eastern coastlines of the United States and Newfoundland before crossing the Atlantic Ocean. The process of intensification from the west causes the Gulf Stream to be a northward accelerating current along the east coast of North America. At about 30°W, 40°N, the Gulf Stream splits into two, with the northern stream crossing to northern Europe and the southern stream recirculating off West Africa. The Gulf Stream influences the climate of the east coast of North America from Florida to Newfoundland, and the west coast of Europe. Although there has been debates recently, there is a consensus that the climate of Western Europe and Northern Europe is warmer than it would otherwise be, and that this is due to the North Atlantic drift, one of the branches from the tail of the Gulf Stream. It is part of the North Atlantic Subtropical Gyre. Its presence has led to the development of strong cyclones of all types, both within the atmosphere and within the ocean. The Gulf Stream is also a significant potential source of renewable power generation.

Think about the question: How does the Gulf Stream come into being?

# Chapter Two  Government and Politics

*The Irish government has three parts: the Executive, the Legislative and the Judicial. And each part has its own powers and functions. Develop a general introduction to its political system.*

The government is constitutionally limited to fifteen members. No more than two members of the government can be selected from the Senate (the *Seanad* in Irish). The Prime Minister (the Taoiseach, Tánaiste in Irish) and the Minister for Finance must be members of the House of Representatives (the Dáil in Irish). The government consists of a coalition of three parties: Fine Gael, Fianna Fail, and Green Party. The last general election to the House of Representatives took place in February, 2016, and Sean O'Fearghail as the head. While the last general election to the Senate took place in April, 2016, and Denis O'Donovan as the head.

Ireland joined the European Union in 1973 but has chosen to remain outside the *Schengen Treaty*. Citizens of the United Kingdom can freely enter Ireland without a passport thanks to the Common Travel Area, but some forms of identification are required at airports and seaports. Ireland has vetoed a number of European treaties. In a referendum on 12 June, 2008, Ireland rejected the *Lisbon Treaty*, which has caused much controversy within the European Union and may affect the future of it.

## Part One  Constitution

On 29 December, 1937, the Constitution of Ireland came into force. It replaced the Constitution of the Irish Free State and created a new state called simply *Éire* or "Ireland" in English. The former **Irish Free State** government had taken steps to formally abolish the Office of Governor-General some months before the new Constitution came into effect.

Although the Constitution of Ireland established the office of President of Ireland, Ireland was not a real republic between 1937 and 1949. This was because the principal key role, possessed by a head of state that symbolically represented Ireland internationally, remained vested under statutory law in the King of Ireland as an organ of the Irish government.

The Constitution of Ireland of 1937 took the Catholic Church as the church of the majority, but also recognised other Christian denominations and Judaism. Along with other predominant Catholic European states, the Irish state underwent a period of legal secularisation in the late 20th century. In 1999, the Good Friday Agreement signed by the Ireland and Britain came into effect. The Irish government amended the Constitution, giving up the territorial sovereignty of Northern Ireland.

## Part Two  Political System

### The Executive

Ireland is a republic, with a parliamentary system of government. The head of state is **President of Ireland** who serves for seven years a term and can be re-elected only once. The president is largely a figurehead but can still carry out certain constitutional powers and functions, aided by the Council of State. The President is entitled to summon and dissolve the Parliament (Orireachtas in Irish) and is empowered to propose certain bills to the Supreme Court for a final decision on their constitutionality and to the people for referendum. He also has the power to appoint the Prime Minister nominated by the House of Representatives and appoint other members of the government on the nomination of the Prime Minister with the approval of the House of Representatives.

The **Prime Minster** is the head of the government of Ireland who is responsible only to the House of Representatives. Most Prime Ministers have been the leader of the political party winning the most seats in the national elections. It is a common case for coalitions to form a government and there has not been a single-party government since 1989.

### The Legislative

All the legislative powers are vested in the **Parliament** (Oireachtas) which has the sole power of making laws. The parliament consists of two Houses: the **Senate** (Seanad Éireann), being the upper House and the **House of Representatives** (Dáil Éireann), being the lower House. The Senate is composed of

sixty members, among whom eleven are nominated by the Prime Minister, six are elected by two universities and the other forty-three elected by public representatives from candidates established on a vocational basis. The House of Representatives has 166 members called Teachtaí Dála (DTs), elected to represent multi-seat constituencies under the system of proportional representation by means of the Single Transferable Vote. DTs and senators are elected every five years.

### The Judiciary

**Higher court** holds priority on all the cases concerning law. It also can adjudicate the constitutionality of the law. Generally, it is made up of one judge as chairman and 12 jurymen.

**The Supreme Court** is the final court of appeal. It is composed of one chief-judge and six associated judges. It has the power to adjudicate all the bills proposed by the President and passed by the Parliament or to veto them unconstitutional with current law.

## Part Three  Parties

Ireland has a bipolar political party system with two major parties: the Irish Republic Party (Fianna Fáil) and Fine Gael. Minor parties include the Green Party, the Progressive Democrats and the Labour Party.

**The Irish Republic Party** founded in 1926 is the second largest party in Ireland. Originally, it was conservative and insisted on unification of Ireland. It advocates reducing tax and increasing jobs at home and stands for neutrality internationally. Its economic policies include supporting the European Community, and raising public expenditure to reduce unemployment.

**Fine Gael** established in 1933 is the largest party in Ireland. It insisted on free socialism since the 1970s. It also supported equality in politics, expansion of social services, an open-door economy and reduction of public expenditures, tax rates and denationalisation.

The third largest political party is the **Labour Party** which was set up in 1912 and is the oldest political party in Ireland. With the belief that man is born equally, it favours establishing a fair and democratic society.

**The Progressive Democrats** splitting from the Republic Party in 1985 has been the largest minor party since the general election of 1987. The Progressive Democrats holds 14 seats as compared with the Labour Party's 12 seats. The Progressive Democrats advocates establishing modern society on the basis of European models and improving the role the government plays in national economy and social life.

> **? Questions for discussion:**
> Which political party is in office now? And what policy does it follow domestically as well as abroad?

### Exercises

**I. Fill in the blanks.**
1. Ireland is a _____ republic and a unitary state under the Constitution of 1937.
2. The current government consists of a coalition of three parties: the Irish Republic Party, the _____ _____ and the _____ _____.
3. On 29 December, _____, the Constitution of Ireland came into force.
4. The head of state is President of Ireland who serves for _____ years a term and can be re-elected _____ _____.

**II. Define the following terms.**
1. Fine Gael
2. the Irish Republic Party

**III. Multiple choice.**
1. Ireland has a bipolar political party system with two major parties. They are _____.
   A. Sinn Fein and the Republic Party
   B. Sinn Fein and Fine Gael
   C. the Irish Republic Party and Fine Gael
   D. IRA and Sinn Fein
2. _____ is the oldest of all the parties in Ireland.
   A. The Labour Party
   B. The Progressive Democrats
   C. the Republic Party
   D. Fine Gael
3. In Ireland, the Republic Party and Fine Gael are both descended from _____.
   A. the Irish Labour Party
   B. Sinn Fein
   C. IRA
   D. the Progressive Democrats

**IV. Translate the following terms into English.**
1. 爱尔兰自由邦

2. 天主教会
3. 进步民主党

## V. Answer the following questions in a few sentences.

1. What kind of government system does Ireland have?

2. What powers does the president have?

  Mini-task:

The Constitution of Ireland is the second constitution of independent Ireland and replaced the Constitution of the Irish Free State. It came into force on 29 December, 1937 after having been passed by a national plebiscite on 1 July, 1937.

The constitution falls broadly within the liberal democratic tradition. It establishes an independent state based on a system of representative democracy and guarantees certain fundamental rights, along with a popularly elected president, a separation of powers and judicial review. The constitution may only be amended by referendum.

Please search for the information about the differences between the Constitution of Ireland and the Constitution of the Irish Free State.

# Chapter Three  Economy

> In the past decades, the economy of Ireland has undergone a rapid growth, accompanied by an unavoidable high level of inflation. Major changes took place in the national economy during this time. Research materials about the current situation of its national economy.

The economy of Ireland has shifted its focus from agriculture to modern knowledge in recent years, emphasizing services and high-tech industries and becoming dependent on trade, industry and investment. Economic growth in Ireland averaged 5.3% from 2004 to 2007, but fell into recession during economic crisis in 2008. The industry, which accounts for 38.6% of GDP and about 80% of exports, now takes the place of agriculture as the country's leading economic sector.

The landscape of Ireland determines that livestock farming is the main form of agriculture, especially cattle farming. Though nearly 60% of the whole territory is being cultivated, the production of crops is too small to meet domestic demands.

The long history of agricultural production coupled with modern intensive agricultural methods has put pressure on the biodiversity in Ireland. Agriculture is the main factor determining current land use patterns in Ireland, leaving limited land for preservation of natural habitats, particularly for larger wild mammals with greater territorial requirements.

Ireland's economic growth mainly relied on exports, which led to an increase in consumer spending, construction and business investment brought about by exports. On the surface, the country is the largest exporter of software-related goods and services in the world. In fact, a lot of foreign software, sometimes music, is filtered through the country to avail businesses of Ireland's tax-free policy of royalties on copyrighted goods.

By the 1980s, underlying economic problems became apparent. High unemployment, more emigration, a growing public debts became severe again. Middle income workers were taxed as high as 60% of their marginal income and unemployment rate was up to 20%. Annual emigration reached over 1% of total population and public deficits was up to 15% of GDP. The Irish Republic Party, which was largely responsible for the spending increase in the late 1970s that caused much of the **economic turmoil**, was elected in 1987 and shocked everyone when it announced a swing toward small government.

After the Irish Republic Party was in office, public spending and taxes were reduced quickly. Ireland promoted competition in all areas. For instance, Ryanair made use of Ireland's deregulated aviation market, showing to European regulators the benefits of competition in transportation markets. The more competitive economy attracted more foreign investment. Intel invested in 1989 and was followed by numerous technology companies, such as Microsoft and Google, who have found Ireland an excellent investment location. Political parties have maintained consensus about the economic development policy.

The construction sector, inherently cyclical, accounts for a significant component of Ireland's GDP. A recent downturn in residential property market has highlighted the over-exposure of the Irish economy to construction, which now poses a threat to its economic growth. Several successive years of economic growth have led to an increase in equality in Irish society and a decrease in poverty. Figures showed that 6.8% of population in Ireland suffers from "consistent poverty".

High growth in economy usually brings about high levels of inflation, particularly in the capital city. Prices in Dublin, where nearly 30% of Ireland's population lives, are considerably higher than elsewhere around the country, especially in the real estate market, but property prices have fallen rapidly following the downturn in the world economy and its adverse effects on Ireland. At the end of July 2008, the annual rate of inflation was running at 0.9% measured by the Consumer Price Index and the inflation actually dropped slightly from the previous month.

However, after a construction boom in the last decade, the economic growth slowed down. There has been a significant fall in house prices but the cost of living is rising. The huge reduction in construction has caused Ireland's massive economic downturn. If construction was excluded in the economic outlook, Ireland would still grow by about 5.5%, for it now has the second-highest level of household debt in the world, at 126% of household income.

Despite a forecast for slower economic growth in 2008, Ireland ranked fifth in terms of Gross Domestic Product (GDP) per capita and Human Development Index in the world. The country also boasts the highest quality of life in the world, ranking first in the **Economist Intelligence Unit**'s Quality-of-life index. Ireland ranked sixth on the **Global Peace Index**. Ireland also has high rankings for its educational system, political freedom, civil rights, press freedom and economic freedom. Ireland has emerged as an attractive destination for foreign immigrants who now make up approximately 12.5% of the population. Ireland's population is the fastest growing in Europe with an annual growth rate of 1.3%.

The Financial Crisis of 2008 affected the Irish economy severely and domestic economic problems were compounded and related to the collapse of the Irish property bubble. Ireland was the first country in the European Union to officially enter a recession as declared by the **Central Statistics Office**. Ireland had to accept an 85-billion-euro bailout from the European Union and the International Monetary Fund, and quitted the aid programme in 2013. Since then, Ireland witnessed a rapid economic growth, up to 21.7% from 2015 to 2017.

### ? Questions for discussion:
1. What measures did the Irish government take to cope with the problems caused by the financial crisis of 2008?
2. What impacts did the measures have on people's daily life?

## Exercises
### Ⅰ. Fill in the blanks.
1. The economy of Ireland has transformed in recent years from an _____ focus to a modern knowledge economy, focusing on _____ and _____ industries.
2. The landscape of Ireland determines that _____ farming are the main form of agriculture.
3. _____ now takes the place of agriculture as the country's leading sector.
4. In 2008, Ireland has the _____ highest gross domestic product per capita and the fifth highest Human Development Index rank in the world.
5. On paper, the country is the largest _____ of software-related goods and services in the world.

### Ⅱ. Translate the following terms into English.
1. 经济学家情报单位
2. 世界和平指数
3. 国内生产总值
4. 中央统计局
5. 经济动荡

### Ⅲ. Answer the following questions in a few sentences.
1. What are the two types of farming in Ireland?
2. What are Ireland's chief exports?

### ✓ Mini-task:

Electrical generation from peat consumption, as a percent of total electrical generation, was reduced from 18.8% to 6.1% between 1990 and 2004. A forecast by Sustainable Energy Ireland predicts that oil will no longer be used for electrical generation but natural gas will be dominant at 71.3% of the total share, coal at 9.2%, and renewable energy at 8.2% of the market. New sources of supply are expected to come on stream after 2009 and 2010, including the Corrib gas field and potentially the Shannon Liquefied Natural Gas (LNG) terminal. In addition to gas supplies, energy exports have the potential to transform Ireland's economy.

Energy is a severe problem faced by the whole world. How to invent and explore new energy resources becomes a great challenge. How can Ireland deal with the problem of energy?

## Chapter Four   History

> *Religion plays an important role in people's daily life, especially in western countries. However, more and more younger generations in Ireland describe themselves as having "no religion". Explain the reason for this change from the perspective of younger generations.*

From the ***Act of Union*** on 1 January, 1801 until 6 December, 1922, Ireland had been a part of the United Kingdom of Great Britain and Ireland. During the Great Famine from 1845 to 1849, the island's population of over 8 million fell by 30 percent. One million Irish died of starvation and another 1.5 million emigrated, which set the pattern of emigration for the century to come, resulting in a constant population decline until the 1960s. From 1874, particularly from 1880, under Charles Stewart Parnell, the Irish Parliamentary Party gained prominence through widespread agrarian agitation that secured improved tenant land reforms, and with its attempts to win two ***Home Rule Bills***, which would have granted Ireland limited national autonomy within the United Kingdom. These events nevertheless led to the control of national affairs under the ***Local Government (Ireland) Act of 1898*** previously in the hands of landlord dominated grand juries.

On 6 December, 1922, Ireland became a Dominion called the Irish Free State when all the islands of Ireland seceded from the United Kingdom of Great Britain and Ireland. However, the following day the Parliament of Northern Ireland exercised its right under the ***Anglo-Irish Treaty*** to go back into the United Kingdom. This action, known as the **Partition of Ireland**, followed four attempts to introduce decentralised autonomous government over the whole island of Ireland.

The Free State was a constitutional monarchy over which the British monarch reigned. The Representative of the Crown was known as the Governor-General. The Free State consisted of a bicameral parliament and a cabinet, called the "**Executive Council**" answerable to the lower house of parliament, the Free State House of Representatives. The head of government was called the **President of the Executive Council.**

The *Anglo-Irish Treaty* provided that should Northern Ireland choose not to be included in the Free State, a Boundary Commission would be set up to revise the borders between the two jurisdictions. The Irish perspective was that this provision was intended to allow largely nationalist areas of Northern Ireland to join the Free State. Shortly after the establishment of the Free State, this commission came into being. However, the commission concentrated on economic and topographic factors, rather than on the political aspirations of the people who would be living near the new border. In 1925, the Boundary Commission report, contrary to expectations, proposed ceding some small areas of the Free State to Northern Ireland.

Irish independence in 1922 was preceded by the **Easter Uprising** of 1916, when Irish volunteers and the **Irish Citizen Army** took over sites in Dublin and Galway under terms expressed through the Proclamation of the Irish Republic. The seven signatories of this proclamation were executed, along with nine others and thousands were arrested, precipitating the Irish War of Independence. The Irish Free State was abolished when the Republic of Ireland was formally established on 29 December, 1937, the day its Constitution came into force. At the same time, the Governor-General was replaced by a President of Ireland and a new more powerful Prime Minister, called the "Taoiseach", came into being, while the Executive Council was renamed the "Government". Though it had a president, the new state was not a republic. The British Monarch continued to reign theoretically as King of Ireland and was used as an "organ" in international and diplomatic relations, with the President of Ireland relegated to symbolic functions within the state but unknown to the world.

The state was nominally neutral during World War II, a period known within the state as the "Emergency". Though it did not appear in the battlefield, it worked closely with the Allies. For example, the date of the Normandy landings was decided on the basis of transatlantic weather reports provided by the Irish state. It is estimated that about 100,000 men from Ireland participated in the war, with that number roughly evenly divided between Northern Ireland and the southern state. Conversely, following the suicide of Adolph Hitler and the diplomatic protocol, De Valera controversially offered condolences to the German ambassador. The state's decision to adopt neutrality was influenced by memories of the Anglo-Irish War and the Civil War and the state's lack of military preparation for involvement in a war.

On 1 April, 1949, the **Republic of Ireland Act** was enacted, which described Ireland as the Republic of Ireland but did not change the country's name. The international and diplomatic functions previously exercised by the King were now vested in the President of Ireland who finally became unambiguously the Irish head of state. Under the Commonwealth rules then in force, the declaration of a republic automatically terminated the state's membership of the British Commonwealth. Unlike India, becoming a republic shortly afterwards, Ireland chose not to reapply for admittance to the Commonwealth. However, after a long time, the British Government recognised that the Republic of Ireland had "ceased to be part of His Majesty's dominions".

The state joined the **United Nations** in December 1955, after a lengthy debate and veto by the Soviet Union. Turned away by France's veto in 1961, the state finally succeeded in joining the European Economic Community (now known as the European Union) in 1973.

The period of economic crisis of the late 1970s was a difficult time for Ireland. Budget of the Republic Party's government, the abolition of the car tax, borrowing to fund spending, and global economic conditions had caused high unemployment and mass emigration. One possible reason for these outcomes was even more borrowing by the Charles Haughey and Garret FitzGerald governments, and increases in tax rates by 60% (with one Fine Gael finance minister suggesting people were not being taxed enough). There were widespread tax evasion and political corruption. Political power alternated between the Republic Party and Fine Gael, with some governments not even lasting a year. In one case, there were three elections in one year.

Starting in 1989, there were significant policy changes like economic reform, tax cuts, welfare reform, an increase in competition, and a ban on borrowing to fund current spending. This policy was started by the Republic and Progressive Democrat government in office from 1989 to 1992 with the support of the opposition Fine Gael and continued by the subsequent several governments. It has been debated whether the tax cuts caused the "boom" or just followed it.

Although Ireland maintains a neutral policy in dealing with foreign affairs and does not join in any military alliances, it did become a member of North Atlantic Treaty Organization (NATO) in December 1999. In September 2005, the Irish Republican Army was announced to disarm and enter the peace era.

Gripped by the effects of poverty and emigration for most of its existence, the state became one of the fastest growing economies in the world by the 1990s, a phenomenon known as the **Celtic Tiger**. By the early 2000s, the Republic had become the second richest (in terms of GDP per capita, adjusted for purchasing power parity) member of the European Union and had moved from being a net recipient of European Union funds to a net contributor, and from a position of net emigration to one of net immigration.

The Celtic Tiger started in the mid-1990s and boomed right on up to 2001, when it slowed down, only to pick up again in 2003. It slowed again in 2007 and in June 2008, the **Irish Economic and Social Research Institute (ESRI)** predicted that Ireland would go into recession briefly before growth would resume.

According to the preliminary results of the 2022 census, the population of the Republic of Ireland has increased by 7.6% in the six years from 2016 to 2022. According to the data from the Central Bureau of Statistics in April, 2022, the number of people living in Ireland reached 5,123,536.

In June, 2020, the General Assembly of the United Nations voted Ireland as a non-permanent member of the Security Council from 2021 to 2022.

The trading volumes of China and Ireland have substantially improved since the establishment of diplomatic relations. However, the US – China trade war in 2019 negatively affected Ireland's export goods to China. Ireland is known for exporting high-end chips that mainly export to China to make final products which are frequently shipped on to the US. The trade war impacts both Chinese and Ireland's economic growth.

Due to the **"Agreement for the Avoidance of Double Taxation"** signed in 2000 and **"Agreement on Scientific and Technological Cooperation"** signed in 2001, Ireland and China developed their foreign relations and economic growth by increasing job opportunities and wages. By 2019, there are about 37 Chinese companies in Ireland that have 3,200 employees in total. One of the well-known Chinese companies established offices in Ireland is Huawei, the most-used cellphone brand by Chinese people. On the other side, some Irish companies also expanded their market in China. By 2019, more than 400 Irish companies have successfully entered into the Chinese market.

The friendly diplomatic relations between China and Ireland promote cultural exchange and travelling over the years. In recent years, Ireland becomes one of the hottest recommended countries to travel to. By 2019, almost 40,000 Chinese travellers visit Ireland a year according to the official data. Furthermore,

Hainan Airline from China opens direct flights between Dublin and three Chinese cities—Beijing, Shenzhen, and Hong Kong.

On the ceremony of the 40th anniversary of diplomatic relations held in June 2019 in Dublin, Minister for Justice and Equality Charlie Flanagan announced that the Irish government welcomes Chinese visitors and would issue a five-year multi-entry visa option for Chinese people, which started in July 2019.

By 2019, this bilateral relationship had boomed to a high point, and a ceremony of their 40th anniversary of diplomatic relations was held in Dublin, Ireland in June 2019.

However, in July 2019, Ireland together with other 21 ambassadors from United Nations signed a joint letter to the United Nations Human Rights Commission condemning China's mistreatment of the Uyghurs and other minority groups, urging the Chinese government to close the Xinjiang re-education camps.

Concerning the Taiwan question, Ireland follows a One-China policy and emphasises Taiwan question being best settled through dialogue "between the parties concerned". Ireland does not establish official diplomatic relations with Taiwan but a Taipei Representative Office was set up to deal with issues in relation to economic and cultural promotion.

On 1 July, 2020, the Irish Ministry of Foreign Affairs and Trade released a statement on its website, accusing China of unprovoked accusations about Hong Kong National Security Law, and China strongly resented and firmly opposed, saying that no country can override its interests in Hong Kong over China's sovereignty and security interests and Hong Kong's peace, tranquility and prosperity. Like the Irish people, the Chinese people, including the people of Hong Kong, will never again swallow the bitter pill of foreign oppression and national division. China looks forward to working with Ireland to promote the healthy and stable development of China-Ireland relations based on the principle of mutual respect and equal treatment.

> **Question for discussion:**
> The Irish government followed a neutral policy in dealing with foreign affairs and refused to join in any military alliances, which is similar to China. Research the relationship between the Republic of Ireland and the People's Republic of China.

## Exercises

### Ⅰ. Fill in the blanks.
1. When all the islands of Ireland seceded from the United Kingdom of Great Britain and Ireland on _____ _____, 1922, Ireland became the Dominion called the Irish Free State.
2. On 1 April, 1949, the _____ was enacted. That legislation described Ireland as the Republic of Ireland but did not change the country's name.

### Ⅱ. Define the following term.
1. Partition of Ireland

### Ⅲ. Translate the following terms into English.
1. 地方自治条例
2. 联合国
3. 凯尔特虎
4. 爱尔兰经济和社会研究所

> **Mini-task:**
>
> Trinity College, Dublin, corporately designated as the Provost, Fellows and Scholars of the College of the Holy and Undivided Trinity of Queen Elizabeth near Dublin, was founded in 1592 by letters patent from Queen Elizabeth I as the "mother of a university" and is the only constituent college of the University of Dublin. Located in Dublin, Ireland, it is Ireland's oldest university.
>
> Trinity is now surrounded by Dublin and is located on College Green, opposite the former Irish Houses of Parliament. The college occupies 190,000 square metres, with many of its buildings as ranged around large quadrangles (known as squares) and two playing fields.
>
> Academically, Trinity is divided into three faculties comprising 24 schools, offering degree and diploma courses at both undergraduate and postgraduate levels. It is consistently ranked as the best university in Ireland and as the 108th best worldwide THES-QS World University Rankings of universities (2019). The Library of Trinity College is a legal deposit library for Ireland and the United Kingdom, containing over 4.5 million printed volumes and significant quantities of manuscripts, maps and music.
>
> Try to search for more information about Trinity College through other resources available.

# Appendix: Supplementary Materials for Reference

## 1. 英国历代国王、女王世系表

| 英王 | 世系 | 在位期间 |
|---|---|---|
| | **（一）诺曼底王朝（House of Normandy）** | |
| 威廉一世（William I） | 法国诺曼底公爵，"征服者威廉" | 1066—1087 |
| 威廉二世（William II） | 即红发威廉，威廉一世次子 | 1087—1100 |
| 亨利一世（Henry I） | 威廉一世之子 | 1100—1135 |
| 斯蒂芬（Stephen） | 亨利一世之侄，亦即威廉一世之外孙，亨利一世之女马蒂尔达（Matilda）对斯蒂芬继承王位持有异议 | 1135—1154 |
| | **（二）金雀花王朝（House of Plantagenet），又称安茹王朝（House of Anjou）** | |
| 亨利二世（Henry II） | 马蒂尔达和她的第二个丈夫法国安茹伯爵杰弗里之子 | 1154—1189 |
| 理查一世（Richard I） | 即十字军战士"狮心王"理查，亨利二世之子 | 1189—1199 |
| 约翰（John） | 亨利二世之子 | 1199—1216 |
| 亨利三世（Henry III） | 约翰之子 | 1216—1272 |
| 爱德华一世（Edward I） | 亨利三世之子 | 1272—1307 |
| 爱德华二世（Edward II） | 爱德华一世之子 | 1307—1327 |
| 爱德华三世（Edward III） | 爱德华二世之子 | 1327—1377 |
| 理查二世（Richard II） | 爱德华三世之孙 | 1377—1399 |
| | **（三）兰开斯特王朝（House of Lancaster）** | |
| 亨利四世（Henry IV） | 兰开斯特公爵约翰·冈特（John of Gaunt）之子，亦即爱德华三世之孙 | 1399—1413 |
| 亨利五世（Henry V） | 亨利四世之子 | 1413—1422 |
| 亨利六世（Henry VI） | 亨利五世之子 | 1422—1461, 1470—1471 |
| | **（四）约克王朝（House of York）** | |
| 爱德华四世（Edward IV） | 约克公爵理查之子，亦即爱德华三世的玄孙 | 1461—1470, 1471—1483 |
| 爱德华五世（Edward V） | 爱德华四世之子，在位两个月 | 1483 |
| 理查三世（Richard III） | 约克公爵理查之子，亦即爱德华四世之弟 | 1483—1485 |
| | **（五）都铎王朝（House of Tudor）** | |
| 亨利七世（Henry VII） | 埃德蒙·都铎（Edmund Tudor）和爱德华三世的曾孙女玛格丽特·博福特（Margaret Beaufort）之子 | 1485—1509 |
| 亨利八世（Henry VIII） | 亨利七世与爱德华四世之女约克的伊丽莎白之子 | 1509—1547 |
| 爱德华六世（Edward VI） | 亨利八世和其第三个妻子简·西摩（Jane Seymour）之子 | 1547—1553 |
| 玛丽一世（Mary I） | 亨利八世和其第一个妻子阿拉贡的凯瑟琳（Katharine of Aragon）之女 | 1553—1558 |
| 伊丽莎白一世（Elizabeth I） | 亨利八世和其第二个妻子安妮·博林（Anne Boleyn）之女 | 1558—1603 |
| | **（六）斯图亚特王朝与共和国（House of Stuart and the Commonwealth）** | |
| 詹姆斯一世（James I） | 苏格兰国王詹姆斯六世继承英格兰王位后改称詹姆斯一世，其母苏格兰女王玛丽·斯图亚特为亨利七世的曾孙女 | 1603—1625 |
| 查理一世（Charles I） | 詹姆斯一世之子，被斩首 | 1625—1649 |
| 议会执政（Council of State） | 共和国时期（1649—1660） | 1649—1653 |

| | | |
|---|---|---|
| 奥利弗·克伦威尔(Oliver Cromwell) | 以护国公(Lord Protector)名义执政 | 1653—1658 |
| 理查德·克伦威尔(Richard Cromwell) | 奥利弗之子，以护国公名义执政 | 1658—1660 |
| 查理二世(Charles II) | 查理一世之子，复辟 | 1660—1685 |
| 詹姆斯二世(James II) | 查理一世之子，查理二世之弟 | 1685—1688 |
| 威廉三世与玛丽二世(William III and Mary II) | 威廉三世是荷兰奥兰治亲王威廉二世(William II, Prince of Orange)之子，玛丽二世之夫；玛丽二世是詹姆斯二世之女，玛丽二世卒于1694年 | 1689—1702 |
| 安妮(Anne) | 詹姆斯二世和安妮·海德(Anne Hyde)之女,玛丽二世的妹妹 | 1702—1714 |

**（七）汉诺威王朝(House of Hanover)**

| | | |
|---|---|---|
| 乔治一世(George I) | 德国汉诺威选帝侯埃内斯特(Ernest, Elector of Hanover)和詹姆斯一世的孙女索菲娅(Sophia)之子 | 1714—1727 |
| 乔治二世(George II) | 乔治一世之子 | 1727—1760 |
| 乔治三世(George III) | 乔治二世之孙 | 1760—1820 |
| 乔治四世(George IV) | 乔治三世之子 | 1820—1830 |
| 威廉四世(William IV) | 乔治三世之子，乔治四世之弟 | 1830—1837 |
| 维多利亚(Victoria) | 乔治三世之第四子肯特公爵爱德华(Edward, Duke of Kent)和德国萨克森—科堡公主维多利亚之女，维多利亚女王于1840年与其表兄萨克森-科堡-哥达亲王阿尔伯特(Prince Albert of Saxe-Coburg-Gotha)结婚 | 1837—1901 |

**（八）萨克森-科堡-哥达王朝(House of Saxe-Coburg-Gotha)**

| | | |
|---|---|---|
| 爱德华七世(Edward VII) | 维多利亚女王和阿尔伯特亲王之子 | 1901—1910 |

**（九）温莎王朝(House of Windsor)**

| | | |
|---|---|---|
| 乔治五世(George V) | 爱德华七世之子，1917年以温莎为姓 | 1910—1936 |
| 爱德华八世(Edward VIII) | 乔治五世之长子，1936年1月即位，同年12月逊位 | 1936 |
| 乔治六世(George VI) | 乔治五世之次子，1923年与伊丽莎白·鲍斯-莱昂(Elisabeth Bowes-Lyon)结婚 | 1936—1952 |
| 伊丽莎白二世(Elizabeth II) | 乔治六世之长女 | 1952—2022 |
| 查尔斯三世(Charles III) | 伊丽莎白二世之长子 | 2022— |

## 2. 英国历届首相一览表

| 首相 | | 任期 |
|---|---|---|
| 罗伯特·沃波尔 | (Sir) Robert Walpole | 1721—1742 |
| 威尔明顿伯爵 | Earl of Wilmington | 1742—1743 |
| 亨利·佩勒姆 | Henry Pelham | 1743—1754 |
| 纽卡斯尔公爵 | Duke of Newcastle | 1754—1756 |
| 德文希尔公爵 | Duke of Devonshire | 1756—1757 |
| 纽卡斯尔公爵 | Duke of Newcastle | 1757—1762 |
| 比特伯爵 | Earl of Bute | 1762—1763 |
| 乔治·格伦维尔 | George Grenville | 1763—1765 |
| 罗金厄姆侯爵 | Marquis of Rockingham | 1765—1766 |
| 查塔姆伯爵 | Earl of Chatham | 1766—1768 |
| 格拉夫顿公爵 | Duke of Grafton | 1768—1770 |
| 诺思勋爵 | Lord North | 1770—1782 |
| 罗金厄姆侯爵 | Marquis of Rockingham | 1782 |
| 谢尔本伯爵 | Earl of Shelburne | 1782—1783 |
| 波特兰公爵 | Duke of Portland | 1783 |
| 威廉·皮特 | William Pitt | 1783—1801 |
| 亨利·阿丁顿 | Henry Addington | 1801—1804 |
| 威廉·皮特 | William Pitt | 1804—1806 |
| 威廉·格伦维尔勋爵 | Lord William Grenville | 1806—1807 |
| 波特兰公爵 | Duke of Portland | 1807—1809 |
| 斯宾塞·珀西瓦尔 | Spencer Perceval | 1809—1812 |
| 利物浦伯爵 | Earl of Liverpool | 1812—1827 |
| 乔治·坎宁 | George Canning | 1827 |
| 戈德里奇子爵 | Viscount Goderich | 1827—1828 |
| 惠灵顿公爵 | Duke of Wellington | 1828—1830 |
| 格雷伯爵 | Earl Grey | 1830—1834 |
| 梅尔本子爵 | Viscount Melbourne | 1834 |
| 惠灵顿公爵 | Duke of Wellington | 1834 |
| 罗伯特·皮尔 | Sir Robert Peel | 1834—1835 |
| 梅尔本子爵 | Viscount Melbourne | 1835—1841 |
| 罗伯特·皮尔 | Sir Robert Peel | 1841—1846 |
| 约翰·罗素勋爵 | Lord John Russel | 1846—1852 |
| 德比伯爵 | Earl of Derby | 1852 |
| 阿伯丁伯爵 | Earl of Aberdeen | 1852—1855 |
| 帕默斯顿子爵 | Viscount Palmerston | 1855—1858 |
| 德比伯爵 | Earl of Derby | 1858—1859 |
| 帕默斯顿子爵 | Viscount Palmerston | 1859—1865 |
| 约翰·罗素伯爵 | Earl Russel | 1865—1866 |
| 德比伯爵 | Earl of Derby | 1866—1868 |
| 本杰明·迪斯雷利 | Benjamin Disraeli | 1868 |
| 威廉·尤尔特·格莱斯顿 | William Ewart Gladstone | 1868—1874 |
| 本杰明·迪斯雷利 | Benjamin Disraeli | 1874—1880 |
| 威廉·尤尔特·格莱斯顿 | William Ewart Gladstone | 1880—1885 |
| 索尔斯伯里侯爵 | Marquis of Salisbury | 1885—1886 |
| 威廉·尤尔特·格莱斯顿 | William Ewart Gladstone | 1886 |

| | | |
|---|---|---|
| 索尔斯伯里侯爵 | Marquis of Salisbury | 1886—1892 |
| 威廉·尤尔特·格莱斯顿 | William Ewart Gladstone | 1892—1894 |
| 罗斯伯里伯爵 | Earl of Rosebery | 1894—1895 |
| 索尔斯伯里侯爵 | Marquis of Salisbury | 1895—1902 |
| 阿瑟·詹姆斯·鲍尔福 | Arthur James Balfour | 1902—1905 |
| 亨利·坎贝尔-班纳曼 | Sir Henry Campbell-Bannerman | 1905—1908 |
| 赫伯特·亨利·阿斯奎斯 | Herbert Henry Asquith | 1908—1916 |
| 戴维·劳合·乔治 | David Lloyd George | 1916—1922 |
| 安德鲁·博纳·劳 | Andrew Bonar Law | 1922—1923 |
| 斯坦利·鲍德温 | Stanley Baldwin | 1923—1924 |
| 詹姆斯·拉姆齐·麦克唐纳 | James Ramsay MacDonald | 1924 |
| 斯坦利·鲍德温 | Stanley Baldwin | 1924—1929 |
| 詹姆斯·拉姆齐·麦克唐纳 | James Ramsay MacDonald | 1929—1935 |
| 斯坦利·鲍德温 | Stanley Baldwin | 1935—1937 |
| 内维尔·张伯伦 | Neville Chamberlain | 1937—1940 |
| 温斯顿·斯宾塞·丘吉尔 | Winston Spencer Churchill | 1940—1945 |
| 克莱门特·理查德·艾德礼 | Clement Richard Attlee | 1945—1951 |
| 温斯顿·斯宾塞·丘吉尔 | Winston Spencer Churchill | 1951—1955 |
| 安东尼·艾登 | Sir Anthony Eden | 1955—1957 |
| 哈罗德·麦克米伦 | Harold Macmillan | 1957—1963 |
| 亚历克·道格拉斯-霍姆 | Sir Alec Douglas-Home | 1963—1964 |
| 哈罗德·威尔逊 | Harold Wilson | 1964—1970 |
| 爱德华·希思 | Edward Heath | 1970—1974 |
| 哈罗德·威尔逊 | Harold Wilson | 1974—1976 |
| 詹姆斯·卡拉汉 | James Callaghan | 1976—1979 |
| 玛格丽特·撒切尔 | Margaret Thatcher | 1979—1990 |
| 约翰·梅杰 | John Major | 1990—1997 |
| 托尼·布莱尔 | Tony Blair | 1997—2007 |
| 戈登·布朗 | Gordon Brown | 2007—2010 |
| 大卫·卡梅伦 | David Cameron | 2010—2016 |
| 特雷莎·梅 | Theresa Mary May | 2016—2019 |
| 鲍里斯·约翰逊 | Boris Johnson | 2019—2022 |
| 伊丽莎白·特拉斯 | Elizabeth Truss | 2022 |
| 里希·苏纳克 | Rishi Sunak | 2022— |

# 3. 美国主要地名表

## （一）美国各州及首府名称

| 州名 | | 首府 | |
|---|---|---|---|
| 亚拉巴马 | Alabama | 蒙哥马利 | Montgomery |
| 阿拉斯加 | Alaska | 朱　诺 | Juneau |
| 亚利桑那 | Arizona | 菲尼克斯 | Phoenix |
| 阿肯色 | Arkansas | 小石城 | Little Rock |
| 加利福尼亚 | California | 萨克拉门托 | Sacramento |
| 科罗拉多 | Colorado | 丹　佛 | Denver |
| 康涅狄格 | Connecticut | 哈特福德 | Hartford |
| 特拉华 | Delaware | 多　佛 | Dover |
| 佛罗里达 | Florida | 塔拉哈西 | Tallahassee |
| 佐治亚 | Georgia | 亚特兰大 | Atlanta |
| 夏威夷 | Hawaii | 火奴鲁鲁（檀香山） | Honolulu |
| 爱达荷 | Idaho | 博伊西 | Boise |
| 伊利诺斯 | Illinois | 斯普林菲尔德 | Springfield |
| 印第安纳 | Indiana | 印第安纳波利斯 | Indianapolis |
| 艾奥瓦 | Iowa | 得梅因 | Des Moines |
| 堪萨斯 | Kansas | 托皮卡 | Topeka |
| 肯塔基 | Kentucky | 法兰克福 | Frankfort |
| 路易斯安那 | Louisiana | 巴吞鲁日 | Baton Rouge |
| 缅　因 | Maine | 奥古斯塔 | Augusta |
| 马里兰 | Maryland | 安纳波利斯 | Annapolis |
| 马萨诸塞 | Massachusetts | 波士顿 | Boston |
| 密歇根 | Michigan | 兰　辛 | Lansing |
| 明尼苏达 | Minnesota | 圣保罗 | St. Paul |
| 密西西比 | Mississippi | 杰克逊 | Jackson |
| 密苏里 | Missouri | 杰斐逊城 | Jefferson City |
| 蒙大拿 | Montana | 海伦娜 | Helena |
| 内布拉斯加 | Nebraska | 林　肯 | Lincoln |
| 内华达 | Nevada | 卡森城 | Carson City |
| 新罕布什尔 | New Hampshire | 康科德 | Concord |
| 新泽西 | New Jersey | 特伦顿 | Trenton |
| 新墨西哥 | New Mexico | 圣菲 | Santa Fe |
| 纽　约 | New York | 奥尔巴尼 | Albany |
| 北卡罗来纳 | North Carolina | 罗利 | Raleigh |
| 北达科他 | North Dakota | 俾斯麦 | Bismarck |
| 俄亥俄 | Ohio | 哥伦布 | Columbus |
| 俄克拉荷马 | Oklahoma | 俄克拉荷马城 | Oklahoma City |
| 俄勒冈 | Oregon | 塞勒姆 | Salem |
| 宾夕法尼亚 | Pennsylvania | 哈里斯堡 | Harrisburg |
| 罗得岛 | Rhode Island | 普罗维登斯 | Providence |
| 南卡罗来纳 | South Carolina | 哥伦比亚 | Columbia |
| 南达科他 | South Dakota | 皮　尔 | Pierre |
| 田纳西 | Tennessee | 纳什维尔 | Nashville |
| 得克萨斯 | Texas | 奥斯汀 | Austin |
| 犹他 | Utah | 盐湖城 | Salt Lake City |
| 佛蒙特 | Vermont | 蒙彼利埃 | Montpelier |

| 弗吉尼亚 | Virginia | 里士满 | Richmond |
| 华盛顿 | Washington | 奥林匹亚 | Olympia |
| 西弗吉尼亚 | West Virginia | 查尔斯顿 | Charleston |
| 威斯康星 | Wisconsin | 麦迪逊 | Madison |
| 怀俄明 | Wyoming | 夏　延 | Cheyenne |

### （二）主要山脉

| | |
|---|---|
| 阿巴拉契亚山脉 | Appalachian Mountains |
| 科迪勒拉山脉 | Cordillera Range |
| 喀斯喀特山脉 | Cascade Range |
| 海岸山脉 | Coast Range |
| 落基山脉 | Rocky Mountains |
| 内华达山脉 | Sierra Nevada |

### （三）主要河流

| | |
|---|---|
| 哈得逊河 | Hudson River |
| 密西西比河 | The Mississippi River |
| 密苏里河 | Missouri River |
| 俄亥俄河 | Ohio River |

### （四）国际河流

| | |
|---|---|
| 科罗拉多河 | Colorado River |
| 哥伦比亚河 | Columbia River |
| 格朗德河 | Rio Grande |
| 圣劳伦斯河 | St. Lawrence River |

### （五）五大湖

| | |
|---|---|
| 伊利湖 | Lake Erie |
| 休伦湖 | Lake Huron |
| 密歇根湖 | Lake Michigan |
| 安大略湖 | Lake Ontario |
| 苏必利尔湖 | Lake Superior |

### （六）尼亚加拉瀑布　　Niagara Falls

### （七）主要城市

| | |
|---|---|
| 巴尔的摩 | Baltimore |
| 伯明翰 | Birmingham |
| 波士顿 | Boston |
| 芝加哥 | Chicago |
| 克利夫兰 | Cleveland |
| 底特律 | Detroit |
| 休斯敦 | Houston |
| 堪萨斯城 | Kansas City |
| 洛杉矶 | Los Angeles |
| 明尼阿波利斯 | Minneapolis |
| 新奥尔良 | New Orleans |
| 纽约（市） | New York City |
| 费城 | Philadelphia |
| 匹兹堡 | Pittsburgh |
| 圣地亚哥（圣迭戈） | San Diego |
| 旧金山 | San Francisco |
| 西雅图 | Seattle |
| 圣路易斯 | St. Louis |
| 华盛顿（市） | Washington（D.C.） |

## 4. 美国历届总统一览表

| 任次 | 任职年份 | 姓名 | 所属党派 |
|---|---|---|---|
| 1 | 1789—1797 | 乔治·华盛顿（George Washington） | 联邦党 |
| 2 | 1797—1801 | 约翰·亚当斯（John Adams） | 联邦党 |
| 3 | 1801—1809 | 托马斯·杰斐逊（Thomas Jefferson） | 民主共和党 |
| 4 | 1809—1817 | 詹姆斯·麦迪逊（James Madison） | 民主共和党 |
| 5 | 1817—1825 | 詹姆斯·门罗（James Monroe） | 民主共和党 |
| 6 | 1825—1829 | 约翰·Q·亚当斯（John Q. Adams） | 民主共和党 |
| 7 | 1829—1837 | 安德鲁·杰克逊（Andrew Jackson） | 民主党 |
| 8 | 1837—1841 | 马丁·范布伦（Martin Van Buren） | 民主党 |
| 9 * | 1841 | 威廉·H·哈里森（William H. Harrison） | 辉格党 |
| 10 | 1841—1845 | 约翰·泰勒（John Tyler） | 辉格党 |
| 11 | 1845—1849 | 詹姆斯·K·波尔克（James K. Polk） | 民主党 |
| 12 * | 1849—1850 | 扎卡里·泰勒（Zachary Taylor） | 辉格党 |
| 13 | 1850—1853 | 米勒德·菲尔莫尔（Millard Fillmore） | 辉格党 |
| 14 | 1853—1857 | 富兰克林·皮尔斯（Franklin Pierce） | 民主党 |
| 15 | 1857—1861 | 詹姆斯·布坎南（James Buchanan） | 民主党 |
| 16 * | 1861—1865 | 亚伯拉罕·林肯（Abraham Lincoln） | 共和党 |
| 17 | 1865—1869 | 安德鲁·约翰逊（Andrew Johnson） | 共和党 |
| 18 | 1869—1877 | 尤利塞斯·S·格兰特（Ulysses S. Grant） | 共和党 |
| 19 | 1877—1881 | 拉瑟福德·B·海斯（Rutherford B. Hayes） | 共和党 |
| 20 * | 1881 | 詹姆斯·A·加菲尔德（James A. Garfield） | 共和党 |
| 21 | 1881—1885 | 切斯特·A·阿瑟（Chester A. Arthur） | 共和党 |
| 22 | 1885—1889 | 格罗弗·克利夫兰（Grover Cleveland） | 民主党 |
| 23 | 1889—1893 | 本杰明·哈里森（Benjamin Harrison） | 共和党 |
| 24 | 1893—1897 | 格罗弗·克利夫兰（Grover Cleveland） | 民主党 |
| 25 * | 1897—1901 | 威廉·麦金莱（William McKinley） | 共和党 |
| 26 | 1901—1909 | 西奥多·罗斯福（Theodore Roosevelt） | 共和党 |
| 27 | 1909—1913 | 威廉·H·塔夫脱（William H. Taft） | 共和党 |
| 28 | 1913—1921 | 伍德罗·威尔逊（Woodrow Wilson） | 民主党 |
| 29 * | 1921—1923 | 沃伦·G·哈定（Warren G. Harding） | 共和党 |
| 30 | 1923—1929 | 卡尔文·柯立芝（Calvin Coolidge） | 共和党 |
| 31 | 1929—1933 | 赫伯特·C·胡佛（Herbert C. Hoover） | 共和党 |
| 32 * | 1933—1945 | 富兰克林·D·罗斯福（Franklin D. Roosevelt） | 民主党 |
| 33 | 1945—1953 | 哈里·S·杜鲁门（Harry S. Truman） | 民主党 |
| 34 | 1953—1961 | 德怀特·D·艾森豪威尔（Dwight D. Eisenhower） | 共和党 |
| 35 * | 1961—1963 | 约翰·F·肯尼迪（John F. Kennedy） | 民主党 |
| 36 | 1963—1969 | 林登·B·约翰逊（Lyndon B. Johnson） | 民主党 |
| 37 * | 1969—1974 | 理查德·M·尼克松（Richard M. Nixon） | 共和党 |
| 38 | 1974—1977 | 杰拉尔德·R·福特（Gerald R. Ford） | 共和党 |
| 39 | 1977—1981 | 吉米·卡特（Jimmy Carter） | 民主党 |
| 40 | 1981—1989 | 罗纳德·里根（Ronald Reagan） | 共和党 |
| 41 | 1989—1993 | 乔治·布什（George H. Bush） | 共和党 |
| 42 | 1993—2001 | 比尔·克林顿（Bill Clinton） | 民主党 |
| 43 | 2001—2009 | 乔治·W·布什（George W. Bush） | 共和党 |
| 44 | 2009—2017 | 巴拉克·奥巴马（Barack Obama） | 民主党 |
| 45 | 2017— | 唐纳德·特朗普（Donald Trump） | 共和党 |

备注：

9 * 哈里森 1841 年 4 月病故，由副总统泰勒继任。
12 * 泰勒 1850 年 7 月病故，由副总统菲尔莫尔继任。
16 * 林肯 1865 年 4 月被刺身亡，由副总统约翰逊继任。
20 * 加菲尔德 1881 年 9 月被刺身亡，由副总统阿瑟继任。
25 * 麦金莱 1901 年 9 月被刺身亡，由副总统罗斯福继任。
29 * 哈定 1923 年 8 月病故，由副总统柯立芝继任。
32 * 罗斯福 1945 年 4 月病故，由副总统杜鲁门继任。
35 * 肯尼迪 1963 年 11 月被刺身亡，由副总统约翰逊继任。
37 * 尼克松 1974 年 8 月 9 日辞职，由副总统福特继任。